Rediscovering the Democratic Purposes of Education

STUDIES IN GOVERNMENT AND PUBLIC POLICY

Rediscovering the Democratic Purposes of Education

Edited by Lorraine M. McDonnell,
P. Michael Timpane, and Roger Benjamin

 University Press of Kansas

Published by the University Press of Kansas (Lawrence, Kansas 66049), which was organized by the Kansas Board of Regents and is operated and funded by Emporia State University, Fort Hays State University, Kansas State University, Pittsburg State University, the
University of Kansas, and Wichita State University.

Library of Congress Cataloging-in-Publication Data

Rediscovering the democratic purposes of education / edited by Lorraine M. McDonnell,
    P. Michael Timpane, and Roger Benjamin.
        p. cm. — (Studies in government and public policy)
    Includes bibliographical references and index.
    ISBN 0-7006-1026-X (cloth : alk. paper) — ISBN 0-7006-1027-8 (paper: alk. paper)
        1. Politics and education—United States. 2. Education—Aims and objectives—
    United States. 3. Democracy—Study and teaching—United States. I. McDonnell,
    Lorraine, 1947– II. Timpane, P. Michael, 1934– III. Benjamin, Roger W. IV. Series.

    LC89.R43 2000
    370.11—dc21   00-026689

British Library Cataloguing in Publication Data is available.

Printed in the United States of America

10 9 8 7 6 5 4 3 2 1

Contents

Preface

This volume grew out of our shared concern about the state of education research, particularly the scholarly neglect of schooling's political dimensions. From different vantage points as researchers, university teachers, administrators, and policy advisers, we saw a lack of attention to education's democratic pur poses in policy, school practice, and research. The economic purposes of education are the ones typically highlighted in policy debates, even as education remains one of the most politicized policy arenas with increasingly diverse (and often divisive) constituencies vying to define what the nation's children should learn and to decide who should bear the costs and receive the benefits of the American educational system.

As we discussed our misgivings about the sidelining of democratic purposes in policy debates and educational practice, we also realized that few researchers are studying the politics of education, and that education school faculty have become increasingly isolated from disciplinary perspectives that would allow them to examine political questions productively. Consequently, we sought to begin a process in which the democratic purposes of education could be emphasized, and faculty and students in disciplinary departments and in education schools could jointly consider different conceptual frameworks for examining the politics of education. Our hope was to provide a starting point for renewed scholarly attention, in teaching and research, to how democratic values are transmitted in schools and to how the educational enterprise is governed.

The Spencer Foundation generously supported a small working conference on the democratic purposes of education and the preparation of the commissioned papers that constitute this volume. Many of the formulations presented in the first chapter originated among the participants at the 1996 conference, organized by RAND and the Aspen Institute. We are grateful to the chapter authors and to Gary Fenstermacher, Edmond Gordon, Patricia Graham, Joseph

Kahne, Michael O'Keefe, Sharon Robinson, David Steiner, and David Tatel for ideas and insights that helped frame the project. Robert Reich was an active participant in our discussions and prepared a synopsis of the conference that was invaluable in focusing subsequent writing and revisions; Nancy Pelz-Paget skillfully handled the conference logistics; and Thurese Bonneville and William Ford ably prepared the final manuscript. We were also fortunate to be the beneficiaries of the encouragement and high-quality editorial support provided by Fred Woodward and his colleagues at the University Press of Kansas.

1

Defining Democratic Purposes

Lorraine M. McDonnell

Highlighting the democratic purposes of education at the beginning of the twenty-first century may seem hopelessly romantic or quaintly outdated. After all, democratic purpose is a vague concept that appears to have little relevance for schools desperately trying to raise students' academic achievement and prove themselves to a skeptical public more concerned that youth become economically self-sufficient than be good citizens. Democratic purpose may also seem like a hollow concept when the overwhelming majority of the public report having little trust in government, formal political participation is declining, and the democratic promise of political equality has eluded a sizable group of Americans.

Despite these reasons for downplaying the concept, we hope to demonstrate that the democratic purposes of education are not outmoded ideas. We argue in this book that they should continue as primary rationales for public education, influencing classroom teaching and school governance, and that social science research should focus once again on how well schools fulfill their democratic mission. In this chapter, we define what we mean by the democratic purposes of education; we then argue why scholarly attention should be paid to such goals of schooling while acknowledging the significant barriers to achieving democratic purposes; and we preview subsequent chapters by outlining theoretical and empirical approaches that scholars might use in studying democracy and education.

THE DEMOCRATIC PURPOSES OF EDUCATION: SOCIALIZATION AND GOVERNANCE

The original rationale for public schooling in the United States was the preparation of democratic citizens who could preserve individual freedom and engage in responsible self-government. For the Founders, public schools were to serve

1

democratic purposes not only in how they educated students but also in how they were organized. That ideal was embodied in Jefferson's notion of the local ward, or "little republic," with its school built and governed by local citizens.

As initiators of the first large-scale experiment in democratic government, the Founders recognized that the survival of America's political institutions depended on citizens' ability to participate in public life and to exhibit civic virtues such as mutual respect and prudent judgment. Yet in the aristocratic world of the late eighteenth century, the Founders found few models of how to instill democratic values in citizens. Consequently, they had to devise an entirely new approach to education. In Chapter 2, Lorraine Smith Pangle and Thomas L. Pangle outline how the Founders, including Jefferson, Franklin, Washington, and Webster, conceived of the goals of democratic education, its curriculum, and school organization. Their purpose in doing so is to argue that the Founders' writings on democratic education are relevant today and to draw from their ideas a set of principles for focusing contemporary schools more clearly on the task of shaping democratic citizens.

The Founders' ideas were not immediately translated into widespread practice. Citizens' unwillingness to pay school taxes combined with the population sparsity of a predominantly rural country meant that most areas did not have a public school system until well into the nineteenth century.[1] Nevertheless, concern about citizenship formation in the United States led to universal primary schooling (at least for white males) earlier than in western European countries.[2] However, the rationale for public schooling was never completely political. From the very beginning of the republic, political and economic motivations were intertwined. The Founders assumed that citizens' economic self-sufficiency was necessary for the nation's political survival, and the focus on instilling skills and virtues useful in the workplace grew stronger as the nation industrialized. In describing the common school movement, James notes that it "brought together Protestant-style civic religion and a republican fervor carried forward from the American Revolution, along with socially and politically conservative values stressing nativism, work discipline, time control, sobriety, and other traits associated with the maintenance of moral order and civic cohesion in a nascent capitalist economy."[3] Still, those who worked to spread public schooling "stressed civic and moral values that they claimed could only be maintained through public education. The nation could fulfill its destiny only if each rising generation learned those values together in a common institution."[4]

Although the federal government, through the Northwest Ordinance of 1787, provided new states with land grants to support schools, the spread of public schooling was largely due to the actions of states and local communities. The states provided constitutional frameworks and what James has called "a feeble administrative apparatus and grudgingly ceded, poorly implemented tax laws."[5] But it was local citizens who actually established and maintained the primary school in each local community. The process by which public schooling spread reinforced the notion that it should be popularly controlled, and locally elected school trustees became an integral part of the emerging system. Schools were not governed exactly as Jefferson had envisioned for his little republics, but they were a focal point for residents of local communities to come together in common purpose. "The mainstream of American public education during most of the nineteenth century was rural, chiefly unbureaucratic in structure, exhibiting only rudimentary professionalism, and dependent on the actions of hundreds of thousands of lay promoters and school trustees."[6]

The Founders' notion of using education as a tool for creating a stable political and social order was mirrored in later concerns about maintaining a shared sense of civic values amid geographic dispersion, industrialization, and the growing religious and cultural diversity of the population. In response to these challenges and the patchwork of public and private schools that had emerged, the common school movement worked to implement a uniform model of schooling financed by state and local governments, controlled by lay boards of education, and enrolling all social groups in the same school building. It was designed to provide nonsectarian moral education and nonpartisan political instruction. Later progressive educators such as John Dewey, Henry Adams, and Charles Merriam also viewed civic education as the keystone of democracy, and they argued that it required a well-developed public sphere where civic discourse among a broad spectrum of the population was actively encouraged.[7]

The common school, affording broad-based access and a curriculum to prepare students for citizenship, has been an enduring ideal in American education. However, that ideal seems to have faded as the economic purposes of schooling have become more prominent. In the third chapter, Carl F. Kaestle examines the historical development of the common school concept to determine whether there was indeed a time when citizenship education took precedence over preparation for the workplace. Kaestle concludes that there is a plausible case for deciding that civic education has receded in the face of increasing emphasis on preparation for work. In his view, however, the idea of separate political and economic sectors spawning distinct purposes for education is simplistic. Rather, he argues, we need to conceive of "a political economy that generates purposes for education, all of which have political, economic, and cultural functions."

Although the socialization of students in civic values and skills and the democratic governance of schools are less explicit goals today than they were in the nineteenth century, they continue to define the democratic purposes of education. Large majorities of parents and the public believe that it is essential for schools to teach habits of good citizenship.[8] Similarly, despite a reliance on professional educators for the day-to-day running of schools, the ultimate responsibility for them continues to be shared among elected officials at the state and local levels, with a significant measure of local control still a defining attribute of American public education. Current demands that schools and educators be held publicly accountable for their performance and that groups outside the educational establishment participate in defining curricular standards are only the most recent examples of a tradition that assumes schools should be subject to the strictures of democratic politics.

Socialization and governance reinforce each other as democratic purposes. The politics of education, or the way schools are governed, determines how students are socialized, for it is in this arena that decisions are made about what should be taught and who is entitled to educational benefits. That same politics is also an object of students' learning because it demonstrates the rules of political access and participation, the methods by which conflicts are resolved, and the weight given to different political interests. How students are socialized, in turn, determines the future vitality of education politics. Although socialization and governance are closely linked, they are still conceptually distinct, with one focused on the individual student and the other on schools as educational institutions. Under some conditions, the two purposes may even exist independently of one another. For example, private schools that are not democratically controlled typically teach citizenship skills. In contrast, some public schools, while under the control of elected officials, make little effort to prepare students for their public responsibilities. Despite a lack of perfect congruence between the two purposes, there is a strong presumption that public schools will instill civic values in students and that they will be democratically controlled.

This latter goal raises the question of what constitutes democratic governance. Although they differ in their portrayal of the system, Terry M. Moe (in Chapter 6) and Lorraine M. McDonnell and M. Stephen Weatherford (in Chapter 8) identify serious flaws in how schools are currently governed, pointing to the strong incentives for organized interests to dominate education politics, the lack of broad-based participation, and the gridlock resulting from fragmented governance. Here the question is whether there are alternative ways of organizing schools that would still constitute a form of democratic governance. For example, how much market competition can be introduced and still maintain democratic accountability? Can politics, as Moe argues, be removed from most educational decisions and still ensure that students are socialized consistent with democratic purposes and that schools are answerable to the larger polity? These dilemmas of democratic purpose raise normative questions about where the boundaries between the public and private spheres should be drawn and about who should decide the aims of schooling. But they also raise practical questions about how to evaluate a diverse array of policy options (e.g., vouchers, charter schools, bilingual education, and common curricular standards) in light of the core democratic purposes of education.

BARRIERS TO DEMOCRATIC PURPOSES

Despite a continuing focus on democratic purposes, a variety of indicators suggest that they are peripheral to today's schooling. Not only is formal civics instruction just a small part of the curriculum, but that instruction also tends to focus on static descriptions of governmental institutions and less on the deliberative skills that students will need to make informed political judgments and to participate actively in the public life of their communities.[9] Democratic purposes are also noticeably absent from elite and public discourse about education. As Westbrook notes, "Many have decried the shortcomings of American public schools, but few have attributed their difficulties to a weakness of democratic imagination, will, and purpose. Few of the many reports on the dire condition of schooling in the United States which have filled bookshelves recently have anything to say about the education of citizens."[10]

Although competent citizenship is mentioned in public speeches and documents as a goal of schooling, it is typically ancillary to arguments about workforce skills. President Clinton's recommendation in his 1994 State of the Union address that "we measure every school by one high standard: Are our children learning what they need to know to compete and win in the global economy?" exemplifies the rhetorical preeminence of economic goals.

Four major factors have contributed to the sidelining of democratic purposes. The first is the ascendancy of the private, individual goals of schooling over its collective, public purposes. Those who study the history of American education and its underlying values have defined its goals in a variety of ways.[11] But all agree that there are both private purposes aimed at providing individuals with the knowledge, skills, and status they need to pursue economic and social position, and public goals associated with maintaining and enhancing the wider community. The growing shift away from the democratic purposes of schooling reflects a broader move from public goals to private ones.

David F. Labaree defines three alternative goals for public education: democratic equality that focuses on citizenship formation; social efficiency or workforce preparation; and social mobility that assumes schools should prepare individuals to compete for social position. Although he acknowledges critical differences between the democratic equality and social efficiency goals, Labaree argues that distinguishing between them as political and economic purposes may be less important than seeing both as public goals needed to sustain the economy and the polity, and fundamentally different from the third goal of social mobility, which views education as a private, consumption good. Using such developments as the spread of school choice options and the growing stress on credentialism in higher education as evidence, Labaree concludes that the social mobility goal has grown in prominence: "From this perspective, the most striking thing about that history is the way the consumer conception of education has gradually come to dominate the structure of American schooling as well as the policy talk about schools. It seems increasingly that no reform is possible, and neither of the other two goals can be advanced effectively, without tapping into the concerns raised by social mobility: the need for education to maintain its value as a consumer good that can provide individuals with social advantage."[12]

This analysis suggests that the diminution of education's political purposes may be part of a broader shift away from collective goals, whether they be economic or political, to a focus on individuals pursuing their own self-interest and interacting with schools as consumers rather than as citizens.

A second barrier stems from the current state of political participation. Because participation in politics and civic life has become less important, political socialization may be a less central focus in schools. Trend data on adult political participation present a mixed picture, but most analysts agree that political activity has not expanded at rates that might be expected given the significant increases in educational attainment among Americans.[13] Participation rates for those political acts that only a minority of the public engage in remained relatively stable or increased between 1967 and 1987. For example, the proportion of respondents reporting that they had contacted local officials about an issue increased from 14 to 24 percent; the proportion reporting that they contributed money to a political campaign showed a similar increase; and those reporting that they worked with others on a local problem remained stable at about 30 percent.[14]

However, the proportion of respondents reporting that they voted in a national election declined over the same period from 66 to 58 percent, and in local elections from 47 to 35 percent.[15] Another indicator of declining participation in civic life is Americans' decreasing membership in a variety of voluntary associations. Robert D. Putnam uses participation in bowling leagues as illustrative of an overall decline in civic engagement.[16] For Putnam, the solitary bowler is symbolic of a widespread decline in associational life: although the number of bowlers increased by 10 percent between 1980 and 1993, bowling in organized leagues decreased by 40 percent. This somewhat fanciful example mirrors a variety of other membership statistics. Weekly church attendance has declined from close to 50 percent in the 1950s to 32 percent in the late 1980s; PTA membership fell by more than half between 1960 and 1976 and has not recovered. Similarly, membership in organizations such as the League of Women Voters, the Elks, and the Masons has declined by 20 to 40 percent over the past thirty years. Many of these organizations are not expressly political in purpose, but they build social capital and norms of civic engagement by connecting their members to the larger community.[17]

Although we lack the evidence to establish a causal connection, it seems reasonable to assume that the decline in political participation and associational membership may contribute to a reduced emphasis on the political purposes of education. Schools reflect the values of the larger society, and they can only pursue those goals permitted and supported by the broader polity. Consequently, the schools face a conundrum: political socialization is unlikely to be central to schooling until civic participation among adult Americans increases, yet that change depends at least partly on equipping future adults with the values and skills needed for active citizenship.

Increased uncertainty about whether Americans can respect and accommodate cultural and political diversity while still espousing shared values is a third factor explaining why political socialization is not a high priority for schools. Civic education assumes that despite diverse religious beliefs, ethnic cultures, and political views, the vast majority of citizens subscribe to a set of common values that allow them to trust each other in their public lives. However, a number of commentators are now asking whether the United States has passed a threshold of diversity that makes a shared civic identity impossible.

The question has been tested most recently in state and local debates over what should be included in social studies and language arts curricula. In his dissent to a report on the New York social studies curriculum that he viewed as promoting a "cult of ethnicity," Arthur M. Schlesinger Jr. wrote: "The new ethnic gospel rejects the unifying vision of individuals from all nations melted into a new race. Its underlying philosophy is that America is not a nation of individuals at all but a nation of groups, that ethnicity is the defining experience of most Americans."[18]

In contrast, the San Francisco school board recently considered a proposal from two of its members mandating that more than half the required reading included in the city's high school literature courses be books written by nonwhite authors. Despite passionate public testimony in favor of the idea (with a smaller number of speakers opposing it), the board rejected imposing a numerical quota and instead ordered that students be required to read nonwhite authors and that "writers who are lesbian, gay, bisexual and transgender be identified."[19] Similar controversies have ensued over the inclusion of religious and political content in the curriculum, and recent debates over bilingual education have revolved, at least partly, around what learning experiences should be common to all students as members of a broader community and which, if any, should reinforce their unique ethnic, cultural, and religious identities.

Often lost in the fervor of these controversies is evidence of considerable agreement about the values that schools should teach. Large majorities of white, African-American, and traditional Christian parents agree that schools should teach mutual respect for others regardless of their racial or ethnic background or their sexual identity, that students should learn that living in integrated neighborhoods is good, and that they should be taught about the black struggle for civil rights.[20] Similarly, the overwhelming majority of respondents in another national survey reported that they believe the public schools should not promote "one common, predominant cultural tradition," but rather should give equal emphasis to "both a common cultural tradition and the diverse cultural traditions of the different population groups in America."[21]

Although poll data suggest that most Americans believe we can share common civic values while still respecting each other's unique identities and history, implementing that goal has often proven difficult. In a few well-publicized cases, the result has been wrenching controversies that tear communities apart. The more common response, however, has been bland textbooks designed, as one recent analysis of U.S. history texts concluded, "to meet the demands of the multicultural left and the conservative religious right."[22] Neither resolution provides a strong basis for moving beyond vague platitudes to a set of civic values on which most people can agree and that can be conveyed concretely to students.

A fourth factor, making the pursuit of democratic purposes more difficult, stems from value conflicts inherent in education and democracy. One example is the tension between popular and professional control of schooling. Since the advent of the Progressive era, reforms emphasizing professional expertise, democratic governance, and professionalism have coexisted in an uneasy truce. Most people view professional and political norms as equally legitimate, but balancing their respective claims represents a challenge to achieving democratic purposes.

Democratic control assumes that as a governmental institution, schools derive their legitimacy from the consent of the electorate and that they should be held publicly accountable. It further assumes that as public employees, educators' behavior should be constrained and that those constraints should be externally imposed.[23] In contrast, professionalism assumes that educators possess a specialized body of knowledge and that, because their work poses complex and nonroutine problems, their application of that knowledge should be regulated by a code of ethics internal to their profession.[24] In other words, educators should be held accountable through standards and procedures collectively specified and enforced by their peers, not by externally defined and enforced criteria.

Under the political model, those served by schools act as constituents able to challenge educational authorities when they deem it necessary. In contrast, under the professional model, constituents are transformed into clients who are expected to defer to expert judgment. As teaching has become more professionalized, educators have been reluctant to accept parental and public participation in education governance on an equal basis and instead have encouraged parental involvement on limited terms that they define (viz., parental assistance with homework, participation in the PTA, classroom volunteering). Educators typically view themselves as caring professionals, rather than public servants answerable to the public and its elected representatives. The most recent manifestation of the tension between professional and political values has been debates over curriculum standards in states and local school districts. They have often revolved around differences between what professional educators argue that students should be taught and the content and pedagogy that parents and the public think are most appropriate.

Although we have argued that governance and socialization are tightly linked, their underlying values may conflict at times and give rise to a second tension. Democratic control is typically exercised through the majority decisions of legislators and school board members and by citizens voting in elections. However, this form of control can undermine other liberal democratic principles, such as equal political standing regardless of one's resources and the protection of minorities against majority tyranny. These latter values are critical to ensuring that all students have access to an education that adequately prepares them for active citizenship, but they may not always be the outcome produced through popular democratic control.

Nowhere in education has this dilemma been more apparent than in the case of school desegregation. The arguments in favor of desegregation rest on liberal principles of social justice and equal educational opportunity, values that lie at the heart of socialization for democratic citizenship. Intertwined with these principles are notions of popular control: liberal values are translated into policy and practice through the collective choices of officials held electorally accountable by their constituents. Yet, whether because of racism or for other reasons, popular control has worked against broad-based desegregation. As Jennifer L. Hochschild has argued, "Roughly speaking, popular control works: elected executives and legislators do less to facilitate and more to impede desegregation success than do nonelected judges and bureaucrats. . . . There are more whites than minorities; whites register and vote more than minorities do; whites oppose mandatory school desegregation more than minorities do. Thus it is a rare school district indeed in which majoritarian elections yield policies requiring racial balance. The more perfect the means of popular control, the worse for racial equity."[25] To the extent that various kinds of resource disparities work against political equality, popular control is more likely to operate at odds with liberal principles rather than reinforcing them.

Acknowledging the inherent tensions between professional norms and democratic accountability and between liberalism and popular control is not to argue that these values cannot be reconciled. Rather, it points out how difficult pursuing the democratic purposes of education truly is. The requirement that education prepare both workers and citizens and that it serve public and private purposes places the democratic focus of schooling in continuing (and often losing) competition with other goals. Declining political participation means that the schools can count on only passive support from the larger society as they address their collective mission, and increasing cultural and political diversity make any collective goals and strategies for achieving them considerably more complex and contentious. Finally, democratic socialization occurs within a governance framework that at times may encourage the pursuit of goals directly at odds with liberal democratic citizenship.

WHY FOCUS ON DEMOCRATIC PURPOSES AND WHY NOW

These significant barriers are precisely why we believe a strong case can be made for refocusing American education and the academic study of it on democratic purposes. The arguments in favor of such a shift stem from the current state of American civic life and from evidence that attention to democratic purposes can make a positive difference. The growing diversity of the population, our inability to reach consensus on key social and cultural values or even to deliberate about our differences, and the weakening of other societal institutions all suggest a stronger role for education in maintaining social comity. Schools, acting alone, cannot be expected to reenergize political participation or help citizens find common ground in their public lives. Nevertheless, with the exception of the family, education is the only major social institution in which all Americans participate over a sustained period and that also focuses on the values and skills necessary to maintain a civil society. In essence, these barriers—the ascendancy of private over public purposes, declining political participation, a weakened common civic identity—are the strongest arguments in favor of paying renewed attention to the democratic purposes of education.

As we have argued, focusing on the democratic purposes of education means paying attention to how students are socialized and to how schools are governed. Arguments for the latter focus also stem from the shortcomings of the current system. Chapter 8 summarizes a variety of public opinion data suggesting that while support for the schools is at least as strong as it is for other large public and private institutions, there are signs that the public is becoming disengaged. Only a small proportion of voters have school-age children; parents and the public differ significantly from education reformers in their views about what should be taught and how it should be taught; and support for using public funds to allow children to attend private schools has grown considerably over the past decade. Some have suggested that these trends point to a legitimacy crisis. While that may be an overstatement, there is no question that schools need to be reconnected to the broader community. Even if the current governmental monopoly over publicly funded schooling was replaced with a mixed system, public support would still be necessary. Without such support, public funding will decline, whether it be for the current system or for one that includes vouchers. More important, the interests of the larger polity will not be served if the public's views are not reflected in an institution critical to the nation's political and economic survival.

Concrete ideas for how the goals, structures, and processes of education governance can be made more democratic are discussed throughout this volume. Although the chapter authors take different perspectives on the topic, they agree on the need for a sharper focus on education's collective purposes, a more even balance between professional and public values, and reconfigured structures and processes to make educational decisions more accessible to those most affected by them.

It is easier to make the case that current problems with political participation and civic identity require a greater emphasis on schooling's democratic purposes than to demonstrate that such attention will solve these problems or even make significant inroads in addressing them. The difficulty lies in the lack of research on the topic. As Judith Torney Purta notes in reviewing two major studies of the relationship between education and political knowledge and participation, virtually no research has investigated the "black box" of formal education. Although political scientists have analyzed the effect of years of formal education on adult political knowledge, attitudes, and participation, they rarely consider the influence of curricula, pedagogy, or informal school experiences on these factors.[26]

However, the limited data available suggest a positive relationship. Using a variety of nationally representative survey data, Delli Carpini and Keeter found that years of formal education play a central role in promoting the acquisition of political knowledge. The greatest impact of formal education is on knowledge of rights. However, large differences by level of education are evident across a range of topics and demographic groups. With regard to civic education specifically, they found that respondents' self-reports of having studied civics in high school were weak predictors of political knowledge compared with other factors such as years of education, race, gender, and strength of party identification. However, civics instruction closely approached "statistical significance on the knowledge domain most likely to be taught in such classes—the rules of the game" (i.e., political institutions and processes).[27]

As might be expected, researchers have found a stronger relationship between political knowledge and civics instruction when they examine that effect on youth rather than on adults. In contrast to earlier studies that were based on limited tests of political knowledge (typically, fewer than ten items) and found little or no relationship between civics coursework and political knowledge and attitudes, Niemi and Junn analyzed the civics portion of the 1988 National Assessment of Educational Progress (on which each student answered fifty to seventy-five items) and found a quite different effect. Even after controlling for a variety of demographic and home environmental factors, they found that the amount and recency of civics coursework had a significant and positive effect on students' civic knowledge and on their attitudes about governmental responsiveness. Similarly, the variety of substantive topics covered in a civics course and the extent to which teachers incorporate discussions of current events into the curriculum mattered to students' level of knowledge.

Also especially significant was their finding that participation in student government and students' interest in studying the subject had a stronger positive effect than either parental education, the amount of television students viewed, or the availability of reading materials in the home. Niemi and Junn conclude that "the most important message to come out of our study of the political knowledge of high school seniors is that the school civics curriculum does indeed enhance what and how much they know about American government and politics. Furthermore, these educational effects on civic knowledge persist even after accounting for other powerful predictors of knowledge.[28] In addition, Niemi and Hepburn list seven other studies of students in the United States and abroad that identified positive effects of civics instruction.[29]

Some may argue that without an extensive research base the case in favor of greater attention to the democratic purposes of education is tenuous. However, we believe that the need for such an emphasis is well-documented, and that although the existing research is only suggestive, it provides sufficient evidence that greater attention to students' political socialization can raise their level of political knowledge and help them forge a stronger connection to the polity. At the same time, the lack of recent, in-depth research on all aspects of political socialization and education governance represents a compelling case for greater attention not only to the democratic purposes of education but also to how scholars understand those purposes and their effects on citizens' relationship to government.

REBUILDING THE INTELLECTUAL INFRASTRUCTURE

A number of political theorists have recently highlighted the need to strengthen civil society and to create a more inclusive, deliberative politics, often citing the educational system as one of the most critical institutions in building social capital and making democracy more deliberative.[30] Within education, groups such as Public Agenda and the Kettering Foundation have concerned themselves with the divisiveness and narrow interests reflected in contemporary education politics even as large segments of the general public remain disengaged from the schools. Despite this renewed attention to schools as a focus of democratic politics, neither practical recommendations for reconnecting schools with their communities nor scholarship on political socialization and the politics of education have matched rhetorical expressions of concern.

The study of how youth learn to be citizens has languished for twenty years, and conceptual thinking and empirical research on the politics of education have also been scant. This volume represents an initial step in rebuilding the intellectual infrastructure for understanding schools as political institutions. In commissioning the papers that constitute it, we acted on three assumptions. First, schools are political institutions. Along with the academic knowledge and skills that students acquire in schools, they are also exposed to classroom teaching, extracurricular activities, and interactions with other students that shape their values and actions as adult citizens. In addition to this socializing role, schools are the focal point for major political debates about what should be taught, who is entitled to educational benefits, and who should govern the schools.

Second, knowledge about schools as political institutions has withered because so little research has been conducted over the past twenty years on the politics of education. Researchers have largely confined their studies to determining how politics affects policy outcomes. Other functions of politics, such as mobilizing citizen participation, serving as a focal point for deliberation, and exposing participants to the values and interests of others, have largely been ignored. We believe that empirical research on these neglected topics is needed to inform efforts to reconnect schools to their communities and to prepare professional educators to act as public servants in shaping future democratic citizens. Finally, theoretical frameworks for explaining education politics have atrophied because little attention has been paid to how newer theories from relevant disciplines such as political science and organizational sociology might be applied to explaining education politics. Without such an infusion of new ideas, empirical work on the democratic purposes of education will be shallow.

With these assumptions in mind, we convened a group of distinguished researchers representing a variety of academic disciplines and theoretical perspectives. Most of them work in disciplinary departments outside schools of education, but they are all familiar with public schooling and have written on topics related to education. The purpose was to have them think about how the democratic purposes of elementary and secondary education might be redefined.

This volume is divided into three parts, reflecting our concern with civic education, the politics of education, and the implications of a focus on democratic purposes for education policy. The second and third chapters provide a philosophical and historical context for contemporary discussions of civic education. In Chapter 4, Amy Gutmann outlines a perspective to inform such a discussion. In her past work, Gutmann has argued both for a more deliberative approach to politics and for a democratic theory of education that has as its goal student attainment of the skills needed for active citizenship. Here she joins the two themes by focusing on the three major ways that democracies deal with political disagreement: procedurally through majority rule, constitutionally through the application of fundamental democratic values, and deliberatively through civil public discussion. She then connects these approaches to corresponding skills of democratic citizenship and argues that recommitting public schooling to education for citizenship would be one important strategy for reducing our current democratic deficit where sound bites and self-interested bargaining often substitute for deliberation on the merits of an issue. However, taking civic education seriously is a necessary, but not sufficient, condition for sustaining a publicly defensible school system. Gutmann explores three other conditions—decreasing bureaucracy in schools, increasing parental choice, and developing the distinctive potential of every child—as a basis for arguing that even as they focus on civic education, schools can also address the serious problems plaguing them.

The fifth chapter, by Pamela Johnston Conover and Donald D. Searing, reports initial findings from a major new study of political socialization. The theoretical perspective guiding Conover and Searing's research emphasizes citizen identities and the process by which individuals come to understand their mutual obligations as members of a political community. Because this study was designed to understand how students develop a sense of citizenship and the practices associated with that status, it needed to study political socialization in particular political, economic, and social contexts. Therefore, high school students, their parents, teachers, community leaders, as well as a sample of adult citizens were interviewed in each of four communities—a rural farm community in Minnesota, an urban, blue-collar community in Philadelphia, a suburban community in North Carolina, and a Hispanic community in San Antonio. Among the most notable findings is that students in all four community samples demonstrate a clearer, more well-defined understanding of their basic rights as citizens than of their civic responsibilities. In addition, few students have concrete notions about what they might do to become better citizens in the future. The study results suggest not only that civic engagement and school discussions are critical in developing a sense of citizenship among students, but also that coursework outside the formal civics curriculum has a significant influence in shaping how students view the practice of citizenship.

In part two, we move away from a focus on how individual students are prepared for citizenship to a consideration of different approaches for understanding how educational institutions are governed. Even though the frameworks presented in part two focus on the politics of education and institutional questions, they link back to themes raised in the section on civic education. For example, James G. March and Johan P. Olsen argue that different institutional theories of politics have contrasting implications for how citizens are educated, and in their own work they adopt a perspective similar to Conover and Searing's, with its focus on developing citizen identities and a sense of mutual obligation.

In Chapter 6, Terry Moe elaborates on the theory of political institutions that guided his earlier comparison of public and private schools and his advocacy of vouchers. From this perspective, schools are viewed as public agencies whose design and performance are rooted in a political logic that subjects them to the control of multiple authorities and their constituents. According to the assumptions of the model, those with the greatest stake in policy outcomes tend to be the best organized and to lock in their political victories through institutional rules and structures that favor their interests even when they may no longer constitute a majority. The effect of this institutional system on schooling is twofold. First, the role of parents is reduced because they tend to be less well organized than economic interests such as teacher unions and textbook publishers, and they represent only a small part of the diverse constituencies that collectively have a right to govern any given school. Second, the logic that institutionalizes the gains of political winners through organizational structures and rules results in schools that are overly bureaucratic. Moe's model leads him to conclude that "the schools have difficulty contributing to the quality of democratic government precisely because they are democratically controlled."

Like Moe, James March and Johan Olsen propose an institutional perspective for understanding the relationship between education and democracy. However, the model they present in Chapter 7 rests on a set of assumptions very different from Moe's. Rather than emphasizing competition among interests and the formation of coalitions to advance those interests, they focus on the identities and rules that encourage the development of shared meanings within a political community. In this model, the purpose of education is to create in students political identities that encourage preferences and beliefs consistent with democratic processes and discourage ones that do not; to help mold a comprehensible and accountable political system where historical events can be understood and interpreted in ways that maintain a democratic culture; and to aid in creating an adaptive political system that learns from experience and matches its resources and processes to a changing political environment. March and Olsen view the schools as playing a vital role in shaping citizens who take a critical stance toward the actions of elected officials and who can enter into informed deliberations about their own and the community's interest, but who also are constrained by the shared obligations of political equality, mutual respect, and the rules of reasoned discourse.

In Chapter 8, Lorraine McDonnell and Stephen Weatherford connect several themes raised in earlier chapters. They argue that the politics of education determines whether and how schooling promotes democratic purposes. However, because little research has been conducted on this topic over the past twenty years, we have only a fragmentary understanding of the values that underlie education politics, the public's attitude toward the schools, and the diverse institutional actors that define the political arena in which democratic purposes are debated and decided. McDonnell and Weatherford document major trends in contemporary education politics through a review of public opinion data and empirical studies of the political institutions responsible for public education. They then return to a consideration of the institutional and deliberative models outlined by Moe, March and Olsen, and Gutmann to suggest that such models not only constitute distinctive theoretical frameworks for guiding future research but also different normative standards for judging the political performance of the education system.

In part three, the volume's dual focus on education for citizenship and the politics defining and structuring that education comes together in an analysis of the value conflicts they pose and their implications for education policy. The American system of public education is designed to accomplish two goals: provide the knowledge and skills that individuals need to succeed and pursue collective purposes such as instilling democratic values, providing a mechanism for equal opportunity, and establishing a sense of national community. During various periods in our history, and particularly in the past decade, some Americans have also demanded that schools satisfy the distinctive needs of particular groups and demonstrate respect for their identity. Although these three goals sometimes fit together quite well, the possibility for conflict between them increases when resources are scarce and priorities need to be set, and when the system is perceived as failing and change must start somewhere. The final chapter, by Jennifer L. Hochschild and Nathan Scovronick, focuses on several policy controversies—desegregation, equitable funding, school choice, and debates over when it is appropriate to separate students—and examines how policymakers have tried to resolve the conflict between individual groups and collective goals. The authors argue that for the next several decades, collective goals should take precedence. Three demographic trends lead them to this judgment: the huge cohort that will soon reach retirement age, the large growth in school enrollments, and the increasing diversity of the population. Hochschild and Scovronick conclude that the coming competition for public resources will make it essential for education advocates of all kinds to defend the central role of education in a democracy.

Like politics itself, the chapters in this volume represent diverse perspectives on the role of education in a democratic society. They start with different normative assumptions about the purposes of education, and the theoretical lenses they present span political philosophy, history, sociology, and political science. Yet they share a common focus on education politics broadly defined, and they illustrate both how far we are from truly understanding this critical domain of political life and how rich the possibilities are for fruitful inquiry.

NOTES

1. Lorraine Smith Pangle and Thomas L. Pangle, *The Learning of Liberty: The Educataional Ideas of the American Founders* (Lawrence: University Press of Kansas, 1993).

2. Ira Katznelson and Margaret Weir, *Schooling for All: Class, Race, and the Decline of the Democratic Ideal* (New York: Basic Books, 1985).

3. Thomas James, "State Authority and the Politics of Educational Change," *Review of Research in Education* 17 (1991): 178.

4. David B. Tyack and Elisabeth Hansot, *Managers of Virtue* (New York: Basic Books, 1982), 23.

5. James, "State Authority," 179.

6. Tyack and Hansot, *Managers of Virtue*, 17.

7, Michael X. Delli Carpini and Scott Keeter, *What Americans Know About Politics and Why It Matters* (New Haven, CT: Yale University Press, 1996).

8. For example, see Jean Johnson et al., *Assignment Incomplete: The Unfinished Business of Education Reform* (New York: Public Agenda Foundation, 1995). In "The 28th Annual Phi Delta Kappa/Gallup Poll of the Public's Attitudes Toward the Public Schools," *Phi Delta Kappan* 78, 1 (1996): 41–59, 86 percent of the public rated preparing students to be responsible citizens as a very important purpose of the nation's public schools, while a smaller proportion (78 percent) rated helping people become economically self-sufficient as very important. However, the authors (Stanley M. Elam, Lowell C. Rose, and Alec M. Gallup) note that when the public is asked an open-ended question about the goals or purposes of public education, their responses are quite different from what they offer when presented with a list of objectives. In the open-ended responses, they emphasize material goals such as "to get better jobs," "to make more money," or "to achieve financial success" (55).

9. As mentioned in Lee Anderson, Lynn B. Jenkins, James Leming, Walter B. MacDonald, Ina V. S. Mullis, Mary Jane Turner, and Judith S. Wooster, *The Civics Report Card* (Princeton, NJ: Education Testing Service, National Assessment of Educational Progress, 1990). Unfortunately, national data about the type of civics instruction provided to American students and their knowledge of the topic are now a decade old. However, examinations of the civics textbooks used in high school courses typically find that they describe governmental institutions and define democratic concepts, but minimize the degree of

conflict inherent in the political process, thus failing to present a realistic picture of politics in a diverse society. See Lorraine M. McDonnell, Leigh Burstein, Tor Ormseth, James M. Catterall, and David Moody, *Discovering What Schools Really Teach* (Santa Monica, CA: RAND, 1990), and John R. Hibbing and Elizabeth Theiss-Morse, "Civics Is Not Enough: Teaching Barbarics in K–12," *PS: Political Science and Politics* 29 (1996): 57–62. According to Hibbing and Theiss-Morse, "currently used curricular material does little to help students develop an appreciation of actual democratic processes" (60). Delli Carpini and Keeter, *What Americans Know*, 279, make a similar point with regard to instruction in the earlier grades: "the disjuncture between the overwhelmingly positive view of government provided by primary school socialization and the reality of clashing interests that the young adult sees when viewing the real world of politics is apt to result in cynicism and withdrawal."

10. Robert B. Westbrook, "Public Schooling and American Democracy," in *Democracy, Education, and the Schools,* ed. Roger Soder (San Francisco: Jossey-Bass, 1996), 126.

11. In Chapter 9, Jennifer L. Hochschild and Nathan Scovronick outline three purposes that public schools have traditionally served in the United States and illustrate how tensions among them have shaped several recent policy debates. For another perspective on the purposes of public education, see David C. Paris, *Ideology and Educational Reform: Themes and Theories in Public Education* (Boulder, CO: Westview Press, 1995).

12. David F. Labaree, "Public Goods, Private Goods: The American Struggle over Educational Goals," *American Educational Research Journal* 34 (1997): 59.

13. Sidney Verba, Kay Lehman Schlozman, and Henry E. Brady, *Voice and Equality* (Cambridge, MA: Harvard University Press, 1995).

14. Ibid.

15. Ibid.

16. Robert D. Putnam, "Bowling Alone: America's Declining Social Capital," *Journal of Democracy* 6 (1995): 65–78.

17. Ibid.

18. Author M. Schlesinger Jr., *The Disuniting of America: Reflections on a Multicultural Society* (New York: W. W. Norton, 1992), 16.

19. Maria L. LaGanga, "S.F. Board Oks Reading of Works by Nonwhites," *Los Angeles Times*, 21 March 1998.

20. Jean Johnson and John Immerwahr, *First Things First: What Americans Expect from the Public Schools* (New York: Public Agenda Foundation, 1994).

21. Stanley M. Elam, Lowell C. Rose, and Alec M. Gallup, "The 26th Annual Phi Delta Kappa/Gallup Poll of the Public's Attitudes Toward the Public Schools," *Phi Delta Kappan* 76, 1 (1994): 41–64.

22. Alexander Stille, "The Betrayal of History," *New York Review of Books* 15–16 (11 June 1998): 15.

23. Robert A. Dahl, *Dilemmas of Pluralist Democracy: Autonomy vs. Control* (New Haven, CT: Yale University Press, 1982), and Judith E. Gruber, *Controlling Bureaucracies: Dilemmas in Democratic Governance* (Berkeley: University of California Press, 1987).

24. Bernard Barber, "Some Problems in the Sociology of Professions," in *The Professions in America*, ed. K. S. Lyn (Boston: Houghton Mifflin, 1965), 15–34.

25. Jennifer L. Hochschild, *The New American Dilemma* (New Haven, CT: Yale University Press, 1984), 143–44.

26. Judith Torney Purta, "Links and Missing Links Between Education, Political Knowledge, and Citizenship," *American Journal of Education* 105 (August 1997), 447–57.

27. Delli Carpini and Keeter, *What Americans Know*, 144.

28. Richard G. Niemi and Jane Junn, *Civic Education: What Makes Students Learn* (New Haven, CT: Yale University Press, 1998), 147.

29. Richard G. Niemi and M. A. Hepburn, "The Rebirth of Political Socialization," *Perspectives on Political Science* 24 (1995): 7–16.

30. For example, see Amy Gutmann and Dennis Thompson, *Democracy and Disagreement* (Cambridge, MA: Belknap Press of Harvard University Press, 1996); Robert D. Putnam, *Making Democracy Work: Civic Traditions in Modern Italy* (Princeton: Princeton University Press, 1993); and Michael J. Sandel, *Democracy's Discontent: America in Search of a Public Philosophy* (Cambridge, MA: Belknap Press of Harvard University Press, 1996).

PART I
The Philosophy and Practice of Civic Education

2

What the American Founders Have to Teach Us About Schooling for Democratic Citizenship

Lorraine Smith Pangle and Thomas L. Pangle

Our prosperity, liberty, and dignity depend on the healthy maintenance of our democracy. And democracy, as "government of the people, by the people, and for the people," depends ultimately on the political wisdom and civic spirit of the people. But prudence and patriotism, mutual respect and fraternal concern, zeal for public service and an admiration for those who make such service their vocation, are not natural or innate human qualities; they are rare and acquired characteristics. They are civic virtues that are the products of education, democratic-civic education. In our time, education has come to be centered on schooling. Yet in the contemporary controversies over what ought to be done to improve the sad state of our public schools, little is said about the need to restore the capacity of schools to serve as seminaries of civic virtue, which is not altogether surprising. It is a mark of the grave difficulties into which our democracy has fallen that the very idea of civic virtue has passed out of currency—and that, as a natural consequence, for the past few years we have been witnessing, and some of us have been participating in, ever more desperate attempts to revive awareness of this crumbling cornerstone of democracy and of the role schools ought to play in forming sound democratic civic character.

Those who take this enterprise of retrieval seriously will profit from a reconsideration of the perspective afforded by the leading Founders, who put down in writing their thoughts on education in the new republic. These Founders exhibited a concern akin to ours and felt the absence of democratic civic education in America. As initiators of the first large-scale democratic experiment in human history, they were well aware of the scarcity not only of democratic educational institutions and practices but above all of democratic educational theory. They confronted a monarchic and aristocratic world that offered very inadequate models and principles to guide their practical reflections on the construction of a new, more democratic American educational philosophy.[1] They therefore had to think the problem through in an original way and under the sobering discipline of practical urgency. As a consequence, their reflections are refreshingly free of traditional antidemocratic prejudice.

On the other hand, the Founders' clearest superiority to us, as theorists of democracy and of democratic education, is a direct consequence of the fact that they did not grow up in a democracy; they were thus immunized against the pious embrace (and even flattery) of democracy and "the people" that so constantly threatens to restrict our attempts to liberate ourselves from current or reigning convention in order to theorize in a truly critical spirit.[2] To be sure, another consequence is that their thought is remarkably diverse, evolving, and tension-ridden: a far greater range of alternatives in democratic theorizing was examined during the founding era than has ever been (or likely ever will be) in our lifetimes.

Yet for all the divergences among and transformations within the various Founders' writings on education, a common set of principles and aims around which all converge is readily discernible. All agree on striving to convince their stingy and shortsighted, but shrewd and attentive, fellow countrymen of the need for serious attention to a new kind of civic education, the outlines of whose character they believe to be pretty clear. At the same time, the Founders seek to show how democracy can approach the standards of excellence that have been set by the great, previous high points of aristocratic educational theory and practice. These first American democrats have a deep appreciation for the considerable virtues, as well as a sharp distaste for the demeaning and narrowing vices, of traditional aristocratic education—the education that all of them are most familiar with or have received in one form or another. They are determined to prove to themselves and to the world that democracy does not have to entail the sacrifice of excellence in the life of the mind or the vulgarization of moral standards in the life of action.

However, they also know that they have their work cut out for them.[3] They know from the testimony and the experience of ages that democracy contains within it powerful tendencies toward majoritarian tyranny, class resentment and hatred of natural superiority, and a narrowing, greedy individualism, debased by what Tocqueville was to diagnose as the inordinate "love of material enjoyments in the centuries of democracy."[4] Even as they struggle with the practical needs of the moment, the Founders seek to give guidance for the ages to come and to delineate the essential features and abiding problems of democracy. We do not distort their thought, then—on the contrary, we do it justice—if we try to distill from their manifold remarks those abiding principles and arguments that continue to apply to schooling for civic education in our time or that pose the most provocative challenges to our assumptions and consensus about such schooling.

This approach means that for our present purposes we are only incidentally or tangentially interested in how the thought of the Founders was shaped by or meant to deal with the peculiar character of American society at the time of the founding. We are seeking here to distill from the Founders' writings on democratic education those lessons that are applicable to democracy in all times and places. In other words, we write not as historians but as political theorists. We view the Founders' thought on education in the perspective afforded by the philosophy of civic and democratic education as that philosophy has been formulated and contested by Plato and Aristotle, Locke and Rousseau, Dewey and Whitehead. It is only when we approach the educational thought of the Founders in this philosophic context and spirit that we begin to escape the stultifying constraints of historicism and thus can appreciate the incisiveness of criticism, and the promise of civic renewal, that the Founders' liberal republican vision poses to our current and rather impoverished intellectual framework.

We live today in a polity dominated by a public philosophy that "lacks the civic resources to sustain self-government."[5] The great synthesis of liberal and republican principles that characterized the founding and continued to define America's public philosophy up until at least the early days of the New Deal—the synthesis that in the twentieth century gave Brandeis and Wilson and the Progressives and the early New Dealers their agenda—has been ever more steadily disappearing from our public school curricula and therefore from our moral horizon in the past fifty years. Government and public policy increasingly have come to be seen as lacking any legitimate concern with the formation of the character of the citizenry. Yet this development does not mean that law and legally sanctioned coercion have not been fostering conformity to a very specific and very narrow morality. Quite the contrary. Law, and public education sanctioned by law, has been instilling with intensifying moralism that specific moral outlook that requires the liberation of the individual from all ties of solidarity, responsibility, tradition, and obligation that are not autonomously chosen. The balances delicately articulated in our original, founding public philosophy have been decisively tilted: rights have eclipsed responsibilities, freedom has obscured virtue, tolerance has rendered suspicious the passing of moral judgments, and concern for autonomous choice has come to outweigh concern for human fulfillment found in dedication and devotion.

The result is a public philosophy, embedded in coercive law as well as in public discourse, that leaves our political life in general and our public education in particular increasingly bereft of the capacity to foster those specific traits of character that are essential not only for a vigorously deliberative self-governing people, but even for the more modest bonds of mutual caring and obligation, the more restricted sense of responsibility and capacity for sacrifice, that are required to sustain the contemporary family and the modern welfare state.

At a more profound level, this contemporary public philosophy of ours leaves us with a conception of our souls or selves as narrow, fragmented, isolated, powerless—and hence naturally prone to apathy or resentment. Our public philosophy lacks a vocabulary in which we might articulate those longings and dimensions of existence that we experience as beings situated in larger social wholes entailing strong bonds of affection, duty, and obedience that are not merely chosen but instead are discovered, grown into, and accepted as essential.

And this crippling of our moral vocabulary frustrates our need to express these dimensions of our civic and moral existence in our public actions, in our laws and institutions, and in the narratives that weave together the fabric of our common lives. This inarticulateness has grave communal consequences. It conduces to a tolerance that is a "mere" toleration: a thin pluralism of coexisting but mutually indifferent or hostile multicultural posturings rather than a rich diversity of spiritual strivings, mutually respectful and attentive, teaching and learning, affirming and nurturing, even while criticizing and arguing—because all share a common dedication to fundamental principles of democracy and human rights, and all share a thirst for ever deeper spiritual completion.

What our predicament calls for is a massive effort of intellectual and cultural retrieval: not an effort to return to some golden age, not the reverent recitation of a rosary of supposedly eternal verities, but rather a critical and self-critical confrontation with the most challenging civic-educational views of earlier thinkers—and especially the Founders, who laid down the basic moral foundation of our civic tradition and vocabulary. It is such an "essay in retrieval" (to borrow a phrase from C. B. Macpherson) that this chapter aims to help launch; and it is this ambition that guides our highly selective encounter with a few of the Founders.

GOALS

The overarching aim of the education the Founders promote is moral: the formation of character. And the character the Founders have in view is of a new or specifically "modern" kind.[6] The Founders seek a society of self-reliant individuals, deeply concerned with reputation, exhibiting mutual respect, capable of fraternal cooperation, and inclined to charitable benevolence, all on the basis of a shared self-confidence solidly rooted in the rational capacity to take responsibility for oneself and one's own life. Two principal objects of concern animate and ground the lives of these equally free and rational individuals: property and family. God enters the picture chiefly as a support and source of protective sanctions for these two secular cynosures. But, in the words of James Wilson, "Property, highly deserving security, is, however, not an end, but a means. How miserable, and how contemptible is that man, who inverts the order of nature and makes his property not a means, but an end!"[7] Property provides the foundation for freedom, for self-reliance, and for stable family life.

Meaningful independence and security must be rooted in the training and the self-discipline that allow one to succeed in the economic competition and cooperation of the free enterprise system. The classical republican tradition had tended to see property as the "equipment" that made possible a life of political participation and virtue. But this ordering of priorities is no longer so evident in the American founding. Addressing the women of the new nation, Wilson goes on, in the oration we have just quoted, to declare: "You have, indeed, heard much of publick government and publick law: but these things were not made for themselves: they were made for something better; and of that something better, you form the better part—I mean society—I mean particularly domestick society."[8] The good democratic citizen, in the Founders' understanding, is one who can be trusted to enter into permanent ties of marriage, to accept the lasting responsibilities of parenthood, and to subordinate political as well as economic interest to love of family.

Hence, the Founders see no tension but rather a complementarity between moral education and job or career training.[9] The acquiring of the capacity for sustained hard work, culminating in a sense of satisfaction with a job well done; the achievement of integrity, accompanied by contempt for dishonesty; the practice of frugality and the habit of long-range planning for one's family as well as one's own personal future; the experience of organizing and maintaining extrafamilial associations for the promotion of all sorts of social goods; the prizing of the satisfactions and the obligations of parenthood and of spousal fidelity: these are all regarded as contributing simultaneously to both moral maturity and economic self-sufficiency or prosperity.

Now since much or most of moral education is a matter not of intellectual discovery or rational conviction but of habituation, emotional attachment, and cultivation of the heart, it follows, for the Founders, that by far the most important part of education takes place in family life rather than in school life. Still, schooling is an essential supplement to and completion of the more basic and decisive formative influence of the home. As Jefferson put it in his most public statement on (emphatically coeducational) elementary schooling, the goals of such schooling are:

> To give to every citizen the information he needs for the transaction of his own business;
>
> To enable him to calculate for himself, and to express and preserve his ideas, his contracts and accounts, in writing;
>
> To improve, by reading, his morals and faculties;
>
> To understand his duties to his neighbors and his country, and to discharge with competence the functions confided to him by either;
>
> To know his rights; to exercise with order and justice those he retains, to choose with discretion the fiduciary of those he delegates; and to notice their conduct with diligence, with candor, and judgment;
>
> And in general, to observe with intelligence and faithfulness all the social relations under which he shall be placed.[10]

The specific civic spirit that the Founders aim to cultivate is thus one that springs from and reflects the predominantly private concerns of the new model human being. Americans are to be familial and economic beings first, civic or political animals second or secondarily—and largely in order to protect and advance their economic and familial interests.[11] The chief end of government is understood to be the securing of the individual rights to life, liberty, and the pursuit of happiness as each sees fit, but with a massive stress on the ever increasing accumulation of personal economic power and the material satisfactions and comforts that such power brings: "The first object of government," Madison declares in *Federalist* 10, is "the protection of different and unequal faculties of acquiring property."

What makes American republicanism contrast so profoundly with the previous or classical tradition of republicanism is precisely this reordering of priorities: the older, classical republican idea of liberty entailed the primacy of the political, or the notion that participation in government was the chief constituent of human fulfillment and dignity. This traditional, classic conception of human nature reflected and promoted the idea that republics, and especially democratic republics, were necessarily restricted to a single city or to a very small scale and required an intense degree of homogeneity and self-sacrificing patriotic devotion. The framers, led by Madison in the famous *Federalist* 10, argue, on the contrary, that freedom is better promoted by "enlarging the orbit" of republican life, by diversifying the citizen body and encouraging economic competition. But this approach means that the freedom in view is not principally the freedom treasured by the ancients, the freedom to share directly in sovereign governmental deliberations, and even to assist, to some degree, in the execution of public policy. The freedom of most concern to the framers is rather the security from oppression, either by factions within society or by the government, acting as an agent for oppressive factions or as its own self-serving tyranny.

The ancient republics, *The Federalist Papers* argue, were riven by class conflict; ancient democracy tended to degenerate into mob rule, goaded by demagogues. "The true distinction between these and the American governments lies *in the total exclusion of the people in their collective capacity,* from any share in the *latter.*" The new constitution is "strictly republican" in that it establishes "a government which derives all its powers directly or indirectly from the great body of the people, and is administered by persons holding their offices during pleasure for a limited period, or during good behavior." The people express their will through majority vote and public opinion. But the federal government itself is placed entirely in the hands of the tiny minority of representatives, who, acting as the people's agents or servants, are not merely to reflect but also to "refine and enlarge," to moderate and stabilize, the will of their constituents. Yet, while the Founders believed it reasonable to hope that representatives would be chosen with a view to their superior education, experience, breadth of vision, and care for the common good, they also devised a complex system of institutional checks and balances that set the representatives in competitive watchfulness over one another.[12]

Accordingly, the civic virtues to be fostered in the vast majority of Americans as national and also as state citizens are not so much virtues enabling participation in rule as they are virtues enabling vigilant judgment of the few representatives who are to participate in rule. What is required in the mass of the people is an appreciative understanding of how the system works and an attentive, selective, and critical partisanship[13]—supporting and opposing, praising and blaming, judging and choosing among those few politically ambitious citizens who put themselves forward as candidates for public office and trust. This expectation implies a call for more than a passive or merely occasional interest in federal and state politics. What is needed is a steady and sustained civic awareness, and no one stated this preeminent goal of education more forcefully or clearly than President George Washington in his First Annual Message to Congress (8 January 1790). Civic education, he insisted, was a first order of business for the new national government: what was needed was support for an education that would consist of:

> teaching the people themselves to know and to value their own rights; to discern and provide against invasions of them; to distinguish between oppression and the necessary exercise of lawful authority; between burthens proceeding from a disregard to their convenience and those resulting from the inevitable exigencies of Society; to discriminate the spirit of Liberty from that of licentiousness—cherishing the first, avoiding the last; and uniting a speedy, but temperate vigilance against encroachments, with an inviolable respect to the Laws.[14]

This civic sophistication is understood to require from the populace a genuine respect for those few who do respond to the political vocation, a respect that holds representatives to high standards of practical wisdom, responsiveness to voters, and concern for the public good. The founding vision does not, then, unqualifiedly relegate politics or the political calling to the status of a means; there is not, and there can never be, a simple abandonment of the classical conception of politics as a high, if not the highest, manifestation of human excellence and flourishing. A public servant is to be regarded not merely as a servant, as an inferior who has to be paid somehow to neglect his or her own business in order to attend to the common business. The politician cannot be adequately understood as someone who for some obscure reason fails to recognize the preeminent importance of private life with its economic and familial satisfactions. Public service is to continue to be regarded as ennobling. The citizenry is to continue in some measure to demand leaders it can look up to with gratitude, pride, even reverence. Moreover, the Founders assume that at the local level of government, direct participation by a substantial portion of the citizenry is both an essential safeguard of personal security—above all through citizen-jury control of judicial decisions—and a key component of human dignity. It is no accident that the same framer, Thomas Jefferson, who writes most influentially concerning education also writes most emphatically concerning the value of local participatory democracy. These two themes go hand in hand in Jeffersonian democratic thought—and, we may add, in the kindred thought of John Dewey.

We encounter here one of the deepest ambiguities or tensions in the Founders' republican ideal: political life and those few who live that life most fully are to be regarded as somehow both means and ends, as somehow both secondary and primary. Liberty is to mean both freedom to pursue one's private, familial welfare in security (or freedom to live as one pleases so long as one allows others to do the same) *and* the freedom constituted by life in a community permeated and elevated by a proud sense of indirect as well as direct participation in self-government.

The fundamental distinction between the more modest civic role of the mass of the citizenry, who hold ultimate sovereignty but exercise that sovereignty in mainly indirect ways, and the more active civic role of the few who the people select to be their governing representatives informs every aspect of the Founders' educational conceptions. In explaining the purpose of his proposal for a new kind of academy, Benjamin Franklin stresses the goal of supplying "the succeeding Age with men qualified to serve the Publick with Honour to themselves, and their Country." Thomas Jefferson's most important educational writing, the preamble to his proposed Bill for the More General Diffusion of Knowledge (1779), explains that the deepest (and somewhat tension-ridden) twofold civic goal of his educational philosophy is, on the one hand, "to illuminate, as far as practicable, the minds of the people at large, . . . that . . . they may be enabled to know ambition under all its shapes, and prompt to exert their natural powers to defeat its purposes," and, on the other hand, to see to it "that those persons, whom nature hath endowed with genius and virtue, should be rendered by liberal education worthy to receive, and able to guard the sacred deposit of the rights and liberties of their fellow citizens, and that they should be called to that charge without regard to wealth, birth, or other accidental condition or circumstance." He goes on to declare that these latter, "whom nature hath fitly formed and disposed to become useful instruments for the public," are more likely to come from the poor than from the rich or middle class.[15]

Jefferson therefore proposed publicly funded scholarships for higher education: "By this means," he explains in *Notes on the State of Virginia,* "the best geniuses will be raked from the rubbish annually." It is these few of whom Jefferson later speaks, in a famous letter to John Adams, as "the natural aristocracy": "The natural aristocracy I consider as the most precious gift of nature, for the instruction, the trusts, and government of society. . . . May we not even say that that form of government is the best which provides the most effectually for a pure selection of these natural aristoi into the offices of government?"[16]

CURRICULUM

The spirit of the Founders' curricular thinking is seen most vividly if we focus first on Benjamin Franklin's famous and influential proposals, supplementing them with the later, more explicitly democratic ideas of Webster, Jefferson, and others. At the heart of Franklin's and Jefferson's conception of moral education is the emphatic conviction that the moral dimension of schooling should not be a separate aspect but rather be intimately integrated into all aspects of the curriculum.[17] This integration is best accomplished, in Franklin's judgment, by putting the study of English at the heart of the curriculum. Appealing explicitly to the authority of John Locke's treatise on education, Franklin argues that only by becoming adept in speaking, writing, and reading their own language will young people be equipped to function as economically independent and politically sophisticated citizens.[18]

Indeed, Franklin and his disciple Webster name their newly envisaged school "the English School" to distinguish it from the "Latin School" idea that had previously been predominant. In accordance with the guiding moral intention of the curriculum, the texts selected for students' reading and study as well as the writing exercises that they practice should habituate them to the kinds of reading and writing they will need to do as adults engaged in business, responsible for families, and partisan in politics. The stress should therefore be on prose rather than on poetry, on expository rather than on creative writing: "The Stiles principally to be cultivated," Franklin remarks, "being the *clear* and *concise*." The content of readings should be weighted less toward fiction and entertainment and more toward history (especially political and economic history), biography, and serious contemporary journalism commenting on real issues and questions of the day.

Still, this approach does not mean that children should not use language to express and reflect upon their own lives and experiences. Explicitly following again the lead of Locke's educational treatise, Franklin advocates constant practice in letter writing and diary keeping.[19] But the students need guidance in focusing and giving useful content to their self-explorations and self-expressions. Franklin suggests that students be required to write to one another regularly, giving accounts of their reading and of their judgment on that reading and discussing current controversies in public and school life. He recommends that letters by great letter writers, perhaps in juxtaposition with biographies of those writers, be used as models for students' own letter writing.

Almost equally important in Franklin's new republican curriculum is training in public oratory and debate. He believes that the capacity to speak up in public, and to judge critically the rhetoric of others who speak, is essential to informed citizenship and to effective self-assertion in an egalitarian and hence freely competitive world. There is, moreover, a continuum between oral rhetoric and journalistic rhetoric. In the modern republic, Franklin observes, the rhetoric that has the greatest influence is not that of the rostrum but rather that of the printed periodical page. In general, the Founders saw in journalism one of the pillars of the republicanism they were creating. Jefferson could not emphasize too much his concern that familiarity with newspapers and journals "should penetrate the whole mass of the people: The basis of our government being the opinion of the people, the first object should be to keep that right; and were it left to me to decide whether we should have a government without newspapers or newspapers without a government, I should not hesitate a moment to prefer the latter. But I should mean that every man should receive those papers, and be capable of reading them."[20]

As for Franklin, he urges that students be required to read newspapers and journals of opinion on a regular basis, and that they be incited to debate and to argue over both the issues and the modes of presentation of the various contesting parties in major controversies of the day.[21] The goal here is not only to develop the students' capacity and admiration for sound and eloquent expression but also to instill in them a gimlet eye for sophistic fallacies and methods of manipulation. Opportunities afforded by burning political issues ought to be seized upon in order to organize classroom debates in which students practice advancing and defending what they think is right in the rough-and-tumble arena of free and frank exchange. Franklin observes that these kinds of passionate competitions provide occasions for introducing the principles of logic and of political philosophy, where students can start to sense the value of appeal to great classics in moral and political theory. The great books can begin to come to attractive life when students see that they are more likely to win their arguments if they have sound and deep arguments.

> On Historical Occasions, Questions of Right and Wrong, Justice and Injustice, will naturally arise, and may be put to youth, which they may debate in Conversation and in Writing. When they ardently desire Victory, for the Sake of the Praise attending it, they will begin to feel the Want, and be sensible of the use of Logic, or the Art of Reasoning to discover truth, and of Arguing to defend it, and convince Adversaries. This would be the Time to acquaint them with the Principles of that Art. Grotius, Pufendorf, and some other Writers of the same Kind, may be used on these occasions to decide their Disputes. Publick Disputes warm the imagination, whet the Industry, and strengthen the natural Abilities.

What Franklin favors here is not primarily the encouragement of debating clubs and teams, where the winning of arguments is prized as a kind of sport. Rather, he means to promote serious moral and political controversy in which students learn to make disciplined arguments expressing genuine conviction and inspired by the quest for clarity and truth.[22]

What is more, we see here, in Franklin's emphasis on the didactic importance of appealing to the desire for victory and for praise, a striking example of a leitmotiv of the Founders' education philosophy. The Founders again and again stress the value of schools in arousing ambition and cultivating emulation through mutually inspiring intellectual competition. As the young Jeffersonian Samuel Harrison Smith put it in his prizewinning 1797 essay on education in the new republic, "the great argument which may be called the center of all others urged is the production of emulation by a public education."[23] The love of victory, the zest for political and historical controversy, ought to be whetted and exploited in order to give students a strong incentive to develop the intellectual tastes and tools they will need if they are to become forceful citizens in their communities. Another competitor in the same national essay contest, the French immigrant Lafitte du Courteil, went further, arguing that competition and emulation among the teachers as well as the students ought to be the mark of a truly free and democratic public school. Regular prizes and rewards, both monetary and honorific, for teachers whose classes best succeed intellectually will spur both teachers and students.[24]

Admiration for those who excel at argument and a provocative need and desire to imitate such students ought to be central aspects of the atmosphere in an effective democratic school. It is inevitable in a truly free and democratic society, where rank is not assigned by ascriptive qualities and where in principle opportunity is open to all, that young people will rank themselves on some basis; that there will be a few leaders and many followers, a few admired ones and many striving or wishing to emulate their success. It is crucial, then, that as much as possible the basis for such ranking be constructive: students should be encouraged to compete for preeminence and to take pride not only or even mainly in their looks or their sports abilities or their material possessions or their dancing and singing talents, but above all in those intellectual and moral strengths, those capacities to think and argue and exercise critical judgment, that will enable them to stand up for themselves and lead or cooperate with others in effective community action.

It is obvious from what has been said that, in the Founders' view, the study of English is intimately associated with the study of history. It should be further evident that the history to be stressed is political, not social. Moreover, the study of political history ought to be guided by a specific inspirational goal. Rather than learning how individuals and groups are shaped by their times and circumstances, students ought to be taught how individuals and groups can change and shape their own destinies by dint of the gradual discovery of the true political and moral principles. The emphasis should not be on how people have been oppressed or marginalized or victimized but rather on how they have successfully struggled against and overcome adversity and injustice, how they have transformed and even revolutionized their circumstances.[25] Above all, the liberating power—and the limits—of the specifically American republican principles ought to be conveyed.

It is in this context that the Founders stress the educational value of biography and autobiography. There is perhaps no species of literature that more effectively and directly affords to the young arresting models of aspiration and deeply provocative sources of reflection.[26] Here again it is Benjamin Franklin who sets the standard. His *Autobiography* is as perfect an exemplar of what the Founders were looking for from biography as can be imagined. With ingenuous charm and nobly guileful simplicity, Franklin succeeds in telling a life that is the story of an American democrat: proud in hard-won independence and ascent from lowly origins, disarmingly modest in confession of faults, pervaded by joyful philanthropy and love of communal action, and proof of the riches to be found in a life of reason and rational self-control. It is revealing to note how difficult it has been for Europeans, forged in an undemocratic world (the key examples are the German Max Weber and the Englishman D. H. Lawrence),[27] to appreciate this work, and how immensely popular and influential it has been with generations of young Americans.

Nor was it only Franklin, among the Founders, who self-consciously left behind either autobiographical writing or abundant materials for future biographers. The Founders were themselves formed in large part by Plutarch, and they carried through their lives a keen sense of the role they were playing on the stage of local and world history. Washington with his obsessive concern for a reputation established by public actions and speeches, Jefferson in his highly self-conscious letters, James Wilson in his famous lecture series, are only the most prominent examples. When John Marshall wrote his biography of Washington, he was carrying into execution the kind of edifying biographical scholarship that the founding generation promoted and expected. As Webster wrote in his 1787 essay "On the Education of Youth in America":

> Every child in America should be acquainted with his own country. . . . As soon as he opens his lips, he should rehearse the history of his own country; he should lisp the praise of liberty and of those illustrious heroes and statesmen who have wrought a revolution in her favor.
>
> A selection of essays respecting the settlement and geography of America, the history of the late revolution and of the most remarkable characters and events that distinguished it, and a compendium of the principles of the federal and provincial governments should be the principal schoolbook in the United States.[28]

Indeed, Webster went on to write just such an elementary schoolbook, which influenced generations. Beginning with editions published in 1787, the epigraph is a quotation from Mirabeau: "Begin with the infant in the cradle; let the first word he lisps be Washington."[29] However much Jeffersonian Republicans and Hamiltonian Federalists like Webster may have disagreed over the interpretation of events, both parties were in passionate agreement about the need to make the biographies and the political history of the American revolutionary era focal points to which every history class in the schools ought ceaselessly to return.

For the Founders there is no aim of the curriculum that is more important than this: the enormous advantages of modern constitutional democracy, that is, of the kind of civil society created by the founding, over previous or traditional societies and forms of government should be unashamedly explained and illustrated. This can and should be done even or especially while showing how often Americans have failed to live up to or have distorted the basic principles and aspirations laid down in the founding. The aim of education in history ought to be the inculcation of a sober pride in and a reasonable sense of inspiration by our national heritage. Of the two dangers most likely to occur, it is far better to run the risk of arousing the naive virtues of civic pride, enthusiasm for action, and hope for continued progress than it is to court the disaster of instilling the debilitating and enslaving vices of cynicism and resentful apathy.[30]

The constant refrain of the Founders' concern with education in political history is the need to bring the young step by step to a steadily clearer and more sophisticated grasp of the truth and the intrinsic superiority of the most basic principles of political philosophy that underlie the American Constitution: first and foremost, natural rights and the natural laws that flow from those rights;[31] the idea of consent or the social compact as the basis of legitimacy; the arguments by which one refutes claims to rule not based on consent, and especially the arguments that refute divine right claims; the precise meaning of the "moral sense"; the reasons for indirect rather than direct democracy at the national and state levels; the nature and importance of separation of powers and of federalism; the meaning of the specific civil rights proclaimed in bills of rights, both state and national; the moral justification of property rights and of the free enterprise system and the arguments by which one refutes the moral claims for competing notions of property; and the arguments for religious liberty and for separation of church and state.

To make lively the significance of these most basic principles of political philosophy, the Founders recommend the study of tyranny and despotism in past and present societies. Such study is of unique value, they suggest, both in providing gruesome case studies of the price humanity pays for its ignorance or neglect of the true principles of liberty and in exposing the young to sharp pictures of those conspiracies and cajolings and machinations, of governments and of unscrupulous politicians, that Americans must learn to be vigilant against. As Jefferson put it in his preamble to the Bill for the More General Diffusion of Knowledge, the key purpose of the education of the people is "especially to give them knowledge of those facts, which history exhibiteth, that, possessed thereby of the experience of other ages and countries, they may be enabled to know ambition under all its shapes, and prompt to exert their natural powers to defeat its purposes."[32]

Benjamin Franklin was of course one of the greatest scientists of his age, and we are not surprised to find that science plays a major role in his and Jefferson's curricular proposals. But once again, science finds its place and plays its role in an emphatically moral and civic scheme. The science youngsters should learn is not theoretical but practical; the goal is not to make them scientists but to help them to understand the mechanical principles that explain the natural environment and the machinery and technology that Franklin and other commentators such as Samuel Knox[33] are convinced will increasingly pervade the lives of

Americans. Youngsters should be so equipped in their mechanical and technical knowledge, and in their grasp of the nature of their own health, that they are the masters, rather than the creatures, of the technology that surrounds them.

The very first subject Franklin recommends that students learn is drawing: not chiefly for aesthetic reasons, but—following Locke once again—as a way of enabling children to begin at an early age to comprehend, retain, and communicate the basic principles of architecture and the workings of machinery: "How many Buildings may a man see, how many Machines and Habits met with, the Ideas whereof would be easily retain'd, and communicated by a little Skill in Drawing; which being committed to Words, are in danger to be lost, or at best but ill retained in the most exact Descriptions?" Closely linked with early training in drawing are lessons in arithmetic. Franklin strongly endorses Locke's proposal that children be expected from an early age to keep their own cash or "Merchants accounts" and learn the arithmetic principles that govern such accounts, starting with the simplest ledgers. The idea here is not only to give compelling motivation for the study of the precise use of numbers, but to instill in young people a habit of economy and frugality and a sense of how important arithmetic is in learning how to manage one's fortune. Following Locke, Franklin dismisses the objections of those who think it unseemly thus to tarnish little folks' minds with concerns for lucre; the fact is, Locke and Franklin insist, the constant husbandry of one's finances is an essential basis for independence in a free society.[34]

As we have discussed, the study of history is to be carried out primarily with a view to understanding the principles of government and politics; but a strong secondary—and, in Franklin's eyes, complementary—goal is the introduction of students to and the whetting of their appetite for mechanical science and technological understanding. Consequently, economic history, and the history of economic and technological development, is to be conjoined with political history; students are to be shown the intimate connection between progress in political and economic liberty and advances in prosperity and scientific and technological knowledge, including military technology and weaponry:

> The History of *Commerce,* of the Invention of the Arts, Rise of Manufacturers, Progress of Trade, Change of its Seat, with the reasons, Causes, etc. may also be made entertaining to Youth, and will be useful to all. And this, with the accounts in other History of the prodigious Force and Effect of Engines and Machines used in War, will naturally introduce a Desire to be instructed in Mechanicks, and to be inform'd of the principles of that Art by which weak men perform such Wondours, Labour is sav'd, Manufactures expedited, etc. etc. This will be the Time to show them Prints of antient and modern machines, to explain them, to let them be copied, and to give Lectures in Mechanical Philosophy.[35]

Franklin links this kind of study of the history and progress of technology to the student's growing awareness of the need, and the spiritual rewards, of service to mankind, or of "that *Benignity of Mind* which shows itself in *searching for* and *seizing* every Opportunity to serve and to *oblige.*" In other words, Franklin anticipates John Dewey's argument that there is a close link between the cultivation in the young of the modern scientific spirit and the cultivation of the sort of character that modern democracy needs. Franklin, and Jefferson as well, would strongly agree with Dewey that the scientific spirit breeds "fairmindedness, intellectual integrity, the will to subordinate personal preferences to ascertained facts and to share with others what is found"; they would fervently endorse Dewey's insistence that "the future of democracy is allied with the spread of the scientific attitude," or that the spread of the scientific attitude "is the sole guarantee against wholesale misleading by propaganda." They would join with Dewey in stressing that "an experimental philosophy of life in order to succeed must not set less store upon methodic and organized intelligence, but more."[36] As a consequence, it is reasonable to surmise, they would join with Dewey in deploring as a most serious threat to democracy current "deconstructionist" and "postmodern" currents of thought insofar as those currents seek to draw into question the possibility of objectivity and of the discovery of truly objective, rational, and scientific standards of inherent or inalienable right.

On the other hand, few of the Founders were as sanguine as Dewey about the potential of the scientific spirit to foster the necessary republican virtues in the absence of supports of a very different and not simply rational kind. George Washington gave the classic expression of their concerns in his farewell address:

> Of all the dispositions and habits which lead to political prosperity, religion and morality are indispensable supports. In vain would that man claim the tribute of Patriotism, who should labour to subvert these great Pillars of human happiness, these firmest props of the duties of Men and citizens. The mere Politician, equally with the pious man ought to respect and to cherish them. A volume could not trace all their connections with private and public felicity. Let it simply be asked where is the security for property, for reputation, for life, if the sense of religious obligation desert the oaths, which are the instruments of investigation in Courts of Justice? And let us with caution indulge the supposition, that morality can be maintained without religion. Whatever may be conceded to the influence of refined education on minds of peculiar structure, reason and experience both forbid us to expect that National morality can prevail in exclusion of religious principle.[37]

Washington's views on religion were echoed by such men as John and Samuel Adams, John Marshall, Noah Webster, and Benjamin Rush. These views were also shared by most of the Anti-Federalists and by many of those who voted to ratify the Constitution while calling for a bill of rights. Like Washington, the Anti-Federalists on the whole were persuaded that the liberty of Americans depended on their moral fiber, and that their moral fiber depended largely on religion. In their desire to secure good government, the Anti-Federalists generally put less faith than the Federalists did in the competition of factions orchestrated by shrewd constitutional arrangements and saw more need for "prepossessing the people in favour of virtue by affording *publick* protection to religion." Charles Turner, who voted finally and with reluctance to ratify the new constitution, admonished the Massachusetts ratifying convention that

> without the prevalence of Christian piety and morals, the best republican Constitution can never save us from slavery and ruin. . . . Nor have I an expectation of a greater prevalence of Christian moral principles, unless some superiour mode of education shall be adopted. It is EDUCATION which almost entirely forms the character, the freedom or slavery, the happiness or misery of the world. And if this Constitution shall be adopted, I hope the Continental Legislature will have the singular honour, the indelible glory, of making it one of their first acts . . . to recommend to the several States in the Union, the institution of such means of education, as shall be adequate to the divine, patriotick purpose of training up the children and youth at large, in that solid learning, and in those pious and moral principles, which are the support, the life and SOUL of the republican government and liberty.[38]

On the question of direct governmental support for religious education, however, the Founders were deeply divided. Thomas Jefferson echoed the view that liberty requires a foundation in faith when he wrote: "Can the liberties of a nation be thought secure when we have removed their only firm basis, a conviction in the minds of the people that these liberties are of the gift of God? That they are not to be violated but with his wrath?"[39] Yet he denied that government has any legitimate role in actively supporting the people's faith and at times denied government any legitimate part in shaping opinions of any kind.[40] A similar stand was taken by James Madison, who believed that liberty was only safe when government abstained from all involvement with religion and who therefore advocated an impenetrable "wall of separation" between church and state. He went so far as to oppose not only state support for religious instruction but also tax exemptions for churches, chaplains in the armed services, and national observations of days of thanksgiving.[41]

Madison's extreme views were far from representative of the majority of the Congress who passed the First Amendment. Indeed, as Michael J. Malbin has argued, the peculiar wording "Congress shall make no law respecting an establishment of religion" is best understood as a compromise intended both to prevent the establishment of a national religion and to prevent federal interference with the practice of offering multidenominational support for churches and religious schools then current in many of the states.[42] The same Congress that passed the First Amendment showed its consensus on the need for direct or indirect governmental support for religious education when it framed the Northwest Ordinance of 1787, which included the provision that "Religion, morality, and knowledge being necessary to good government and the happiness of mankind, schools and the means of education shall forever be encouraged."[43] But while the majority of the Congress of 1787, like the majority of their countrymen, agreed that some religious content to publicly funded education was appropriate, they were divided on the question of how and by whom such education should best be delivered.

SCHOOL ORGANIZATION

In colonial America and in the republic's early decades, the chief means by which state governments supported education was by grants to sectarian schools of various denominations. Although this arrangement had provided Puritan New England with an impressive level of education, schools in most of the country remained seriously inadequate both in number and in quality. Thus, leading Founders turned their thoughts increasingly to providing free, universally available public schools that would bring citizens of all sects under one roof, set high standards, and develop a curriculum tailored expressly to the practical and political requirements of the new democracy.

But while many of the leading Founders agreed that universal, publicly funded civic education was an urgent national priority, they turned away from centralized, nationalized, or even uniform educational schemes, which certainly was not because such schemes were unheard of at the time. As we have had occasion to note, in 1797 the American Philosophical Society held an essay contest on the best proposal for a national system of education. The contestants, including the Jeffersonian Samuel Harrison Smith, embraced with alacrity the idea of a nationalized educational system. Knox proposed standardized textbooks, curricula, and requirements; Smith similarly proposed nationally standardized textbooks, in part out of alarm at the lamentable stinginess of state legislatures and at the absence or very poor quality of local standards for teachers. In addition, Smith suggested the establishment of a national board of educational standards that would supervise the creation and governance of a national university, award prizes and honors for writings and discoveries, found libraries, and assign the works to be studied at every level of education.

The leading Founders, however, were wedded to federalism as regards the organization of formal schooling and, moreover, were strongly inclined to assume that the American people would insist on state control over education. When Madison observed in *Federalist* 46 that it was "beyond doubt that the first and most natural attachment of the people will be to the governments of their respective states," one of his principal reasons was that "all the more domestic and personal interests of the people will be regulated and provided for" by the state rather than the national government.[44] To some extent, the Founders welcomed this assignment of responsibility for public education to the state governments. They recognized the virtues of local experimentation and of responsiveness to the diversity of local conditions and hoped for some benefits from competition and emulation among states and localities.[45] In the case of Jefferson and Franklin above all, they saw in local control a greater likelihood of involving parents, or principal local citizens, directly in the management as well as the funding of the schools. Whereas Franklin stressed the administration of his proposed academy by prominent local citizens, who might but normally would not be parents of the students in the school, Jefferson placed more emphasis on the involvement of parents. The experience of Franklin's academy suggests the greater wisdom of Jefferson's insistence on parental control. In later years Franklin openly confessed, with shame and self-recrimination, that he and the other nonparent trustees of his academy had failed miserably to exercise the intimate supervision required.[46]

For his own state of Virginia, Jefferson made the famous, if in the event forlorn, proposal for the organization of the coeducational elementary schools by "wards" or "hundreds." Each such subdivision was to be made up of enough families to provide men for one company of the state militia; the wards would thus be rooted in the citizen army and the patriotic public service, and manly bearing of arms, such a militia entailed. Each ward, Jefferson suggested, would be in effect "a little republic within the republic of the county." The ward would first be empowered and directed to build a schoolhouse and appoint a school board. But these locally administered schools were supposed to become, in Jefferson's vision, the seeds of vigorous local governments: inspired by its success in establishing and maintaining a local school, the ward society was eventually to take responsibility for the police, for arranging the selection of juries, for appointing a judge to the county court, for the roads, and for the care of the local poor. Jefferson thus saw in the involvement of local adults in the establishment of schools for their children an educational experience valuable above all for the adults themselves—and, through their example as active citizens, valuable to their children. Schools were to become educational not merely in the obvious sense but in a more profound and unobtrusive sense: they were to become for the parents the basis for and the spur to an education in self-organization and self-government. Local and neighborhood government, centered on parental authority over the elementary schools, were regarded by Jefferson as absolutely essential for the flourishing of democracy.[47]

It is this crucial link between local government and education that John Dewey rediscovered through his reading of Jefferson: "One of the most serious of present problems regarding democracy," Dewey observed, is "the way in which individuals at present find themselves in the grip of immense forces whose workings and consequences they have no power of affecting." Since "vital and thorough attachments are bred only in the intimacy of an intercourse which is of necessity restricted in range," it follows that "democracy must begin at home, and its home is the neighborly community." What is needed is a civic education that is an "apprenticeship in the practical processes of self-government, which

Jefferson had in mind." Democratic civic education "involves development of local agencies of communication and cooperation, creating stable loyal attachments, to militate against the centrifugal forces of present culture."[48]

For Jefferson, however, parental control over the administration of local elementary schools was not only supremely valuable as the basis of an adult education in participatory democracy. He also was convinced that parents can and will do a better job of managing their children's schools than any educational bureaucracy or professional elite. As Jefferson wrote to Cabell in the famous letter of 2 February 1816, "If it is believed that these elementary schools will be better managed by the governor and council . . . than by the parents within each ward, it is a belief against all experience. Try the principle one step further, and . . . commit to the governor and council the management of all our farms, our mills, and merchants' stores." Yet he did not mean to give parents or local authorities total or unsupervised control. State government was needed to provide essential leadership, to set and maintain general standards, and to mandate minimum spending levels. Besides, Jefferson was acutely aware of parents' widespread disinclination, for many reasons, to shoulder the task of building and managing local schools. He was convinced that local school initiative and self-government were possible, but he was equally convinced that they required the spark of inspiration from and the guidance of leaders like himself. As Lawrence A. Cremin has rightly observed, "for all of Jefferson's emphasis on local control, it was, after all, the Virginia legislature to which he had turned in his effort to effect educational improvement."[49]

If the leading Founders were convinced that the new republic did not need a national school system, they were equally sure that the republic sorely needed a national school vision and national educational goals. Thus, the same Founders who eschewed national school organization felt keenly, and tried to answer, the need for informal but dynamic national educational leadership. Noah Webster's ambitious project of writing and publishing texts, spellers, and his great dictionary is probably the most notable and successful of these efforts. Jefferson saw his promotion of ward schools and his more successful founding of the University of Virginia in part as attempts to establish precedents for other states; and he welcomed Governor George Clinton's efforts in New York, hoping they would provoke emulation in Virginia as well as in other states. Other Founders such as Washington employed exhortation and set the conspicuous public example of spending their own funds on the promotion of educational institutions.

But while Jefferson had powerful reasons to call for a universal system of public, nonsectarian schools, others among the Founders who were deeply religious or deeply concerned about the moral character of the citizenry—most notably Benjamin Rush—believed that denominational schools and colleges should be the mainstay of the republic's education. Rush shared Jefferson's and Madison's concern about creating institutions that would help unify the people into one nation. But Rush was more impressed than Jefferson and Madison by the need for lower schools to provide bulwarks of faith and morals. With Noah Webster, Rush thought much could be done through a common curriculum; and with George Washington, he placed special hopes in the proposed National University, as a postgraduate institution, to bridge what he and Washington saw as the most serious divide in the nation, the divide not of religion but of North and South.

To be sure, the proponents of public schools, including even Jefferson, did not attempt to exclude religion from the schools altogether, which would have been politically impossible at the time. Jefferson did insist, however, that the public schools should not teach religious tenets that were inconsistent with the faith of any sect in the community. But as Rush observed in the case of the University of Philadelphia (and as Jefferson likewise observed, but without the same dismay), attempts at interdenominationalism invariably produce tepidity in religious faith. Although American schools in the nineteenth century managed an uneasy synthesis between inclusiveness and piety by teaching a nondenominational, watery Protestantism, this solution was unsatisfactory to many even among the Protestants, was always unfair to Catholics, and is quite untenable in a society as diverse as ours has become.

It is tempting to speculate on how the Founders' comparatively sparse reflections on school organization, considered in light of their more capacious discussions of goals and curriculum, might be brought to bear on our rather heated contemporary arguments over school organization. Such lessons as we may glean here can only remain at the level of speculations and suggestions. Indeed, one of the Founders' lessons for us may consist precisely in demonstrating the diversity of thoughtful approaches to how republican education can best be delivered. In particular, a study of their disagreements tends to foster the humbling recognition that the most serious cultivation of spirit and character, and the most serious inculcation of tolerance and openness, will not often be found under the same roof, that both are needed, and that thoughtful citizens will, if given a choice, seek different ways of balancing the twin goals of commitment and openness. Perhaps, then, the best answer lies in the paradoxical direction suggested by Theodore Sizer's phrase, "a loose system that has rigor."[50]

The Founders' suggestions would seem to point toward a school system that allows for substantial parental involvement in schools, with administrations that, if not directly overseen by parents, will be imbued with a keen sensitivity to parental concerns about curriculum as well as about discipline and pedagogy. The Founders' suggestions point to a system centered on nonsectarian neighborhood schools but also lend support to sectarian schools of all kinds for those who find in them a more promising soil for the nurture of character and spirit. In contemporary urban conditions, parental freedom to choose among truly diverse schools, in light of the fullest possible information about the relative quality of educational achievement in each school, would perhaps foster not only the sort of parental involvement and control that Jefferson deemed crucial, but also the bracing competition and emulation that the Founders argued was so essential for widespread excellence in education. A Jeffersonian approach would have state governments set spending levels and standards, defining broad curricular goals and guidelines, but allowing great latitude to and diversity among local schools in their adoption of various pedagogical methods to reach those goals and standards.

The strongest message from the Founders is that organization must follow and support curriculum and that curriculum must be unified around a specific and substantial notion of the sorts of character traits that need to be nurtured in young future citizens. Every modern society, including Stalin's, requires productive and technically efficient workers; modern *democratic* society is distinguished by the need to make its highest priority the development of productive workers who are also citizens—energetic, responsible, and capable of sustaining deliberative self-government.

NOTES

1. For eloquent expressions of the problem, see Noah Webster, *A Grammatical Institute, of the English Language, Comprising, an Easy, Concise, and Systematic Method of Education, Designed for the Use of English Schools in America,* pt. 1 (1783; reprint, Menston, England: Scolar Press, 1968), 3, 4, 14; Webster, "On the Education of Youth in America" (1790), in *Essays on Education in the Early Republic,* ed. Frederick Rudolph (Cambridge: Harvard University Press, 1965), 45, 66–67, 70; Benjamin Rush, "Thoughts Upon Female Education, Accommodated to the Present State of Society, Manners, and Government in the United States of America" (1787), in Rudolph, *Essays on Education,* 27–28, 36; Rush, "Address to the American People" (January 1787), in *Benjamin Rush and His Services to American Education,* ed. Harry G. Goode (Berne, Ind.: Witness Press, 1918), 198; and the documents collected in Edgar W. Knight, *A Documentary History of Education in the South Before 1860,* 5 vols. (Chapel Hill: University of North Carolina Press, 1950), vol. 2, chap. 1, especially Jefferson's letter to J. Banister Jr., 15 October 1785.

2. The Jacksonian Democrat James Fenimore Cooper argued for democracy "on account of its comparative advantages, and not on account of its perfection"; his treatise in democratic political theory stressed especially the evils and imperfections peculiar to democracy, because he held to the Aristotelian principle that "under every system it is more especially the office of the prudent and candid to guard against the evils peculiar to that particular system, than to declaim against the abuses of others" (*The American Democrat* [Indianapolis: Liberty Fund, n.d.], author's preface, "On the Disadvantages of Democracy," and conclusion, xxiv–xxv, 80–86, 243; cf. Aristotle, *Politics* 1310A12–35); see Nathan Tarcov, "The Meanings of Democracy," in *Democracy, Education, and the Schools,* ed. Roger Soder (San Francisco: Jossey-Bass, 1996).

3. Cf. the remarkably gloomy assessment by John Dewey, writing in 1929: "American Education and Culture," in *John Dewey on Education,* ed. Reginald D. Archambault (Chicago: University of Chicago Press, 1974), 289–94.

4. Alexis de Tocqueville, *De la Démocratie en Amérique,* ed. Eduardo Nolla (Paris: J. Vrin, 1990), vol. 2, pt. 2, chap. 11, 120–22.

5. Michael J. Sandel, *Democracy's Discontent: America in Search of a Public Philosophy* (Cambridge: Harvard University Press, 1996); what follows draws on and responds to Sandel's provocative thesis. For a fuller discussion, see Thomas L. Pangle, "The Retrieval of Civic Virtue: A Critical Appreciation of Sandel's Democracy's Discontent," in *Michael Sandel's America: Essays on Politics, Law, and Public Philosophy,* ed. Anita L. Allen and Milton Regan (Oxford: Oxford University Press, 1998), 17–31.

6. Cf. Ralph Lerner, "Commerce and Character: The Anglo-American as New-Model Man," *William and Mary Quarterly,* 3d ser., 36 (1979): 3–26.

7. "On the Study of Law in the United States" (1790), in *Selected Political Essays of James Wilson,* ed. R. Adams (New York: Knopf, 1930), 206.

8. Ibid., 210.

9. See especially Noah Webster, "A Letter to the Author, with Remarks," in *A Collection of Essays and Fugitiv Writings* (Boston: Thomas Andrews, 1790), 248, and the definition of "education" given in Webster's 1828 edition of his famous *American Dictionary of the English Language:* "The bringing up, as of a child: instruction; formation of manners. Education comprehends all that series of instruction and discipline which is intended to enlighten the understanding, correct the temper, and form the manners and habits of youth, and fit them for usefulness in their future stations; to give children a good *education* in manners, arts and sciences, is important; to give them a *religious* education is indispensable; and an immense responsibility rests on parents and guardians who neglect their duties."

10. Report of the Commissioners Appointed to Fix the Site of the University of Virginia" (the Rockfish Gap Report), in *The Complete Jefferson,* ed. Saul Padover (New York: Duell, Sloan, and Pearce, 1943), 1097–98.

11. See especially Noah Webster, "An Examination into the Leading Principles of the Federal Constitution Proposed by the Late Convention Held at Philadelphia. With Answers to the Principal Objections That Have Been Raised Against the System," in *Pamphlets on the Constitution of the United States Published During Its Discussion by the People, 1787–88,* ed. Paul L. Ford (Brooklyn, N.Y.: n. p., 1888), 59–61.

12. James Madison, Alexander Hamilton, and John Jay, *The Federalist Papers,* ed. Clinton Rossiter (New York: New American Library, 1961), nos. 9, 10 (pp. 78–84), no. 12 (p. 91), nos. 14, 22 (p. 146), nos. 35, 37 (pp. 226–27), no. 39 (pp. 240–41), nos. 51, 63 (p. 387). See also James Wilson, speech at the Pennsylvania Ratifying Convention, 24 November 1787; and "Of the General Principles of Law and Obligation," in Adams, *Selected Political Essays,* 179–81, 228–35.

13. For the notion of constructive partisanship at the heart of *The Federalist Papers'* conception of vigorous republican political life, see David Epstein, *The Political Theory of The Federalist* (Chicago: University of Chicago Press, 1984), 125, 136, 170, 195–96.

14. *The Writings of George Washington from the Original Manuscript Sources,* ed. John C. Fitzpatrick, vol. 30 (Washington: Government Printing Office, 1939), 493. See also the eloquent formulation of the goals of the new American national civic education in the prize-winning essay by the young Jeffersonian Samuel Harrison Smith: "Remarks on Education, Illustrating the Close Connection Between Virtue and Wisdom" in Rudolph, *Essays on Education,* 220–21.

15. Franklin, "Paper on the Academy" (1750), in *The Papers of Benjamin Franklin,* ed. Leonard Labaree et al., vol. 4 (New Haven: Yale University Press, 1959–), 36, and Jef-

ferson, *The Papers of Thomas Jefferson,* ed. Julian Bond et al., 2 vols. (Princeton: Princeton University Press, 1950–), 2:526–27. See Jefferson's statements of the aim of elementary and of higher academy education in the Rockfish Gap Report in Padover, *The Complete Jefferson,* 1097–98. See also Jefferson's letter to Joseph Cabell, 14 January 1818, in *The Works of Thomas Jefferson ,* 12 vols., ed. Paul L. Ford (New York: G. P. Putnam's Sons, 1905), 12:85–86, and Webster, "On the Education of Youth in America," in Rudolph, *Essays on Education,* 55–57.

16. Jefferson, *Notes on the State of Virginia,* query 14 (New York: W. W. Norton, 1972), 146; Jefferson to John Adams, 28 October 1813, in *The Adams-Jefferson Letters,* 2 vols., ed. Lester J. Cappon (Chapel Hill: University of North Carolina Press, 1959), 2:388. Contrast Lawrence A. Cremin, *The Genius of American Education* (Pittsburgh, Pa.: University of Pittsburgh Press, 1965), 41–47. Jefferson did indicate that he regarded universal elementary education as more important than higher education; see Jefferson to Joseph Cabell, 13 January 1823, in *Early History of the University of Virginia as Contained in the Letters of Thomas Jefferson and Joseph Cabell,* ed. Nathaniel Francis Cabell (Richmond, Va.: J. W. Randolph, 1856), 267–68.

17. See similarly John Dewey, "Ethical Principles Underlying Education," in Archambault, *John Dewey on Education,* 112–17, 129–30.

18. Franklin, "Proposals Relating to the Education of Youth in Pennsylvania" (1749), in *Papers,* 3:405–6 (quoting sec. 168 of Locke's treatise on education). See similarly Webster, "On the Education of Youth in America," in Rudolph, *Essays on Education,* 46–48, but contrast Jefferson's continued insistence on the study of Latin and Greek as the core of high school education: *Notes on the State of Virginia,* query 14, 147–48, and letters to John Brazier, 24 August 1819, in Padover, *The Complete Jefferson,* 1087, and to Joseph Priestley, 27 January 1800, in Ford, *The Works of Thomas Jefferson,* 9:103. Also see Samuel Knox's even more emphatic plea for a national curriculum centered on literary education in the classical languages (Knox was an academy principal and pamphleteer whose essay shared with Samuel Harrison Smith's the 1797 prize given by the American Philosophical Society for the best essay on a national system of education): "An Essay on the Best System of Liberal Education," in Rudolph, *Essays on Education,* 312–14.

19. Franklin, in *Papers,* 3:408, 4:106.

20. Letter to Edward Carrington, 16 January 1787, in *The Life and Selected Writings of Thomas Jefferson,* ed. Adrienne Koch and William Peden (New York: Random House, Modern Library, 1944), 411–12. See also letter to Adamantios Coray, 31 October 1823, in *The Writings of Thomas Jefferson,* ed. Andrew A. Lipscomb and Albert E. Bergh, 20 vols. (Washington, D.C.: Thomas Jefferson Memorial Association, 1903), 15:489; Noah Webster's editorial in the opening issue of his journal *Minerva* (9 December 1793; quoted in Willard Bleyer, *Main Currents in the History of American Journalism* [Boston: Houghton Mifflin, 1927], 113); and Franklin, *The Autobiography of Benjamin Franklin,* ed. Leonard W. Lebaree (New Haven: Yale University Press, 1964), 165.

21. Franklin frequently refers with admiration to the examples of *The Spectator* and *Cato's Letters,* but he also has in mind, of course, his own great contributions to a native American journalism of the first order. Contemporary parallels might be *The New Republic, Commentary, Dissent, National Review,* or nationally syndicated newspaper columnists with antagonistic political leanings.

22. Franklin, "Idea of the English School," and "Proposals," in *Papers,* 3:413–15,

4:104; on Franklin's precise conception of healthy argument, see Labaree, *Autobiography,* 60, 65, 212–13.

23. Samuel Harrison Smith, "Remarks on Education," in Rudolph, *Essays on Education,* 205. See also George Washington, letter to William A. Washington, 27 February 1798, in *Writings,* 36:172; Franklin, "Idea of the English School," in *Papers,* 4:102, 105, 107; and Jefferson, Bill for the Establishment of District Colleges and a University (1817), in Padover, *Complete Jefferson,* 1080. Contrast John Dewey, "Ethical Principles Underlying Education," in Archambault, *John Dewey on Education,* 119–20.

24. Amable-Louis-Rose de Lafitte du Courteil, "Proposal to Demonstrate the Necessity of a National Institution in the United States of America, for the Education of Children of Both Sexes" (1797), in Rudolph, *Essays on Education,* 244–45.

25. On this key point, the Founders stand with Tocqueville's educational thought (*De la Démocratie en Amérique,* vol. 2, pt. 1, chap. 20), and at the opposite pole from Emile Durkheim (*Moral Education,* trans. E. K. Wilson and H. Schnurer [New York: Free Press, 1961], 275–78).

26. "Everything set before the young must be rooted in the particular and the individual. . . . We must make students learn by contact." (Alfred North Whitehead, *The Aims of Education and Other Essays* [New York: Free Press, 1967], 72).

27. For these well-known bitter attacks on Franklin, and, by implication, on the very essence of American democracy, see Max Weber, *The Protestant Ethic and the Spirit of Capitalism,* trans. Talcott Parsons (New York: Charles Scribner's Sons, 1958), esp. 47–56, 64, 70–71, 75–78, 151, 180, 193 n. 6, 194; and the two essays by D. H. Lawrence, both entitled "Benjamin Franklin," in *English Review* 27 (1918): 397–408, and *Studies in Classic American Literature* (1923; reprint, New York: Viking Press, 1961), 9–21.

28. Webster, "On the Education of Youth in America," in Rudolph, *Essays on Education,* 64–65.

29. Noah Webster, *An American Selection of Lessons in Reading and Speaking* (Philadelphia: Young and M'Culloch, 1787); for a well-documented account of the evolution and influence of Webster's textbooks, see Harry R. Warfel, *Noah Webster: Schoolmaster to America* (New York: Macmillan, 1936), and E. Jennifer Monaghan, *A Common Heritage: Noah Webster's Blue-Back Speller* (Hamden, Conn.: Archon Press, 1983).

30. Compare Whitehead's pregnant remarks on the dialectical "rhythm" of "growth" that alternates "romance" and "precision," or "freedom" and "discipline," and that ought to be reflected in an education that inspires: "Moral education is impossible apart from the habitual vision of greatness. . . . The sense of greatness is the groundwork of morals. We are at the threshold of a democratic age, and it remains to be determined whether the equality of man is to be realised on a high level or a low level" (*The Aims of Education,* 21–22, 27–28, 29–41, and 69).

31. Compare John Dewey, confessing in light of current events in 1939 his earlier fundamental mistake: "In the past I have concerned myself unduly with the English writers who have attempted to state the ideals of self-governing communities. If I now prefer to refer to Jefferson, the chief reason is that Jefferson's foundation is moral through and through." Dewey found "the heart of Jefferson's faith" in "his words 'Nothing is unchangeable but the inherent and inalienable rights of man,'" and he stressed and praised the fact that in these words of Jefferson, it is "the *ends* of democracy, the rights of *man*— not of men in the plural—which are unchangeable" (*Freedom and Culture* [New York:

G. P. Putnam's Sons, 1939], 131ff., 155–57). See also Dewey, *Democracy and Education* (New York: Free Press, 1966), 91–93, 96, and Dewey's *Introduction to the Living Thoughts of Thomas Jefferson* (New York: Longmans, Green, 1940).

32. Jefferson, *Papers,* 2:526–27; see also Jefferson, *Notes on the State of Virginia,* query 14, p. 148.

33. Samuel Knox, "An Essay on the Best System of Liberal Education," in Rudolph, *Essays on Education,* 371; see also Franklin, "Proposals," in *Papers,* 3:416–17, and Dewey, *Democracy and Education,* 286–88.

34. Franklin, "Proposals," in *Papers,* 3:404–5 (quoting Locke, *Some Thoughts on Education,* secs. 161 and 210). Compare Dewey, "Ethical Principles Underlying Education," in Archambault, *John Dewey on Education,* 129: "One of the absurd things in the more advanced study of arithmetic is . . . to train the child in these operations, while paying no attention to the business realities in which they will be of use, and the conditions of social life which make these business activities necessary."

35. Franklin, "Proposals," in *Papers,* 3:417–18.

36. Dewey, *Freedom and Culture,* 148–49, *German Philosophy and Politics,* rev. ed. (New York: G. P. Putnam's Sons, 1942), 46–47, 142, and *The Public and Its Problems,* rev. ed. (Chicago: Gateway Books, 1946), x, as well as *Liberalism and Social Action* (New York: G. P. Putnam's Sons, 1935), 70–73, 87, *Experience and Education* (New York: Collier Books, 1963), 81, and *Democracy and Education,* 318–19.

37. Washington, *Writings,* 35:229.

38. "Letter by David," in Herbert Storing, ed., *The Complete Anti-Federalist* (Chicago: Unversity of Chicago Press, 1981), 4.24.2; Charles Turner, in ibid., 4.18.2.

39. Jefferson, *Notes on the State of Virginia,* query 18, p. 163.

40. See esp. Jefferson's Bill for Establishing Religious Freedom, 12 June 1779, in vol. 5, *The Founders' Constitution,* ed. Philip Kurland and Ralph Lerner (Chicago: University of Chicago Press, 1987), 77.

41. See esp. Madison's "Memorial and Remonstrance" on a 1785 Virginia bill to provide support for "teachers of the Christian Religion," in *The Mind of the Founder,* ed. Marvin Meyer (Indianapolis: Bobbs-Merrill, 1973), 8–16; Madison to Edward Livingston, 10 July 1822, ibid., 432–33; and "detached memoranda ca. 1817," in Kurland and Lerner, *Founders' Constitution,* 5:103–4.

42. Michael J. Malbin, *Religion and Politics: The Intentions of the Authors of the First Amendment* (Washington, D.C.: American Enterprise Institute, 1978), 7. For the text of the debate in the House of Representatives on 15, 17, and 20 August 1798, see Kurland and Lerner, *Founders' Constitution,* 5:92–94; for a fuller discussion of the debate and the Founders' views on religion, see Lorraine Smith Pangle and Thomas L. Pangle, *The Learning of Liberty: The Educational Ideas of the American Founders* (Lawrence: University Press of Kansas, 1993), chap. 9.

43. Kurland and Lerner, *Founders' Constitution,* 1:27–29.

44. *The Federalist Papers,* no. 46, pp. 294–95.

45. Letters of James Madison to W. T. Barry, 4 August 1822, to Richard Rush, 22 July 1823, and to George Ticknor, 6 April 1825, in *Letters and Other Writings of James Madison,* 4 vols. (Philadelphia: J. B. Lippincott, 1865), 3:276–81, 332, 486; letter of Jefferson to Joseph Cabell, 28 November 1820, in Ford, *The Works of Thomas Jefferson* 12:170.

46. Franklin, "Observations Relative to the Intentions of the Original Founders of the Academy in Philadelphia" (1789), in *The Works of Benjamin Franklin*, 10 vols., ed. Jared Sparks (London: B. F. Stevens, 1882), 2:133–34, 140–42, 144, 153, 156.

47. Letter of Colonel Coles (Jefferson's private secretary) to Joseph Cabell, 17 July 1807, in Cabell, *Early History of the University of Virginia,* n18; Jefferson to Joseph Cabell, 31 January 1814, in Ford, *The Works of Thomas Jefferson* 11:382, and to Cabell, 2 February 1816, in Koch and Peden, *Life and Selected Writings,* 660–62; to Governor Wilson C. Nicholas, 2 April 1816, in Lipscomb and Bergh, *The Writings of Thomas Jefferson,* 14:454.

48. Dewey, *Freedom and Culture,* 159–61.

49. Lawrence A. Cremin, *The Genius of American Education* (Pittsburgh, Pa.: University of Pittsburgh Press, 1965), 90.

50. See Theodore Sizer, *Horace's School: Redesigning the American High School* (Boston: Houghton Mifflin, 1992).

3

Toward a Political Economy of Citizenship: Historical Perspectives on the Purposes of Common Schools

Carl F. Kaestle

What happened to civic education? Many people believe that the focus on train-ing citizens that was prominent in the nineteenth century gave way in the twen-tieth century to a focus on training workers, and that this shift parallels a decline in political knowledge and political participation. The impression is reinforced by the choice of the two periods most commonly compared, the early national period and America since the 1950s. The political self-consciousness and nation-building mentality of the early nineteenth century contrasts with the role of schools as the arbiter between families and the economy in the information soci-ety of late corporate capitalism.

In this chapter I explore that hypothesis, concluding that at a surface level there does appear to have been a shift from the eighteenth- and nineteenth-century emphasis on the political functions of schools to a post–World War II emphasis on the economic functions of schools, and that indeed the economic functions have become more salient and more consequential in the past fifty years. It is less clear that these shifts are paralleled, as some have claimed, by a decline in political knowledge among the population. I will argue further that the earlier ideas about the functions of schools were not simply political but rather were based on a no-tion of the political economy of the country, whether an agrarian republic in the case of Jefferson or an industrial democracy in the eyes of Dewey. Furthermore, these were contested views. Alexander Hamilton challenged Jefferson's vision of the relationship between the economy and the polity, and Dewey had profound dis-agreements with such theorists as Edward L. Thorndike. All, however, believed that the polity and the economy were inextricably linked and that civic education both flowed from and sustained the economic institutions and practices of the country. This chapter, then, has a dual purpose: to synthesize the existing literature about the history of citizenship and civic education and to reconceptualize the hy-pothesis about a shift from political to economic purposes in education, arguing

47

instead that it would be helpful to reintroduce the notion of the political economy into discussions of civic education.

NATION-BUILDING AND THE
CREATION OF COMMON SCHOOLS

The fountainhead of ideas about civic education in early American political thought is Thomas Jefferson. No one in American history felt more passionately or argued more persuasively about the connection between education and republican government. Jefferson sometimes wavered in his belief that the people would see things right, but when he was in the democratic mood, he was eloquent. He advised his friend George Wythe to "preach a crusade against ignorance," to "let our countrymen know that the people alone can protect us."[1] But Jefferson was only one among many of the leaders of his day to underscore the primacy of citizenship education among the functions of schools. Ruminating on popery, dictators, and the Stamp Act in 1765, young John Adams wrote that "wherever a general knowledge and sensibility have prevailed among the people, arbitrary government and every kind of oppression have lessened and disappeared in proportion."[2] And in a prizewinning essay in 1797, the Jeffersonian editor Samuel Harrison Smith argued that "an enlightened nation is always most tenacious of its rights," and that in a republic a "man feels as strong a bias to improvement as under a despotism he feels an impulse to ignorance and depression."[3]

To be sure, there was a strain between liberty and order. Men of both parties were subject to anxieties about untutored participation and undisciplined learning, as we can glean from Jefferson's often quoted proposition that the ultimate repository of power is in the people, and "if we think them not enlightened enough to exercise their control with a wholesome discretion, the remedy is not to take it from them, but to inform their discretion by education."[4] The Federalists were even more nervous about popular education and thus tended to emphasize the necessity of moral training, discipline, and patriotism. In the most quoted set of authoritarian remarks on republican education in America, Benjamin Rush declared it "possible to turn men into republican machines. . . . Let our pupil be taught that he does not belong to himself, but that he is public property."[5]

Whatever their tone, the state education plans of the republican theorists of the early national period fell mostly on deaf ears.[6] New state legislatures were strapped for funds, the electorates they represented were opposed to new taxes, and there was no tradition of state intervention in matters as local and domestic as the education of children. As Richard Brown has recently pointed out, the "expansive, innovative agencies of public instruction" of this period—newspapers, subscription libraries, academies, debating clubs, and lyceums—were private and voluntary.[7] The point is not that this sense of urgency from leaders of both parties led to the establishment of public school systems, but that they agreed on the central importance of education for citizenship in the new nation. The politics of education was about education for politics.

POLITICS AND PRINT

It is not surprising that Americans focused on citizenship education in the early national period. They had just fought a war with Britain to establish a nation; following this upheaval they had vociferously debated the nature of their constitution. But nation-building went well beyond formal constitutions; the unity and stability of the federated colonies were far from automatic or secure. The former colonialists were engaged in a process of cultural and political innovation described insightfully by Benedict Anderson. Referring to the Americas in general, he wrote: "Out of the American welter came these imagined realities: nation-states, republican institutions, common citizenships, popular sovereignty, national flags and anthems . . . and the liquidation of their conceptual opposites: dynastic empires, monarchical institutions, absolutism, subjecthoods, inherited nobilities, serfdoms."[8] Literacy, public discourse, and education were central to this creation of "imagined realities." And the shift to political concerns was not just a function of the revolutionary moment in American history. It was the culmination of a process that had been evolving throughout the eighteenth century, a shift in the nature of public life and the functions of literacy.

The print culture of seventeenth-century British America had been centrally religious. This was quintessentially true in New England, Calvinism's "City on a Hill," but it was also true to a greater or lesser degree in the central and southern colonies. There was a modest commercial book trade based on English steady sellers; and gradually there developed a small stream of American-produced almanacs. But the acquisition of literacy was enmeshed in religious text, and the great bulk of print culture was godly.[9] As the colonies developed and diversified, and as the colonists became more engaged in imperial politics, a culture of political discussion slowly emerged, centering on newspapers and pamphlets. Beginning timidly in the 1720s and more boisterously by the 1760s, America developed what Jürgen Habermas called a "public sphere," the legitimation of competing ideas in print, an arena in which white males from a wide range of circumstances could participate, a forum for dispute on matters of trade, politics, and emerging American institutions.[10]

The purposes of literacy were public and political. By the mid-nineteenth century, this "sphere" was challenged by new modes of reading and new genres of reading material, epitomized by the private, individualistic readers of novels and the eclectic, extensive readers of magazines. Habermas lamented the same processes of erosion of the public sphere in nineteenth-century Germany: the commercialization attendant upon capitalism and the manipulation of ideas with the advent of interest group politics and bigger government. Print culture was driven increasingly by the market: the profession of authorship, the subsidization of print by advertising, and the commodification of formula fiction all undermined the dedication of print to public discourse. Summarizing the net effect of these two changes from religion to politics and from politics to the market, Richard D. Brown has written that from 1700 to 1865 America "had gone from a society where public information had been scarce, and chiefly under the control of the learned and wealthy few, to a society in which it was abundant and under no control other than the interests and appetites of a vast, popular public of consumers."[11]

But if these were geological changes in print culture, there were nonetheless sturdy layers from the preceding systems: many authors and readers continued to use text principally as the revealed and authoritative Word; and the press continued to accommodate political dialogue despite various media transformations and information explosions, even as commerce governed the bulk of print production. There is a danger of romanticizing the "public sphere" and mistaking Habermas's ideal for a historical reality, yet with all the necessary caveats about restricted access to high-level rational discourse, it remains true that in the early national period, when writers discussed the purposes of literacy and of education, they often focused on republican citizenship. Conversely, occupational preparation was accomplished largely through family or through apprenticeship. In a nation where most children received only a modest elementary education in basic literacy and numeracy, work was learned on the job.

TOWARD A POLITICAL ECONOMY OF CITIZENSHIP

The relevance of republican political theory for citizenship in our own time has been prominently asserted recently. In this book, Lorraine and Thomas Pangle argue that the political thought of the founding generation provides a rich basis for thinking about citizenship education as we move into the twentieth century. They criticize schools for failing to instill character, a sense of unity, and mutual obligations.[12] Michael J. Sandel has placed the now common distinction between republican and liberal thinking at the center of his advocacy of a public philosophy based on republican values emphasizing collective responsibility and substantive character building as a foundation for citizenship education in contrast to the emphasis he sees in liberal thinking on procedural questions and group rights.[13]

Many historians have averred that liberalism and republicanism were intertwined in the early national period. Both republican theorists and liberal theorists talked about rights, and both talked about substantive goals. Jefferson himself forged a liberal republicanism drawing more upon ideas from Locke and Smith than from classical republicanism.[14] In this chapter I do not aim to make a contribution to the ample literature on republicanism and liberalism except to assert that the distinction is neither historically accurate nor very helpful in reflecting on citizenship education today.

I hasten to endorse, however, a different point that Michael Sandel makes: when Jefferson defended an agrarian republic and Hamilton advocated commercial development, they both understood that the nature of the economy in the new nation would help shape the nature of its politics—in other words, that the two spheres were linked.[15] As Drew McCoy wrote nearly twenty years ago, the Republican "revolution" of 1800 inaugurated "a sustained Jeffersonian attempt to secure the requisite conditions for a republican political economy."[16] That the economic system and the political system were interwoven can be seen in plans for education in the early national period. In Benjamin Rush's *Plan for the Establishment of Public Schools,* the first two purposes of education are devotion to liberty and knowledge of government, but the next two are to serve agriculture, the "basis of national wealth," and manufacturing, which "owe their perfection chiefly to learning."[17] Robert Coram's essay on education calls for the government to "furnish the people with means of subsistence."[18]

Many discussions today about the decline of civic education imply that there are two separate sectors and two sets of purposes for education: one political, the other economic. But the two are so frequently and tightly intertwined that it suggests a need to reevaluate the relationship of these two spheres to civic education. We should strip the term "political economy" of the garments it has acquired on its journey from the late eighteenth century to the modern political science department, and we should restore it to discussions of citizenship. Of course, economics and politics are not synonymous. The purpose of the economy is the production of goods, and the structure of authority in the workplace is for the most part unapologetically hierarchical. The purpose of democratic politics is collective decision making, and the structure of authority, in theory, is participatory and egalitarian. As Judith Shklar said, "The individual American citizen is in fact a member of two interlocking public orders, one egalitarian, the other entirely unequal."[19]

In practice, though, the two spheres are intertwined in many ways. Politics in the United States has been less than fully democratic. The franchise has been substantially limited historically, and hierarchy has emerged in government, both because government reflects power relationships and because the practical business of governing requires lines of authority. Furthermore, politics from Jefferson's day to our own has been profoundly influenced by economic issues and interests. Conversely, economic enterprise is influenced by politics in the form of regulatory legislation, tax laws, the assertion of constitutional rights in the workplace, and in countless other ways. In the future, the more potent the global economy becomes, the more citizens will need to address the interpenetration of politics and economics.

Politics and economics in an industrial democracy, then, are connected but often in tension. The recent dominance of economic purposes in educational rhetoric has led many to advocate a revival of the political purposes of education, emphasizing their distinctness and the urgent necessity that we train citizens, not just workers. In this chapter I argue that a more truly democratic civic education

should address both the political and the economic spheres and the tensions between them. A political economy of citizenship would strive to achieve in both
spheres the best elements of the falsely dichotomized republican and liberal
value systems: civic capacity, participation, equity, tolerance, and shared values.

To think of economic preparation as work skills and political preparation as
electoral participation seems naive at best, disingenuous at worst. Certainly it is
crucial that students learn in depth about the Constitution and the workings of government, but I am skeptical about the effectiveness in the long run of conceiving
of civic knowledge, skills, and participation as a separate sphere, competing with
the economic sphere but isolated from it. I am skeptical for two reasons: one, I believe that most concepts of citizenship have flowed implicitly or explicitly from a
sense of political economy; and two, I believe that if civic education stops at the
workplace door, it will be both intellectually and ideologically inadequate.

A new civic education stemming openly from a notion of the political economy could be perilous. It certainly would be difficult. It invites critical thinking, addresses the tensions between group rights and collective obligations, and aims
implicitly at an expansion of democratic participation. Even when civic education
is based on the conventional notion that it is only about political participation, civics
teachers have had to face the difficulty of teaching controversial issues. Schools un-
derstandably shy away from political controversy, and broaching issues of the political economy would present additional challenges. There is much to celebrate in
the history of the American political economy, but many problems remain. Teaching controversies is difficult, but it is also an opportunity to model democracy.

We have touched upon some of the complexities lurking behind the nostalgia for the Founders' ideas about civic education. Jefferson's ideas about education in a republic were rooted in an understanding of the political economy, not
on the primacy of politics over economics. And his ringing endorsements about
the wisdom of "the people" must be understood in the context of a very limited
franchise. Still, the founding generation provided us with inspiring concepts and
traditions to reflect upon—elegant ideas about the nature of liberty, virtue, and
knowledge and about rights and obligations. In this chapter I do not argue that
the nostalgia for the Founders' educational ideas is misplaced, but that we should
focus instead on their insight that citizenship was defined by the political economy. How did citizenship work out in subsequent periods? Did political concepts
recede as the economic purposes of education came to the fore? What have recent historians learned about concepts of citizenship and political participation
when they turned to the years beyond the early national period?

CAVEAT: CITIZENSHIP FOR WHOM?

It is essential when we think of the history of citizenship in the United States that
we ask "whose citizenship?" The electorate of the early national period was a

small minority of the people being governed, and this situation did not change drastically with the expansion of the franchise to more white males in the nineteenth century. For many groups, the history of citizenship is a history of exclusion. In a recent symposium on the history of American citizenship, Linda Kerber thus spoke of a "braided" narrative of citizenship history that must be seen from different eyes: women, African slaves and their descendants, Native Americans, Mexicans whose homelands were incorporated into the United States, people in U.S. possessions, voluntary migrants eligible for citizenship, voluntary migrants ineligible for citizenship, and refugees. Defined vaguely in the Constitution, citizenship has been for many groups "what they made it mean," in Kerber's phrase, when they tried to join the democratic state.[20]

Even among citizens, the features of citizenship differed, involving different legal rights, voting rights, property rights, and other key elements. In a striking retelling of the narrative, Rogers M. Smith has recently argued that American citizenship stems not just from the value systems of republicanism and liberalism but also from various forms of racial and gender supremacy. He recounts the legal history of exclusion from citizenship or its privileges, and the cultural and economic views that shaped unegalitarian civic education.[21]

FREE SCHOOLS AND CITIZENSHIP IN ANTEBELLUM AMERICA

Historians are divided about how rapidly and pervasively the market affected thinking about the political economy in the early nineteenth century. Richard Brown argues that a shift to market orientation began very early: "The self-sacrificing classical republican commitment to the public over the private good that was prominent in 1780's rhetoric waned with each passing decade."[22] Others, such as Drew McCoy, emphasize the continuing ambivalence of the Jeffersonians toward the market, while Sean Wilentz has shown that classical "commonwealth" ideas, with an emphasis on unity rather than individualism, informed an emerging working-class version of republicanism in the early decades of the nineteenth century.[23]

Whatever the impact of the market on republican political thought, the role of schools in training citizens survived into the antebellum period in a fairly robust form. It was during this period, from the late 1830s to the late 1850s, that state school systems were established in the Northeast and the Midwest. The first report of the Michigan superintendent of education declared in 1837: "Among other nations, especially where ignorance prevails in the body politic, violent commotion, anarchy and bloodshed have often followed in the wake of a mere change in the administration of government, whilst we procure reforms and effect quiet revolutions at many of our important elections. Reposing under the standard of civil and religious liberty, we offer to the oppressed of every clime a safe retreat."[24]

However, citizenship education increasingly shared center stage with general moral training and with preparation for productive work, reflecting an Anglo-American ideology uniting three sources of values: republicanism, Protestantism, and capitalism.[25] In Horace Mann's hugely popular *Fifth Report,* he related education to economic productivity. Maris A. Vinovskis has argued that Mann was usually motivated more by political ideals and that the arguments of the *Fifth Report* were a minor issue with Mann, thrown in to protect his besieged board by soliciting the support of industrialists. Indeed, at the end of that report Mann declared that economic profitability "dwindles into insignificance when compared with those loftier and more sacred attributes of the cause."[26] Yet by the time he produced his twelfth and final report as secretary to the Massachusetts Board of Education in 1848, the economic functions of education had become more explicit and prominent, and he seems to have seen the political functions as pro forma, declaring that "the necessity of general intelligence, under a republican form of government, like most other very important truths, has become a very trite one. . . . Almost all the champions of education seize upon this argument, first of all."[27]

The interpenetration of politics and economics in the rhetoric of educational purposes is apparent in this *Twelfth Report.* It weaves together the benefits of education to the elimination of vice and crime, the elimination of poverty, the promotion of social stability, the prevention of radicalism and violent political protest, and the prevention of class hostility. The creation of common schools was an integral part of the Whig Party's program of development, a program that featured a strong state role in fostering the economy and in producing virtuous citizens. The ideology presented in school texts attempted to inculcate and harmonize the traits deemed necessary for the two spheres: respect for property, acceptance of the central role of hard work and restraint, the superiority of republican government, the grand destiny of the United States, and other propositions.[28] That this ideology could be applied with enthusiasm to the polity and the economy simultaneously is illustrated by the plans of the New England Emigrant Aid Company in 1855 for the settlement of Kansas with antislavery emigrants devoted to free labor, free soil, economic enterprise, and the Republican Party. This approach to the settlement process, they said, represented "a new discovery in Political Economy."[29]

These are examples of people who thought the economy and the polity could walk arm in arm if we would only get it right, but of course the two sectors were frequently in tension. The expansion of the franchise and the simultaneous expansion of wage labor in the nineteenth century raised new questions about the relationship of citizenship and work. Although the development of free soil and free labor ideology in the antebellum North helped tie many workers to the social system, there was much anxious talk about "wage slavery" and "factory slavery." Faced with the right to vote and highly undemocratic workplaces, American workers were forced to confront a contradiction. Of course, elite Americans could adhere to concepts of economic and political participation that were compatibly hierarchical. But the working class, argues David Montgomery, faced a tortuous paradox when they pondered how "to preserve the community welfare through both spheres."[30] Recognizing the "limits of bourgeois individualism," in Sean Wilentz's phrase, some fashioned a political ideology around traditional republican values emphasizing solidarity and mutual obligation.[31] But the nineteenth century witnessed the development of other popular beliefs that portrayed work in an open market more positively. The dignity of labor, self-improvement, the self-made man, and the work ethic eased the contradictions of the political economy, though Daniel T. Rodgers has demonstrated how a belief in the work ethic could serve both radical and conservative agendas.[32]

What did the expanding franchise mean? Historians used to characterize the period from 1840 to 1900 as the golden era of political participation in United States history. Recently, revisionists have emphasized that voter turnout was fluctuating and depended heavily on intense mobilization by political parties, that party loyalty was based on factors other than political content, and that voting was therefore largely ritualistic, not an example of rational discourse and choices.[33]

This style of campaigning—featuring spectacular display, symbols, picnics, marches, and party mobilization—characterized the years of greatest voter participation. Issues were not absent, of course; the heyday of participation also produced the most substantial third-party and radical alternatives in American political history. And elections that involved issues of great popular interest, such as that of 1896, attracted larger turnouts. Finally, of course, electoral politics did not exhaust the possibilities of political engagement for ordinary people. But the mainstream election style was oriented toward spectacle and party loyalty, even among third parties. Gradually, from the 1870s to the 1890s, a reform movement began, beginning with Samuel Tilden's "Literary Bureau" in 1886 and broadening among reformers in the 1880s and 1890s. According to Michael E. McGerr, the often cited historian of this transition, the move to make voting more issue-oriented and intelligent served to diminish voter participation. Though ironic, it was also logical. The "educational" style was more challenging, required more work, and was less focused on mere party mobilization. Other factors combined to reduce voting: large-volume immigration, cumbersome voter registration laws, increasing class tensions and stratification, and other possibilities were discussed at the time.[34]

EXACERBATING THE CONTRADICTIONS OF THE POLITICAL ECONOMY: THE "PROGRESSIVE" ERA

Progressive reformers responded to declining political participation with proposals to make voter registration easier, to provide Americanization classes for immigrants, and to gain acceptance for procedures they thought would make participatory democracy more democratic: women's suffrage, referenda, the recall of public officials, and the direct election of the Senate, innovations familiar to us from our high school history textbooks. At the same time, however, the country was undergoing severe labor strife, rapid immigration, and economic consolidation, which produced the "search for order" familiar to us from our college textbooks.[35] Thus, while education was expanding and various forms of political participation were opening up, many Americans were facing workplaces, schools, and courts devoted to efficiency and the primacy of business. Structural changes in the economy gave rise to various theories about how elites could gain control of a complex industrial society. Faced with these problems and armed with these tools, schools focused more on students' preparation for work.

As corporate capitalism increased the demand for white-collar labor, and as child labor declined, secondary school attendance increased. In 1890 the proportion of youths age fourteen to seventeen who were in high school fell just short of 7 percent. By 1920 it was 32 percent, and by 1970, 94 percent.[36] As the century progressed, school attainment increased dramatically, and schools changed in the process. The curriculum at the secondary level diversified, and schools increasingly became the arbiters between families and the economy. The proportion of students taking a full-scale track called "vocational education" was never very great; but as Marvin Lazerson and W. Norton Grubb argue, schools became more generally "vocationalized," guiding students through diverse courses of study toward predicted futures.[37] Taylorism in industry, expertise in the professions, stratification in the social structure, theories of social control in the social sciences, the creation of more bureaucracies—many developments increased the forces of hierarchy in the early twentieth century.

The blending of educational purposes that we observed in the antebellum period can also be found in the late nineteenth and early twentieth centuries: education can promote productivity, moral conduct, individual mobility, and the survival of the American political system. The image of the well-behaved, hardworking, Americanized immigrant took on more and more prominence, and the union of economics and citizenship was tight. The Factory Inspectors of Illinois declared in 1895 that the "children of immigrant toilers need the best educational facilities which any American city can provide, if they are to develop into useful citizens of value to the industrial life of their generation."[38]

As schools became the arbiters between families and the economy, reformers advocated a new sort of civic education. The "new civics" shifted the emphasis in citizenship education from electoral participation to good community membership. Julie A. Reuben argues that beyond the clichéd interpretation of social control (which nonetheless makes some sense), this shift was grounded in two features. First, the school curriculum was catching up with legal and cultural developments that disconnected citizenship from the franchise. Various late-nineteenth-century legal cases made a sharp distinction between citizenship and voting, and the new civics texts of the Progressive era made this clear. Second, many political theorists and civics textbook writers thought that the nineteenth-century emphasis on voting rights and political participation impeded the building of powerful state institutions. Civics texts thus emphasized the provision of government services in such areas as health and recreation. Citizenship included all people, including children, and it covered all aspects of life.[39] We do not know how many schools ignored the new civics texts and continued to teach about the Constitution and the machinery of government, but the message from the theorists and the professional spokespeople was clear: citizenship was about being a good community member.

The stratification of the secondary school curriculum and the role of the schools in guiding children toward occupational destinations may seem to provide the perfect evidence for a narrative about the increasing prominence of economic purposes of schools and the declining importance of civic education. Alternatively (and I believe more usefully), it can be seen as a perfect example of a political economy that generated ideas about civic education as well as occupational training. The prevailing view of the political economy in the Progressive era was strongly hierarchical, and the new civics was consistent with that central belief. It emphasized responsibility and community over rights and participation.

We have, then, two interpretations of the history of civic education. One is that civic education declined as occupational training rose. The other is that educators' understanding of the political economy generated their ideas about both civic and occupational preparation. Next I will apply these two alternative interpretations to our own time: the United States since World War II. Is it helpful to think of how the political economy generates purposes for political and economic participation in the society, or is it more accurate to see a decline in civic education at the hands of increasing emphasis on education for work?

FROM POLITICS TO MARKETS IN THE TWENTIETH CENTURY

Adding to the impression of a decline in civic education in our own time, the necessity of an educated citizenry has receded into the background in discussions about education while the necessity of improved education for work has come to the fore. In the 1960s, politics was melded with economics when issues of equality focused on equal opportunity in training and work and when the government chose education as the chief weapon in the "war on poverty." After the recessions of the 1970s and 1980s, it became apparent that American economic growth would not sail into the twenty-first century with its cargo of an ever-enhanced standard of living intact. At that point the concern for training smarter and more productive workers spread to the population as a whole. In the famous *Nation at Risk* manifesto of 1983, the National Commission on Excellence in Education barely mentioned citizenship; its central theme was economic. America's "preeminence in commerce, industry, science, and technological innovation is being overtaken by competitors throughout the world." America is witnessing "a redistribution of trained capability throughout the globe. Knowledge, learning, information, and skilled intelligence are the new raw materials of international commerce and are today spreading throughout the world. . . . If only to keep and improve on the slim competitive edge we still retain in world markets, we must dedicate ourselves to the reform of our educational system."[40]

A decade later Ray Marshall and Marc Tucker wrote a book whose title announced the school-to-work theme—*Thinking for a Living: Education and the Wealth of Nations*. Arising from the work of the Carnegie Corporation's Forum on Education and the Economy, the book was influential during the early years of the Clinton administration. It argued that "more than ever before, nations that want high incomes and full employment must develop policies that emphasize the acquisition of knowledge and skills by everyone, not just a select few. The prize will go to those countries that are organized as national learning systems. . . . Our most formidable competitors know this."[41] Another prominent commission, the Secretary's Commission on Achieving Necessary Skills, began its 1991 report with assurances that other functions of education were important, not just readiness for work. Preparing students to "participate in their communities" was as close as they got to civic education. The titles of the commission's first two reports reflect the nation's central preoccupation with education in the 1990s: *What Work Requires of Schools* (1991) and *Learning a Living: A Blueprint for High Performance* (1992).[42]

One can find a myriad of statements about the purposes of education, scattered around and ritually repeated. More examples, then, would further illustrate but not "prove" that there was a shift from political to economic purposes. Most people familiar with the literature on education seem to agree that there is a difference of emphasis between the early national period and the present era. The post–World War II emphasis on education for work skills seems unsurprising in a world in which work demands more thinking, where equal opportunity is defined as access to work, where the central postwar *political* preoccupation—the Cold War—has evaporated, and thus where international rivalry has come to be measured by trade balances and math scores. Was the apparent shift to economic purposes accompanied by a decline in Americans' political knowledge?

THE PARALLEL DECLINE: POLITICAL KNOWLEDGE

This sense of a decline in civic education has been reinforced by data suggesting that students are studying less history and government, and that they *know* less about these subjects. As chair of the National Endowment for the Humanities, Lynne V. Cheney lent her voice to the decline theme, arguing that the culprit in the decline of history learning was "process," an undue emphasis on skills over substance, attributable largely to the problem orientation of the "social studies" rubric under which history is often subsumed.[43] In an article on "the precarious state of history," Diane Ravitch traced the conclusions of major commissions empaneled to assess the study of history and social studies since the 1890s, showing the gradual retreat from a commitment to traditional historical content.[44] Also, in an assessment of factual knowledge of literature and history, she and her coauthor, Chester E. Finn Jr., admitted in passing that they did not have any data from any previous time, but they implied a decline thesis when discussing the disappointing results of their 1985 assessment of knowledge in history and literature. There is, they argued, "ample reason to wonder whether the younger generation is culturally illiterate." The spread of remedial courses, they said, "has contributed to the sense that our society is breeding a new strain of cultural barbarian," informed only by television.[45]

LAMENTING THE DECLINE

This sense that not only the rhetoric but the reality of schools has shifted away from the training of citizens for democratic government has prompted some extensive commentaries in our time. In the 1980s, Morris Janowitz called for a return to patriotic civic education in the schools and the establishment of voluntary national service to inculcate civic obligation in young Americans. In *The Reconstruction of Patriotism* he painted a stark contrast between the way civic education had been conducted in public schools from 1890 to 1940 and the deterioration he saw from 1945 onward. In the earlier period, he points out, immigrant training in the English language, American political culture, and American history were high goals. According to Janowitz, the patriotism, acculturation, and English dominance demanded by the schools were mild, fair, and widely accepted. Civics instruction emphasized obligations as well as rights, and history texts were strongly nationalistic, venturing little or no criticism of the country.

In the 1930s, two elements interrupted this mode of civic education, which, in Janowitz's eyes, had been successful and appropriate. First, the Depression spawned criticism of American society and left-leaning materials for schools that drew upon social realism. These were only adopted by a minority of the teaching profession, but, according to Janowitz, it portended ill for the coherence of the system of civic education that had prevailed to that point. Second, at American universities some students began to be vocal in opposition to mainstream policies. These tendencies, submerged in the 1940s and 1950s, flowered by the 1960s into what Janowitz called the "new communalism," by which he meant an emphasis on group or individual rights, ethnic insularity, and separatism, epitomized by black power and especially by bilingual education, all accompanied by the breakdown more generally of education for civic obligation.[46]

Janowitz's views are very conservative but relevant to contemporary debate seventeen years after he wrote *The Reconstruction of Patriotism*. Among these views are his conviction that the expansion of group rights was corrosive rather than salutary, that early-twentieth-century schools were mild about assimilation and respectful of immigrants' cultures, that schools in recent decades have emphasized group rights and not citizens' obligations, that "Latinos are the most pronounced exception to the absorptive capacity of the American social structure," and that "Mexican Americans are more concerned with their rights than their obligations."[47] Considerable evidence could be brought to bear against each of these generalizations, yet such views still retain much popularity.

Another proposal, from a more moderate position, for the revival of civic education came from R. Freeman Butts. Like Janowitz he broke his narrative into two periods. One, from 1820 to 1930, he characterized as a period of pluralism and modernization; the second, from 1930 to the present, was simply a period of the "decline of civic purposes." Unlike Janowitz, Butts recognized that there had been a demand for "rapid assimilation to a stridently nationalistic Americanism" in the face of increasing immigration in the late nineteenth and early twentieth centuries.[48] He seems agnostic about the results of civic education in the early twentieth century but notes positively that schools tried to keep civic education central in the social studies curriculum. Butts sees the decline of civic values proceeding as much from neoconservatives' attacks on the welfare state and their advocacy of privatization and choice as he does from the divisive effects of cultural pluralism. He bemoans the lack of emphasis on citizenship in the "excellence" reports of the 1980s, as well as in E. D. Hirsch's advocacy of memorized cultural facts and William Bennett's advocacy of private school choice. Butts is a traditionalist; he wants common public schools, and he wants them to revive the teaching of civics.

Other voices for the revival of civics came from prominent liberals like Ernest Boyer. In *High School: A Report on Secondary Education in America,* released by the Carnegie Foundation for the Advancement of Teaching in 1983, Boyer argued for a high school course in American history to deepen students "understanding of our national heritage . . . with special emphasis on the people, ideas and issues that have shaped the nation." In addition, he proposed a one-year course on American government, citing public distrust in institutions, the complexity of public issues, and the need to have "as a central goal of education" ways for students to "learn about their social memberships." "Civic illiteracy is spreading," warned Boyer. He feared that ignorance might lead to an undemocratic rule by experts. In addition to more coursework in history and government, he proposed that all high school students volunteer to do community service to learn "that they are not only autonomous individuals but also members of a larger community."[49]

CRITIQUING THE DECLINE THESIS: NO NEW BARBARIANS, NO GOLDEN AGE

We have seen that the nineteenth century's "golden age" of political participation is largely a myth: higher percentages of voters went to the polls than today, but there is not much evidence that they deliberated on the issues. Is it possible that the twentieth-century decline in political knowledge is also a myth?

In 1976, on the bicentennial of the American Revolution, some distinguished historians were asked by the *New York Times* to rate political knowledge among the general public. They gave a multiple-choice quiz that demanded fairly subtle reasoning and knowledge. The widely publicized results were disappointing, and many people scored poorly. Less noticed was the historians' inclusion of a batch of items from a similar survey in 1943, so that they could assess whether there had been a decline. The levels of ignorance were indistinguishable over the thirty-year span.[50] Surveys of assessed knowledge that *do* look at data over time have led some observers to two debatable conclusions: first, that the level of general public knowledge about history and politics is shockingly low both in earlier and recent periods; and second, that despite increased educational attainment, the levels are slightly less now.[51] Similar efforts more recently have yielded comparable results. Dale Whittington has mustered much relevant data and concludes that there has not been much change in history knowledge over time.[52] Other emerging work, particularly Lawrence C. Stedman's studies of trends in academic knowledge over time, suggest that there has been little or no decline in knowledge in successive cohorts of American students, and that the problem for our society is the stagnation of knowledge and literacy skills in the face of escalating demands as well as the gaps in achievement across racial and income groups.[53]

In a recent monograph on trends in political knowledge, Michael X. Delli Carpini and Scott Keeter conclude that public knowledge of politics has been remarkably stable over the past fifty years.[54] Yet this stability has persisted during a time of great increases in educational attainment when one might have expected increasing knowledge of history and politics. They explain the stasis as a function of countertrends: there has been increasing educational attainment but deteriorating trust in government; increasing media information but declining newspaper reading and other trade-offs.

What are the implications of this and other recent work on the public's knowledge of civics and its relationship to education? Samuel L. Popkin has argued that people are more knowledgeable than is alleged and that measuring facts is not a good indicator of how we use knowledge; rather, we employ various "short-cuts" and substitutes for knowledge (like recommendations from trusted friends, public endorsements, or a candidate's previous positions and character) and have other strategies for making rational decisions on low amounts of information. "My theory," he writes, "redeems the voter from some of the blame heaped upon him or her by contemporary criticism. . . . There is more meaning to voting and less manipulation of voters than either media-centered analyses or the traditional civics-information focus would have us believe."[55] Claims about a decline in political knowledge, resulting in a public not only indifferent but ignorant, should be treated with caution. Nevertheless, the schools must do much more than they are now doing if we are to create the kind of "strong democracy" Benjamin Barber has advocated—vigorous, pervasive, participatory democracy.[56] For this task, civic education does not need to be "revived" but rather redefined. The redefinition should be based on the presumption that civic education proceeds from a concept of the political economy and that civic education and workplace preparation should be related in much more reflective ways. Before summarizing that argument, however, one further "decline" must be assessed.

PARTY POLITICS AND PUBLIC SCHOOLS: THE DEPOLITICIZATION OF EDUCATION

Running parallel to the perceived decline of democratic education in the schools is a demise in the democratic control of education. Conceptually they are distinct, and historically they can be analyzed separately. Yet as a matter of policy, I believe they should be related; at least, in postmodern fashion, they should "interrogate" each other. The question of democratic control of education leads necessarily to a related question, the involvement of political *parties* in educational governance.

As we have seen, both Jeffersonian Republicans and Federalists placed a high value on education in their political rhetoric about the fledgling republic. Differences in emphasis were not great and, as it turned out, were inconsequential for policy because their plans for education were too ambitious for cautious state legislatures. Fifty years later, the variations in party positions on public education made a much greater difference in the United States. In the twenty years preceding the Civil War, state governments in the Northeast and the Midwest intervened in unprecedented ways in support of local schooling, which was largely a victory for the distinctive views of the Whig Party. Both the Jacksonians and the Whigs, to be sure, approved of free public schooling and an educated white male citizenry. In the Whigs' view of the world, however, the state needed to play a strong role in education. Whigs drew upon the dominant Protestant evangelical culture, were more uniform and more Anglo-American in their constituency, and developed a program for national development and collective moral improvement. They were thus more interventionist and more urgent about discipline, character, and cultural assimilation.[57]

The Democrats, in contrast, were more culturally diverse in their constituency, more tolerant about cultural differences, and more laissez-faire about government action. They tended to favor local school control. The key reforms of the antebellum period—state school superintendents, mandatory local property taxes for free schools, state school funds for modest local aid—were in general passed by Whig legislatures. In many states the battles were fierce and partisan. Orestes Brownson accused Horace Mann of attempting to "Prussianize" the public schools of Massachusetts; Mann responded that the "political madmen [were] raising voice and arm" against him and his state board.[58] In a vote in the Massachusetts legislature in 1840 on Mann's possible ouster, the strongest predictor was party affiliation.[59] In New York, Vermont, Ohio, Connecticut, and elsewhere, the parties played out the same struggle, with the Whigs attempting to erect new state systems of education and the Democrats striving to preserve local control with minimal state involvement.

In the later nineteenth century, the politics of education became more complicated and submerged. In large cities, school boards contracted for textbooks, city governments saw school systems as part of the patronage system, and in various ways education became a business. At the same time, educational administration was becoming professionalized and the systems bureaucratized. The hydra-headed "Progressive" education movement began in this context, reacting to these developments. In its dominant mode—guided by notions of efficiency, expertise, and professionalization—the reformers moved to centralize schools. It was a political agenda, often carried forward by Republicans or Progressive Party members fighting Democratic urban "machines," and it expressed ethnic and class tensions.[60] But the reformers did not present it that way; they proposed that education had nothing to do with politics, should not be a party issue, and should be insulated from the formal political process through such devices as nonpartisan elections and appointive boards. This was a politics of antipolitics.

William Estabrook Chancellor established this belief as orthodoxy in a 1904 text, arguing that the best board members, those who could see the good of the whole, were manufacturers, merchants, and professional men.[61] These ideas elicited opposition not only from ward politicians but also from many teachers, parents, and trade unionists. And in the 1920s, George S. Counts, in a study of school board membership, called this image of disinterested professionals serving everyone's interests a "pious fraud."[62] But it prevailed. The general drift toward centralization and professionalization did diminish the direct involvement of political parties in school governance, and the growing myth that education should be insulated from politics seems to have worked. It is an ironic myth, as Roscoe C. Martin has remarked, because it distanced the schools from participatory politics even as they promoted themselves as the training ground for future citizens.[63]

These developments received a provocative interpretation in a book by Ira Katznelson and Margaret Weir entitled *Schooling for All: Class, Race, and the Decline of the Democratic Ideal* published in 1985. *Schooling for All* is relevant to our interest in the relationship between democratic governance of schools and schooling for democratic citizenship. Katznelson and Weir demonstrate through two urban case studies that workers were active in the politics of education in the late nineteenth and early twentieth centuries, in San Francisco through the lens of ethnic identity and in Chicago as organized labor. But in order to gain ground on some of their key objectives, workers allied themselves with professionals and middle-class reformers; in this process they narrowed and limited their goals.[64] At the same time, the reformers and professionals sought to depoliticize education, masking the political nature of centralized administration and stratified curriculum. "The domestication of class and the depoliticization of reform went hand in hand."[65] But it was an unstable coalition, and the effort to keep party politics out of the schools was quixotic.

In both of the cities studied by Katznelson and Weir, patronage was reestablished, but again in limited areas and with limited goals. The central premise of *Schooling for All* is that full democratic participation should have aimed for two goals of truly common schools: universal access and the same curriculum for all children.[66] The first goal, they conclude, has largely been met: access has dramatically improved and is nearly universal. The second goal has receded farther and farther from reach over the course of the century as schools became more segregated and more stratified.[67] *Schooling for All* is a fascinating read and a stirring call for renewed equality and participation in our schools. It needs a more robust explanation about how nonelites acceded to the professionalization, depoliticization, and stratification of the schools. And, despite its subtitle ("the Decline of the Democratic Ideal"), it mainly emphasizes the failure of workers to oppose differentiated school programs and touches lightly upon the connection between democratic participation and training for democracy. In the nineteenth century, the authors argue, the local politics of education "created a common forum of citizens" that has largely disappeared.[68]

In several important ways, as Katznelson and Weir and others have argued, both the centralization of administration and various potent market forces have increased segregation and different treatment of students in schools while they diminished dialogue and participation by adults on these issues. In some other regards, however, the politics of education has made another revival, at a much more public level than the submerged political deals of the 1930s and 1940s that Katznelson and Weir note. The 1950s witnessed a flurry of educational politics: widespread criticism of the weak "Life Adjustment" variant of Progressive education, then the Cold War scare dramatized by Sputnik and the subsequent curriculum reforms spawned by the National Defense Education Act of 1958. This insertion of international politics into American education led to bipartisan support, helping to escalate the federal government's role in shaping elementary and secondary education in local school districts.

More important, the federal government's themes and goals shifted dramatically in the 1960s, and this time the educational debate had partisan overtones. Leaders of the maturing civil rights movement pressured President John F. Kennedy on racial issues, the federal courts put teeth into the desegregation process begun slowly by the *Brown* decision, and urban riots bore out the prophetic phrase of James B. Conant that there was "dynamite in the slums."[69] Six brief years after the passage of the National Defense Education Act, President Lyndon Johnson had shepherded the Civil Rights Act of 1964 followed by the Elementary and Secondary Education Act of 1965 through a Democratic Congress.

Thus, the 1960s and 1970s witnessed the resurrection of education as a partisan political arena at the national level. The Democrats took the more interventionist, reformist positions, while the Republicans either reacted defensively, opposing such measures, or, eventually, developed their own program of reform, informed by an agenda of excellence and rigorous academic content as well as various proposed mechanisms for parental choice. As in the antebellum period, one political party decided to use education to further its vision of a better, reformed society, and it tried to use central authority to impose its program on local government. In the antebellum period, it was the Whigs at the state level; in the 1960s and 1970s, it was the Democratic Party at the national level. Both had a view of the proper citizen for the republic, and both proceeded from their respective understanding of the political economy of their day.

The Whigs were more culturally conformist than today's Democrats, although in terms of their own time, they thought they were being cosmopolitan, trying to integrate more people into the mainstream culture, creating a single system for people of different classes, and eliminating sectarian religious views from schools. It is always easier to see the cultural narrowness of an ideology when it is farther back in time. The liberal Democratic program of the 1960s and 1970s was more pluralistic, and in some regards more coercive, and it upset many traditional interests and beliefs. The backlash against this program in the 1980s has been chronicled many times, and it continues into the 1990s.[70] One legacy of the liberal, federal effort, however it turns out, is that educational policies and philosophies have once again become connected with the major political parties, and, for better or for worse, educational issues have also been highly political at the state and local levels in recent decades.

One ironic possibility, painful to liberals, is that resurgent educational politics could lead to public subsidies for private schooling. Democratic participation does not guarantee that the outcome will move in the direction of common school systems. One author who raises an alarm about this possibility is Jeffrey R. Henig. He not only connects democratic participation in the control of schools with the necessity of maintaining a common school system but also connects both of those features with civic education. In a book-length argument against private-school choice, Henig articulates this relationship: "Responding to the failures of our schools by turning away from government, politics, and public deliberations . . . almost certainly will make things worse. . . . Democratic government plays an absolutely critical role in airing alternative visions, encouraging compromise, and enticing disparate groups to redefine their interests and find common ground." More to the point of our inquiry about civic education, Henig argues that "education is a process through which individuals come to richer and broader understandings of their interests and how they relate to those of others. . . . Government policy toward public schools is the major opportunity that democratic societies have for upgrading the quality of insight and sensitivity on which future majority decisions will rely."[71]

THE MAIN ARGUMENT RESTATED

I have presented some of the evidence for the view that civic education, a central purpose in the early years of our public schools, has in the twentieth century receded in the face of an increasing emphasis on the preparation for work, and that some underlying structural realities shaping schools in the twentieth century suggest that the rhetorical shift is matched by some changing functions. In important ways, however, the rhetorical shift is a distraction, likely to mislead the search for a revival of schools as democratic institutions. The premise of a sectoral shift from political to economic functions should be qualified in three ways. First, educational leaders of the early republic saw economic purposes related to their political goals, and, conversely, the economic functions of schools in the twentieth century are inextricable from political considerations. Second, more incidentally, the jeremiads about declining political knowledge are exaggerated, and the nostalgia for a golden age of political participation is misplaced. Third, the idea of distinct sectors of politics and economics, sectors that could generate distinct purposes for education, is simplistic. It would be more fruitful to think of a political economy that generates purposes for education, all of which have political, economic, and cultural functions.

TOWARD A POLITICAL ECONOMY OF CITIZENSHIP: IMPLICATIONS FOR CIVIC EDUCATION

We need a vision of civics education that acknowledges how economics and politics overlap. The leaders of the Revolutionary generation had such a vision, as did the reformers of the Progressive era. The political economy of the early republic and the political economy of early corporate capitalism are evident in the educational reforms of the early nineteenth and early twentieth centuries. One finds their manifestation at the rhetorical level, at the structural level, and at the curricular level. For an adequate civic education we need an understanding of our political economy, the political economy of the information society and of advanced corporate capitalism. We need a vision of civic education that will include economics and politics, work life and political life.

One beginning point lies in the parallels we observe in separate discussions about what is needed for effective work life and what is needed for effective citizenship in the contemporary United States. Commentators underscore the need for problem-solving, critical thinking, flexibility, and reasoning.[72] Whether most workplaces actually prize such abilities is a difficult question, but the trend is in this direction, and it is more than a fad. At a topical level, some scattered elements of political economy are already taught in many schools—such as civil rights in the workplace, government regulation pertaining to work conditions and the environment, issues regarding international trade, and other matters. One could provide many further opportunities for students to reflect upon the intersections of democracy and capitalism, some controversial, some not, some historical, some contemporary. A political economy of citizenship would promote the idea in schools that both the polity and the economy need citizen workers who can solve problems, who are anxious to participate, and who have both broad knowledge and broad tolerance.

Some educators fear that when talk turns to a tighter fit between work and school, it means that businesspeople will be calling the shots for education, as in the Progressive era, when some educators asked business leaders to specify what they wanted from the schools. Indeed, there are impatient spokespeople on the current scene who think that schools are doing a lousy job providing the kind of workers that industry needs. The concept of a political economy of citizenship would be a different approach. Rather than an invasion of schools by hierarchically minded businesspeople, it would seek to capitalize on the best impulses of workplace theorists and invade the workplace with an expanded notion of democratic participation.

I do not believe that calls for a "revival of civic education" will get much attention. It has been tried many times without much success, and it largely overlooks the interpenetration of economics and politics. We need instead an analysis of the simultaneously economic and political nature of public issues, and we need to breed such a sense in students' analytical repertoires. We need a vision of a good, empowered citizen in a corporate capitalist world, with elements of appropriate knowledge, critical thinking, collaborative skills, ethics, and sense of obligations. The sense of ethics and obligations must pervade all sides of power relationships and not be aimed principally at the duties of subordinates toward those in power. With such a concept of the political economy of citizenship, we need not bemoan the preoccupation of schools with training for the workplace. We can embrace it and transform it.

NOTES

For research assistance and astute comments during the gestation of this essay, I wish to thank Sarah Hodges and Nicholson Collier of the University of Chicago, Edward Rafferty and Adam Nelson of Brown University, as well as the conference participants, in particular Rob Reich of Stanford. Two of the editors of this volume, Lorraine M. McDonnell and P. Michael Timpane, also provided valuable encouragement and prodding to more complex thinking during the revision. The remaining inadequacies are entirely mine.

1. Thomas Jefferson to George Wythe, August 13, 1786, in *Crusade Against Ignorance: Thomas Jefferson on Education,* ed. Gordon C. Lee (New York: Teachers College Press, 1961). On Jefferson's periodic doubts about popular wisdom, see Richard D. Brown, *The Strength of a People: The Idea of an Informed Citizenry in America, 1650–1870* (Chapel Hill: University of North Carolina Press, 1996), 87–89.

2. John Adams, "A Dissertation on the Canon and Feudal Law," in *The Works of*

John Adams, ed. Charles Francis Adams (Boston: Charles C. Little and James Brown, 1851), 448.

3. Samuel Harrison Smith, "Remarks on Education" (1797), in *Essays on Education in the Early Republic,* ed. Frederick Rudolph (Cambridge, Mass.: Harvard University Press, 1965), 188–89. Smith shared with Samuel Knox the American Philosophical Society's prize awarded in 1797 for the best plan for a system of education in the new republic.

4. Thomas Jefferson to William Charles Jarvis, September 12, 1820, in *The Works of Thomas Jefferson,* 12 vols., ed. Paul L. Ford (New York: G. P. Putnam's Sons, 1904–1905), 10:161.

5. Benjamin Rush, "A Plan for the Establishment of Public Schools and the Diffusion of Knowledge in Pennsylvania" (Philadelphia: Thomas Dobson, 1786), in Rudolph, *Essays on Education,* 14, 17. Lorraine Smith Pangle and Thomas L. Pangle caution against undue emphasis on this Rush essay in their book, *The Learning of Liberty: The Educational Ideas of the American Founders* (Lawrence: University Press of Kansas, 1993), 290 n. 9, 295 n. 3, where they criticize Frederick Rudolph, Linda Kerber, and Gordon Wood for exaggerating the typicality of such sentiments.

6. I note the modest exceptions to this lack of action in Carl F. Kaestle, *Pillars of the Republic: Common Schools and American Society, 1780–1860* (New York: Hill and Wang, 1983), chap. 1.

7. Brown, *Strength of a People,* 93.

8. Benedict Anderson, *Imagined Communities: Reflections on the Origin and Spread of Nationalism,* rev. ed. (London: Verso, 1991), 81.

9. David D. Hall, *Worlds of Wonder, Days of Judgment: Popular Religious Belief in Early New England* (Cambridge, Mass.: Harvard University Press, 1989), chap. 1.

10. Jürgen Habermas, *The Structural Transformation of the Public Sphere: An Inquiry into a Category of Bourgeois Society,* trans. Thomas Berger (Cambridge, Mass.: MIT Press, 1989); Michael Warner, *The Letters of the Republic: Publication and the Public Sphere in Eighteenth-Century America* (Cambridge, Mass.: Harvard University Press, 1990).

11. Richard D. Brown, *Knowledge Is Power: The Diffusion of Information in Early America, 1700–1865* (New York: Oxford University Press, 1989), 286.

12. See Chapter 2, pp. 36–43, of this book.

13. Michael J. Sandel, *Democracy's Discontent: America in Search of a Public Philosophy* (Cambridge, Mass.: Belknap Press of Harvard University Press, 1996).

14. See Susan Okin, review of Sandel, *Democracy's Discontent,* in *Political Theory 91* (June 1997): 440–42; Joyce Appleby, *Liberalism and Republicanism in the Historical Imagination* (Cambridge, Mass.: Harvard University Press, 1992), 323–38; Linda K. Kerber, "The Republican Ideology of the Revolutionary Generation," *American Quarterly* 37 (1985): 474–95; and Richard E. Ellis, "The Market Revolution and the Transformation of American Politics, 1801–1837," in *The Market Revolution in America: Social, Political, and Religious Expressions, 1800–1880,* ed. Melvyn Stokes and Stephen Conway (Charlottesville: University Press of Virginia, 1996), chap. 6.

15. Sandel, *Democracy's Discontent,* chap. 5. Sandel titled the second section of his book "The Political Economy of Citizenship." Published in spring 1996, it came into my hands in the fall of that year after I had titled this chapter "Toward a Political Economy

of Citizenship." His intention is to tie the phrase "political economy" to the values of early republican thinkers; my intention is to advocate a civic education that addresses the relationship between the economy and the polity.

16. Drew McCoy, *The Elusive Republic: Political Economy in Jeffersonian America* (Chapel Hill: University of North Carolina Press, 1980), 187.

17. Rush, "Plan," in Rudolph, *Essays on Education,* 4.

18. Robert Coram, "Political Inquiries, to which is added, A Plan for the General Establishment of Schools" (1791), in ibid., 113.

19. Judith Shklar, *American Citizenship: The Quest for Inclusion* (Cambridge, Mass.: Harvard University Press, 1991), 63–64.

20. Linda Kerber, "The Meanings of Citizenship," *Journal of American History* 84 (December 1997): 833–54.

21. Rogers M. Smith, *Civic Ideals: Conflicting Visions of Citizenship in U.S. History* (New Haven, Conn.: Yale University Press, 1997). Other notable entries in this burgeoning scholarship include Linda K. Kerber, *No Constitutional Right to Be Ladies: Women and the Obligations of Citizenship* (New York: Hill and Wang, 1998); Dana D. Nelson, *National Manhood: Capitalist Citizenship and the Imagined Fraternity of White Men* (Durham, N.C.: Duke University Press, 1998); and Nancy Isenberg, *Sex and Citizenship in Antebellum America* (Chapel Hill: University of North Carolina Press, 1998).

22. Brown, *Strength of a People,* 105.

23. McCoy, *Elusive Republic,* chap. 8; Sean Wilentz, *Chants Democratic: New York City and the Rise of the American Working Class, 1788–1850* (New York: Oxford University Press, 1984); Kerber, "Republican Ideology," 491–93.

24. *Report of the Superintendent of Public Instruction of the State of Michigan . . . January 5, 1837* (Detroit, 1837), 6.

25. Kaestle, *Pillars of the Republic,* chap. 5.

26. Mann, *Annual Report* (1842), quoted in Maris A. Vinovskis, "Horace Mann on the Economic Productivity of Education," *New England Quarterly* 43 (December 1970): 571.

27. Horace Mann, *Twelfth Report* (Boston: Massachusetts Legislature, 1848).

28. Kaestle, *Pillars of the Republic,* chap. 5.

29. *Herald of Freedom,* March 30, 1855, cited in Gunja SenGupta, *For God and Mammon: Evangelicals and Entrepreneurs, Masters and Slaves in Territorial Kansas, 1854–1860* (Athens: University of Georgia Press, 1996), 80–81.

30. David Montgomery, *Citizen Worker: The Experience of Workers in the United States with Democracy and the Free Market During the Nineteenth Century* (Cambridge: Cambridge University Press, 1993), 12; see also Charles Sellers, *The Market Revolution: Jacksonian America, 1815–1846* (New York: Oxford University Press, 1991), and Eric Foner, "Free Labor and Nineteenth-Century Political Ideology," in Stokes and Conway, *Market Revolution,* chap. 4. Note also, however, Daniel Feller's caution, in "The Market Revolution Ate My Homework," *Reviews in American History* 25 (September 1997): 408–15, that the phrase "market revolution" means so many things to different historians that it must be used with caution.

31. Wilentz, *Chants Democratic,* 101.

32. Shklar, *American Citizenship,* chap. 2; Daniel T. Rodgers, *The Work Ethic in Industrial America, 1850–1920* (Chicago: University of Chicago Press, 1978), chap. 8.

33. Michael Schudson, "Was There Ever a Public Sphere? If So, When? Reflections on the American Case," in *Habermas and the Public Sphere,* ed. Craig Calhoun (Cambridge, Mass.: MIT Press, 1992), chap. 6, and Schudson, *The Good Citizen: A History of American Civic Life* (New York: Free Press, 1998). See also Glenn Althschuler and Stuart M. Blumin, "Limits of Political Engagement in Antebellum America: A New Look at the Golden Age of Participatory Democracy," *Journal of American History* 84 (December 1997): 855–85.

34. Michael E. McGerr, *The Decline of Popular Politics: The American North, 1865–1928* (New York: Oxford University Press, 1986); Schudson, "Was There Ever a Public Sphere?"

35. Robert Wiebe, *The Search for Order, 1877–1920* (New York: Hill and Wang, 1967). Note that school texts deliver the good news in elementary and secondary school and the bad news in college, which says something about the politics of civic education.

36. Ken A. Simon and W. V. Grant, *Digest of Educational Statistics* (Washington, D.C.: U.S. Department of Education, 1970).

37. Marvin Lazerson and W. Norton Grubb, eds., *American Education and Vocationalism: A Documentary History, 1870–1970* (New York: Teachers College Press, 1974), 26, 32, 39.

38. *Third Annual Report of the Factory Inspectors of Illinois* (Springfield, Ill.: H. W. Rokker, 1895), 40.

39. Julie A. Reuben, "Beyond Politics: Community Civics and the Redefinition of Citizenship in the Progressive Era," *History of Education Quarterly* 37 (Winter 1997): 399–420.

40. National Commission on Excellence in Education, *A Nation at Risk: The Imperative for Educational Reform* (Washington, D.C.: U.S. Department of Education, 1983), 1.

41. Ray Marshall and Marc Tucker, *Thinking for a Living: Education and the Wealth of Nations* (New York: Basic Books, 1992), xiii.

42. Secretary's Commission on Achieving Necessary Skills, *What Work Requires of Schools* (Washington, D.C.: U.S. Department of Labor, June 1991); ibid., *Learning a Living: A Blueprint for High Performance* (Washington, D.C.: U.S. Department of Labor, April 1992).

43. Lynne V. Cheney, *American Memory: A Report on the Humanities in the Nation's Public Schools* (Washington, D.C.: National Endowment for the Humanities, 1987).

44. Diane Ravitch, "The Precarious State of History," *American Educator* 9 (Spring 1985): 11–17.

45. Diane Ravitch and Chester E. Finn Jr., *What Do Our 17-Year-Olds Know?* (New York: Harper and Row, 1987), 13.

46. Morris Janowitz, *The Reconstruction of Patriotism: Education for Civic Consciousness* (Chicago: University of Chicago Press, 1983), 73–144.

47. Ibid., 129, 131.

48. R. Freeman Butts, *The Civic Mission in Educational Reform: Perspectives for the Public and the Profession* (Stanford, Calif.: Hoover Institution Press, 1989), 122.

49. Ernest Boyer, *High School: A Report on Secondary Education in America* (New York: Harper and Row, 1983), 101, 104–5, 209–10.

50. Edward B. Fiske, "*Times* Test of College Freshman Shows Knowledge of Americans' History Is Limited," *New York Times,* May 2, 1976.

51. See Stephen Earl Bennett, " 'Know Nothings' Revisited: The Meaning of Political Ignorance Today," *Social Science Quarterly* 69 (1988): 476–90, and "Trends in Americans' Political Information, 1967–1987," *American Politics Quarterly* 17 (October 1989): 422–35; National Assessment of Educational Progress, *Changes in Political Knowledge and Attitudes, 1969–1976* (Washington, D.C.: U.S. Department of Education, March 1978).

52. Dale Whittington, "What Have 17-Year-Olds Known in the Past?" *American Educational Research Journal* 28 (1991): 759–80.

53. Lawrence C. Stedman, "International Achievement Differences: An Assessment of a New Perspective," *Educational Researcher* 26 (April 1997): 4–15; see also Carl F. Kaestle et al., *Literacy in the United States: Reading and Readers Since 1880* (New Haven, Conn.: Yale University Press, 1991), 75–145.

54. Michael X. Delli Carpini and Scott Keeter, *What Americans Know About Politics and Why It Matters* (New Haven, Conn.: Yale University Press, 1996).

55. Samuel L. Popkin, *The Reasoning Voter: Communication and Persuasion in Presidential Campaigns* (Chicago: University of Chicago Press, 1991), 7, 21.

56. Benjamin Barber, *Strong Democracy: Participatory Politics for a New Age* (Berkeley: University of California Press, 1984).

57. See Daniel Walker Howe, *The Political Culture of the American Whigs* (Chicago: University of Chicago Press, 1979), chaps. 1 and 2.

58. Brownson's attack is found in the *Boston Quarterly Review,* October 1839; Mann's response is in his "Journal," January 5, 1840, Horace Mann Papers, Massachusetts Historical Society, Boston.

59. Carl F. Kaestle and Maris A. Vinovskis, *Education and Social Change in Nineteenth-Century Massachusetts* (New York: Cambridge University Press, 1980), 219–30.

60. See David B. Tyack, *The One Best System: A History of American Urban Education* (Cambridge, Mass.: Harvard University Press, 1974).

61. William Estabrook Chancellor, *Our Schools: Their Administration and Supervision,* rev. ed. (Boston: D. C. Heath, 1915), 12–13; see also Ellwood P. Cubberley, *Public School Administration* (Boston: Houghton Mifflin, 1916), 124–25.

62. George S. Counts, *The Social Composition of Boards of Education: A Study in the Social Control of Public Education* (Chicago: University of Chicago Press, 1927), 87.

63. Roscoe C. Martin, *Government and the Suburban School* (Syracuse, N.Y.: Syracuse University Press, 1962), 89.

64. Ira Katznelson and Margaret Weir, *Schooling for All: Class, Race, and the Decline of the Democratic Ideal* (New York: Basic Books, 1985), 84.

65. Ibid., 126.

66. It is curious that Katznelson and Weir react negatively when professionals or academics try to define the participation of workers, but they leave unexamined in their own work the premise that workers should have fought for a uniform curriculum. This position was not self-evident to working-class leaders in the early twentieth century, some of whom advocated vocational education.

67. Katznelson and Weir, *Schooling for All,* 221.

68. Ibid., 215–16.

69. James B. Conant, *Slums and Suburbs* (New York: McGraw-Hill, 1961).

70. See, for example, Rosemary C. Salomone, *Equal Education Under Law: Legal Rights and Federal Policy* (New York: St. Martin's Press, 1986), chap. 6.

71. Jeffrey R. Henig, *Rethinking School Choice: Limits of the Market Metaphor* (Princeton, N.J.: Princeton University Press, 1994), 24.

72. Lauren Resnick, "Learning in School and Out," *Educational Researcher* 16 (December 1987): 13–20; Francis Schrag, *Thinking in School and Society* (New York: Routledge, 1988); Benjamin Barber, *An Aristocracy of Everyone: The Politics of Education and the Future of America* (New York: Oxford University Press, 1992).

4

Why Should Schools Care about Civic Education?

Amy Gutmann

Why should primary and secondary schools in the United States concern themselves with civic education? To begin answering this question, I go back to a basic justification of democracy: the capacity of a democratic society to cope with political disagreements among citizens in a more mutually justifiable way than its alternatives. In the first part of this chapter I highlight three different, though not mutually exclusive, ways that democracy can deal with disagreement: procedurally, constitutionally, and deliberatively. Each of these ways is emphasized by a major conception of American democracy. But at their strongest, proceduralists, constitutionalists, and deliberative democrats recognize that fair procedures, constitutional rights, and moral deliberation about controversial political issues are all necessary, while none are sufficient, to deal well with the wide range of disagreements that are unavoidable in a modern, diverse democracy. The second part of the chapter connects these three ways of dealing with disagreement with corresponding skills and virtues of democratic citizenship. In the third part I compare these skills and virtues with reasons why schools can and should constructively engage in civic education. The fourth and concluding part describes how, contrary to the claims of some prominent defenders of a voucher system, a system of decentralized democratic control is consistent with less bureaucracy, more choice, and explicit recognition of the importance of the civic aims of education in a democratic society.

THREE WAYS OF DEMOCRATICALLY DEALING WITH DISAGREEMENTS

How can democracy best respond to moral disagreements?[1] Procedures are necessary for the fair and peaceful resolution of moral conflicts, and no one has yet proposed a decision-making procedure that is *generally* more justified than majority rule. If political equals disagree on moral matters, the greater rather than the lesser number should normally rule. The alternative imposes the claims of the minority on the majority. The alternative may sometimes be justified, but it calls for a justification of why some citizens' moral convictions count for more than those of others.

When majority rule is justified, the decision of a majority at any particular time is provisional. Subsequent majorities may revise it. Members of the losing minority can accept majoritarianism as a fair procedure even when it yields incorrect results as long as it respects their status as political equals. The results of majority rule are legitimate as long as the procedure is fair, but not because the results are necessarily right. Numerical might does not make a decision morally right. When majority rule is not the fairest procedure, another procedure needs to be justified with a rationale that is compatible with democratic values.

Fair procedures are essential to a healthy democratic society. But for procedures to be fair, citizens must appreciate the value of fairness as well as the value of majority rule (or its cousin, plurality rule). Majority rule is not always fair in itself or by itself. It typically needs to be accompanied by a concern for fairness so that majority decisions do not infringe upon the legitimate claims of individuals. Fundamental constitutional values—including free speech, free press, free association, the rule of law, universal adult suffrage, and religious freedom—serve as constraints on majority rule in American constitutional democracy. Some of these values are justified on procedurally democratic grounds, as necessary to preserve the integrity of the democratic process itself over time. If a majority votes to disenfranchise women, for example, it will be destroying an important precondition of a fair democratic procedure: universal adult suffrage. Something similar can be said if majorities take it upon themselves to restrict political speech, which is necessary, but not sufficient, for majority rule to be a fair process of registering the considered opinions of citizens as free and equal beings.

But it is not only as a condition of a fair democratic process that constitutional constraints on majority rule can be justified. Freedom of religion and of conscience and equal protection under the laws, for example, are valuable independently of any contribution they make to the democratic nature of the political process. Religious freedom is widely recognized as a basic liberty of individuals and deserves protection as such in its own right, not only as a precondition of a fair democratic process. Equal protection under the laws is necessary to protect the basic opportunities of all individuals. As these examples suggest, American constitutional democracy recognizes certain substantive values not only as preconditions to a fair democratic process but also as fundamental values independent of that process, and as such, they represent a second basis for resolving political disagreements.

The Bill of Rights is the primary, although not the only, collective reference point for these substantive values. Not only the judiciary, but legislatures, bureaucracies, private associations, and individual citizens are responsible for respecting and protecting individual rights, to the extent that it is within their legitimate power. Constitutional rights need to be protected against both majorities and minorities who threaten the basic liberties or basic opportunities of individuals.

But the basic liberties and opportunities of individuals are not always easily discernible. In the past, American constitutional democracy did not recognize or respect many of the basic liberties and opportunities that are routinely recognized and respected today, most conspicuously of women and black Americans but also of many other less obviously disadvantaged Americans. It would be hubris on the part of American citizens today—and dangerous—to assume that we and our political institutions are recognizing every basic liberty and opportunity (and only those) that are worthy of protection. Moreover, it is obvious, although too easily overlooked, that we disagree on how to interpret even constitutional protections—including freedom of speech, religious freedom, equal protection, and due process of law—that most Americans would affirm in the abstract. The "we" who disagree, often reasonably, include Supreme Court justices, legislators, public officials in charge of interpreting statutes, and private citizens to whom public officials are supposed to be accountable. We cannot realistically expect to resolve all of our politically relevant disagreements, nor would it be desirable for us to do so unless we resolved them on terms that were clearly justifiable. But who among us can demonstrate that controversies over abortion, affirmative action, capital punishment, pornography, school reform, health care reform, welfare reform, foreign interventions, and terms of trade with foreign countries are resolvable, either for now or once and for all, on clearly justifiable terms?

The third way that democracies can deal with disagreements is by citizens and public officials deliberating over the moral disagreements that proceduralism and constitutionalism, taken alone, leave unresolved. Deliberation is public discussion and decision making that aim to reach a justifiable resolution, where possible, and to live respectfully with those reasonable disagreements that remain unresolvable. James Madison emphasized the importance of deliberation to American democracy, or what he and the other Founders called republican government.[2] Voting is a far more valuable act if preceded by open-minded argument where different sides not only represent their own views but also listen to others and try to reach an economy of moral disagreement, which minimizes rejection of those opposing positions that are worthy of respect.[3]

Defenders of proceduralism, constitutionalism, and deliberative democracy agree that the fundamental values of democratic institutions, such as equal political liberty, must be justified by moral arguments that are in principle acceptable to citizens who are bound by them. All seek to show that democratic institutions protect the equal right of citizens to participate in political processes and to enjoy basic liberties and opportunities. They also agree that individual citizens should be regarded as moral agents who deserve equal respect in any justifications of basic procedures and constitutional rights. Deliberation, rather than being an alternative to procedures or constitutional rights, adds to both proceduralism and constitutionalism a way of explicitly respecting individuals as moral agents as we continue to disagree about important issues in everyday democratic discussion and decision making. Deliberation calls upon citizens and public officials to try to justify our political positions to one another and in so doing to take into account the viewpoints of others who reasonably disagree with us.

To simplify somewhat, democratic procedures require that we count ourselves as one, and no more than one, among equals in political decision making; constitutional rights require that we respect and protect the basic liberties and opportunities of all individuals even against a majority's decision to override those rights; and democratic deliberation requires that we discuss our political disagreements with one another, including our disagreements over fair procedures and constitutional rights, in an attempt to economize on moral disagreements and respect those that invariably remain. If fair procedures, constitutional constraints, and moral deliberation could resolve political disagreements once and for all, a democratic form of government might no longer be necessary. But an end to political disagreement in any modern democracy would signal the rise of repression, not the success of proceduralism, constitutionalism, or deliberation.

SKILLS AND VIRTUES FOR DEALING WITH DISAGREEMENTS

For its effectiveness in dealing well with disagreements, American constitutional democracy has been designed to depend partly on institutions such as an electoral system that secures one person one vote, a judiciary empowered to protect constitutional rights, and a legislature that deliberates before it votes. But people with certain skills and virtues—not those of saints, but those of citizens—are needed to realize the moral promise of the methods of proceduralism, constitutionalism, and deliberation. The methods do not work automatically. They also and importantly depend for their success on citizens and accountable public officials, acting in a spirit of cooperation and understanding. One need only think of a citizenry voting to disenfranchise women and a judiciary deferring to the majority on this decision. Or one might imagine voting on any and all public matters by means of a personal computer terminal without any deliberation among citizens or their representatives. Considering these possibilities serves to indicate the considerable extent to which these three basic ways of dealing with disagreement in American democracy already depend to an important extent on the willingness and ability of individuals to support institutions that try to resolve disagreements consistently with fair procedures, constitutional rights, and public reasoning.

The procedural, constitutional, and deliberative institutions, practices, and policies that exist depend on the ongoing support of citizens and their representatives. But this is only half of the story. Those institutions, practices, and policies that *could improve* the capacity of American democracy to resolve disagreements also depend on citizens and their representatives for collectively identifying and creating them. And those that present obstacles to improving American democracy similarly depend on citizens for changing them. There is no reason to believe that either every existing practice and policy or none of them serves the purposes of proceduralism, constitutionalism, and deliberation well as modes of resolving disagreements on moral terms in American democracy. In light of the reasonable disagreements that undoubtedly exist, citizens and representatives should try to justify controversial political practices to one another. Mutual justification is not only often an effective means to better outcomes, but it is also in itself a manifestation of mutual respect. If deliberation is the greatest political promise of American democracy, it is also one of the greatest challenges, especially as the United States grows in diversity and distrust.

Proceduralism, constitutionalism, and deliberation depend on individuals in ways that therefore call for certain civic skills and virtues that would otherwise be less important. To the extent that these skills and virtues are closely connected to democracy's ways of dealing with disagreement, publicly funded schools should be called upon to cultivate them. I will first describe the skills and virtues that are needed to support proceduralism, constitutionalism, and deliberation and then examine the ways in which schools can be called upon to cultivate these skills and virtues.

Each way of resolving disagreements calls upon citizens to exercise certain civic skills and virtues more than others. Proceduralism requires law-abidingness, respect for fair rules, and reasonable expectations of winning and losing. Fair political procedures cannot possibly guarantee that any one person's opinion will carry the day, even when that person's opinion is correct. Proceduralism therefore also requires a capacity to delay gratification of one's desires, to tolerate dissent, and to persist in pursuing an outcome that one believes is just.

Proceduralism cannot assume that established procedures are fair, so it also calls for the ability of citizens to discern the difference between those that are fair and unfair. Citizens should try to change unfair procedures, just as some Americans opposed the discriminatory poll tax. Citizens also need to discern the difference between procedural outcomes that lie within the bounds of constitutional legitimacy and those that do not. From the perspective of procedural democracy, for example, a majority vote to decrease (or even end) public support of the arts is a qualitatively different outcome from a majority vote to fine or disenfranchise artists whose work offends the moral sensibilities of the majority. The former is within the legitimate power of the majority to legislate, while the latter is not.

Some people are likely to disagree with where I have drawn the line between the legitimate and illegitimate power of the majority. Others may disagree with what you or I take to be fair democratic procedures in today's political context, and any plan of action that is in place for resolving such disagreements over procedure is itself likely to be subject to reasonable disagreement. There is no morally certain escape from the possibility of such an infinite regress. Although proceduralism looks to procedures for resolving disagreements, it must look beyond them in any narrow sense of the term for dealing with moral disagreements about them, such as which are fair and what outcomes are illegitimate even if they followed from a fair procedure. This limitation of proceduralism in dealing with disagreement points to the need for citizens to possess another important set of skills and virtues without which this process will be far less likely to distinguish fair from unfair procedures or legitimate from illegitimate outcomes of fair procedures.

These skills and virtues are closely tied to constitutionalism and deliberation. Constitutionalism calls for the capacity of citizens to distinguish between legitimate and illegitimate outcomes of political procedures as well as between fair and unfair procedures. Citizens must not only discern their own rights but also respect the rights of others. Restraint is often required in order to respect the rights of others, as when someone publicly speaks in terms that are morally offensive. Constitutionalism also calls on citizens to have the courage to stand up for those rights that are being violated, whether by a minority or majority.[4]

Several important constitutional rights—such as free speech and freedom of religion—require citizens to possess the virtue of tolerance. Other constitutional rights—such as equal protection and due process—require citizens to possess and practice the virtue of nondiscrimination in their everyday associations with one another. Americans must not discriminate on the basis of color, gender, religion, or sexual orientation in any business, commercial, or other public contact with each other. And they must be able to discern what kind of behavior nondiscrimination entails: more than just a prohibition on charging more or paying people less but also a prohibition on decreasing or increasing their opportunities because of irrelevant characteristics such as skin color.

Because deliberation involves trying to reason together about public policy in an effort to reach mutually acceptable decisions, it explicitly calls upon citizens who disagree on many moral and political issues not only to tolerate one another but also to develop mutual respect. Mutual respect entails the capacity to discern and respectfully discuss disagreements over what constitutes fair procedures and defensible constitutional rights. Both the procedural and constitutional aspects of democracy have more potential for self-improvement to the extent that citizens and their accountable representatives are willing and able to deliberate about the fairness of procedures and the legitimacy of their outcomes. Although the civic skills associated with democracy also include the ability to negotiate and bargain, the deliberative capacity of citizens is needed to distinguish between those times when bargaining and negotiation are more and less appropriate. Bargaining and negotiation, we might think, are important skills to enlist in situations where agreement on moral terms is unnecessary (because nothing morally important is at stake) or undesirable (because one or another side in the controversy is unwilling to assume a moral perspective and therefore is likely to take advantage of anyone who did). It is the willingness and ability to deliberate that enables citizen to discern when these situations arise. Without the capacity to deliberate, there would be no escaping from power politics, which all moral conceptions of democracy are intent on avoiding.

Why do American citizens need to deliberate about constitutional rights when a written constitution enumerates those rights, and a judiciary is authorized to interpret and enforce them? Any extended discussion of the practical implications of free speech, religious freedom, and nondiscrimination would demonstrate that interpretations of constitutional rights are open to reasonable disagreement. Does the constitutional protection of free speech also protect all forms of pornography? Does the constitutional protection of religious freedom permit parents to exempt their children from any parts of a public school curriculum that offend their religious beliefs? Does the constitutional prohibition on racial discrimination also extend to a prohibition on taking race into account as one factor among many in employment or college admissions? For these disagreements to be resolved on moral terms rather than by self-interested or group-interested bargaining, citizens and their accountable representatives must be willing and able to engage in a politics of reasoning and persuasion rather than a politics of manipulation and coercion. We must be willing and able to engage with one another in public discourse that is empirically informed and morally reasonable. We must be willing and able to recognize and treat other citizens as equals in democratic discourse and decision making on the condition that they extend the same recognition and treatment to us. This capacity is sometimes called civility, but it should not be confused with etiquette or politeness even in the face of oppression. Civility is a moral (not an aesthetic) attitude, which depends on reciprocity: you treat me as an equal provided I treat you as such.

We earn each other's respect as equal citizens in some very basic ways. We show ourselves capable of abiding by the results of fair procedures, honoring the rights of others, and supporting the passage of laws and public policies that we can justify to one another. We develop and defend our political positions by addressing the reasonable concerns of others and having similar expectations of others. Without the civic skills and virtues that allow us to earn each other's respect as equal citizens, a democracy cannot resolve the disagreements that arise among its citizens on moral grounds or expect its citizens to live well with those disagreements that invariably remain.

DEVELOPING CIVIC SKILLS AND VIRTUES THROUGH SCHOOLING

What role should schools play in cultivating the civic virtues of a democratic society? A citizenry without the skills and virtues that support proceduralism, constitutionalism, and deliberation does not bode well for a democratic society. There is a great deal of concern these days that families, schools, and other social institutions are not cultivating such skills and virtues. There is also a great deal of cynicism about whether anybody or any institution has the will or knows the way to make a moral difference. In contemporary democratic politics and political discourse, communicating by sound bite, competing by character assassination, and resolving political conflicts through self-seeking bargaining, logrolling, and pork-barreling too often substitute for moral deliberation on the merits of issues.

Recommitting primary and secondary education in the United States to the value of democratic citizenship would be one important way of reducing this democratic deficit. Although the need for our political life to rely less on sound bites and more on substantive interchange is ever more widely appreciated, the need to improve education in a more democratic direction is still sorely neglected, to the detriment of both education and democracy.[5] Unless American citizens, educators, and public officials alike increase our appreciation of educating all children not merely for literacy, numeracy, economic productivity, and academic excellence but also for the more inclusive goal of democratic citizenship, we will forsake the promise of American democracy before we even begin to try.

Emphasizing the civic responsibilities of our educational system is certainly not the only way or a sufficient way to improve either our educational system or American democracy. Nonetheless, the public justification offered for a publicly funded system of primary and secondary education has long been that of providing educational opportunity for all and educating all to the skills and virtues of democratic citizenship. There is no single realm more distinctively connected to these two purposes, and there is perhaps a greater social need than ever for schools to focus on civic purposes in light of the decline in other civic associations and the increasing demands placed on parents. Parents undoubtedly can have more influence over children than schools, but they also have far broader responsibilities for children than that of education for opportunity and citizenship.

Schools are the major realm in which every nonadult member of society should, if possible, be taught the skills and virtues that are necessary for effective citizenship in an increasingly complex and interdependent society. Well-run schools model some of the most basic skills and virtues that need to be conveyed to students: they institutionalize fair procedures, honor individual rights, and expect everyone who is part of the school to demonstrate mutual respect by doing his or her share to contribute to its educational mission.

There is also evidence, outlined in several excellent studies, that the curriculum of schools can make a difference in teaching some of the more demanding virtues of democratic citizenship, such as toleration and mutual respect.[6] Some of these studies show that diverse groups of students, working together on a mutual project over an extended period of time, effectively increase toleration, and the increases have some staying power over time. A skeptic might still challenge the very idea that teaching toleration by schools can be publicly defended in light of the differing perspectives about right and wrong, good and bad, decent and indecent, worthy and unworthy, that are present in a pluralistic, multicultural democracy. But the skeptical challenge either proves too much or too little.

It proves too much if it doubts that publicly subsidized schools can defend the teaching of any values. Schools cannot help but teach values, even if they do so unconsciously, by who teaches and is taught, what is included and excluded from the curriculum, and how students are taught inside and outside of the classroom. The claim that teaching toleration is controversial proves too little if it simply calls attention to the lack of universal agreement on almost any basic value. The fact that toleration and other fundamental values of American democracy are controversial offers no reason not to defend their teaching. Quite the contrary, if the fundamental values of democracy were uncontroversial, there would be far less reason for schools to concern themselves with teaching civic values.

Publicly subsidized schools, like democratic governments more generally, are public trusts. Democratic citizens have no better alternative than to educate future citizens to those civic values, like toleration, that are procedurally, constitutionally, and deliberatively defensible. Schools in the United States can teach toleration, probably not under all circumstances and against all odds, but in enough situations that the call for civic education in schools is not an idle one. Schools can also teach deliberation. Diane Ravitch offers an excellent example of the way in which a public school in Brooklyn, New York, taught students to deliberate in a history class, taught by Mr. Bruckner. The students were discussing whether it was moral for the United States to drop the atomic bomb on Japan: "The lesson was taught in a Socratic manner. Bruckner did not lecture. He asked questions and kept up a rapid-fire dialogue among the students. 'Why?' 'How do you know?' 'What does this mean?' . . . By the time the class was finished, the students had covered a great deal of material about American foreign and domestic politics during World War II; they had argued heatedly; most of them had tried out different points of view, seeing the problem from different angles."[7]

This kind of teaching makes students exercise and thereby develop their capacities to reason collectively about politics—an ability that is no less essential to democratic citizenship because it is difficult to measure by survey research. Some surveys show that different kinds of teaching do make a difference in the effectiveness of civic education in the classroom.[8] Education is not only a public good. The prerogatives of parental education in the family must also be given their due in a constitutional and deliberative democracy. Parents are a child's primary educators except in the desperately unfortunate situations where children have no families. But just as democratic governments in the United States are constitutionally bound to recognize the rights of parents, so too parents have a constitutional responsibility as American citizens to recognize that their children are also future citizens of a democratic society, with their own rights and responsibilities.

Should schools go beyond teaching the most basic virtue of toleration and also teach mutual respect? Toleration—an attitude of live and let live that entails no positive regard among citizens—is an essential value of American constitutional democracy and one of its great historical accomplishments. Toleration makes peace possible, a precondition for all other democratic accomplishments. But toleration is not enough to create a democratic society with liberty and justice for all, where "all" includes people of differing religions, ethnicities, colors, and cultures. Absent mutual respect, people discriminate against each other on the basis of a host of cultural differences; we fail to take each other's political perspectives seriously; and we therefore treat each other in ways that are not conducive to constructive collective action. If educators do not try to teach future citizens the importance of mutual respect among people whose ideas and perspectives on life differ from their own, who will? Educators can teach mutual respect by encouraging their students to engage in the give and take of argument, as did Mr. Bruckner in the Brooklyn public school. In the process of arguing vigorously but respectfully about a political issue, students learn to reflect, individually and collectively, on both the reasonable differences and commonalties that constitute a pluralistic democracy.

To teach and to learn in this way demand open-mindedness and engagement on the part of both teachers and students with perspectives different from one's own; neither moral relativism nor skepticism is required. Mutual respect can be cultivated by learning from diverse people and perspectives, not by giving up one's own beliefs but by discovering that they are informed by those of others. Learning to learn from others does not promise resolution of all the differences that divide a pluralistic democracy. Such comprehensive unity is surely impossible in a free society and is in all likelihood undesirable. Learning to learn from others is part of the virtue of mutual respect among citizens, and mutual respect expresses the democratic ideal of equal citizenship. Mutual respect is also an instrumental value: it enables a democracy provisionally to resolve as many differences as possible in a mutually acceptable way. Bringing more mutual respect into education addresses the challenge of moral pluralism on democratic terms rather than trying to dissolve differences by either philosophical or political fiat.

A recent study of perspectives on citizenship education suggests that despite varying views among social studies teachers of what citizenship education ideally should be, self-identified conservatives, moderates, and liberals all share a core set of convictions about citizenship education that include the following: encouraging tolerance and open-mindedness, addressing controversial issues, and developing an understanding of different cultures.[9] These are also among the civic virtues recommended by procedural, constitutional, and deliberative ways of resolving disagreements in democracy. I have suggested some ways that schools can teach these virtues and cited several studies that provide an "existence proof" that various methods make a positive difference in teaching some of these virtues. If there was a will among schools to teach the virtues and skills of democratic citizenship, the evidence suggests there would be more than one way to do so.

DEMOCRATIC CONTROL WITH LESS BUREAUCRACY
AND MORE CHOICE

Public schooling in a democracy can and should take civic education seriously, which is intimately connected to taking democracy itself seriously. Civic education is a necessary and central part of a democratically defensible school system.[10] Some critics suggest, however, that public oversight of schools, which is closely associated with public concern for civic education, is educationally counterproductive because it is a recipe for a highly bureaucratized school system.[11]

The critics are certainly correct in thinking that too much bureaucracy in schools is typically an obstacle to achieving desirable ends of democratic education. It takes effective teachers to convey to students the importance and substance of the skills and virtues of citizenship, and teachers often are not very effective in highly bureaucratic schools. The "effective schools research" of the 1970s and early 1980s demonstrated that many of the major characteristics of effective schools (and by extension effective teaching) are incompatible with large bureaucratic structures.

Among the characteristics of effective schools are strong leadership at the school level, teacher participation in educational decision making, active parental support and cooperation, clear goals that are effectively articulated at the school level, rigorous academic standards, high expectations for student performance, regular homework, order, and discipline.[12] Some of these characteristics, such as teacher participation in educational decision making and active parental support and cooperation, are almost impossible to achieve in large, bureaucratic, top-down institutional structures. Others—rigorous academic standards and responsiveness to new ideas—are far easier to achieve in relatively unbureaucratic schools, where teachers are treated as professionals whose academic standards and ideas for improving education make a difference. But no one should conclude from this research that decreasing bureaucracy in schools is a sufficient condition for making schools satisfy even the minimal aims of a democratic education.

Some of the most prominent academic defenders of educational vouchers pose the choice among school systems as a stark one: decentralized market control or centralized public control. But there is a third way, which is neither of these.[13] Defenders of the third way are every bit as critical of the status quo in inner city schools as defenders of a market system. The third way, simply stated, is decentralized and democratic. A decentralized, democratic system can (and ideally probably should) have many variations, subject to the discretion of democratic citizens, such as charter schools, theme schools, neighborhood schools, schools-within-schools, and vouchers that may be used for any public school. The third way supports a variety of decentralized public school systems, the variety being subject to democratic approval at the local level. (Parents may use the public schools at taxpayers' expense or use an accredited private school at their own expense. Poor parents may not have the latter option, but the unfairness inherent in their inability to opt out of a public school system is the unfairness of poverty, not the unfairness of not subsidizing private schools with public tax monies.)

Decentralized democratic control encourages citizens, parents, teachers, and public officials to work together through public institutions to create new and better public schools. This approach has been implemented even in some big cities, for example, in New York, where small, decentralized charter schools have been created in recent years, which are open to parental choice. Parents are free to choose among several public schools for their children even if they do not live in the school's neighborhood, and schools therefore are encouraged to respond to educational needs and demands that are not those of a (more or less) captive neighborhood constituency.

We therefore need to consider two decentralized models rather than one: market and democratic control. In the market model, the government gives parents vouchers redeemable for some part of the cost of their children's schooling. Parents then choose among any accredited school, public or private, that is willing to admit their child. To be accredited as satisfying the state's mandatory schooling requirement, a school must serve civic purposes. Although proponents of vouchers often radically downplay this aspect of the social rationale of publicly subsidized schooling, the market model, taken at its strongest, requires public oversight, at a minimum through the public's accreditation standards. The decentralized democratic model also requires schools to serve important civic purposes, and it too decentralizes the decision of how to implement and to supplement the required civic purposes of schooling in a democratic society. Since schooling is heavily publicly subsidized under both the decentralized market model and the decentralized democratic model, in both cases schools should have an obligation to live up to some publicly agreed-on standards of education. Otherwise, schools forsake their strongest claim to public subsidy.

Some defenders of market control make a far more radical claim for their preferred alternative. They claim that the market model of schooling can and should do without any "higher-order values" that are publicly imposed on schools. They thereby suggest that the market model can and should support almost unconstrained choice by parents and students. According to two prominent defenders of the market model, it is "not built to enable the imposition of higher-order values on the schools, nor is it driven by a democratic struggle to exercise public authority. Instead, the authority to make educational choices is radically decentralized to those most immediately involved. Schools compete for the support of parents and students, and parents and students are free to choose among schools. The system is built around decentralization, competition, and choice."[14]

This characterization of vouchers as doing without "higher-order values" and democratic control as depending on them poses a false and morally dangerous dichotomy between market and democratic control. Decentralized democratic control can and should include some substantial choice among public schools, and decentralized market control can and should include public oversight over publicly subsidized schools. Both models are therefore built around a substantial degree of decentralization, competition, and choice, but in neither case can one say that decentralization, competition, and choice are the ultimate ends rather than the means to other, complex educational ends that must be publicly defended in order for public subsidy of schooling to make sense. For this reason, neither decentralized model can in theory or practice avoid the imposition of some "higher-order values on the schools" or "a democratic struggle to exercise public authority." (Ironically, the market control model offers no explicit safeguard against centralization, while a decentralized democratic system does. Without a public safeguard against monopolization, market control can become at least as bureaucratized and centralized as inner-city public school systems.)

In the case of decentralized democratic control, the "higher-order values" that are democratically imposed on schools include some substantial degree of democratic decision making itself at the local level. Citizens or their accountable representatives are expected to deliberate with one another about an important collective good: education for preserving and improving their democratic society. In the case of market control, the "higher-order" values include the value of market choice and competition. My point here is not to defend one or the other higher-order value but rather to challenge the claim of proponents that vouchers impose no higher-order values on schools, while a model of decentralized democratic decision making does. Both models are driven by and, once implemented, entail the imposition of social values on citizens.

The defense of the market model in schooling is misleading in yet another sense: it cannot guarantee good educational outcomes. However, neither can a decentralized democratic model. Whichever model we as a society choose to govern publicly subsidized schooling, we cannot guarantee that the educational values that matter most for society (such as education for numeracy, literacy, religious toleration, and racial integration) will be the outcome of the chosen procedure of governance. Some of these educational values are themselves controversial; others are not, but how best to implement them is. Only a usurpation of democratic authority could institute a school system that deprives American citizens of their long-standing constitutional right to deliberate about their disagreements over public schooling. And only by assuming a constitutional amendment, which would have to be passed by a supermajority of citizens or their accountable representatives, can critics of decentralized democratic control claim that democratic citizens should not be authorized, as they now are, to deliberate collectively about schooling. The critics cannot therefore consistently assume that the one best system of schooling is a market system.

The most justifiable institution of a market model would therefore be "driven by a democratic struggle to exercise public authority" every bit as much as the institution of a decentralized democratic system. Short of anyone staging a coup, the institution of any school system will be the result of "a democratic struggle to exercise public authority." Some defenders of the market model support the passage of state constitutional amendments that forbid a wide range of democratic control over schools that is now constitutionally legitimate. These proponents of market control would need to engage in democratic struggles to pass such amendments. In suggesting that their model is not driven by a democratic struggle to exercise public authority, they therefore must be imagining a time in the future when they no longer would need to engage in democratic struggles because their side had won, and a market system in schooling was instituted in every state once and for all. But until that time comes, which is unlikely to be soon, they have no better alternative than to act politically as the defenders of a decentralized democratic system. Defenders of the market model must try to convince citizens that the benefits of market control over schools are so large and certain as to justify placing school politics far beyond day-to-day democratic control, and that the public should financially support schools that are placed far beyond democratic control. The most justifiable way to do so is to engage in democratic deliberations with their fellow citizens.

Some proponents of market control seem to deny that there can be any reasonable disagreement over what system of education is most publicly defensible, which may be why they neglect the importance of democratic deliberation over disagreements concerning publicly subsidized schooling. They suggest that instituting a market system is a sure means to all desirable educational ends. Without being "too literal about it," they ask us to "entertain the notion that choice *is* a panacea." They say it is "not like other reforms and should not be combined with them as part of a reformist strategy for improving America's public schools." Instead, choice should be viewed as "a self-contained reform with its own rationale and justification. It has the capacity *all by itself* to bring about the kind of transformation that, for years, reformers have been seeking to engineer in myriad other ways. Indeed, if choice is to work to greatest advantage, it must be adopted *without* these other reforms, since the latter are predicated on democratic control and are implemented by bureaucratic means."[15]

The idea that a single sweeping reform can cure all America's educational ills is as old as the republic itself. What has changed fundamentally over the years in the minds of radical reformers, which may help account for why the general idea of an educational panacea is never entirely discredited, is the nature of the reform itself. But however nonliteral we want to be about it, we do not have anything close to the certain knowledge about the complexities of education that would warrant our saying that school choice (or any other school system for that matter) is a panacea or even close to one. No single structural reform, however radical, can realistically promise to deliver an education adequate for democratic citizenship (broadly understood) to all the children of this country.

The limits of school choice should not lead us to overlook two important challenges that its proponents present to inner-city school systems as they now exist. The first challenge is to make inner-city schools less bureaucratic. This challenge is also presented by a defense of decentralized democratic control in a variety of mixed systems, all of which include competition between and among private and public educational sectors. There are many effective public schools, but almost all are unbureaucratic. Most are small enough so that no students get lost in them; teachers engage their students in small, typically cooperative classes; and principals communicate a clear vision of the school's mission to parents, students, and teachers, who share in shaping and carrying out that mission.[16]

The second important challenge to a substantive conception of civic education is to open up more choices among effective public schools. There are few schools that are "just right" for all students. A public school system that provides relevant information to parents about the distinctive features, successes, and failures of different schools is better than one that tries to fit all children into a single school mold. If this is true, it does not speak in favor of a market model. Markets do not automatically disseminate accurate and relevant information. Proponents of public choice rightly suggest that we cannot rely on the invisible hand of the market to provide accurate information about the performance of schools. Even in theory, the invisible hand does not work in a situation where the "consumers" of a particular service are children and therefore not the same people who need to decide whether to continue "buying" it or to switch to another provider. The public school system of Cambridge, Massachusetts, demonstrates that a parental information center can work. All parents in Cambridge who take advantage of the public schools, and a large proportion of parents, including middle-class parents, do so, must be informed before they choose a school for their child, not an unreasonable requirement insofar as parents are trustees of their children's education rather than the actual consumers.

Will increasing parental choice also increase segregation of the most advantaged and least advantaged students? This question must be raised by anyone concerned about civic education in American democracy. Segregation by class or race in our society is a problem from the perspective of both educating the least advantaged and also teaching all students the civic virtues of toleration and mutual respect in the midst of social diversity. Students learn from each other as well as from their teachers and parents. Publicly subsidized schools are an appropriate place for children of different socioeconomic, ethnic, racial, and religious backgrounds to learn from each other. Students from less educated families also tend to do better by the conventional measures of educational achievement if they attend schools with students from more educated families.[17] "Creaming off" can be controlled by requiring all parents to become informed before choosing a school and requiring all schools to be nondiscriminatory in their admissions. Many private schools are less economically and racially segregated than some public schools, so the latter requirement does not parallel the conventional public-private distinction.

The recent disappointing efforts at privatization in the Hartford, Connecticut, school system and at centralized state control in the Newark, New Jersey, school system suggest that neither private nor public control, taken by itself, can promise effective schools. As one ardent advocate of choice admits, a market approach "might lead to franchised schools that leave relatively little discretion at the school level."[18] Effective education, which includes civic education, cannot be pursued primarily through mechanisms of control, whether market or public control. To educate students effectively for citizenship, a democratic society needs to offer better choices, not only more choices, among less bureaucratic schools.[19] Choice among schools may work as a safety valve, but it is not a solution to the problems that now beset our schools. The market is no substitute for a public commitment to civic education nor is public commitment a substitute for satisfying parental as well as public standards of education.

There is no simple substitute for judging schools, however they are chosen, on their educational merits where those merits include civic education. Civic education—whose aims include the ability to argue and appreciate, understand and criticize, persuade and collectively decide in a way that is mutually respectful even if not universally acceptable—is a central merit of schools in a constitutional democracy. So many political decisions today profoundly affect so many people. The fairness of our political processes, the protection of our constitutional rights, and the quality of our collective deliberations are all the more important in this context. Schools that cultivate the capacity of citizens to deliberate on moral terms about their ongoing disagreements are our best hope for creating such a deliberative democracy.

NOTES

1. I rely throughout this chapter on arguments and evidence presented in Amy Gutmann and Dennis Thompson, *Democracy and Disagreement* (Cambridge: Harvard University Press, 1996).

2. See especially "Jared Sparks: Journal," in *Records of the Federal Convention of 1787,* rev. ed., ed. Max Farrand, vol. 3 (New Haven: Yale University Press, 1966), 479.

3. A discussion and defense of the democratic virtue of economizing on moral disagreement can be found in Gutmann and Thompson, *Democracy and Disagreement,* esp. 82–94.

4. This description and an excellent discussion of virtues attached to constitutional democracy can be found in William Galston, *Liberal Purposes* (New York: Cambridge University Press, 1991), esp. 224–27.

5. There are important exceptions, such as Benjamin R. Barber, *An Aristocracy of Everyone: The Politics of Education and the Future of America* (New York: Oxford University Press, 1992), esp. 230–61. Barber's focus on "teaching democracy through community service" complements the focus of this essay on teaching democratic skills and virtues within schools. Schools themselves may engage students in community service to develop some important democratic skills and virtues.

6. For evidence on the effectiveness of teaching tolerance, see *Review of Education/Pedagogy/Cultural Studies* 16, nos. 3–4, 315–86. See also Patricia G. Avery, Karen

Bird, Sandra Johnstone, John L. Sullivan, and Kristina Thalhammer, "Exploring Political Tolerance with Adolescents," *Theory and Research in Social Education,* 20, no. 4 (Fall 1992): 386–420. The pedagogical techniques that are detailed in these studies include important aspects of teaching mutual respect as well as toleration.

7. Diane Ravitch, *The Schools We Deserve: Reflections on the Educational Crises of Our Times* (New York: Basic Books, 1985), 288.

8. Morris Janowitz discusses some surveys that "indicate that students in classrooms exposed to moderate-to-frequent amounts of classroom discussion about politics did better than those without such discussion" (*The Reconstruction of Patriotism: Education for Civic Consciousness* [Chicago: University of Chicago Press, 1983], 154). Students exposed to political discussion in the classroom demonstrated both better reasoning capacities and more factual knowledge. For another discussion of the desirability and possibility of teaching deliberation in schools, see Amy Gutmann, *Democratic Education* (Princeton: Princeton University Press, 1987).

9. Christopher Anderson, Patricia G. Avery, Patricia V. Pederson, Elizabeth S. Smith, and John L. Sullivan, "Perspectives on Citizenship Education," paper presented at the annual meeting of the American Educational Research Association, San Francisco, April 22, 1995.

10. My discussion here draws on arguments I presented in *Democratic Education,* 64–70. I pursue some positive dimensions of choice here that are not considered in my earlier work.

11. See John E. Chubb and Terry M. Moe, *Politics, Markets, and America's Schools* (Washington, D.C.: Brookings Institution, 1990), 3–6. See also David B. Tyack, *The One Best System: A History of American Urban Education* (Cambridge: Harvard University Press, 1974), who presents a sustained criticism of the movement to create such a system.

12. See, e.g., Michael Rutter et al., *Fifteen Thousand Hours: Secondary Schools and Their Effects on Children* (Cambridge: Harvard University Press, 1979), and M. J. Kyle, ed., *Reaching for Excellence: An Effective Schools Sourcebook* (Washington, D.C.: National Institute of Education, 1985). Compare Stewart C. Purkey and Marshall S. Smith, "Effective Schools: A Review," *Elementary School Journal* 83 (March 1983), 427–52.

13. "It is one thing to know what kind of organization promotes effective education," write John E. Chubb and Terry Moe in their pathbreaking and provocative *Politics, Markets, and America's Schools.* "It is quite another to know how to use public policy to engineer that kind of organization" (p. 18).

14. Ibid., 189.

15. Ibid., 217. The logic of the case for market control rather than democratic control can be summarized as follows: The primary concern of a market institution is to please its clients; to please one's clients means to perform as effectively as possible, and to perform effectively in education—as the effective schools research amply demonstrates—is to avoid being overly bureaucratic as only an institution controlled by the market can.

16. For compelling evidence concerning the educational benefits of small classes, see Frederick Mosteller, "The Tennessee Study of Class Size in the Early School Grades," *Future of Children* 5, no. 2 (1995): 113–27. For a discussion of the characteristics of one of the most successful urban schools, see Deborah Meier, *The Power of Their Ideas: Lessons for America from a Small School in Harlem* (Boston: Beacon Press, 1995).

17. This was a major, although disputed, finding of the pathbreaking study by James S. Coleman et al., *Report on Equality of Educational Opportunity* (Washington, D.C.: Government Printing Office, 1966).

18. Myron Lieberman, *Public Education: An Autopsy* (Cambridge: Harvard University Press, 1993), 10.

19. See Jeffrey R. Henig, *Rethinking School Choice: Limits of the Market Metaphor* (Princeton: Princeton University Press, 1995).

5

A Political Socialization Perspective

Pamela Johnston Conover and Donald D. Searing

The role of public education in the "making of citizens" diminished in the late twentieth century. Preoccupied with preparing students to assume their place in a rapidly changing economy and multicultural society, schools now give inadequate attention to developing the "democratic character" of students and the skills necessary for an active practice of citizenship. If educators are to alter this state of affairs, several related projects should be undertaken: the normative justifications underpinning the democratic purposes of education must be reasserted; the cultural and institutional barriers to fulfilling the democratic purposes of education must be identified and broken down; and the psychological and social contexts of political socialization must be better understood. In this chapter we address the third of these concerns: the psychological and social context of political socialization. After reviewing the pitfalls associated with the traditional study of political socialization, we present empirical data bearing upon the role of schools in political socialization. We conclude by sketching out the implications of our research for educational reform.

THE INADEQUACY OF POLITICAL SOCIALIZATION RESEARCH

One avenue through which political scientists can contribute to educational reform is the study of political socialization. In recent years, however, this field has been in a state of disarray, and the amount of research devoted to it has declined precipitously.[1] Although particular studies stand as exceptions, the field as a whole provides disappointing theoretical and empirical bases for undertaking the educational reforms that might strengthen the role of schools in the making of citizens. The problems become evident when we sketch out what the study of political socialization *should* look like if it is to contribute to educational reform.

Simply put, the democratic purposes of education are to develop in young citizens the motivations, understandings, and skills necessary to engage in a full practice of citizenship once they reach adulthood. What normative and empirical presumptions are embedded in this assertion? Our use of the term "practice" to describe the behaviors of citizens is not a casual one but rather is meant to suggest that, *ideally*, acting as a citizen—leading a public life—involves the self-conscious performance of a collection of behaviors in an attempt to meet society's standards of the "good citizen."[2] Thinking of citizen behavior as a practice points to the importance of a psychological "sense of citizenship," which encompasses citizen identity and understanding. "Citizen identity" is the emotional significance that people give their membership in a particular political community. "Understanding" refers to the framework of beliefs that people develop about their relationship to the state and to other citizens; it encompasses legal rights and duties, informal responsibilities and privileges, as well as perceptions of the role of citizens. Thus, understanding constitutes the cognitive side of a sense of citizenship, while identity comprises the affective side. *Sense of citizenship* is critical, therefore, because it provides the key motivation for a practice of citizenship: identity supplies the emotional energy, while understanding provides the substantive direction for behavior.

Therefore, to argue that the central democratic purpose of education is to instill the motivations, understandings, and skills necessary to engage in a full "practice of citizenship" is to suggest both the substantive core of civic education and the appropriate focus of socialization research. At a minimum, civic education should foster strong citizen identities, develop rich understandings of the role of citizens in our contemporary democracy, and hone the skills necessary for realizing that role.[3] What exactly is that role? In the United States, our shared understanding of the practice of citizenship focuses on those actions and predispositions essential to sustain a representative, liberal democracy in our multicultural society.[4] Central to such a conception are political tolerance, mutual respect, and the skills essential to deliberation.[5] To be a useful basis for educational reform, then, political socialization research should focus, at a minimum, on how students develop a sense of citizenship (citizen identities and understandings), political tolerance, and the ability to deliberate. Unfortunately, this has not been the case. Although considerable research has been devoted to explaining tolerance among adults,[6] for the most part we have ignored the empirical question of how students develop a sense of citizenship, tolerance, and the "deliberative character" that Amy Gutmann, William Galston, and others judge to be so central to a liberal democratic society.

Conceiving of citizenship as a practice has further implications for empirical political socialization research, for the approach taken, the kinds of explanations pursued, and the methods adopted. In approaching the study of citizen behavior, political scientists have focused typically on explaining discrete acts of a single type of behavior, such as whether citizens voted in a particular election or watched a particular debate or gave money to a particular organization. But practices are *not* constituted by single acts of behavior. Consequently, conceptualizing citizen behavior as a practice requires that we consider instead the interrelationships among the multiple citizen behaviors that contribute to the practice as well as the patterns of sustained activity over time. We should study, for example, whether citizens have maintained *patterns* of voting and staying informed and giving money, patterns that are related and reinforce one another over time such that they become part of people's everyday lives. In the case of students, the question becomes are they developing lifelong patterns of political discussion, staying informed, and being tolerant in ways that can sustain a full practice of citizenship?

With regard to citizen understandings, political scientists have typically focused on individual patterns of thinking in categories that citizens define or, far more frequently, that we as researchers define. For example, individuals tell us their conception of citizen duty, or we measure their beliefs in terms of *our* conception of citizen duty. But practices are not defined by individuals alone, be they average citizens or thoughtful political psychologists. They are socially defined over time through the practice itself. Recognizing the inherently social nature of practices requires that we begin the study of citizen understandings by identifying the socially defined standards that govern the practice of citizenship and by asking how the appropriate "role" of citizens is understood. What constitutes excellence in the practice of citizenship? We also must gauge the extent to which students are aware of that socially defined role and motivated to perform it. Do they accept those standards as authoritative guidelines for their behavior? How do students themselves understand their role of citizens? To what extent do their individually defined understandings fit with the socially prescribed role?

Studying citizenship in this fashion places additional demands on the kinds of explanation that we should employ in our study of political socialization. Studying citizenship as a practice encourages us to focus less on general causal explanations of behavior and more on explanations that are both interpretive and developmental. By "interpretive," we mean explanations that make political behavior intelligible by providing an account of its meaning to the participants. This approach involves an account of their desires, beliefs, and actions and an account of the rules they are trying to follow. Thus, interpretive models place a premium on realism and credibility (verisimilitude) as a measure of explanatory power, not predictive ability. Their justification rests on the assumption that learning and understanding are always situated in a cultural setting and facilitated by the use of cultural resources.[7] By "developmental" we mean explanations that make political behavior intelligible by recognizing that behavior is self-transformative over time. With regard to individuals, such explanations require that researchers be sensitive to the ways in which the practice of a behavior evolves over a lifetime. With regard to the evolution of the practice itself, such explanations require attention to context—to the changing conceptions of the practice of citizenship over the course of history and in different locales.

This discussion brings us to the final demand involved in studying the making of citizens. To develop interpretive, developmental explanations, we must study citizenship in context and use methods that are sensitive to the variations in practice that occur between and within cultures, which requires that our research become both more comparative and more qualitative. Let us be clear about our argument here. We are suggesting that interpretive, developmental explanations pursued through comparative analysis provide the richest understanding of political socialization and therefore the best basis for identifying needed educational reforms. This is the perspective from which we have pursued our study of the making of citizens.

STUDYING CITIZENS IN THE MAKING

Data

It is essential to study political socialization in context. Taking account of cultural contexts fosters our understanding of "citizens in the making" as they understand themselves, for their language of citizenship is the key to the best explanations for their developing practice of it.[8] Political, economic, and social contexts are also essential for tracing out how institutional and systemic conditions shape the formation of a sense of citizenship. Often the focus of political socialization research is on microlevel explanations, but these micro explanations must be embedded in cultural, political, economic, and social macrolevel explanatory contexts in order to establish their political and philosophical relevance.

Therefore, our larger study of citizenship encompasses two national contexts—the United States and Great Britain—though our focus here is on the United States alone. The other macro contextual variations in our design are local in nature. People are citizens of nations, but national surveys are insufficiently sensitive to the fact that students learn and subsequently experience most of their citizenship in local communities. Local contexts are the ones in which citizens must be studied if they are to be understood as they understand themselves. Therefore, the research design[9] used local school communities[10] as its basic element.

The local research sites encompassing these "school communities" were selected on the basis of macro community characteristics that condition the psychology of citizenship. Thus, urbanization is a key ecological variable. Similarly, the "openness" of a community (individual mobility) conditions the sense of citizenship directly as well as indirectly through the community's internal social organization. In the same vein, education and social class should be important factors influencing the nature of citizenship. The need to provide considerable variation on these local contextual characteristics determined the choice of four research sites: a rural farm community in Minnesota; an urban, blue-collar community in Philadelphia; a suburban community in North Carolina; and a Hispanic community in San Antonio. In each location, interviews were conducted with 100 students and their parents, teachers, and community leaders, as well as with a random sample of approximately 125 adult citizens.[11] The following analyses focus on the student[12] and teacher[13] samples.

The Learning Environment: Community Descriptions

For present purposes, the context of socialization is defined by the four communities represented in our study. While a full characterization of each location is impossible here, it is useful to provide detailed thumbnail sketches of the communities that we developed during our months of participant observation in each of them. These sketches focus on the socioeconomic nature of the communities, the sense of community that exists, and shared values regarding politics and education.

The farm community in our study is a small, rural town on the edge of the prairie in Minnesota. It is a middle-class place that lacks distinct social classes of either the very wealthy or the very poor. Settled in the nineteenth century by a mix of Norwegian, Swedish, and German immigrants, it is today culturally homogeneous with the one exception of a small group of Mexican Americans who recently migrated to the town. Politically, the citizens proudly identify themselves as conservatives; the majority are Republicans, although partisan politics is not salient at the local level. The citizens are enthusiastically patriotic, especially about their own town. Their love of community— love of place—is reinforced by clear social norms and a sense of civility and decency. In daily life, this strong sense of community is focused on the churches and schools rather than on politics. Eighty percent of the town attends church regularly and takes religion seriously; indeed, church activities are a daily part of most of their lives. The high school is a key focal point for community activities. High school sports events are some of the town's most important civic rituals. Parents and teachers alike are committed to seeing that students do well academically, but there is an ambivalence about the pursuit of individual excellence. A serious problem is that the community is aging; young people go off to college and not enough return to maintain a balance across cohorts. So school life is meant to instill a sense of community, basic work skills, and fundamental knowledge, but not to produce young scholars so curious that they will want to abandon their community.

The suburban community in our study is in the piedmont region of North Carolina. It has only recently grown from a small town into a sprawling collection of "planned unit developments"—clusters of single-family homes with green spaces and shopping areas. Economically, this community is a predominantly upper-middle-class "bedroom suburb" for the Research Triangle, a concentration of high-tech businesses. There are very few poor people in the community, and it is socially homogenous as well: middle-aged, white, rootless, and Protestant. There are few public spaces, civic rituals, or forms of entertainment beyond several large shopping malls and movie theaters; instead the focus is on expensive private recreational facilities—country clubs, tennis clubs, gyms, and the like. Still, there is a great deal of voluntary association activity in the community; for example, parents participate in the PTA, and residents protect their economic investments through neighborhood associations. Politically, this community is solidly Republican; it encompasses aggressive right-wing Republican minorities alongside a more moderate Republican majority. Having moved here from elsewhere in the state and country, many people display little connection or sense of identity with their community; indeed, they seem to view themselves more as residents than community members. Nonetheless, as parents with high aspirations for their children, they focus their energy on the schools, thereby ensuring their academic excellence. Consequently, students receive the attention they need to achieve success as upper-middle-class members of a market economy.

The urban community in our study is located in north Philadelphia. The dying commercial center of the community, an avenue of half-abandoned, dark storefronts, separates its few middle-class and respectable working-class areas from poorer neighborhoods and public housing projects—this is a community in serious economic decline. It is also in social disarray: class and race cleavages erode the vestiges of what was once a close-knit community with strong civic traditions. Thus, the small, middle-class white neighborhood association seeks to rehabilitate the community's parks and main avenue, while across that avenue, the black, Hispanic, and white citizens of the community's poorest neighborhoods struggle with drug trafficking and crime. Civic activity is a luxury that most cannot afford. Politically, the community has a well-organized, though deteriorating, local Democratic Party structure. In contrast to the other communities in our study, the high school here is *not* a strong focal point of community pride and activity for *any* of those involved: students, parents, or teachers. Many students drop out, and those who stay the course often are more interested in school athletics than in the basic, no-frills education they are offered. Some parents are concerned about their children's education, but others are not even aware when their children have been truant for weeks; some teachers are frustrated and discouraged by their students' lack of interest and especially by the failure of parents to "do their job" in socializing their children.

The immigrant community—a socially conservative, respectable, lower-working-class neighborhood—in our study is located in San Antonio. Economically and socially homogeneous, its residents are Mexican American and work at blue-collar, civil service jobs at nearby military bases or in service industries.[14] Politically, citizens are fiercely patriotic to the nation and quite partisan. The community is overwhelmingly Democratic and boasts relatively high participation rates in spite of a prevailing sense of machismo among the men that actively depresses the political participation of women and is probably due in part to a well-organized, successful community organizing program. As in the case of the farming town, there is a strong sense of community that is maintained by the neighborhood's dominant institutions: schools and churches. The churches, particularly the local Catholic church,[15] play a prominent role in maintaining the community. They, rather than the government, have taken responsibility for organizing day-care centers, meal programs, and emergency care for the ill and for the poor, each church taking responsibility for its own members. The high school is the other focal point for the community. Indeed, the school is so embedded in the ethos of the local community that it is less effective than it might be in promoting individual development and achievement. Compared to those in the rural community, parents here are even more wary of their children developing talents that will lead them to abandon the community. Thus, the school focuses on vocational education, and parents encourage their children to take up manual jobs like their own.

CITIZENS IN THE MAKING

Sense of Citizenship

A sense of citizenship is critical to the development of a *practice* of citizenship. Citizen identities foster an emotional "we-ness," a sense of belonging that can be a powerful motivation for action. And "understanding," what it means to act as a citizen, is necessary if people are to act deliberately *as citizens*. Understanding thus provides a necessary direction to the passion of citizen identities.

From the standpoint of political theory, citizen identities are especially important. They have the potential to forge civic relationships by creating bonds of solidarity among citizens; when they are missing, the "social glue" that holds society together must come from elsewhere. Moreover, citizen identities are thought to influence the relationship between citizens and the state. By inspiring patriotism, they help ensure the viability of the state; when they are missing, the foundations of legitimacy must come from elsewhere. Thus, political philosophers presume that citizen identities shape the quality of public life, the strength of civil society, and the success of democratic institutions. Unfortunately, the philosophical importance of citizen identities easily obscures their empirical complexity and leads us to exaggerate their potential power in everyday life.

Therefore, it is often difficult to realize in practice the desirable effects of citizen identities. For one thing, their fundamental psychological nature makes their use less probable. Like all other political identities, the *active use* of citizen identities reflects a process of self-categorization in which we actively identify ourselves as citizens because that category is a valuable one for distinguishing ourselves from others, from noncitizens, at a particular moment. The cultural and historical setting defines the terms in which "citizen" as a category and "citizens" as a group are understood. Ultimately, however, whether or not the category enters our immediate consciousness depends on the framing of the current situation, and therein lies the problem for realizing active citizen identities. We experience our lives locally: the social groups that populate everyday life automatically enter into the framing of particular incidents. Consequently, groups made "visible" by the local context (e.g., ethnic groups) or inscribed on our bodies (e.g., race, sex) are more likely to become salient in the self-categorization process, either as categories for identification or for contrast, where "group visibility" is a function of the number of group members, their concentration, and their distinctiveness.[16] "Citizens," in fact, is one of the most *invisible* political groups because the grounds for determining membership in a political community are so abstract. Citizens qua citizens are especially invisible where citizenship is universal or nearly so.[17]

Ultimately, however, the potential of citizen identities to motivate publicly oriented behavior turns on citizens' understandings of their role as citizens, for such understandings give substantive direction to the emotional force of their identities. When people have relatively undeveloped understandings, they lack a clear sense of their proper roles as citizens; the motivational force of their identities is without direction and thus wasted. Alternatively, understandings of citizenship might be quite developed but overly individualistic in the sense that they privatize the meaning of citizenship: to act "as a citizen" comes to mean behaving as a private individual with rights and not as a public member of the community. In such cases, the emotional force of citizen identities is directed away from publicly and collectively oriented behaviors. Thus, for the sense of citizenship to motivate behavior, individuals must have strong and salient citizen identities, and those identities must be linked to adequate understandings of the role of citizens. It is important to ask, therefore, whether students have strong, salient citizen identities and, if so, whether they have the understanding necessary to act on them.

The key measurement task in determining the presence and centrality of citizen identities is to assess whether this identity is part of the core self, the part of the self easily accessible for frequent use. Accordingly, students were asked "how often, if ever, they thought of themselves as a citizen of the United States."[18] As shown in Table 1, fully 60 percent of the students think of themselves as citizens of the United States "all of the time," which is a high level of identification compared to other possible identities. Nearly 75 percent of the students report thinking of themselves as Americans "all of the time," but for most students, this is the only identity that is more central than "citizen." Only 28 percent of our respondents think of themselves as "students" all of the time, while 59 percent describe themselves as a friend, 41 percent as a neighbor, 16 percent as a member of a social class, and 40 percent as a member of a religion "all of the time"; only 9 percent view themselves as a member of a political party "all of the time."

Moreover, there are significant differences between communities in the level of identification: only 56 percent of the students in the suburban community think of themselves as citizens all of the time compared to 71 percent in the immigrant community where the everyday contrasts between citizens and nonciti-

Table 1. Strength of Citizen Identity by Community Type

| Strength of Identity | Community | | | | |
	Suburban	Rural	Urban	Immigrant	Total
All of the Time	56.0%	60.0%	55.7%	71.4%	60.8%
Most of the Time	17.0	10.5	20.3	12.4	15.0
Some of the Time	18.0	17.9	12.7	8.6	14.3
Occasionally	8.0	10.5	6.3	1.9	6.7
Never	1.0	1.1	5.1	5.7	3.2
Total	100	100	100.1*	100	100
(Weighted N)	(100)	(100)	(100)	(100)	(400)

*Percentages do not total to 100 due to rounding.

zens are likely to be more vivid and the category of "citizen" consequently more visible. Thus, most students have core citizen identities, but will such identities necessarily motivate an active practice of citizenship? The answer depends upon both their understanding of citizenship and the context of public life in which they find themselves.

With that in mind, we explored their understanding of citizenship. Specifically, do students grasp what it means to be a citizen, and do they apply that understanding to themselves? We used two types of questions to gauge our students' understanding of citizenship. First, to tap their general sense of what it means to be a citizen, respondents were asked: "The term 'citizen' means different things to different people. When you hear the word 'citizen' what do you think of *first?* A person who is a member of the community? Or a person who has legal rights and duties?" Four percent of the students volunteered that they automatically thought of citizens in both terms.[19] The remainder, however, were quite willing to choose between these two alternatives. Their responses are presented in Table 2. The prevalent influence of our rights-oriented[20] political culture is evident in the students' definition of a citizen. Nearly 60 percent of the students in three of the four communities say that a citizen is a "person who has legal rights and duties." The one exception to this pattern occurs in the rural community, where a slim majority of the students report that a citizen is "a member of the community." Such a response is not surprising given the tightly knit, communal nature of this rural town. Here, then, is clear evidence of the importance of local culture in structuring understandings of the practice of citizenship.[21]

A more in-depth picture of our students' understanding of citizenship emerges from two sets of questions dealing with the rights and duties of citizens. Using a card sort, students were first asked to identify their basic rights as an American citizen; items identified as a right were scored "1," those rejected as rights were scored "0."[22] Note that our emphasis was on what *are* one's rights as a citizen, not what *should be* one's rights. Presented in Table 3 are the means and standard deviations for the perceived rights by community. The closer the mean is to 1, the greater the consensus that the item is a right. Variation *within* communities, as indicated by the standard deviations, suggests ambiguity in the local,

Table 2. Basic Meaning of "Citizen" by Community

	Community				
Meaning	Suburban	Rural	Urban	Immigrant	All
Member of the Community	38.0%	52.6%	36.7%	33.3%	40.2%
Person with Rights and Duties	60.0	45.3	58.2	58.1	55.4
Both (Volunteers)	2.0	2.1	5.1	7.8	4.4
Total	100	100	100	99.2*	100
(Weighted N)	(100)	(100)	(100)	(100)	(400)

*Percentages do not total to 100 due to rounding.

Table 3. Perceived Citizen Rights by Community

	All		Suburban		Rural		Urban		Immigrant	
Rights	M	SD	M	SD	M	SD	M	SD	M	SD
I. Civil										
Freedom of Speech	.99	.11	.99	.10	.98	.14	1.00	.00	.98	.14
Freedom of Religion	.97	.16*	.98	.14	1.00	.00	.99	.11	.92	.27
Privacy	.91	.29	.87	.34	.89	.31	.94	.24	.92	.27
Read Anything	.69	.46*	.75	.44	.72	.45	.70	.46	.59	.49
Equal Treatment Under the Law	.95	.22	.98	.14	.95	.22	.95	.22	.92	.27
Fair Trial	.97	.17*	.99	.10	.99	.10	.97	.16	.93	.25
Protection from Bodily Harm	.87	.34	.87	.34	.88	.32	.85	.36	.87	.34
Being Homosexual	.59	.49*	.68	.47	.64	.48	.58	.50	.45	.50
Abortion	.56	.50*	.75	.44	.60	.49	.27	.50	.42	.50
Choice to Emigrate	.82	.38*	.90	.30	.89	.31	.70	.46	.79	.41
Protection of Private Property	.89	.31	.93	.26	.84	.37	.87	.33	.92	.27
Join Any Group	.90	.30	.94	.24	.86	.35	.92	.27	.87	.34
II. Political										
To Vote	.97	.16	.99	.10	.97	.18	.95	.22	.98	.14
Demonstrate Against the										
Government	.72	.45*	.81	.39	.80	.40	.56	.50	.70	.46
III. Social										
Opportunity for Education	.97	.17	.97	.17	.96	.20	.97	.16	.97	.17
To Work	.91	.29	.91	.29	.86	.35	.95	.22	.91	.28
Help from the Government	.80	.40*	.72	.45	.80	.40	.78	.41	.63	.49
Adequate Health Care	.71	.45*	.61	.49	.75	.44	.77	.42	.71	.45
Provision of Basic Food	.66	.47*	.54	.50	.68	.47	.70	.46	.73	.44
Adequate Housing	.64	.48*	.63	.50	.60	.49	.72	.45	.71	.45
Help from Other Citizens	.57	.50*	.41	.49	.53	.50	.62	.49	.71	.45

*Indicates significant differences between communities.

shared understanding; variation *between* communities suggests the extent to which shared understandings may be localized.

It is clear in Table 3 that there is a core set of rights recognized by most students in each community. Mostly, these are basic civil rights having to do with freedom of expression (speech, religion, privacy), government procedures (equal treatment, fair trials), protection of private property, and organizational rights to join and form groups. Voting is widely acknowledged as a core political right, and the opportunity to get an education and to work are viewed as primary social rights.

Beyond this core set of rights, there is considerable disagreement, some of which undoubtedly reflects real, contemporary political debates. There is, for example, substantial ambiguity within communities and disagreement between communities over whether abortion and sexual orientation constitute basic civil rights. On these two items, students in the suburban community have the clearest shared understandings and are most likely to view the two as basic rights; students in the urban and immigrant communities demonstrate the most ambiguity and are least likely to consider abortion and sexual orientation as basic rights, viewpoints in keeping with the working-class, Catholic ethos that is strong in both those communities. There is also much skepticism about the existence of basic social rights in the United States. Here again, shared understandings differ across communities, with students from the suburban community being most doubtful, which is consistent with the strong individualism and Republican influence that permeate that community. In sum, students in all four communities possess a fundamental adultlike understanding about their basic rights as citizens.

But an understanding of citizen rights alone cannot provide sufficient guidance for an active practice of citizenship, particularly when the understanding is focused on civil rights that define the grounds upon which people can live their *private* lives free from interference by the government and other citizens. Students need a richer understanding if they are to have sufficient guidance about how they should live their *public* lives. A full practice of citizenship also demands an understanding of the responsibilities or duties of citizenship.[23] To assess our students' understanding of the duties of a citizen, they were asked to execute a second card sort. Specifically, they were given thirty-six kinds of behavior that citizens might perform and then asked to divide them into four categories: legal duties of citizens, moral duties of citizens, "above the line of duty" but desirable activities for citizens, and activities irrelevant to the practice of citizenship.

At a minimum, students should have a well-defined sense of their legal duties as citizens, but this expectation is only partly realized. Although over 90 percent of the students recognize paying taxes and obeying "major" laws as legal duties of citizens, only 72 percent consider "obeying minor laws" to be a legal duty. And the status of other legal duties is even more equivocal: 50 percent consider being a "witness at a trial" a legal duty; 56 percent see "serving on a jury" as a legal duty; 35 percent think "reporting a crime" is a legal duty; but only 30 percent consider respecting the legal rights of others to be their legal duty. Moreover, there is considerable variation across communities in the shared understandings of what constitute the legal duties of citizens. For example, in the urban community where crime is substantial, only 14 percent of the students identify six or seven of the preceding items as legal duties; in contrast, 43 percent of the students in the suburban community do so. Given that compliance with the law is heavily influenced by normative beliefs about one's duty to obey the law, this failure in socialization may be a contributing factor to the rising crime rate in this urban community.

A practice of citizenship based only on legal duties would be very thin. Other citizen responsibilities are equally or more important. To what extent are these other responsibilities recognized by the students? As shown in Table 4, beyond their legal duties, students are most likely to identify *patriotic* acts as central to the practice of citizenship. Three-quarters mention military service during wartime, respecting the flag, and loyalty to the country as legal or moral duties of citizens, albeit there are differences between communities, with the immigrant neighborhood placing the heaviest emphasis on patriotic acts. Immigrants are often called upon to demonstrate their allegiance to their new country. Moreover, in this case, many members of the community are affiliated with the air force base near San Antonio.

Table 4. Perceived Citizen Duties by Community

Duty (legal or moral)	Community				
	Suburban	Rural	Urban	Immigrant	All
I. Political					
Vote in Elections	87.0	81.1	79.7	85.7	83.4
Defend Rights of Minorities	46.0	48.5	57.0	61.9	53.3
Protest Bad Laws	55.0	46.4	49.4	46.6	49.3
Stay Informed	40.0	32.7	31.7	40.0	36.0
Participate Actively in Politics	27.0	22.1	30.4	37.2	29.1
Participate in Public Discussion	23.0	22.1	26.3	30.0	28.1
Be Tolerant	18.0	17.9	16.5	26.7	19.7
II. Communal					
Protect the Environment	74.0	70.5	65.8	62.4	65.7
Promote the Good of the Community	46.0	34.7	37.9	46.7	41.3
Preserve Traditions	35.0	32.6	41.7	49.5	39.8
Put the Public Interest First	22.0	36.2	26.9	37.9	30.7
Participate in Community Organizations	23.0	11.6	21.6	34.3	22.6
Speak English	12.0	13.7	29.1	28.6	20.8
III. Social					
Educate the Next Generation	68.0	69.4	67.1	76.1	70.2
Be Willing to Work	42.0	47.4	62.0	63.8	53.8
Help Strangers in an Emergency	57.0	54.7	43.0	50.5	51.3
Care for the Elderly/Sick	48.0	47.8	46.9	49.6	45.6
Stop the Cruelty in Public	43.0	43.2	40.6	43.8	42.6
Help the Needy	42.0	39.0	41.7	41.9	41.1
Help the Homeless	43.0	35.8	39.3	44.7	40.7
Being Civil in Public	37.0	41.1	34.2	45.7	34.5
Be a Good Neighbor	35.0	35.8	36.7	45.7	38.3
Give to Charities	26.0	14.8	21.6	30.5	23.2
Insist on Civility from Others	9.0	15.8	19.0	40.0	20.9
IV. Patriotic					
Be Loyal to Your Country	79.0	82.1	76.0	75.2	78.0
Respect the Flag	73.0	76.9	81.0	76.2	76.7
Military Service in Wartime	81.0	73.6	63.3	81.9	75.0
Support President During Crisis	41.0	36.9	50.7	57.1	46.4
Military Service in Peacetime	25.0	30.6	35.4	55.2	36.6

Note: Entries are the percentage saying that behavior is a legal or moral duty of citizenship.

Beyond these patriotic activities, however, there are relatively few that the students think of as responsibilities of citizens. A liberal political culture would define an adequate practice of citizenship as including, at a minimum, certain fundamental *political* duties: voting, staying informed, participating in the public discussion of political issues, and being tolerant of people with whom you disagree. But, amazingly, the majority of students fail to recognize most of these activities as central to a practice of citizenship. Voting is the only political activity understood as a legal or moral duty by most students. And though a bare majority (53.3 percent) believe that "defending the rights of minorities" is a duty of citizens, less than 20 percent characterize being tolerant as a duty. In fact, 26 percent of all students describe tolerance as irrelevant to the practice of citizenship, and nearly 40 percent of the urban students see tolerance as having nothing to do with being a citizen. Similarly, less than 30 percent of the students think of public discussion as a citizen duty, and nearly 20 percent think it irrelevant. Moreover, there are consistent differences between communities, and again it is in the immigrant community where students are most likely to perceive political acts as responsibilities of citizenship, while students in the rural and urban communities have less active views of citizenship.

Consistent with these minimalist perspectives, virtually all of the activities that would characterize a more participatory or communitarian practice of citizenship are categorized by students as being either "above the line of duty" or, in many cases, irrelevant. Thus of the *communal* activities, those benefiting the community in general, only "protecting the environment" is identified by a majority of students as a duty of citizenship. Similarly, of the *social* behaviors, which pertain to how citizens act toward one another, only "educating the next generation" and "being willing to work" are judged as citizen duties by a majority of students. Again, students in the immigrant community have the broadest understanding of their communal and social responsibilities as citizens: for example, 40 percent believe that citizens have a duty to insist on civility from their fellow citizens. In contrast, only 9 percent of the students in the suburban community feel the same way.

In sum, these students' understanding of their responsibilities as citizens is far less well defined than their understanding of their rights and is limited to a few legal duties, voting, and acts of patriotism. However, context matters. The immigrant community, in particular, stands out from the others. There students live in the midst of grassroots community organizing and are socialized into a citizen ethos that stresses the importance of community ties and loyalty to the nation. In a conscious effort to make its children into "super-Americans," this community has actually instilled a deeper understanding of citizenship. In contrast, the relatively thin understanding of citizen responsibility that typifies the other communities can sustain only a very passive, minimal practice of citizenship. On this understanding, all the real action in citizenship is optional—virtuous acts that only the truly exceptional citizens need perform. Still, minimal as they are, such understandings might nevertheless guide a rudimentary practice of citizenship, but only to the degree that students are able to apply them to themselves.

Do students apply to themselves their grasp of what it means to be a citizen? In psychological terms, the question becomes have students developed a self-schema or self-conception as citizens? To answer this question, we asked them to categorize the quality of their own citizenship. Only about 8 percent claim to be "particularly good citizens." Most (50 percent) say they are simply "good citizens," while 40 percent modestly report they are only "ordinary citizens." Very few labeled themselves negatively as "not so good citizens."

Then students were asked to explain in an open-ended format what they did or did not do that made them the kind of citizens they were. Here, we are exploring the students' self-understandings, trying to understand them as they understand themselves. Although all students offered some minimal explanation, less than 3 percent offered more than a sentence or two, and most of the explanations were quite elementary and general. Thus, most students describe themselves as "particularly good" or "good" citizens simply because they obey the laws and participate minimally in their school or community. To these students, being a "good citizen" does *not* mean engaging in those behaviors that are seen as being "above the line of duty"; it means only doing the bare minimum, the few real "duties" of citizenship. Those who characterize themselves as "ordinary" citizens generally do so because they obey the law and nothing else.

In most cases, the students' responses give no sense of a well-organized, richly developed self-conception of themselves as citizens, the kind of self-conception that is essential to guide an active practice of citizenship. More troubling still, most students have little conception of their "possible selves" as future citizens. When asked what they might do to become better citizens in the future and what they might do differently when they become adults, few students have anything concrete or specific to say. Their "future" or "possible" selves as citizens are nebulous at best and nonexistent at worst. For the most part, they do not draw on their understanding of the "virtuous" citizen to create an image of their possible selves as citizens.

This finding is particularly troubling because, as psychologists make clear, when we contemplate changing ourselves we must think about alternatives in a concrete and particularistic way and imagine realistic "possible selves." These possible selves can only be truly meaningful when they are compelling visions of what we might become, visions that actually give personal meaning to the alternative roles under consideration.[24] Possible selves not only provide an evaluative and interpretative context for considering new roles for the self; they also are essential for actual change.[25] Thus, it is not enough for students to muse, "I'll just be a better citizen in the future." Instead, they must imagine themselves acting like a citizen in specific ways: voting in local elections, engaging in political discussions at home, joining particular organizations. Only if students are capable of envisioning such possible "citizen selves" can they be sufficiently motivated to become active citizens. Finally, it is important to recognize that the ability of students to imagine meaningful possible citizen selves is heavily dependent on the particular historical and sociocultural contexts in which they live, on the alternative citizen selves embedded in those contexts, as well as on personal experiences.[26] Students being raised in the immigrant community, for example, are presented with a different set of possibilities (e.g., more law-abiding, patriotic, and participatory) than those living in the urban community.

Thus, students do develop citizen identities, and many have some understanding of what it means to be a citizen. But in most of these communities their understandings are minimal and portray the good citizen in passive terms. Most troubling, however, these students have little sense of their future or possible selves as adult citizens; they lack clear visions to guide personal change. They simply do not grasp how to apply their minimal understanding of citizenship to themselves or of what it will mean for them to act as citizens in the future.

The Practice of Citizenship

Fifteen-year-olds are citizens in training. As such, they are developing a practice of citizenship. Two of the essential elements in that practice should be an ability and willingness to engage in political discussion and the capacity for tolerance.

The importance of political discussion lies in its contribution to creating some of the essential conditions for successful democratic states: good representation, political legitimacy, and a democratic community.[27] Discussion promotes good representation by helping citizens to judge intelligently the talent, character, and performance of candidates vying for office.[28] Political discussion contributes to political legitimacy when public dialogue helps us discover both how fundamental our disagreements are and how we might build up sufficient consensus to create acceptable solutions.[29] Finally, political discussion is the process through which a public-regarding communal will develops by enabling citizens to discover what they have in common, to understand one another, and to create shared visions of a common good.[30]

To what extent are students developing the skills and motivation necessary to sustain regular political discussion? We used two measures for assessing the amount of political discussion: one based on the issues talked about and the other on the settings of the discussions. The issues measure was derived from a series of questions that focused our respondents' attention on "serious" discussions or conversations about a range of different topics during a fixed time period (one month).[31] The settings measure was built from a series of questions that asked respondents to judge how frequently they had serious political discussions in various settings (home, church, social settings with strangers, and social settings with friends) and with various people (parents, relatives, and friends).[32] Both measures are additive scales on which high scores indicate substantial political discussion.

As shown in Table 5, relatively few students engage in a high level of discussion, as tapped by our issues measure, though nearly one-third report a moderate level of discussion. Most, however, talk infrequently or only occasionally about political issues. Moreover, there are significant differences among communities. Discussion of issues is highest in the rural community, where just over 50 percent report moderate to high levels of discussion, and lowest in the immigrant community, where less than a third do so.

The settings measure of discussion produces an even sharper picture of community differences, though the overall level of discussion is similar to that found with the issues measure. As illustrated in Table 6, the immigrant community is again lowest in levels of discussion. The suburban community emerges with highest levels—over 50 percent report high or moderate levels—followed by the rural community. These differences run contrary to those found earlier in the students' understanding of citizenship. In particular, students in the immigrant community expressed the most participatory and demanding understanding of citizenship, but they are nonetheless least likely to have developed an active practice of political discussion. In sum, the practice of discussion varies across communities, and in all communities large numbers of students, ranging from 50 percent to 85 percent depending on the measure, are not actively developing the skills essential for public discussion.

Political tolerance is also critical to the practice of citizenship in a liberal society. Using a variation on the content-controlled measure of tolerance,[33] we asked students to tell us which of ten different groups they "disapproved of the

Table 5. Frequency of Discussion (Issues Measure) by Community Type

| Amount of Discussion | Community | | | | |
	Suburban	Rural	Urban	Immigrant	All
Almost Never (0–6)	7.0%	8.4%	21.5%	34.3%	17.8%
Some (7–13)	49.0	41.1	45.6	35.2	42.7
Moderate (14–20)	38.0	36.8	29.1	24.8	32.2
High (21–28)	6.0	13.7	3.8	5.7	7.3
Total	100	100	100	100	100
(Weighted N)	(100)	(100)	(100)	(100)	(400)

Table 6. Frequency of Discussion (Settings Measure) by Community Type

| Amount of Discussion | Community | | | | |
	Suburban	Rural	Urban	Immigrant	All
Almost Never (0-5)	8.0%	27.4%	26.6%	39.0%	25.2%
Some (6-11)	39.0	38.9	50.6	45.7	43.6
Moderate (12-17)	46.0	31.6	20.3	13.3	27.8
High (18-24)	7.0	2.1	2.5	1.9	3.4
Total	100	100	100	99.9*	100
(Weighted N)	(100)	(100)	(100)	(100)	(400)

*Percentages do not total to 100 due to rounding.

most" as a means of selecting the target group for our series of tolerance questions. Three groups garnered most of the responses: the American Nazi Party (21.3 percent); white supremacists groups such as the Ku Klux Klan (47.7 percent); and groups campaigning for the rights of homosexuals such as the National Gay and Lesbian Task Force (14.2 percent). Although there were some differences between communities in the selection of a target group, by far the most notable was the marked homophobia in the immigrant community: 30 percent of those students most disapproved of gay rights groups, as compared to around 7 percent of the students in the suburban and rural communities and 13 percent in the urban school. This result is not surprising, however, given the context: the immigrant community is socially conservative, heavily religious, and strongly influenced by a tradition of machismo.

Students were then asked five tolerance questions about their "most disapproved of group."[34] As shown in Table 7, the level of tolerance among these students is disappointingly low and varies markedly across communities. In both the immigrant and urban communities, a majority of the students would *not* engage in at least four of the five acts of tolerance. The same is true of nearly a third of the students in the suburban and rural communities. By far, the most tolerant students were found in the suburban community: 36 percent of them would engage in at least four of the five acts of tolerance. Thus, as in the case of discussion, relatively few students are rehearsing their adult roles as citizens. Why?

For a true "practice" of citizenship to develop, one's sense of citizenship needs to be related to one's behavior as a citizen. A grasp of what it means to be a citizen should combine with one's citizen identity to motivate actions in keeping with the understanding. Does this occur in the case of our students? Is there a connection between the strength of students' citizen identities, their understandings of their rights and duties pertaining to tolerance and discussion, and their actual levels of discussion and tolerance? Unfortunately, there is not.

Citizen identities are *not* significantly correlated with either levels of discussion or tolerance except in the urban community, where students with strong

Table 7. Levels of Tolerance by Community Type

Number of Tolerant Acts Toward Most Disliked Group	Community				
	Suburban	Rural	Urban	Immigrant	All
0	14.0%	10.5%	29.1%	41.9%	23.9%
1	17.0	22.1	30.4	24.8	23.6
2	13.0	18.9	15.2	7.6	13.7
3	20.0	23.2	12.7	9.5	16.3
4	21.0	11.6	5.1	9.5	11.8
5	15.0	13.7	7.6	6.7	10.7
Total	100	100	100.1*	100	100
(Weighted N)	(100)	(100)	(100)	(100)	(400)

*Percentages do not total to 100 due to rounding.

citizen identities are more tolerant (Pearson's r = .32). Similarly, most students' understanding of their duties to discuss political issues publicly and stay informed is *not* significantly related to their levels of discussion. The one exception to this pattern occurs in the rural community, where students with a sense of duty about these activities engage in more discussion.[35] The more typical mismatch between the students' understanding of these duties and their actual practice is illustrated in both the suburban and immigrant communities. Specifically, students in the immigrant community are most likely to believe that "staying informed" and "participating in public discussions" are duties of citizenship, and yet they have the lowest levels of discussion. Conversely, students in the suburban community are less likely to view participating in discussions as a duty of citizenship but are nonetheless the most likely actually to engage in such discussions. Similarly, the students' understanding of their duties to be tolerant is not significantly related to their actual levels of tolerance. But their recognition of rights pertaining to tolerance[36] is significantly correlated with their actual level of tolerance (Pearson's r = .30), and this finding holds true in every community.

This disjuncture between sense of citizenship and performance is understandable. While most students identify themselves as citizens, their grasp of what it means to act as citizens is rudimentary and dominated by a focus on rights, thus creating a privately oriented, passive understanding. Moreover, the fact that their *self*-understandings as citizens are often thin and overly general makes it even more unlikely that their sense of citizenship will be consciously applied to shaping their own public behaviors. In the immigrant community, students have a somewhat fuller sense of citizenship, but it still is not reflected in their actions in everyday life, in part because their sense of citizenship is an abstraction; they do not know how to apply it to their own lives. Their performance is also shaped by the community context: ironically, social norms that emphasize civility and respect for one's elders discourage students in the immigrant community from discussion; likewise, intolerance for homosexuals and other "extreme" groups is engendered in social norms emanating from their religious and ethnic heritage. To what extent does the educational experience help to ameliorate these deficiencies? That question is our next topic for discussion.

The School Experience

What is the role of the high school in contributing to students' sense of citizenship and nurturing their practice of it? And to what extent can that role be changed? To answer these questions, we focus on four elements of the school experience: the sense of a school community, the students' level of civic engagement in school and extracurricular activities, the level of political discussion at school, and the curriculum.

Schools provide students with their first opportunity to experience a community. Belonging to a school community can afford significant training in getting along with others and working together. Thus, to the extent that schools generate a genuine sense of community, they should be better able to develop a sense of citizenship and its practice. To assess our students' sense of a school community, we measured both their identification with the school community and their sense of shared interests.[37] Half of the students report strongly identifying with their school community; the levels of identification are strongest in the rural community (60 percent) and weakest in the urban community (42 percent).

The civic engagement of students is a second factor associated with school life that might contribute to the making of citizens. We use the term "civic engagement" to refer to the students' connections with both the school and outside communities. Through involvement in extracurricular activities, students develop relationships with one another and thus create social networks. These networks are themselves a form of "social capital," and they make possible other kinds of social capital   social norms and trust.[38] Thus, the emergence of norms of tolerance and discussion as well as their actual enforcement might be stimulated by the civic engagement of students. To assess our students' levels of civic engagement, we read them a list of different types of organizations and activities.[39] For each type, we asked them to tell us the name of any organizations that they belonged to or with which they had done any activities during the last five years. The total number of groups named in this fashion constitutes our measure of civic engagement.

As shown in Table 8, there is enormous variation among students in the level of civic engagement. Although nearly half of the students report belonging to three or fewer groups, 30 percent say they are members of six or more. The differences between communities are also quite striking: 50 percent of the students in the immigrant community belong at most to only one group, but the same is true of only 4 percent of the students in the suburban community. Conversely, while nearly a third of the students in the suburban and rural communities belong to eight or more groups, none of the students in the urban community can say the same. The comparatively low level of civic engagement in the urban and immigrant communities suggests that school life, broadly construed, makes variable contributions to the development of social capital. Where the social capital of students is higher, the making of citizens should be more successful.

Political discussion is the third element of the school experience on which we focus our attention. The importance of discussion in the school setting is twofold. First, it allows students to develop the skills necessary for discussion in different settings. Frequent discussion should be transformative and self-reinforcing: the more that students discuss at school, the more skillful they should become at it and thus the more willing to discuss in the future in other settings. Second, political discussion allows for the transmission of information through active learning, and thus it can enrich students' understanding of political issues and their roles as citizens. To measure the amount of political discussion that goes on in the school setting, we asked students how often they had discussions

Table 8. Civic Engagement by Community

Number of Groups Mentioned	Community				
	Suburban	Rural	Urban	Immigrant	All
0–1	4.0%	6.4%	25.4%	53.3%	22.2%
2–3	22.0	17.9	40.8	30.5	27.7
4–5	25.0	20.0	23.9	8.6	19.3
6–7	17.0	23.2	9.8	3.8	13.4
8–10	22.0	26.3	0	3.8	13.4
Greater than 10	10.0	5.3	0	0	3.9
Total	100	99.1*	99.9*	100	99.9*
(Weighted N)	(100)	(100)	(100)	(100)	(400)

*Percentages do not total to 100 due to rounding.

Table 9. School-Related Discussion by Community Type

Amount of Discussion	Community				
	Suburban	Rural	Urban	Immigrant	All
Low (0–3)	9.0%	8.4%	31.6%	25.7%	18.7%
Moderate (4–8)	62.0	70.5	59.5	60.0	63.0
High (9–12)	29.0	21.1	8.9	14.3	18.3
Total	100	100	100	100	100
(Weighted N)	(100)	(100)	(100)	(100)	(400)

or serious conversations about political issues (1) at school in a class; (2) at school, but not in a class; (3) at after-school activities; and (4) with teachers. Responses to these four questions were summed to produce a scale ranging from zero to twelve. The frequency distribution for this scale, by community, is presented in Table 9.

As shown in Table 9, the range of political discussion in the school setting varies substantially among students and across communities. In the suburban and rural communities, 29 percent and 21 percent, respectively, of the students say that they experience high levels of discussion. Conversely, discussion is much more infrequent in the urban and immigrant communities.

A fuller picture is presented in Table 10, where the discussion levels in the four different school settings are presented, and it is apparent just how important the classroom is as a setting for discussion. Forty-five percent of the students recount that they often talk about political issues in class, and another 35 percent say that they sometimes do, though disparities among communities are sizable. Specifically, 68 percent of the rural students and 50 percent of the suburban students report frequent in-class discussion compared to 34 percent of the immigrant students and only 25 percent of the urban students. Given the relative frequency of in-class discussion, it is not surprising that discussion levels with teachers are also substantial: 25 percent of the students report often talking with teachers, and another 39 percent say that they sometimes discuss politics with their teachers. Again, there are differences between communities, as frequent dis-

Table 10. Discussion Levels in Various School Settings

Amount of Discussion	Setting			
	In Class	Outside of Class	During After-School Activities	With Teachers
Never	7.2%	29.4%	52.6%	14.2%
Rarely	13.2	34.1	28.3	22.6
Sometimes	35.0	25.4	15.4	38.5
Often	44.5	11.0	3.8	24.7
Total	99.9*	99.9*	100.1*	100
(Weighted N)	(100)	(100)	(100)	

*Percentages do not total to 100 due to rounding.

cussion with teachers is highest in the rural community and lowest in the urban community.

Discussion outside the classroom setting is less frequent and is particularly unlikely during after-school activities; indeed, a majority of the students report never having such discussions. No doubt, part of the explanation is that many students do not have the opportunity for such discussions because they simply do not engage in such activities. There is, however, a clear exception to this pattern: 36 percent of the suburban students report frequently or sometimes discussing political issues during extracurricular activities. Finally, approximately one-third of the students report sometimes or often having discussions at school but outside the classroom.[40] Although some of these discussions might be with teachers, most appear to be with friends, for there is a very strong correlation between out-of-class discussion and talk with friends (Pearson's r = .50). Thus, to the extent that students talk together informally about politics, the school may be the primary setting for such conversations. Still, the classroom emerges as the key site for political discussions at school.

The fourth, and final, element of the school setting that we shall explore, therefore, is the type of class or curriculum that facilitates political discussion. Traditionally, the assumption has been that civic education goes on primarily, if not solely, in civics, government, and American history classes. Over 90 percent of our students report having had at least one such class during their high school careers. But when asked if there were other classes besides these that might have influenced their citizenship, 27 percent of the students reported affirmatively. The differences between communities are significant here, with 40 percent of the suburban students and only 12 percent of the immigrant school students reporting that they have had such a class.

Based on the students' reports, English courses proved to be one of the major arenas for "informal civics education," that is, talking about political issues *outside* the context of a civics or American history class. Beyond this common thread, there is considerable variation between schools. In the suburban school, world civilization, biology, and foreign language classes were mentioned as venues for informal lessons about citizenship. In the rural school, science courses received frequent mention, as did health courses in the urban school. And in the immigrant school, religion and ROTC courses were identified as sites for informal civic education.

It is important to recognize that *within schools* there are significant differences in the extent to which teachers of nongovernment courses consciously engage in informal civic education by discussing public issues and promoting "democratic character." In our teacher interviews, we asked to what extent they deliberately attempted to include materials dealing with government and politics, international affairs, vulnerable and less fortunate members of society, rights and duties as a citizen, tolerance, and patriotism. Even within the same school, the range of responses was remarkable, highlighting the importance of teacher discretion in informal civic education. For example, some English teachers had clearly given a great deal of thought to these topics and could explain in considerable detail the way in which their lesson plans were designed to incorporate such material; for others, our questions seemed to prompt them to think for the first time about these issues as part of *their* teaching.

In sum, the school experiences of our students vary across the four communities and are *not* a simple reflection of the community's socioeconomic makeup. Despite substantial socioeconomic differences, for instance, the suburban and rural school experiences share a number of similarities. Students in both communities identify with their school and have relatively high levels of civic engagement, school discussion, and civic education, both formal and informal. Similarly, though the urban and immigrant communities differ substantially, the school experiences they offer their children are similar in important ways: social capital is low, school discussion of political issues is infrequent, and informal civic education is uncommon.

The key question that remains to be answered is to what extent these elements of the school experience contribute to the students' sense and practice of citizenship. Let us be clear here about our explanatory strategy. We are not testing causal relationships: whether these school experiences actually *cause* students to develop a particular sense or practice of citizenship. Instead, we are exploring developmental models by considering whether particular school experiences are associated with the evolution of the students' sense of citizenship and practice of it. For this reason, we focus on the correlations between school experiences and the students' sense and practice of citizenship; these are presented in Table 11. The pattern of results is clear in identifying how school experiences matter: they are bound up in the actual practice of citizenship much more than in the development of a sense of citizenship. With that in mind, we will briefly consider each facet of the school experience.

At first glance, a sense of school consciousness would appear to be the least important element of the school experience.[41] But that judgment is perhaps too hasty, for school consciousness is the only thing that is related to citizen identity.

Table 11. Correlations Between School Experiences, Sense of Citizenship, and the Practice of Citizenship

	School Experiences				
	School Consciousness	Civic Engagement	School Discussion	Political Class	Nonpolitical Class
Sense of Citizenship					
Citizen Identity	.11*	.00	.00	.05	-.06
Tolerance Rights	.11*	.12*	.11*	.07	.14**
Legal Duties	.02	.19**	.15*	.11*	.07
Tolerance Duties	.08	-.13**	-.02	.02	-.09
Discussion Duties	.06	-.03	.05	.03	.03
Practice of Citizenship					
Discussion (Issues)	.08	.35**	.45**	.11*	.23**
Discussion (Setting)	.02	.27**	.56**	.03	.20**
Tolerance	.03	.26**	.19**	.17**	.14**

Entries are Pearson product moment correlation.
 * = p ≤ .05
** = p ≤ .01

Thus, developing a sense of communal consciousness toward the school community may facilitate developing a sense of citizen identity with the nation.

As suggested earlier, civic engagement creates social capital that can promote the practice of citizenship. It is positively associated with recognition of the rights underpinning the practice of tolerance and legal duties although negatively related to viewing as *duties* those activities grounding a practice of discussion—namely, discussing political issues publicly and staying informed. In effect, the more students are embedded in their school and civic communities, the more likely they are to see discussing political issues and staying informed as activities of the particularly virtuous citizen. That said, civic engagement is more strongly related to the *practices* of discussion and tolerance.

Exactly how is it bound up with learning these practices? The substantial relationship between civic engagement and discussion reflects the fact that participation in such activities provides the opportunity—the setting and the partners—for political discussions to take place.[42] Thus, while the team is suiting up, the orchestra tuning, and the yearbook being planned, some students are talking to one another about the political issues of the day. The social capital embodied in civic engagement fosters discussion in other ways as well. Civic engagement encourages the formation of norms favorable to discussion; it is positively correlated with the students' perception that talking about politics at social occasions is "perfectly suitable" as opposed to being "best avoided." And civic engagement enhances both students' sense of political competence and especially their perceptions that the political system is responsive; in turn, these senses of internal and external efficacy are likely to facilitate discussion in other settings.

The connection between civic engagement and tolerance is also readily understandable. To the extent that students are involved with one another in extracurricular activities, they must develop norms of cooperation and tolerance if their group activities are to be successful. In addition, such activities bring students into contact with people whose views might not agree with their own, as suggested by the moderate correlation between civic engagement and discussing political issues with people who have different views (Pearson's r = .24). Such contact creates opportunities for understanding those differences. This process, too, is evolutionary: civic engagement promotes tolerance, and the more tolerant students become, the easier they will find it to join in new extracurricular activities in the future.

Like civic engagement, school discussion is positively related to a recognition of the rights underpinning tolerance and a citizen's legal duties, but it is unrelated to the recognition of obligations to discuss politics or to citizen identities. Not surprisingly, discussion at school is very strongly correlated with our measure of the discussion of issues (Pearson's r = .45), suggesting that much of the students' discussion of contemporary political issues takes place at school. But discussion at school is also strongly correlated with our measure of discussion in different settings (Pearson's r = .56). In part, this strong connection reflects the fact that "discussion with friends" is part of the discussion settings measure, and much of the discussion with friends presumably goes on in school-related settings. The correlation remains strong, however, even when that item is removed.

In thinking about the connection between discussion at school and in other settings, it is most useful to think in terms of a developmental explanation rather than a causal one. It is empirically difficult, if not impossible, to sort out the causal direction in this association. Instead, it makes more sense to think about the connection between discussion at school and in other settings as representing a point in the evolution of a practice of discussion. Discussion in one setting develops the skills and motivations for discussion in other settings. When students discuss political issues at school, they become better able and more likely to discuss them at home; such discussions at home and at other social occasions further develop the students' skills and motivations, thus facilitating even more discussion at school. Over time, as discussion in one setting eases discussion in other settings, a practice of discussion begins to emerge more and more as a part of everyday life, which is not to suggest that the developmental process moves steadily forward regardless of the norms governing different settings. If social norms discourage discussion at home or in social settings, this can retard the development of the practice of discussion begun at school. But even in the immigrant community where discussion is lowest and the norms against it are strongest, there is a strong positive link between discussion at school and in other settings, suggesting that schools can play an important role in beginning the developmental process.

Also like civic engagement, school discussion is related to tolerance. This relationship deserves some exploration. Earlier we suggested that the value of political discussion lies in its positive effects in creating good representation, political legitimacy, and a sense of community. But there is another important political function of discussion that is less frequently mentioned: its role in fostering political recognition. Many people are hesitant to engage in discussion because they view it as too self-revealing, requiring them to make their issue positions public. This reticence is problematic because our issue positions often say something fundamental about who we are, about our core selves.[43] Therefore, to have our issue positions challenged or criticized in a public discussion can seem like having our basic identities questioned. Conversely, when people choose to discuss political issues, they willingly make their basic identities public and in a fundamental sense may be seeking political recognition. Thus, discussion can be a central act in the politics of recognition.[44] It is politically important that such discussions be characterized by civility, listening, and mutual respect; discussions that are contentious and disrespectful will likely end quickly and leave the participants hurt and angry. Therefore, the more we discuss, the more we learn the necessity of mutual respect and tolerance.

Next, we will consider the impact of formal civic education in civics and American history classes compared to informal civic education in noncivics courses that take up citizenship issues. Most striking is the finding that taking civic courses bears virtually no relationship to the students' sense of citizenship, with one exception: having a civics course makes students more aware of their legal duties as citizens. This finding is explained, in part, by the fact that most students have had such a course, and thus there is little variation in the experience. Still, the finding that most students have emerged from such a course with a very thin understanding of what it means to be a citizen is testimony to the extent to which civics and American history courses may be failing in one of the core tasks of civic education as we understand it: helping students to understand what it means to be a citizen in our society and to develop a self-understanding capable of guiding a satisfactory practice of citizenship.

In thinking about improving such courses, we might learn from how civic education is proceeding informally in noncivics classes. As shown in Table 11, noncivics classes that informally take up citizenship issues are related to the development of tolerance and the practice of discussion. Many of these classes are English courses, and the teachers' comments about how they structure these lessons provide insight into the source of the courses' influence. Specifically, English teachers use the narratives about life found in fiction to give concrete, real-life meaning to the messages about citizenship that they wish to convey. As suggested earlier, one of the most troubling voids in these students' sense of citizenship is their lack of rich, concrete conceptions of themselves as future citizens. The use of narratives, fictional or real, can help students more easily construct meaningful "future selves" as citizens.

In sum, school experiences are clearly a factor in the evolution of a practice of citizenship. Civic engagement, school discussion, and civic education create an environment that fosters political discussion and tolerance. Two questions remain:

Are these relationships a by-product of the socioeconomic status (SES) of students, and to what extent do these relationships vary by community? The relationships between school experiences and the practice of citizenship (e.g., tolerance and discussion) are *not* merely reflections of socioeconomic differences between students. Indeed, they are relatively unchanged when controlled for the students' SES and other background factors.[45]

There are, however, some notable variations between the communities, as might be expected given that their school experiences vary. The connection between civic engagement and political discussion is strongest in the suburban and rural communities; indeed, much of the correlation between civic engagement and discussion (settings measure) is due to the strong relationship in the suburban community.[46] This finding is not surprising given the relatively low civic engagement, and thus lack of variation, in the other two communities. Moreover, it underscores the social nature of the evolution of a practice of citizenship: students are best socialized to citizenship in an environment rich in social capital. Similarly, the link between civic engagement and tolerance is nonexistent in the immigrant community, reflecting the prevailing low level of civic engagement among those students, and the fact that school experiences may have difficulty competing with the political biases emanating from other social institutions such as the family and the church.

At the same time, the potential role of the school in compensating for other institutions in socializing students to citizenship is highlighted by the fact that the connection between school discussion and more general discussion is stronger in the urban and immigrant communities.[47] Adults in both of those communities have relatively low levels of political discussion, and parents discuss politics infrequently with their children. The schools help compensate for this deficiency. Unfortunately, school discussion apparently does not compensate for the relatively low levels of tolerance in those two communities and is only related to tolerance in the rural and especially suburban communities. Similarly, the ties between formal civic education and political discussion and especially tolerance are notably stronger in the suburban community, suggesting that there may be an important curriculum difference between that community and the others. Finally, the relationship between informal civic education (e.g., in noncivics classes) and discussion occurs primarily in the suburban and rural communities and is largely nonexistent in the other two communities.[48] The relationship between informal civic education and tolerance is also strongest in the suburban community, though it is also significant in the immigrant community.

In sum, an examination of the correlations presented in Table 11 by community suggests that the connection between school experiences and the practice of citizenship among students varies a great deal with the context. Civic engagement and civic education, both formal and informal, are more closely tied to the practice of citizenship (e.g., tolerance and discussion) in the rural and especially suburban communities. This is not to suggest that school experiences are unconnected to the practice of citizenship among students in the other two communities, but only that the connections are more limited. For example, school discussion is most closely tied to discussion in the urban and immigrant communities, and civic education promotes tolerance, though not discussion, in the immigrant community. In effect, the school experience in the suburban and rural communities creates the kind of environment most conducive to the development of a practice of citizenship in keeping with the demands of our liberal polity. Thus, as we have argued, to understand the contribution of school experiences to the making of citizens we must consider the context.

CONCLUSIONS: TOWARD EDUCATIONAL REFORM

We have painted a sobering portrait of the "making of citizens" in four American communities. Although most students have strong citizen identities, these identities are experienced as free-floating abstractions that are not tied to the students' understanding of what it means to be a citizen or to their behaviors. Similarly, most students have thin understandings of what it means to be a citizen, understandings dominated by a focus on rights and deficient in a sense of obligation. For most, being a good citizen requires only that one obey the law, vote, and act patriotically. All public activity beyond this falls to the "virtuous citizen" to perform. Particularly troubling is the finding that few students have a clear sense of their "future selves" as adult citizens. Without well-defined images of who they wish to become as citizens, it will be difficult for them consciously to construct a practice of citizenship and a rich public life. Of course, this narrow conception of citizenship does not preclude them from engaging in citizen behaviors without thinking of them as such. But even given that possibility, there is reason for concern. Political discussion and tolerance are two behaviors central to the health of a liberal, democratic state. Yet, many of the students we interviewed discuss political issues infrequently, if ever, and display a remarkable level of intolerance.

What can be done to change this state of affairs? Our analysis suggests several areas for reform concerning the substance, the method, and the institutional context of civic education. If students are to become adults who actually *practice* citizenship, they must come to understand the meaning of citizenship and develop a self-understanding of what being a citizen will mean in the conduct of their own lives. This knowledge is not currently the norm. Of course, civic education is by no means the only source of this problem. Many have suggested that the discourse of citizenship characterizing our political culture itself reflects a very thin, passive, rights-oriented conception of citizenship.[49] Still, by altering the *substance of civic education*, schools can act as agents of change. In so doing, they need to convey to students shared understandings about the specific privileges and obligations of citizenship and help them translate these shared expectations into a concrete vision for their own lives.

In tackling these tasks, schools ought not limit themselves to the arena of civics and American history courses as traditionally conceived. Instead, the civic education curriculum should become more interdisciplinary, multicultural, and community-oriented. Ideally, the practice of citizenship permeates every facet of our everyday life; students must learn, therefore, concrete lessons about what it means to be a citizen in different realms. Civic education must become more interdisciplinary. Biology courses, for example, might—as some already do—take up issues concerning the responsibility of citizens toward the environment, or health courses might—as some already do—teach lessons of tolerance through a discussion of AIDS. Similarly, the practice of democratic citizenship in the United States demands tolerance and respect for cultural differences, which is best promoted through a civic education curriculum that is multicultural in nature.[50] Finally, because the practice of citizenship is rooted in the local community, civic education must familiarize students with their local communities and help them forge connections with that community and its members. One of the best ways to do this is through community- and service-based learning.[51]

In addition to altering the substance of civic education, the *methods of civic education* might also be examined. First, our study suggests the importance of civic engagement and school discussion in fostering the development of a sense and practice of citizenship. These facets of the school environment share a common method: they both encourage active learning through social interaction. Educators have long asserted that active learning is more effective than passive learning. Our assertion is more specific: we are suggesting that social interaction is essential to developing a democratic character and learning the basic skills of citizenship. Tolerance is learned by having to interact and get along with people with whom we disagree; confidence in our political preferences is generated when we successfully defend our positions; understanding of issues is enhanced through discussion; and shared citizen identities are nurtured by working together toward common goals. Second, our study suggests the importance of narratives in helping students to translate shared understandings about citizenship into concrete terms that they can relate to their own lives.[52] Many students mention English classes as having influenced their understanding of citizenship, because it is in those classes that they read narratives in which fictional characters confront real-life dilemmas.

Finally, our findings have institutional implications. First, there is variation *within schools* in the extent to which teachers of similar classes make a conscious effort to incorporate themes and lessons relevant to civic education. Although this diversity is especially true in noncivics courses, there is variation even among civics teachers, which suggests a potential conflict between the goals of teacher autonomy and civic education. Second, there are clear variations *between communities* not only in the sense and practice of citizenship demonstrated by students but in the school environments in which civic education takes place. While it is tempting to reduce these differences to a question of economics, it would be a mistake to do so. Instead, our participatory observation and community studies suggest that the differences we have noted here reflect the influence of a variety of subtle and not so subtle community differences in shared understandings about the meaning of citizenship, the importance of community, and the goals of education. And all of this discussion suggests the importance of *local* understandings of the practice of citizenship that necessarily must inform any attempts at reforming civic education.

NOTES

This chapter is a revised version of a paper originally presented at the Aspen Conference on Democratic Education in 1996. We thank the participants in that conference for their helpful comments. Of course, any shortcomings in the paper are our responsibility. Finally, we gratefully acknowledge the generous support of the Spencer Foundation in the collection and analysis of these data.

1. For a review see Pamela Johnston Conover, "Political Socialization: Where's the Politics?" in *Political Behavior,* vol. 3 of *Political Science: Looking to the Future,* ed. William Crotty (Evanston, Ill.: Northwestern University Press, 1991), 125–52; and Timothy E. Cook, "The Bear Market in Political Socialization and the Costs of Misunderstood Psychological Theories," *American Political Science Review* 79 (1985): 1079–93.

2. Although some consider the concept of a practice to be "deeply elusive," the core of this concept—the notion of a tacit understanding shared by a group—is a useful one. See Stephen Turner, *The Social Theory of Practices* (Chicago: University of Chicago Press, 1994). Alasdair MacIntyre, *After Virtue* (Notre Dame, Ind.: University of Notre Dame Press, 1984), suggests that practices are coherent, collective human activities in which people attempt to achieve certain aims or "standards of excellence" that are appropriate to and partially definitive of that activity. In the process of doing so, people realize certain goods—internal goods—which cannot be had in any other way but by engaging in the activity, and their conceptions of the goods and ends served are transformed and enriched by their activity. We adopt an even more general understanding of practices; see Elizabeth Frazer and Nicola Lacey, "MacIntyre, Feminism and the Concept of Practice," in *After MacIntyre: Critical Perspectives on the Work of Alasdiar MacIntyre,* ed. John Horton and Susan Mendus (Notre Dame, Ind.: University of Notre Dame Press, 1994), 265–82. In arguing that citizenship be conceived as a practice, we view it as human action that is socially based and underpinned by informal and formal institutions. While they can be articulated, the procedures and standards governing the practice of citizenship are mostly informal, though some of the legal aspects of citizenship are enforced by governmental authorities. The practices of citizenship are connected to a public discourse that shapes them and, in return, is shaped by the practices. The practices and discourses of citizenship preexist individual citizens.

3. Our argument is consistent with that recently made by Norman Nie, Jane Junn, and Kenneth Stehlik-Barry, *Education and Democratic Citizenship in America* (Chicago: University of Chicago Press, 1996). They demonstrate that education furthers the practice of democratic citizenship by promoting "political engagement" and "democratic enlightenment."

4. See William A. Galston, "Liberal Virtues," *American Political Science Review* 82 (1988): 1277–92, and Galston, *Liberal Purposes* (New York: Cambridge University Press, 1991). Although some may argue for a strong participatory democracy, we do not think this normative argument was reflected in the dominant understandings of citizenship that characterized public discourse in the 1990s. See Benjamin R. Barber, *Strong Democracy: Participatory Politics for a New Age* (Berkeley: University of California Press, 1984).

5. Barber, *Strong Democracy,* 1984; Amy Gutmann, *Democratic Education* (Princeton, N.J.: Princeton University Press, 1987); Gutmann, "Undemocratic Education," in *Liberalism and the Moral Life,* ed. Nancy L. Rosenblum (Cambridge, Mass.: Harvard University Press, 1989), 71–88; Gutmann, "The Virtues of Democratic Self-Restraint," in *New Communitarian Thinking: Persons, Virtues, Institutions, and Communities,* ed. Amitai Etzioni (Charlottesville: University Press of Virginia, 1995), 154–69; James S. Fishkin, *Democracy and Deliberation: New Directions for Democratic Reform* (New Haven, Conn.: Yale University Press, 1991); and Yael Tamir, ed., *Democratic Education in a Multicultural State* (Oxford: Blackwell Publishers, 1995).

6. See Herbert McClosky and Alida Brill, *Dimensions of Tolerance: What Americans Believe About Civil Liberties* (New York: Russell Sage Foundation, 1983); George Marcus, John L. Sullivan, Elizabeth Theiss-Moore, and Sandra L. Wood, *With Malice Toward Some: How People Make Civil Liberties Judgments* (Cambridge: Cambridge University Press, 1995); and John L. Sullivan, James Piereson, and George Marcus, *Political Tolerance and American Democracy* (Chicago: University of Chicago Press, 1982).

7. Jerome Bruner, *The Culture of Education* (Cambridge, Mass.: Harvard University Press, 1996).

8. See Alexander Rosenberg, *Philosophy of Social Science* (Oxford: Oxford University Press, 1988).

9. We followed a quasi-experimental research design, a variation of the "non-equivalent comparison group" design. See Thomas D. Cook and Donald T. Campbell, *Quasi-Experimentation: Design Analysis Issues for Field Settings* (Chicago: Rand McNally, 1979). Country (United States and Great Britain) and community type (suburban, rural, urban, and immigrant) constituted the "treatments" in this design. For the purposes of our analysis, the samples from the individual communities are combined. This design allows the separate effects of community type to be examined. At the same time, however, the combination of the local samples does *not* constitute a random national sample. Thus, while the direction of influence of national culture can be identified, the precise percentage within a country cannot be specified.

10. Definitions of "community" abound. For our purposes, we focused on the local communities geographically defined by a single high school district. Thus, *all* students in each community sample attended the same high school.

11. The interviews in the Philadelphia and San Antonio communities were conducted by a professional survey organization, while the interviews in the other two communities were done by interviewers recruited, trained, and supervised by the investigators. The interviewing began during the spring of 1990 and was completed by the end of the year.

12. Due to minor variations in the student population size and response rates, the number of respondents in the student samples varies somewhat between communities. Al-

though the target sample size was 100 in each community, the actual Ns are: 95 in the Minnesota community, 79 in Philadelphia, 100 in North Carolina, and 105 in San Antonio. Because of this variation, the samples have been weighted to produce an N of 100 students in each community.

13. The teacher sample is composed of between eighteen to twenty teachers from each school. In each case, the teacher sample includes the civics, history, and English teachers for the respondents in the student sample, as well as a sampling of teachers of other subjects taken by the respondents comprising the student sample.

14. Less than 10 percent of the residents identify themselves as Anglo. Within the Mexican-American population, there is a mix of people who are first-generation immigrants to this country and those whose families have been living in the community for several generations.

15. Although there are several Protestant churches, the local Catholic church claims 75 percent of the residents.

16. Pamela Johnston Conover and Barbara Hicks, "The Psychology of Overlapping Identities: Ethnic, Citizen, Nation, and Beyond," in *National Identities and Ethnic Minorities in Eastern Europe,* ed. Ray Taras (New York: Macmillan, 1998).

17. The category of citizen can be made more visible in several ways. When some residents are denied citizenship and their exclusion is linked to visible categories, status as a citizen becomes more important. The framing of political discourse can also ameliorate the relative invisibility of citizens as a group in everyday contexts. Through public discussion, political leaders can raise the immediate salience of "citizen" as a category and thereby make it more likely that it will enter into the current self-categorization process. When public discussion does *not* include such references, citizen identities are more likely to remain unused.

18. Specifically, the following question frame was used to ask the students about the centrality of eleven different identities, including "a citizen of the United States": "People think of themselves in different ways at different times. For example, at different times people may think of themselves as a friend, a neighbor, a citizen or a member of a community. I'm going to run through a list of different ways in which people have told us they sometimes think of themselves, and I'd like you to tell me for each, how often, if ever, you think of yourself that way. . . . All of the time, most of the time, some of the time, occasionally, or never?"

19. Less than 1 percent were unable to answer the question.

20. Mary Ann Glendon, *Rights Talk: The Impoverishment of Political Discourse* (New York: Free Press, 1991).

21. Our study also suggests substantial crossnational variations. In Great Britain, a substantially higher number of students describe a citizen as a member of the community.

22. The question frame for the card sort was: "People often talk about their rights as citizens. On each of the following cards is listed an item that might or might not be a right. Please divide the deck of cards into two stacks. One stack for those items that *are* your rights as an American citizen. And one stack for those items that *are not* your rights as an American citizen." Students were then presented with a deck of twenty-three possible rights.

23. Amitai Etzioni, *The Spirit of Community: Rights, Responsibilities, and the Communitarian Agenda* (New York: Crown Publishers, 1993); Glendon, *Rights Talk;* Galston, *Liberal Purposes.*

24. Nancy Cantor, Hazel Marcus, Paula Niedenthal, and Paula Nurius, "On Motivation and the Self Concept," in *Handbook of Motivation and Cognition*, ed. Richard M. Sorrentino and E. Tory Higgins (New York: Guilford Press, 1986); Hazel Markus and Paula Nurius, "Possible Selves," *American Psychologist* 41 (1986): 954–69; and Daphna Oyserman and Hazel Rose Markus, "Possible Selves and Delinquency," *Journal of Personality and Social Psychology* 59 (1990): 112–25.

25. Markus and Nurius, "Possible Selves."

26. Ibid.

27. For a lengthier discussion, see Pamela Johnston Conover and Donald Searing, "Political Discussion and the Politics of Identity," paper presented at the annual meeting of the Midwest Political Science Association, Chicago, April 1998.

28. Galston, "Liberal Virtues," 1283.

29. See Fishkin, *Democracy and Deliberation,* 1991; Bruce Ackerman, *Social Justice in the Liberal State* (New Haven, Conn.: Yale University Press, 1980); and Ackerman, "Why Dialogue?" *Journal of Philosophy* 86 (1989): 5–22.

30. Barber, *Strong Democracy,* 170; Michael J. Sandel, *Liberalism and the Limits of Justice* (Cambridge: Cambridge University Press, 1982); Thomas A. Spragens, *Reason and Democracy* (Durham, N.C.: Duke University Press, 1990).

31. Specifically, we asked them the following: "Please tell me how many times, *if ever,* you have had a discussion or serious conversation of five minutes or more about each topic *during the last month.* The first topic is the economy, that is, things like interest rates, unemployment, and rising prices. In the *last month* how many times have you had a discussion or serious conversation about the economy . . . not at all, once or twice, or often?" This question was repeated for thirteen more issues. This question format represents a significant improvement over previous attempts to measure political discussion. First, we focus only on serious discussions; the interviewers stress that we are not interested in brief comments about issues. Second, this format encourages the respondent to search through his or her memory in a systematic fashion, thus increasing the likelihood of accurate reporting. Finally, the format identifies for the respondent the range of issues that are considered "political," thus eliminating one extraneous source of individual variation that is typically present in measures of political talk.

32. Immediately after asking about their discussion of different issues, we asked the following question: "People also discuss politics in different places and with different kinds of people. I'm going to read you a list of *places* where people sometimes talk about public issues. For each one, please tell me how often you usually have discussions or serious conversations of more than five minutes about political issues *like those just mentioned.* The first is at home. Generally speaking, how often would you say you have discussions or serious conversations about political issues at home? . . . Never, rarely, sometimes, or often?"

33. Sullivan, Piereson, and Marcus, *Political Tolerance.*

34. The activities include teach in a local school, form a local branch of the group, campaign to remove the group's books from the library, allow a member of the group to run for the town council, and allow a group member to organize and speak at a public march.

35. The Pearson's correlation between discussion in different settings and a measure combining a duty to stay informed and to discuss political issues publicly is .28.

36. To create a measure of "tolerance rights," students were given a point for each of the following rights that they recognized as such: freedom of speech, being homosexual, freedom of religion, the right to demonstrate against the government, the right to join whatever groups and organizations one wants, the right to read whatever one wants (including pornography), and the right to privacy.

37. Identity was measured by asking, "How strongly do you think of yourself as belonging to the *(name of the school)* community—very strongly, fairly strongly, not so strongly, or don't you think of yourself in those terms?" A sense of shared interests was measured by four agree-disagree questions asking whether students want the same things in life; whether the school doing well has an impact on the student's life; whether people can depend upon one another in the school; and whether the student has much in common with people at the school. Responses to these four questions were summed to form an additive scale on which high measures signify a strong sense of shared interests.

38. James S. Coleman, *Foundations of Social Theory* (Cambridge, Mass.: Harvard University Press, 1990), and Robert D. Putnam, "Tuning In, Tuning Out: The Strange Disappearance of Social Capital in the United States," *PS: Political Science and Politics* 28 (1995): 664–83.

39. The following types of organizations were asked about: sports teams or groups or activities; school clubs like the Spanish club, dramatics club, cheerleaders, and so on; youth organizations like Scouts, Future Farmers of America, 4-H; musical groups or activities like choirs, orchestras, bands, and dance groups; groups connected with their church or synagogue or other religious groups; neighborhood groups or gangs; political groups such as the Young Republicans or the Sierra Club; art and other cultural organizations and activities; and any other formal or informal organization.

40. The differences between communities are not substantial.

41. Our measure of school consciousness was created by multiplying together the measures of school identity and sense of belonging to the school that were discussed earlier.

42. The data bear this out. Civic engagement is significantly related to the two specific measures tapping discussion with friends (Pearson's r = .21) and during after-school activities (Pearson's r = .19).

43. See Conover and Searing, "Political Discussion." The empirical basis of this argument is our analysis of twelve focus group discussions in the United States and Great Britain in which the participants discussed their reasons for and for not discussing politics.

44. For a discussion of the politics of recognition, see Charles Taylor, "The Politics of Recognition," in *Multiculturalism,* ed. Amy Gutmann (Princeton, N.J.: Princeton University Press, 1994).

45. We ran four sets of partial correlations between the five school experiences and the seven sense and practice of citizenship variables presented in Table 11: one each controlling for student's gender; student's race; father's SES (income and social class) and politicization (political participation and political discussion), and mother's SES and politicization. Of the significant relationships in Table 11, none is rendered insignificant by the controls; indeed, few are reduced at all in their magnitude.

46. The Pearson's r between civic engagement and discussion (issues measure) is .21 in the suburban community and .39 in the rural community compared to .16 in both

of the other two communities. Similarly, the Pearson's r between civic engagement and discussion (settings measure) is .32 in the suburban community and nonsignificant in the other communities.

47. This is particularly true for the correlation between school discussion and discussion (settings), which is .59 for both the urban and immigrant communities.

48. Pearson's r between discussion in noncivics classes and discussion (issues measure) is .21 for the suburban community, .36 for the rural community, .10 for the urban community, and .02 for the immigrant community. Pearson's r between discussion in noncivics classes and discussion (settings measure) is .27 for the suburban community, .19 for the rural community, .03 for the urban community, and –.01 for the immigrant community.

49. Barber, *Strong Democracy;* Glendon, *Rights Talk;* Etzioni, *Spirit of Community.*

50. Tamir, *Democratic Education.*

51. Benjamin R. Barber, *An Aristocracy of Everyone: The Politics of Education and the Future of America* (New York: Oxford University Press, 1992).

52. Martha C. Nussbaum, *Poetic Justice: The Literary Imagination and Public Life* (Boston: Beacon Press, 1995).

PART II

Approaches to Studying the Politics of Education

6

The Two Democratic Purposes
of Public Education

Terry M. Moe

Those who think and write about education have long been concerned with the democratic purposes of schooling, and particularly with the contribution public schools ought to be making to a successful, well-functioning democratic political system. The notion is that the schools are important building blocks of democracy. When they are guided by the right values, and when they are properly designed to do their jobs, they pass on knowledge, skills, and values that not only prepare the nation's children for productive lives and careers, but also prepare them to be active, informed citizens in a democratic polity.[1]

Whether the schools can do this job well, and indeed what it even means for them to try, is a complicated issue that turns on a variety of factors. Of these, the most important—and the most unappreciated, in my view—is that the public schools have a second democratic purpose that is even more fundamental than the first.

In this second role, the public schools are agencies of democratic government, created and controlled by democratic authorities. They are not free to do what they want. They are not even free to be what they want. Everything about them, from goals to structure to operations, is a legitimate matter for decision by their democratic superiors and subject to influence by the political processes that determine who those superiors are and how they exercise their public authority.

This is another way of saying that the schools are endogenous to the democratic political system. They are what the system makes them. Concerned scholars may offer their considered judgments about how the schools ought to contribute to American democracy. Indeed, they may offer their considered judgments about how the schools ought to do most anything, from teaching sex education to promoting the arts to inculcating the loftiest of moral values. It does not matter. For the fact is that how the schools are designed, and what they actually do as a result, will be determined by the institutions and politics of democratic

127

government, whose outcomes may have little to do with, or be dramatically different from, those that scholars think are best.

If we want to explore how schools might shape democracy for the better, we have to begin by trying to understand how democracy shapes the schools—for better or for worse. There are different ways to do this, but the most productive, in my view, is to recognize that the schools are typical public agencies—no more, no less—and to rely on the positive theory of political institutions to show how their creation, design, and performance, like those of all agencies, are rooted in the political logic of the democratic system.[2]

I have already taken some steps in this direction in an earlier book with John Chubb entitled *Politics, Markets, and America's Schools*.[3] The theoretical argument of that book, which is rooted in more general work I have done on the theory of political institutions,[4] has unfortunately been lost in all the fury and passion surrounding the voucher debate, and it has been branded as nothing more than ideology or policy advocacy.[5] In my view, this reaction says more about the education field than it does about the book. To my knowledge, *Politics, Markets, and America's Schools* represents the first attempt to apply the positive theory of political institutions to the study of schools. In this chapter, I will use the same general logic, updated and expanded, to address the questions that face us here.

DIVERSITY, SOCIAL CHOICE, AND COMMUNITY VALUES

It is important not to take a romantic or wistful view of democracy, to associate it with consensus or civic values, or to think that democracy somehow allows citizens to act cohesively as a group.[6] If people agreed on important social issues, we would not need democracy. Nor would we need democracy if, in James Madison's terms, people were angels and could be trusted to act in the common interest. The bedrock fact of life is that people have very different interests and values, especially in a society as diverse as the United States. As any poll, political campaign, or effort to pass substantial legislation starkly reveals: Americans disagree. And, needless to say, they are not angels.

It is a mistake to think that, if only people would participate more, and if only they would deliberate the issues with their fellows, they could overcome their disagreements. To my knowledge, the empirical evidence does not even come close to justifying this sort of optimism. People may adjust their beliefs and even their values as a result of participating in democratic forums, especially on issues they have thought little about or that are remote from their own experience. They may compromise and negotiate and moderate what they are willing to accept.[7] But no amount of participation is going to turn a Catholic into a Muslim or even, in most cases, a Democrat into a Republican. And no amount of deliberation or deep thought is going to convince a teachers' union official that vouchers are a good idea.

The presumption cannot be, then, that if we designed a democratic system well, people would agree on the major issues that face them. On the contrary, the presumption must be that people are different, and that the fundamental task of democracy is to aggregate diverse individual preferences into social choices.

What can we say about the social choices that democracy produces? Several points stand out. First, whatever the social choice may be—a particular policy on bilingual education, say—it automatically creates winners and losers in a context of diverse preferences. The winners are those who agree with the policy, the losers are those who disagree, which does not mean that the losers will be worse off in absolute terms, but in many cases this is precisely what will happen. In a democracy, if the winners have the votes, they can do anything they want (as long as it is constitutional) to pursue their own values and interests, and there is nothing to guarantee that the losers will not be worse off as a result. At the very least, they will be subjected to policies they do not support.

Another way to state this premise is that democracy is ultimately coercive. On any given issue, the winners of the democratic struggle enact their own preferences into law, and the losers are required to comply with its dictates or be subject to sanctions. The typical public policy is precisely of this sort: a set of values and requirements devised by one portion of the population but imposed on everyone, whether they like it or not. There is nothing voluntary about it.[8]

Some of the sting is taken out of this democratic coercion if we can say that the winners' policies are somehow reflective of civic values or the community. As a general rule, however, there is little basis for such an interpretation, which is true in the obvious sense that, as long as there are people who disagree—and usually there are plenty who do—it is misleading to claim that the winners somehow speak for society. But it is also true for less obvious, more sophisticated reasons that have become the hallmarks of the best-developed theory in all of political science: social choice theory.

Since Kenneth J. Arrow first unveiled his impossibility theorem almost fifty years ago, social choice theorists have been demonstrating that, under a variety of conditions quite common in real-world contexts, majority rule and other democratic voting processes are unstable and socially irrational, leading to cycles and intransitivities that obliterate any straightforward democratic connection between social outcomes and the underlying preferences of individuals.[9] The coup de grâce came with Richard D. McKelvey's chaos theorem, which showed that majority rule generates a chaos of potential outcomes in which, with the right control of the agenda, virtually *any* point in a multidimensional policy space can ultimately be engineered as the majority-rule winner.[10] It follows that the winners in any given instance are not "the" majority, and that they—and their preferences—have no special status as somehow being representative of the community. With the right control of the agenda, other groups with very different preferences could have won.

Special cases aside, there is no democratic solution to this dilemma. Without agenda control, in a perfect democratic world in which everyone participates, everyone's vote counts equally, and every alternative is ultimately paired against every other, there is likely to be chaos and no social choice at all in any meaningful sense. With agenda control—which is the norm, empirically—some group will win, and there will be a stable "democratic" outcome, although that outcome cannot be regarded as a meaningful reflection of the distribution of preferences in the community. It may have won a democratic vote, but it does not necessarily reveal civic values or anything of the sort. More likely, it reveals the values of the agenda controllers.

For democrats—and for education reformers, who think that civic values can somehow guide the democratic education of our children—these social choice results can only be viewed as troubling. For social scientists, on the other hand, these same results have a more positive side, because they point the way toward promising theories that can help us explain how the political world works.

The main impact of the post-McKelvey work on social choice has been to show that the explanation of stable "democratic" outcomes is fundamentally *institutional*. The earlier research, following Arrow, had explored the chaos of democratic voting processes. But important as these works were on logical grounds, it was also empirically evident that chaos is not the normal state of affairs in real-world voting bodies such as legislatures, committees, or school boards. The norm is considerable stability. The post-McKelvey social-choice literature offers an explanation: the chaos inherent in majority rule (and many other voting rules) is rendered stable through agenda control and other institutional mechanisms that structure how issues get recognized and taken up for decision. Institutions bring stability out of chaos, and they explain, in the process, why some outcomes occur and others do not.[11]

It was this recognition, in combination with others described below, that fueled the "new institutionalism" in positive political theory. The result, over the last twenty years or so, has been the fast-paced development of a much more broadly based institutional theory of democratic government that sheds important new light on a whole range of substantive concerns, among them the fundamental features of public agencies, including schools.

INSTITUTIONS, CONSTITUENCY, AND POWER

So far the lesson here is that even if Americans were somehow able to perfect their democracy (which is fanciful anyway), the schools could not reasonably be viewed as reflecting the will of the people, civic values, or other such pleasing concepts. In a diverse society, democracy produces winners and losers. It is the winners who will control the schools, and the winners' preferences that will set educational policy and structure.

Who are the winners? That depends on the institutions by which the schools are governed and the peculiar ways in which those institutions aggregate individual and group preferences into choices for society. Different institutions will favor different constituencies, produce different sets of winners and losers, and generate different outcomes — and thus different schools. Although on normative grounds we might prefer certain arrangements, outcomes, and winners to others, the scientific task is to try to understand how all of this works and thus what we should expect from democratic governance of the schools, whether we like its results or not.

In practice, many forms of governance are regarded as compatible with democracy. Since the early decades of this century, however, the governance of American public education has taken a very specific structural form that is virtually the same in every state in the union. This form is by now so deeply entrenched that, among those in the education community, it has come to be regarded as the only legitimate way to govern the schools democratically.

In this system, the schools are bottom-level subordinates in a huge, complicated structure of democratic authority. Above them at the local level are school boards, superintendents, central office bureaucracies, and county offices of education. Still higher up are the state authorities: state school boards, state school superintendents, state departments of education, state legislatures, governors, and state courts. And then there is the federal government and its education authorities: the Department of Education, Congress, the president, and the federal courts.[12]

This structure is not a neat classical hierarchy. The different levels exercise different types of authority, and their authority overlaps in some domains. For constitutional reasons, ultimate authority on most matters is not vested in the national officials at the top, but rather in the state officials in the middle. In the final analysis, these details matter. Indeed, they are crucial, for they determine which constituencies will have influence, and who the winners and losers will be on every dimension of policy and structure reachable by public authority — which is to say, virtually every dimension imaginable.

Details aside, the more general point is that the schools are subject to control— legitimate democratic control—by lots of superiors at all three levels of government simultaneously. All of them have the legal right to govern the schools. And the schools, in turn, are responsible to each and every one of these authorities and thus to their constituents, whomever they might be and whatever they might want.

If we take this system as a given for now, there are two ways to approach the typical public school's "democratic constituency." What is it in principle, and what is it in practice? Both are avenues for gaining perspective on the kinds of preferences, people, and groups that are likely to have influence over the schools in this democratic system and those that are not.

Normally, I would not bother much with the "in principle" part, but here it serves an important function. All of us are jaded by the crass realities of politics and are not much surprised to hear that democratic ideals get violated in practice. So it is valuable to point out that, even when the existing democratic system is working properly and players throughout the control structure are doing their jobs well, these ideals are *not even supposed* to be realized.[13] I am talking, in particular, about two myths that undergird the democratic folklore of the public schools: local control and parental control. It should be clear that both are incompatible, in principle, with the basic institutional design of the existing system.

In this system, there is nothing special about local control. Authority is authority wherever it may lie, and the governance of America's local schools is properly shared by all legitimate authorities at all three levels. Right away, then, it should be clear that local control is just part of a much larger system of control in which the local authorities have to contend with state and national authorities in shaping the schools. The locals are actually worse off, however, than even this three-way split suggests, for they are at the bottom of the hierarchy. Unless state constitutions give them a measure of autonomy, they are simply creatures of the state government: their structure, powers, and responsibilities are subject to determination by state officials, and they must follow whatever policies, rules, and regulations are imposed on them by the state. Similarly, in those areas where the federal government has authority, the locals must follow federal requirements. Any notion that local constituencies are privileged in this scheme of democratic government, then, is quite wrong.

This same conclusion follows even more strongly for parents. The parents of children who attend a particular public school are part of the local constituency, and for that reason alone are but a small part of the larger democratic constituency with a legal right to govern that school. Even within the local constituency itself, however, parents find themselves submerged in two additional respects. First, they are typically far outnumbered by people who do not have school-age (or any) children, and who thus have very different interests—in not taxing and not spending, among other things—when it comes to the schools. Second, while parents clearly have a special interest in their own children's schools, this does not carry over into special governing rights: the entire democratic constituency governs each school. Parents with children in that school carry the same weight as anyone else.

The current democratic structure of American education, then, is simply not set up to provide local or parental control of the schools in any meaningful sense. Local control is subordinate to state (especially) and national control. The parents associated with a given school are a tiny, insignificant part of the huge, heterogeneous constituencies at local, state, and national levels that collectively have a right to govern that school. This is what democratic control means under the current system. It is the way the system is supposed to work.

Now let's turn to the second issue: which authorities, constituencies, and groups actually have power? There is much that could be said here, but a few basic points deserve emphasis—each of them, it seems to me, painfully obvious to anyone familiar with the politics of education.

First, power is heavily skewed in favor of organized interests, particularly those whose members' careers and livelihoods are tied to the educational system.

The "500-pound gorillas" in the educational arena are the teachers' unions, but there are countless other groups, whose members range from administrators to bilingual education specialists to book publishers to janitors to building contractors, who are active and influential on issues that concern them. Education is a multibillion-dollar industry, and for groups with a vested interest in the system, the stakes are high—for reasons that have nothing to do with children or quality education or democracy.[14]

In addition to these vested interests, there are other groups, like the NAACP and the ACLU, that have value-oriented, ideological agendas and that are also influential on educational issues. The point is not that vested interests are the only groups that count. The point is that organized interests drive the politics of education, and, of those groups, the ones representing vested interests tend to be the established powers.

Barring radical institutional reform, it is difficult to see how it could be any other way. As Mancur Olson demonstrated long ago, these groups have enormous advantages over more broadly based social interests—notably, those of parents or taxpayers—in organizing and bringing their weight to bear in politics.[15] The logic of collective action favors them overwhelmingly. And so does the logic of politics, in a system where legislators and other elected officials are intensely motivated by a desire to be reelected, and organized groups control the money, manpower, and resources these officials need for reelection.[16] The natural order of things is that American public officials, given their institutional incentives, are disproportionately responsive to organized groups, which is true, I hasten to add, of virtually all areas of public policy, not just education.

Second, most ordinary citizens play little or no role in the politics of education. At best, ordinary people vote. But only about half the electorate votes even in presidential elections, the most salient elections we have, and the percentages decline as the arenas get closer to home. Although democratic theorists like to extol the virtues of small, local settings and often pin their hopes for a vibrant democracy on local decision making, the fact is that local elections—and particularly school board elections—are legendary for voter apathy and low turnout.[17]

In New York City, for instance, where governance was decentralized to put more power in the hands of local citizens, school board elections tend to attract a turnout of about 10 percent. And a good portion of that turnout is doubtless due to the mobilization efforts of candidates, along with unions and other vested interests, who know that, by rounding up small numbers of supporters and getting them to the polls, they can control the outcomes.[18] This situation is not unique to New York City. It is typical: hardly anyone participates in school politics, and those who do are likely to be quite unrepresentative of the public at large and instead a reflection of the power of interest groups.

Third, parents and other local constituents are disadvantaged in fact as well as in principle. Even if all constituents carried equal weight, parents would have little democratic control over the schools their children attend. Empirically, however, given the dominance of interest groups and the apathy and abysmally low participation rates of ordinary citizens, parents actually play a weaker and more marginal role than even this grim portrayal would suggest. All the key decisions are made by other, far more powerful players.

As for local constituencies as a whole, it is clear empirically that they do in fact play subordinate roles in the democratic control structure, and that they are increasingly constrained by the never-ending stream of policies, rules, and regulations generated by state and national authorities. In the distant past, local officials were often granted substantial autonomy. But the authority to violate that autonomy has always existed at higher levels, and as the authorities at these higher levels have chosen to exercise it, animated by organized groups demanding governmental action, the historical trend has been away from local control.

Now let's take a step back and put all of this in perspective. At the beginning of this section, I emphasized that the outcomes of democracy are not a reflection of consensus or civic values or even of the majority, but of winners and their preferences. This assumption raised questions about who the winners are likely to be under the existing system of democratic control, and what we can say about their preferences. Now that I have examined the schools' "democratic constituency," the basic contours of an answer stand out.

The existing democratic system is built to impose social values on the public schools, but the values that get imposed are heavily shaped by organized interest groups, especially those with a vested interest in the existing system, and especially those that are organized at the state and national levels. Because virtually every aspect of the schools is subject to determination by public authority, the political power and active involvement of these groups work to guarantee that their preferences will be intricately woven into the warp and woof of American education. The public schools look the way they do not because that is what "the people" or parents want, but because that is what the group-dominated politics of education has produced.

What, then, can we say about the preferences of these group winners? Four important points deserve emphasis:

Group preferences are not in any sense representative of the larger polity but instead reflect the special interests of group leaders, members, and supporters.

Group preferences often have little or nothing to do with the best interests of children or quality education. Teachers' unions, for example, are primarily concerned with job security, working conditions, and collective bargaining rights, and what is good for unions is not necessarily what is good for children or for education.

Group preferences are usually rooted in basic interests, and they cannot be expected to change much as a result of argument, deliberation, or participation. The groups want what they want, and more "democracy" will not change that.

Group preferences become law because the groups themselves are powerful. The preferences can be unrepresentative, bad, or quite unreasonable and still be adopted—enthusiastically—by public officials, whose institutional incentives orient them to power, not goodness.

Whether we like it or not, these are the preferences that characterize the democratic constituency of the public schools and drive the system of democratic control. When government makes its official decisions about the "democratic purposes" of schooling, or indeed about any aspects of the schools that it wants to specify or regulate, there is no reason to think that some sort of democratic vision or pulse of the people is somehow behind these policies—and every reason to think that the new policies simply reflect the special interests of some set of group winners.

THE POLITICAL FOUNDATIONS OF BUREAUCRACY

Winning is not just a matter of gaining victory on a vote. It is also a matter of seeing to it that the new policy is implemented faithfully and effectively, for failing that, the victory will be meaningless. Thus, when rational actors pursue their interests in the policy-making process, they are concerned not only with fashioning goals and mandates that reflect their own preferences but also with ensuring, as best they can, that those goals and mandates are achieved in practice.

How can they do this? The short answer is that they must think strategically not only about policy but also about the creation, design, control, and oversight of the public agencies—the public schools, in this case—that will be responsible for carrying out policy. In other words, they must think about structure as well as policy. The two problems are really just two sides of the same coin and integral components of the same political calculus.

The long answer is provided by the positive theory of institutions, a fast-growing body of literature that has become the most influential component of the "new institutionalism" in political science. This work arose out of two developments in rational choice theory. The first, as I suggested earlier, was the post-McKelvey recognition by social choice theorists that, because institutions account for the stable outcomes of democratic voting processes, the theory of voting must be expanded to yield a theory of institutions and their effects.[19]

The second development was the meteoric rise of the new economics of organization.[20] This line of work—which roughly consists of transaction cost economics, agency theory, and the theory of repeated games—initially emerged within economics to explain the existence and organizational properties of business firms.[21] Its analytic tools, however, were supremely well suited to generic issues of organization—hierarchy, control, cooperation, specialization—and were quickly adapted by political scientists to the study of their own institutions. The result, over the last fifteen years or so, has been the emergence of a positive theory of institutions that is a hybrid of social choice and the new economics, with growing emphasis on the latter.

Much of this new literature is about how political institutions emerge out of politics and why they take the structural forms they do. It is nothing less than an effort to explain the structure of government. Why, for instance, do kings agree to constitutional checks and balances that limit their powers?[22] What is the political basis of federalism?[23] Why are many public agencies endowed with bizarre structures that make it difficult for them to perform their jobs?[24] Why do legislatures create civil service systems whose personnel they cannot control?[25] Why is Congress organized around committees[26] and legislative parties?[27] Although on substantive grounds these sorts of questions may seem only distantly related to one another, in fact there is a coherent theoretical logic that binds them all together and weaves, in the process, a broadly based theory of political institutions.

AGENCY PROBLEMS, CONTROL, AND BUREAUCRACY

Now let's get back to the issue under consideration, what can the winners in democratic politics do to ensure that their new policies are actually carried out so that the anticipated benefits are realized as fully as possible?

In the institutions literature, the most common starting point for addressing this question is agency theory, which recognizes that the winners face a generic control problem. As principals, they cannot do everything themselves but must delegate authority to agents, who will then be responsible for carrying out policy. These agents, however, will not necessarily act in the principals' best interests. Indeed, they have both the incentive and the opportunity to shirk their responsibilities. They have the incentive because they inevitably have their own values, goals, and interests and therefore stand to gain by engineering policy away from the principals' ideal points and closer to their own. They have the opportunity because they possess resources—notably, information and expertise—that their principals do not have, and that makes it difficult for the latter to know what is being done, why it is being done, and whether it comports with their own interests.[28]

It would be a mistake, then, for political superiors simply to delegate authority to their agents, grant them mandates, and hope for the best. Rational actors will not do that. Instead, the rational strategy is to impose a set of structures on these agents that constrain them to behave in ways that, given the costs and uncertainties, are as desirable as can be expected.[29]

The earliest attempts to apply this theory to politics emphasized the oversight structures associated with *ex post* control.[30] The focus here was on existing public agencies that threatened to drift away from the desired path—to become, in colloquial terms, "runaway bureaucracies"—and solutions took the form of structural tools for getting them back in line: monitoring mechanisms, reporting requirements, budgetary rewards and sanctions, threats of new legislation, and other means of either shaping agency incentives or enhancing the information available to superiors.

Subsequent work, however, recognized that *ex post* control mechanisms are unlikely to be very effective by themselves, and argued that the most powerful means of control are exercised *ex ante,* i.e., prior to any noncompliance by the agency and indeed prior to the emergence of the agency as an actor.[31] This argument makes sense: political superiors need not take agencies as givens, to be dealt with only after they have gone off course. They have the authority to create these agencies and to specify, if they want, virtually every aspect of their organizational structure—their decision-making procedures, who gets to participate, what standards and criteria must be employed, how authority is allocated, how appointments are handled, what decisions can be appealed, who gets to appeal and to what courts, and so on. In these and countless other ways, superiors can take steps to "stack the deck" by building their own interests (and those of their constituents) right into the organization of public agencies, predisposing them, even in the absence of effective oversight, to carry out policy along accepted lines.

In general, then, what this portion of the theory has to say is that "agency problems" are inherent in delegation, and that much of the structure of government arises from—and is explained by—attempts to mitigate them. Some of these structures, such as monitoring and reporting requirements, are obvious control mechanisms, but most are not. They are the hierarchies, rules, procedures, and personnel systems that make up the everyday organization of public bureaucracy.

POLITICAL UNCERTAINTY, PROTECTION, AND BUREAUCRACY

There is much more to the story of government organization, however, than a simple principal-agent perspective can readily tell us, for it misses a feature of democratic politics that is essential to the way rational actors think about and exercise control. What it overlooks is that these actors must operate in a world of "political uncertainty."[32] Players who happen to hold power today have the temporary right to create and control public agencies, but with changes in electoral outcomes and shifts in group strength, their enemies may come to power tomorrow. And if this were to occur, control over these same public agencies would fall into the hands of their opponents, who would have every right to channel agency behavior in very different and undesired directions.

Because today's authorities want their own policies to endure in a politically uncertain future, they must try to assure that, even with shifts in power, their enemies cannot undermine or reverse their achievements, which means when they create and design public agencies, they must be thinking not only about mitigating the usual agency problems, but also about *protecting* their creations from control by other principals in the future. Their task, in more conventional language, is to find ways to insulate their agencies and programs from future democratic control.

The solution is again structural. Civil service, for instance, is an important means of protecting agencies from unwanted control, as are "independent" forms of organization. But a still more general approach is what might be called aggressive formalization. Authorities can specify in excruciating detail all the major factors affecting agency decisions: procedures, criteria, timetables, participating rights, appeal rights, and so on. Not just a matter of stacking the deck as it was for agency problems, this approach is a matter of *locking in* the bias by strictly limiting agency discretion, directing agency behavior through the extensive use of rules, and purposely removing it from the risky realm of politics so that there will be as little as possible for future authorities to influence, and agencies will be formally bound to the "original intent" of their mandates.

A clear trade-off is involved here: whatever the requirements of effective organization might be, political uncertainty will drive proponents to bury their agencies in burdensome rules and restrictions anyway. The purpose of these strategic moves is protective, not productive. As a result, agencies will purposely be burdened with cumbersome, excessive trappings of bureaucracy that impede agency performance. That is the price of political protection.

SEPARATION OF POWERS, COMMITMENT, AND BUREAUCRACY

Political uncertainty is bound up with a larger set of problems, known as "commitment" problems, that are fundamental to the modern theory of institutions.[33] In both public and private settings, commitment problems arise because actors cannot arrive at deals (contracts, bargains) that are enforceable and from which neither party has incentives to renege. To arrive at mutually beneficial arrangements, actors must be able to "commit," in the sense that each must be convinced that the others have incentives to live up to the deal. If they cannot commit, the deal will not happen, and everyone involved will be worse off. To avoid this result and to reap the benefits of cooperation, actors have incentives to find mechanisms that help make credible commitment possible. These often take structural forms, and many real-world structures exist because they make credible commitment possible.

The commitment problem is especially bad in politics largely because of political uncertainty. Consider, for instance, the classic relationship between politicians and interest groups.[34] The groups want certain policies, and thus the stream of future benefits associated with them, and they are willing to provide valuable political support to politicians in return for getting what they want. Politicians, for their part, want interest group support and are willing to supply policy benefits to get it. There is the basis for a mutually beneficial deal here, and these sorts of deals, of course, are the very basis of politics. The problem, however, is that today's politicians cannot automatically commit future politicians to honor the deal, for the latter may be responding to different groups, and they may use their authority to renege. Lacking a solution to this commitment problem, there can be no basis for political deal making, and both politicians and groups would be worse off.

In the American separation of powers system, however, there is a built-in solution to the commitment problem.[35] The key is the simple fact that because there are so many veto points, new laws are extremely difficult to pass, and blocking is relatively easy, which makes life tough on policy proponents. But the bright side is that, should they ever succeed in getting their policies passed, anything they formalize into law will tend to endure, for future authorities will have a difficult or impossible time overturning it.

Thus, if proponents respond to political uncertainty by legally imposing an avalanche of detailed rules and procedures on their agencies, supporters can count on these structures and their effects enduring over time, even with shifts in political power. In general, *formalization works* to solve the commitment problems that plague political transactions, giving everyone in American politics strong incentives to formalize. Because of the multiple veto points built into the separation of powers, whatever is formalized will be protected from subversion or reversal by future authorities, and will tend to endure.

Note that this situation is not necessarily true in other political systems; it turns on the ease of passing laws. In a Westminster parliamentary system, where the majority party has complete control of government and there are essentially no veto points, the party can pass laws at will—and so could the opposing party, should it ever gain power. Thus, any formal restrictions placed in the law as protective devices against political enemies would have little value: they could easily be removed by opponents as soon as they gained power. In a Westminster system, then, there is no point in formalizing agencies beyond what is necessary to manage agency problems, for that would hobble their performance without achieving any gain in political protection. Rational actors therefore have no incentives to impose these excessive burdens on their agencies. They have to solve their commitment problems in other, usually informal ways, since formal structure does not work.[36]

The grand implication, in a nutshell, is that American public agencies are likely to be buried in rules and regulations, and thus excessively bureaucratized, in comparison to agencies in Westminster systems and indeed to most parliamentary systems, since they generally contain far fewer veto points than the American system. These differences are systemic: the separation of powers in the United States has a built-in bias toward excessive bureaucratization that is rooted in the logic of its politics and institutions.

THE BUREAUCRATIZATION OF THE PUBLIC SCHOOLS

As I discussed earlier, there are lots of education authorities with the right to exercise control, and all of them—often acting on behalf of interest groups—can impose their own rules, procedures, and requirements to ensure that the schools comply with their preferences. Even if agency problems were all they focused on, they would have reason to rely heavily on these bureaucratic mechanisms in controlling the schools.

In the first place, they suffer from a critical information asymmetry: they cannot know what principals, teachers, and parents know about what actually goes on in individual schools, and this deficit puts them at a serious disadvantage in trying to exact compliance. In the second place, staff members within the schools have their own views on education, their own values and policy preferences, and they may readily disagree with policies imposed from above. They will have incentives, then, to go their own way and to use the resources at their disposal—particularly, their expertise and their private information about their own schools and activities—to chart their own path, perhaps without superiors even knowing about it. It is up to superiors to see that this divergence does not happen, by imposing all manner of *ex post* and *ex ante* structural devices to generate information, shape incentives, and constrain behavior along acceptable lines. The inevitable result is that the schools get bureaucratized.

The incentives to bureaucratize are far greater than this discussion suggests, however, because of political uncertainty. Educational issues are often contentious, and virtually any important policy initiative—compensatory education, special education, bilingual education, sex education, the choice of textbooks, student testing—can count on having opponents who would change or reverse it if they gained power in the future. Because there are so many authorities at different levels, moreover, these problems of political uncertainty are even more threatening than they might otherwise be, for opponents have a variety of arenas and levels to work through in trying to get at the schools and subvert the winners' "original intent." If today's winners want their education policies to endure, they need to protect and insulate them by formalizing. They need to bureaucratize the schools.

Other things being equal, the farther authorities are from the school site, the greater their incentive to bureaucratize. Authorities in a distant location have a difficult time knowing what is going on in individual schools, and ordinarily have a larger number of schools they are supposed to know about. They also face greater preference diversity among their agents because there are usually more such agents to deal with, and because they are more likely to reflect the dizzying array of geographic, regional, cultural, ideological, economic, and ethnic differences that characterize American society. Primarily for this reason, moreover, the threat of political uncertainty is greater as well: the larger and more diverse the political context, the more likely that active group opponents will seek to change or subvert policy if they gain power and that other education authorities in the picture will try to gain control on their own.

A rule of thumb, therefore, is that national authorities have the greatest incentive to bureaucratize, followed by the states, and then the districts. Similarly, large states and districts should be more prone to bureaucracy than smaller ones, and diverse states and districts should tend to be more bureaucratic than those that are relatively homogeneous.

These are only rules of thumb, however, and other factors have a role to play as well. For instance, because education is largely a state rather than a national function, the states have many more policies and responsibilities to execute, and more situations where they are compelled to bureaucratize in order to promote compliance and protect against political uncertainty. In addition, many of the interest groups active in national politics have their roots in the states; sometimes, rather than demanding a uniform national policy, they put pressure on national officials to grant their states discretion in carrying out policy so that state authorities in conjunction with these same groups can devise their own bureaucratic rules for districts and schools. For these sorts of reasons, then, most of the sheer weight of bureaucracy is likely to come from state authorities, even though national decision makers are at the greatest disadvantage in exercising control and have the greatest incentives to bureaucratize.

However it shakes out, though, the end result for schools is the same: they get heavily bureaucratized. And to say the least, this result is unfortunate, for while it is impossible to run a school of any size, much less a system of schools, without some of the classic components of bureaucracy (division of labor, for instance), extensive bureaucratization is clearly a bad thing for schools. A comprehensive literature currently exists on what it takes for schools to perform their jobs effectively, and the theme running throughout this empirical work is that the schools which work best are flexible, informal, cooperative, professional, team-like organizations that function much like organic communities.[37] Obviously, the rule-bound formalism of bureaucracy is the antithesis of this model of effective schooling, creating a mechanical world in which roles, routines, and paperwork serve as unproductive substitutes for the natural synergies of community.

Scholars who write about the democratic purposes of schooling see much the same kind of dichotomy. The schools they want are ideal training grounds for democracy— small, flexible, participatory communities that encourage active involvement, information exchange, debate, deliberation, and self-governance.[38] Bureaucracy undermines all of these advantages. A bureaucratic "community" is artificial, built on formally specified relationships, rights, and responsibilities that literally obstruct the development of a true community. And when most of the important decisions are made and imposed by higher hierarchic levels, as they are in the education system, there can be little incentive or purpose to democratic involvement at lower levels anyway.

It would be nice to think that somehow the public schools can escape the political logic of bureaucracy, that they are special organizations that cannot rightly be regarded as products of the "politics of structure" in the same way that ordinary agencies are.[39] The fact is, however, that there is nothing special about schools; they are just public agencies. And as public agencies in the American political system, they inevitably get buried in bureaucracy. In the end, therefore, the existing democratic system naturally tends to give us precisely the kinds of schools no one wants: bureaucracies instead of communities.

TOWARD A NEW VISION OF DEMOCRATIC SCHOOLING

It is a fine thing to say that the public schools should serve as training grounds for democracy where participation, political ideals, and civic values are taught and practiced. But the question is whether democracy will allow the schools to do this task well.

If the positive theory of institutions is any guide—and I think it is far and away the best guide we have at this point—the answer is clearly discouraging. The schools are creatures of democracy, and because American democracy works the way it does, the democratic purposes so often ascribed to them are likely to be carried out in ways that do not even come close to meeting the normative ideals of proponents. This is one of the ironies of democracy: the schools have difficulty contributing to the quality of democratic government precisely because they are democratically controlled.

American society is diverse, and it is going to stay diverse however vibrant our democracy may become under the best of circumstances. What a democratic control structure does is to aggregate these differences in such a way that some people win and some people lose. The winners are not necessarily representative of society or the community or even of the majority. Nor are their values necessarily good or admirable or well considered. The winners are the winners simply because they have more political power than the losers.

In the reality of democratic government, it is the winners who tell us what the democratic purposes of schooling will be. What specific values, for instance, should children be taught? What lessons should children learn about good citizenship? What should they be told constitutes a good democracy? What is the proper relationship among ethnic groups in a democratic society? These are questions that do not have objective answers. Philosophers could argue endlessly about them and so could ordinary people. Whatever the analytic or normative merits of the various arguments might be, however, the official answers will be determined in the end by whoever has the most power; the winners get to say.

The identity of the winners can vary, of course, from issue to issue and arena to arena. But the deck is clearly stacked in favor of special interest groups, particularly those with a vested interest in the existing system and those that are organized for action at the state and national levels. It is stacked against local communities and parents, who have little basis for truly governing their own schools. These power asymmetries are not unusual, nor are they accidental. They are predictable facts of political life—reflections of the logic of collective action, the reelection motives of public officials, the unequal distribution of social resources, and the hierarchy of democratic authority.

The preferences of these politically advantaged groups may be couched in the lofty rhetoric of what is best for students and is in the public interest. But in fact these preferences tend to be rooted in basic interests—which often have nothing to do with what is best for kids or society and are unlikely to change as a result of the kinds of deliberation and participation that are sometimes presumed to create greater consensus among people. These are the preferences that, unavoidably, weigh most heavily in defining the democratic purposes of schooling.

Democracy does more than impose the winners' values on the schools. It also allows them to structure the schools in any way they like—and they have incentives to do that, for if they are to see their policy victories translated into desired changes in school behavior, they cannot assume it will happen automatically. They face agency problems, because people in local districts and schools will have incentives and opportunities to go their own ways. And they face political uncertainty, because their opponents may gain power in the future and subvert the original intent of a policy. Both constraints prompt winners to bureaucratize the schools through an array of *ex post* and *ex ante* rules, requirements, and procedures. Thanks to the separation of powers and its multiple vetoes, these sorts of formal mechanisms have staying power and work to ensure that the winners' policies endure in an uncertain political future.

It is difficult to see how schools under this system can serve well as training grounds for democracy. Their democratic missions are not, and cannot be, fashioned in the best interests of society but are simply reflections of the special interests of political winners. And as organizations they cannot be the kinds of informal, interactive communities that facilitate deliberation and participation among equals but are destined instead to be formal, impersonal, and bureaucratic. These characteristics are literally built into the system and will not change as long as the schools continue to be governed through the top-down structure of democratic authority. They come along as part of the package.

What, then, can be done about it? For starters, we need to recognize that these are system problems, and they can only be resolved by changing the system itself. It might help if the United States could shift from a separation of powers to a parliamentary or some other form of government—but this option is clearly impossible. We have no choice but to search for ways of altering the governance of schools within the basic framework of American institutions.

In doing this, it would be a mistake to focus on the schools and to think that, if only the right values could be pursued or participation encouraged, the democratic purposes of schools could be realized. The schools are endogenous to the system, and the focus has to be on the structure of democratic control by which they are governed. As long as the authority to control them remains at higher levels, it will be used by those with power to pursue their own interests. And as long as that authority remains, the schools will get bureaucratized. The solution is to *remove* the schools as far as possible from top-down control and thus, in the process, to remove them from much of politics.

We have to reject the conventional tendency to associate democracy with the current system of top-down governance, which is not the only way to govern schools democratically. Nor is it the only way to have a "public" school system. To appreciate the alternatives, consider the democratic status of the Federal Reserve Board. The Fed was created during the early years of this century because politicians realized that, if monetary policy were directly controlled by Congress and the president, their short-term incentives to manipulate it for political advantage would be bad for the economy. And so the Fed was set up to be highly independent of politics and insulated from most external influences. Is this structure somehow undemocratic? Obviously not. The Fed was set up through a democratic act to achieve democratic purposes, and it so happens that an effective structure for achieving these purposes is one that is highly insulated from political control. Democracy does not require direct, top-down control. The upshot for the schools is that we surely can have a democratic school system without the existing hierarchy of democratic control.

What would such a system look like? There are various possibilities, but let me briefly suggest one that is, by my thinking, the most promising path to reform. This path involves the elimination via constitutional amendment (most likely at the state level) of most top-down authority over the everyday governance of schools and its replacement by a system built around parental choice, school autonomy, competition, and a democratically constructed framework of rules.

Markets are anathema to most education scholars. But they are extraordinarily powerful mechanisms for motivating, controlling, and directing social behavior, and it is unfortunate that the American education system has put them to so little use up to this point. True, markets can lead to undesired consequences under certain conditions—limited information, for instance—but these conditions are well understood by now, and can be addressed through an appropriate structure of rules that constrain and channel how markets operate. This is a job for democratic government: to set up the basic framework. More generally, its job—as it was with the Fed—is to make a democratic decision to remove the schools from politics and to set up a framework of rules that devolves power to parents and schools, regulates their choices, and embodies very basic social values on which there is minimal disagreement.

There is nothing undemocratic about this process. It is just a different way that a democratic people can choose to set up their school system—a way that (if done right) avoids control by special interests, escapes the political pressures that would otherwise bureaucratize the schools, and allows ordinary people (subject to the framework's basic rules) to make their own decisions about what values their children should be taught, how they should be socialized, and what democratic purposes their schools ought to be pursuing.

It would also tend to promote the emergence of schools as true communities. As parents choose their own schools, they are more likely to identify with them, to share their values and missions, to trust one another, to participate, and to have respect for teachers and principals. And to the extent that schools are free from restrictive rules, they are free, among other things, to hire the kinds of teachers who share the school's mission, do their jobs well, get along with one another, have mutual respect, and share power. These are all hallmarks of community, characteristics that arise naturally in an environment of choice and autonomy but that stand little chance under a bureaucratic regime.

This chapter is not about using choice to promote the democratic purposes of schooling, so I cannot address the great variety of issues that this sort of proposal obviously raises—among them, how democratic politics could ever produce such a reform. I will leave it for now as a provocative option. My point is simply that we *do* have options, and a serious concern for the democratic purposes of schooling demands that we exercise them. For too long, the existing structure of democratic authority has been taken for granted. Its problem is not that it is undemocratic, but that its political logic has profoundly negative consequences for the public schools. The way to transform the schools is to transform the system—not by making it "more" democratic, but by shifting from top-down control to other forms of democratic governance that promote rather than undermine the schools' democratic purposes.

NOTES

1. Amy Gutmann, *Democratic Education* (Princeton, N.J.: Princeton University Press, 1987), and Benjamin R. Barber, *Strong Democracy: Participatory Politics for a New Age* (Berkeley: University of California Press, 1984).

2. Terry M. Moe, "The Positive Theory of Public Bureaucracy," in *Perspectives on Public Choice*, ed. Dennis R. Mueller (New York: Cambridge University Press, 1997), and Thomas H. Hammond, "Formal Theory and the Institutions of Governance," *Governance* 9 (1996): 107–85.

3. John E. Chubb and Terry M. Moe, *Politics, Markets, and America's Schools* (Washington, D.C.: Brookings Institution, 1990).

4. See, e.g., Terry M. Moe, "The New Economics of Organization," *American Journal of Political Science* 28 (1984): 739–77; Moe, "The Politics of Bureaucratic Structure," in *Can the Government Govern?* ed. John E. Chubb and Paul E. Peterson (Washington, D.C.: Brookings Institution, 1989); "The Politics of Structural Choice: Toward a Theory of Public Bureaucracy," in *Organization Theory: From Chester Barnard to the Present and Beyond*, ed. Oliver E. Williamson (New York: Oxford University Press, 1990); and "Political Institutions: The Neglected Side of the Story," *Journal of Law, Economics, and Organization* 6 (1990): 213–54.

5. Valerie E. Lee and Anthony S. Bryk, "Science or Policy Argument: A Review of the Quantitative Evidence in Chubb and Moe's *Politics, Markets, and America's Schools*," in *School Choice: Examining the Evidence*, ed. Edith Rasell and Richard Rothstein (Washington, D.C.: Economic Policy Institute, 1993).

6. E. E. Schattschneider, *The Semi-Sovereign People* (New York: Holt, Rinehart and Winston, 1960).

7. James S. Fishkin, *Democracy and Deliberation: New Directions for Democratic Reform* (New Haven, Conn.: Yale University Press, 1991).

8. Moe, "The Politics of Structural Choice."

9. Kenneth J. Arrow, *Social Choice and Individual Values,* rev. ed. (New York: Wiley, 1963).

10. Richard D. McKelvey, "Intransitivities in Multidimensional Voting: Models and Some Implications for Agenda Control," *Journal of Economic Theory* 12 (1976): 472–82.

11. Kenneth A. Shepsle, "Institutional Equilibrium and Equilibrium Institutions," in *Political Science: The Science of Politics,* ed. Herbert F. Weisberg (New York: Agathon Press, 1986).

12. Frederick M. Wirt and Michael W. Kirst, *The Political Dynamics of American Education* (Berkeley, Calif.: McCutchon, 1997), and Roald F. Campbell et al., *The Organization and Control of American Schools,* 4th ed. (Columbus, Ohio: Charles E. Merrill, 1980).

13. Chubb and Moe, *Politics, Markets, and America's Schools.*

14. Myron Lieberman, *Public Education: An Autopsy* (Cambridge, Mass.: Harvard University Press, 1993), and Lieberman, *The Teacher Unions* (New York: Free Press, 1997).

15. Mancur Olson, *The Logic of Collective Action* (Cambridge, Mass.: Harvard University Press, 1965).

16. David Mayhew, *Congress: The Electoral Connection* (New Haven, Conn.: Yale University Press, 1974).

17. Wirt and Kirst, *Political Dynamics.*

18. Matther Purdy and Maria Newman, "Students Lag in Districts Where Patronage Thrives," and "Web of Patronage in Schools Grips Those Who Can Undo It," *New York Times,* 14 May 1996.

19. Shepsle, "Institutional Equilibrium."

20. Moe, "New Economics of Organization."

21. Oliver E. Williamson, *Markets and Hierarchies* (New York: Free Press, 1975), and Williamson, *The Economic Institutions of Capitalism* (New York: Free Press, 1985).

22. Douglass R. North and Barry R. Weingast, "Constitutions and Commitment: The Evolution of the Institutions Governing Public Choice in Seventeenth-Century England," *Journal of Economic History* 49 (1989): 803–32.

23. Barry R. Weingast, "The Economic Role of Political Institutions: Market-Preserving Federalism and Economic Development," *Journal of Law, Economics, and Organization* 11 (1995): 1–31.

24. Moe, "The Politics of Bureaucratic Structure" and "Politics of Structural Choice."

25. Murray J. Horn, *The Political Economy of Public Administration: Institutional Choice in the Public Sector* (New York: Cambridge University Press, 1995).

26. Barry R. Weingast and William Marshall, "The Industrial Organization of Congress," *Journal of Political Economy* 96 (1988): 132–63.

27. Gary Cox and Mathew D. McCubbins, *Legislative Leviathan* (Berkeley: University of California Press, 1994).

28. John W. Pratt and Richard J. Zeckhauser, *Principals and Agents: The Structure of Business* (Boston: Harvard Business School Press, 1985).

29. D. Roderick Kiewiet and Mathew D. McCubbins, *The Logic of Delegation* (Chicago: University of Chicago Press, 1991).

30. Barry R. Weingast and Mark Moran, "Bureaucratic Discretion or Congressional Control: Regulatory Policymaking by the Federal Trade Commission," *Journal of Political Economy* 91 (1983): 765–800, and Mathew D. McCubbins and Thomas Schwartz, "Congressional Oversight Overlooked: Police Patrols Versus Fire Alarms," *American Journal of Political Science* 28 (1984): 165–79.

31. Mathew D. McCubbins, Roger G. Noll, and Barry R. Weingast, "Administrative Procedures as Instruments of Political Control," *Journal of Law, Economics, and Organization* 3 (1987): 243–77; Moe, "The Politics of Bureaucratic Structure" and "Politics of Structural Choice."

32. Moe, "The Politics of Bureaucratic Structure"; Moe, "Politics of Structural Choice"; Horn, *Political Economy of Public Administration.*

33. Horn, *Political Economy of Public Administration.*

34. Ibid.

35. Terry M. Moe and Michael Caldwell, "The Institutional Foundations of Democratic Government: A Comparison of Presidential and Parliamentary Systems," *Journal of Institutional and Theoretical Economics* 150 (1994): 171–95.

36. Ibid.

37. For example, Stewart C. Purkey and Marshall S. Smith, "Effective Schools: A Review," *Elementary School Journal* 83 (March 1983): 427–52.

38. Gutmann, *Democratic Education,* and Barber, *Strong Democracy.*

39. Moe, "Politics of Structural Choice."

7

Democracy and Schooling: An Institutional Perspective

James G. March and Johan P. Olsen

This chapter considers a few aspects of how we think about politics and its implications for the education of democratic citizens. As is usual in such matters, the topic is grander than the text, which is only a minor footnote to Plato, Aristotle, and Dewey. The main point is unsurprising and uncomplicated: How we think about schooling for democracy may depend on how we think about democracy.

AMBITIONS FOR DEMOCRACY

Ideas about the democratic creed have evolved over centuries of discussion and negotiation, and there is no precise agreement on what democracy entails or how to judge its realization. Nevertheless, four things seem particularly essential. First, democracy involves a commitment both to personal privacy and liberty and to individual acceptance of responsibility in their pursuit and exercise.[1] Second, democracy involves the twin principles of popular sovereignty and political equality. Although differences among citizens can be recognized and even glorified, those differences are not to be reflected in differences in political power.[2] Third, democracy involves a faith that human destiny can (and should) be influenced decisively by human will, reason, and intelligence. History is seen as responding to the intentional actions of citizens acting on the basis of reasoned deliberations.[3] Fourth, democracy involves adherence to procedural reliability and the rule of law. Power is regulated by a system of stable institutions and rules that protect citizens from arbitrary exercise of political power, whether by agents of government or by private individuals or groups.[4]

Since they limit not only the routes to political power but also the uses of power, these elements of a democratic creed impose constraints on the institutions of politics and on the actions of both citizens and officials. In societies in which these principles of democracy are well integrated into the normative code of social life, their significance is sometimes obscured. They are, however, the frame and justification of democratic politics, constructed and maintained through a complex structure of social relations and institutions, one of which is the system of formal education.

During the twentieth century, political democracy and mass school-based education have attained extraordinary success. Democracy is virtually unchallenged as a legitimate form of governance, and formal schooling is widely recognized as an indispensable component of democratization and economic development. Despite these positions of dominance (or perhaps because of them), both political democracy and formal schooling are currently undergoing considerable critical examination. Well-established democracies, such as those of western Europe and North America, are viewed as overindulgent, unable to balance budgets or to deal with burgeoning problems of social welfare, globalism, diversity, and technological change. Schools are viewed as archaic, minor contributors to modern education, unwilling to adapt to the realities of social heterogeneity, modern families, television, microprocessor-based instruments of learning, and explosions of knowledge.

Such laments are the normal costs of success, of course, and even a casual reading of the history of commentaries on democracy and schooling suggests that the complaints are hardly novel. In particular, there is no novelty in observations that democratic systems are difficult to sustain, that democratic ideals of political equality, informed consent, and the rule of law are never fully achieved, and that democracy seeks exquisitely prepared citizens but rarely has them. Nor is there novelty in the observation that the possible contributions of schools to civic education are modest. Whatever privileged position nuclear families and formal education may once have had, that combination is now only a small part of a system of institutions and practices by which individuals are educated. Peer groups (particularly age, religious, ethnic, and gender groups), audio and visual media of various sorts, and the paraphernalia of markets are all major contributors to the creation of contemporary political actors. Schooling has a role to play, but it is bounded by the presence of these other major contributors.

Insatiable ambitions for a more perfect democracy condemn a society to an abiding discontent that stimulates a continuing search for ways to improve political institutions by means of schooling. Democracies struggle to define a program for civic education that lies between complete laissez-faire and comprehensive political indoctrination. That struggle, however, is not simply a matter of balancing the risks of anarchy against those of tyranny. It is also a matter of fitting civic education to understandings of the nature of politics. The search for an educational program occurs within a set of taken-for-granted assumptions about political life.

TWO PERSPECTIVES ON DEMOCRATIC POLITICS

Since the 1950s, assumptions about democracy have tended to picture democratic politics in terms that are reductionist, consequentialist, instrumentalist, and functionalist.[5] They have been reductionist in the sense that collective political action has been seen as stemming from the aggregation of individual actions rather than as the consequence of institutions or rules. They have been consequentialist in the sense that they have pictured actions as stemming from calculations and evaluations of the consequences of alternatives. They have been instrumentalist in the sense that they have emphasized the allocative and decision-making aspects of politics and deemphasized the symbolic and meaning aspects. They have been functionalist in the sense that they have tended to portray political institutions as fitting their environments in relatively unique and optimal ways.

These assumptions form a basis for an elementary conception of the nature of a political system, a conception that will be called here an exchange perspective. In such a perspective, political processes are devices for making collective decisions among self-interested actors through negotiation, bargaining, and voluntary exchange.[6] It is a conception that has achieved a certain dominance in political thought, being now widely shared among writers on political systems, particularly democratic political systems.

In recent years, however, discussions of democratic theory have reasserted a set of assumptions that are less reductionist, consequentialist, instrumentalist, and functionalist. These assumptions form the basis for an alternative conception of politics that will be called here an institutional perspective. Although that label has been stretched to cover almost any view of the nature of politics that is not built exclusively on assumptions of conflict and negotiation among rational actors, it is used here to identify a set of ideas that, while conceding the importance of exchange within the constraints of politics, places greater emphasis on the simultaneous evolution of the constraints.[7] These two broad alternative views have somewhat different implications for thinking about the democratic purposes of education.

Exchange Perspectives

Politics can be seen as an arena in which individual actors seek to arrange mutually acceptable exchanges. Using various forms of rational negotiation, individuals locate winning coalitions and policies. In addition to specifying procedures for securing legitimate political authority, the political system imposes certain rules designed to make the discovery and implementation of mutually attractive exchanges feasible and relatively free of transaction costs. It also distributes key political resources (e.g., the vote) in ways that are consistent with broad social norms. The individual political actor within the political arena is expected to pursue his or her own preferences and to secure the best possible combination of policies from the point of view of those preferences. The pursuit by any particular political actor is constrained by the simultaneous pursuit by other actors of their own preferences.

Such ideas are an essential part of political thought dating from Plato and Aristotle. They have been a major part of the modern humanistic canon since the seventeenth- and eighteenth-century elaboration by writers such as Bentham, Mill, and Locke. In their modern form, which borrows heavily from neoclassical microeconomic theory and game theory, exchange perspectives on politics have come to dominate discussions of democratic practice.[8]

Exchange perspectives on politics are special cases of theories of rational behavior.[9] They presume that action is driven by a consequentialist logic. Individuals are assumed to consider alternatives by assessing their consequences in terms of individual preferences or interests. Individual preferences are assumed to be stable and consistent and to arise through processes that are exogenous to the political system. Thus, the process is sensitive to interests, but it is not viewed as affecting them significantly. Similarly, each individual is endowed exogenously with exchangeable resources. Individuals bring these resources to the bargaining table in the service of individual interests. They are willing to make exchanges if and only if such exchanges improve the realization of their own preferences. Thus, there is no assumption of a shared public interest to be used as a basis for collective action. Whether individual actors achieve their desires in such a system depends on the extent to which their desires are consistent with the desires of others and whether they have exchangeable resources of value, including political rights.

Collective action requires agreement among sufficient numbers of independently rational actors to make a change, the numbers required being part of the constitutional structure surrounding the exchanges. The process of negotiation and bargaining is filled with individual strategic action that includes various forms of deceit moderated by the risks and costs of discovery and trust granted to those with reputations for trustworthiness.[10] As a result, devices for locating possible exchange partners and for arranging and enforcing agreements are key parts of the political apparatus.

In company with other theories of rational action, exchange theories of politics recognize the bounded nature of rationality.[11] Information about alternatives is not taken as given but must be obtained. Attention to a particular political arena or policy is problematic.[12] Individuals function politically while attending to a subset of their interests and knowledge.[13] As a result, important parts of the theory are theories of search for alternatives and information about them, as well as theories of political attention, agenda setting, and the mobilization of interests.

This boundedly rational process of realizing winning coalitions and making policies is pictured as regulated by a structure of rules.[14] These rules specify what constitutes a winning coalition and what are legitimate processes for forming them. In democratic societies, these rules include those regulating the allocation, solicitation, and exercise of political rights, particularly the right to vote and rights to participation in the processes of decision. They include limitations on the free exchange of political rights for other commodities, particularly money. And they include rules regulating bargains and their implementation, for example, the rule of law and the neutralization of the civil service.

These rules are normally taken as given and treated as essentially outside the negotiations of day-to-day politics.[15] A common presumption within the rational exchange tradition, however, is that the rules of politics have themselves evolved as an implicit solution to a higher-order rational process that proceeds at a slower pace, and thus they can be treated as constant for many short-run analyses. This presumption of a higher-order rational process stimulates the search for rational interpretations of existing procedures, for if the long-run development of rules can be assumed to produce differential survival of useful rules, enduring rules (even those that appear most bizarre) can be assumed to have some rationality.[16]

This imputation of rationality to long-run evolutionary processes assumes a certain kind of efficiency to historical processes. In an efficient historical process, political institutions come to match their environments and thus are implicit in them.[17] Some control over the short-run course of history may be granted to the political maneuvers and negotiations of current actors, but intentional governance is accorded very little role.[18] Although some modern students of politics in the exchange tradition appear to adopt a strong assumption of historical efficiency, more of them appear to accept at least some degree of indeterminacy in the adaptation of the political system to exogenous pressures, allowing particularly for the effects of attention and multiple winning coalitions.[19] Indeed, the possible equilibria in long-run political processes appear to be so numerous as to make virtually any institution or rule explicable.

Institutional Perspectives

Exchange perspectives on politics capture important aspects of the political system, but they focus on the processes by which coalitions are negotiated to meet the constraints imposed by the distribution of interests and resources, by the subjective interpretations of reality formed by political actors, and by the rules of politics. For the most part, they treat the interests, resource distributions, interpretations, and rules as exogenous to political negotiation. Institutional perspectives, on the other hand, reverse the emphasis, focusing particularly on the ways that interests, resource distributions, interpretations, and rules are formed, modified, and sustained by the processes of politics.[20]

Political action is seen as organized by socially constructed meanings and rules reflected in identities and institutions.[21] It is driven less by calculation of consequences than by a logic of appropriateness that matches identities to situations.[22] The political self is constituted by an identity. The presumption is that most of the time a political actor acts by asking, "What does a person such as I do in a situation such as this?" Action requires matching the rules of that identity to a definition of a situation.[23] Of particular importance are the twin identities of citizen and public official.[24]

Action is rule-based, but it is not thereby necessarily routine. Identities can be inconsistent; they can be complex; they can be ambiguous. Following rules often involves matching an ambiguous rule to an ambiguous situation, and the complications of fulfilling such identities require both energy and tolerance. But the processes of resolving ambiguities and conflicts proceed not by refining knowledge of the consequences of action but by refining understandings of the nature of the situation and the self. They involve modeling of behavior on exemplars, establishing similarities among situations by looking for essential features, and the elaboration and diffusion of meanings.

By focusing on institutionalized identities and rules, an institutional perspective highlights the importance of shared meanings within a political community. In that sense, most institutional treatments of politics are also communitarian to some degree. The emphasis, however, differs somewhat from the primary thrust of much communitarian thought. Where communitarian ideas emphasize the construction of shared values as a route to agreement within a community of consequentialist actors, the institutionalist version emphasizes the shared rules and laws that constitute political institutions in a community of identity-based actors.[25] Particularly in large heterogeneous societies where value homogeneity is difficult to achieve and may be problematic as an objective, institutions, rules, and conventionalized identities become substitutes for communitarian consensus.

Students of politics with an institutional perspective generally have less confidence in the efficiency of history than do students of politics with an exchange perspective.[26] They are less sure that rules will come to match functional imperatives quickly and uniquely.[27] There are lags in adjustment, multiple equilibria, ecological coevolution, and path dependencies. History is a meander[28] in which the directions taken at critical branch points seem almost chancelike even though they may have major effects on future developments.[29]

If the rules of politics are neither the necessary result of a higher-order rational process nor the unique product of environmental conditions, the possibilities for political intervention are increased, To be sure, control over history is limited by the opportunities that arise, and there is no reason to anticipate either that any arbitrary direction can be taken at any arbitrary time or that intentional interventions will serve the intentions that guide them, but institutional theories of politics focus greater attention than do exchange theories on the possibilities for choosing and changing the rules.

Taken together, these aspects of an institutional perspective suggest an important reorientation of democratic thought. The images of an exchange perspective are images of brokerage among contending interests. The images of an institutional perspective are images of the shaping of identities and interests. The images of an exchange perspective are images of voluntary Pareto optimal trading based on initial endowments of resources. The images of an institutional perspective are images of the conscious construction of resource distributions. The images of an exchange perspective are images of action based on calculation of return. The images of an institutional perspective are images of action based on rules and the dictates of identities. Each perspective can easily be made to subsume the other, thus appearing to eliminate the differences; but the differences in emphasis are real and lead to real differences in implications for building democracy and for discovering democratic purposes for schooling.

SCHOOLING AS A FOUNDATION FOR DEMOCRACY

Speculations about the proper role of civic education and the place of schools in building the bases for effective political institutions have been common for as long as either democracy or education has attracted commentary.[30] Defining the democratic purposes of schooling depends, however, on a choice among alternative diagnoses of possible democratic failures and on a choice among alternative perspectives on the nature of democracy.

Alternative Conceptions of Democratic Failures

Different advocates of democratic reform focus on different problems and are led therefore to different solutions, but they share a rough litany of analysis that begins with the simple proposition that the "people" should rule, that current majorities should be able to get what they "want," subject to constitutional limitations designed to protect the rights of current minorities. Insofar as the people are unable to get what they want, democracy is seen as failing. If democracy fails to serve the people in this sense, the most obvious remedy lies in changing either "the people" (including their capabilities for gaining access to and exercising influence over the political system) or their "wants."

The primary difference between traditional radicals and traditional conservatives in their response to democratic failures stems not from conflicting models of democratic politics but from conflicting judgments about the appropriateness of changing an existing distribution of resources. Traditional radicals of democracy focus on redefining "the people" by changing the access to the system or the distribution of resources (endowments), including wealth. For them, the central problem of democracy is to modify the power premises of politics to make the distribution of political resources more equal. They see coercive resource redistribution as essential to democracy. The traditional conservative, on the other hand, sees coercive resource redistribution as a violation of democratic principles. Despite these differences, the two groups share a common analysis of the way to understand politics. Collective outcomes produced by the political system are seen by both as reflecting the weighted wishes of citizens where the weights are given by power and power comes from the possession of relevant exchangeable resources. The quarrel is not over the model but over the sanctity of existing resource distribution.

Any such analysis, however, makes three assumptions that conceal other possible diagnoses of democratic failure. The first is what might be called the *efficiency of politics* assumption, the idea that political systems fairly quickly achieve outcomes that are on the Pareto frontier of possible voluntary exchanges given initial distributions of resources (power) and wants (interests). There are numerous indications that democratic political systems do not achieve efficiency in such a sense, and thus some revisions in the process of exchange might significantly improve the capability of individual citizens to achieve their individual wants even without a modification in either "the people" or the "wants."

The second is what might be called the *antecedence of interests* assumption, the idea that "wants" are exogenous to politics rather than partly a product of politics. Observations of political systems suggest a more complicated, coevolutionary process in which desires are affected by the politics they control. If this assumption of antecedence is dropped, a key consideration in the reform of democracy is the design of political institutions that shape wants (interests) in ways that contribute to democratic aspirations.[31] In this spirit, some modern students of democracy emphasize the importance of treating wants endogenously. They see democratic politics as changing interests, sometimes in a direction of creating more consistent or less consistent wants (thus more or less easily achievable), but somewhat more commonly in the direction of creating wants that fit some conception of democratic virtue.[32]

The third is what might be called the *primacy of consequences* assumption, the idea that human action is determined by choices, and choices are determined by an assessment of the probable consequences of alternatives. Although such a logic seems clearly to capture part of politics, political life is filled with instances in which action seems more accurately characterized as an attempt to match conceptions of self with conceptions of a situation in order to produce behavior that fulfills an identity. If the consequentialist assumption is moderated, the focus shifts to vital democratic identities, such as those of citizen and official, and to rules, such as rules of procedure, and to the processes by which they evolve and are implemented.

For the most part, students of politics who view the political process as rational exchange through bargaining and negotiation are more inclined to emphasize relaxing the first of these asssumptions than the other two. They seek ways of improving the exchange efficiency of politics. Students of politics who approach political processes from an institutional perspective, on the other hand, are less concerned with the first assumption than with the second and third. They seek ways to affect wants and capabilities within the political process itself, and they picture political action as deeply affected by political identities. Consequently, although schooling is pictured by both groups as relevant to reducing the risks of democratic failure, the democratic role of schooling as seen from an institutional perspective is rather different from the role of schooling as seen from an exchange perspective.

The Democratic Role of Schooling from an Exchange Perspective

In an exchange perspective, the objective of politics is to discover and implement winning policy coalitions among individuals whose interests are consistent with one another. Within the constraints of rules, interests, and resource distributions, this objective is accomplished by influencing the flow of attention to particular interests[33] and alternatives[34] and to the organization of political conflict along particular lines of cleavage.[35]

In a political exchange process, success comes from being able to achieve one's desires (satisfy one's interests) through favorable exchanges. Thus, it comes from being able to offer trades that benefit others while benefiting oneself. Such trades are facilitated by having things that others want and by wanting things that others do not want. Things that are wanted by others can be exchanged at favorable rates for things that are desired. Things that others do not want can be obtained at favorable rates. The prototypic exchange in politics is the logroll. In a logroll, each party to a coalition brings three essential things: a political resource (for example, a vote), a desired public action, and a wide range of indifference across actions desired by others. Thus, an effective exchange politics is facilitated by citizens with heterogeneous tastes and large areas of mutual indifference.

The democratic objective within an exchange perspective is to reduce the chance that politically possible policies are overlooked and that some peculiarity of the process allows an inferior set of policies to dominate a superior one (superior, that is, from the point of view of being Pareto preferred). Many of the familiar practices of contemporary democracies are directed to these objectives. They fail particularly when political brokerage is made ineffective. As a general rule, political brokerage functions better in small polities than in large ones (despite the advantage of larger political markets available in large polities);[36] better in polities populated by well-educated, rich individuals with extensive political experience than in those with less-educated, less experienced, and poorer citizens; better in good times than in bad; better in older democracies than in younger ones; and better where there is confidence in shared understandings than where there is not. Thus, a primary objective of schooling is to contribute to the educational, experiential, and shared understanding bases of democratic brokerage.

The political broker's problem is to build a political victory, which involves specifying a policy portfolio that will gain support from a winning coalition of individuals. Policies may attract collections of like-minded people; they may also represent logrolls among individuals with quite different interests. In either case, policy-based coalitions are habitually plagued by complications stemming from the way any coalition combines symbolic and substantive demands, from the difficulties of mobilizing resources and sustaining mobilization over time, and from the difficulties of specifying and enforcing political agreements that stretch over time.

Effective exchange is facilitated by the diffusion of information about interests and resources. Although each participant in the process may see some advantage in falsifying information about his or her own tastes and resources and thereby gaining a trading advantage, the efficiency of the process depends on those efforts being frustrated by the equally compelling needs of others for seeing through such falsifications and by the development of political institutions and practices that result in the spread of accurate assessments. Within an exchange perspective, the primary purpose of political discourse is to refine political markets. Citizens form coalitions and negotiate bargains by developing precise information about preferences and resources.

There is much to be admired in this refinement of political markets. Democratic political systems have sometimes seemed to be more effective at providing employment to officials and encouraging meddling in other people's business than at contributing to social welfare, and political markets offer some relief from such corruptions. At their best, political markets allow autonomous actors to discover and exercise opportunities for choice and mutual tolerance that are difficult to provide within a more centralized and bureaucratic system.

In many respects, contemporary education in the United States and other developed countries is preeminently designed to further effective exchange politics. Recent discussions of democracy tend to subordinate political processes of discussion and debate to processes of information exchange leading to mutually acceptable trades, and recent discussions of schools tend to see them as institutions that prepare individuals for such markets and marketlike politics. Contemporary education is infused with metaphors of markets. For example, the system is commonly rationalized in terms of its contribution to labor markets. Students are seen as economic instruments to be refined for productive labor, and educational experiences are portrayed as opportunities to secure training relevant to remunerative employment. Much of the practical training of schooling is training in dealing with markets of exchange. Students learn how to enter a market to secure their own desires, the role of the possession of resources in that process, and procedures for exchanging information within markets. Such an orientation is frequently extended to simulated politics, where an emphasis is placed on campaigning and advertising.

Similarly, even among people disinclined to embrace "vouchers" as a solution to the ills of schooling, contemporary metaphors of schooling itself are metaphors of market exchange. Students (or parents) are pictured as "customers" who make choices that maximize their own well-being, choices of schools, curricula, and specific courses. "Good" teachers and "good" students enter into mutually satisfactory exchanges that are defined as "good" schools. Students and parents use whatever economic and political resources they have to obtain an education as close to what they think is optimal for themselves. Teachers and educational administrators use whatever economic and political resources they have to obtain an educational setting as close to what they think is optimal for themselves. School boards are brokers who fashion policy portfolios that attract mutually consistent customers and producers. This exchange conception of schools is a triumph of contemporary worldviews and cannot help but shape the political conceptions of participants in education. The school becomes a training ground in market exchange thinking and capabilities not only for students but also for teachers, parents, and administrators.

THE DEMOCRATIC ROLE OF SCHOOLING
FROM AN INSTITUTIONAL PERSPECTIVE

Institutional conceptions of politics share with exchange perspectives a dedication to reducing the frictions on bargaining and negotiation within democratic constraints. Thus, they endorse procedures to provide adequate information about possible coalition partners and their preferences and about the conditions of the world that might affect the attractiveness of options to citizens as they pursue their interests. In either perspective, effective governance involves creating and maintaining institutions that make political exchange efficient in discovering and implementing Pareto-preferred trades.

In addition, however, an institutional perspective on democracy solicits a conception of education that is activist with respect to shaping the constraints of politics. In particular, securing democracy is seen as involving three tasks that are less significant in an exchange vision: *Creating political identities.* The institutions of democratic politics seek to sustain preferences, expectations, beliefs, identities, and interests that are consistent with democratic processes and to discourage those that are not. *Molding a comprehensible and accountable political system.* Democratic institutions seek procedures for interpreting the events of political history in ways that facilitate understanding, maintenance of a democratic culture, and accountability. *Making a political system adaptive.* Democratic institutions seek to provide the processes, resources, and abilities necessary to learn from experience and to match the changing political environment.

Creating political identities. In an institutional perspective, the citizen and the official are not only key determinants of a political system but also some of its products.[37] In that sense at least, democracy is not merely an arena for contending interests but also a primary source of those interests. It is not merely constrained by conceptions of appropriate political norms but is also a primary source of such conceptions. Schooling in a democracy contributes to the creation of citizens and officials, to the construction of their preferences, values, senses of civility, and capabilities. It is a contribution that is facilitated by the autonomy of the school classroom. Although there are instruments of central control over schooling that powerfully constrain learning, particularly learning relevant to political behavior, the elementary practices, culture, and values of individual classrooms are difficult to control without draconian measures. Even under an authoritarian regime, pupils can often learn something about democratic values and identities if a teacher wishes to teach them and is appropriately clever about doing so.

This role of schooling is patently a delicate one. On the one hand, democracy is enjoined to be responsive to the wishes of its citizens and becomes a sham when those wishes stem excessively from indoctrination by instruments of the polity, such as schools. On the other hand, it is clear that the values of citizens are not produced by some immaculate process but are molded by social learning and pressures. The social construction of meaning involves many different kinds of political players whose effectiveness depends less on their value to the society than on their possession of the instruments of persuasion. The question is not whether schools should produce citizens but whether they should add their relatively small voice to the choruses of influence that do so, and if they should participate, what kinds of themes their teachings should sustain.

While shaping citizens who are autonomous, independent, and thoughtful, schooling needs to mold them to a set of conceptions that are consistent with democratic institutions and procedures. Democracy is a particular form of governance, a form that depends on an ethos that is not guaranteed and on values that are not universal.[38] Democratic institutions require a sense of common destiny and identity, a civic solidarity.[39] This solidarity permits trust, affection, and loyalty among citizens, thus encouraging an awareness of mutual obligations. It stimulates tolerance for principled deviation (within the group) and allows for a productive exchange of views, the suspension of conflict once a democratic resolution is made, and the delegation of administrative authority to officials. It permits empathic consideration of the feelings of others and attention to the concerns of those who are not present, such as the unborn or the unrepresented.

Solidarity is, however, also a threat to democracy if it is not civilized by a sense of its limitations. Solidarity is often most easily created by noticing or imagining an external threat, and such solidarity can easily lead to bellicosity and bellicosity, in turn, to adventurous squandering of community resources and loyalties on belligerent endeavors. Moreover, solidarity easily turns into internal intolerance, into the squashing of dissent and the glorification of allegiances. The premise of democratic politics is conflict. Citizens differ with respect to community policies and actions and with respect to their interpretations of proper behavior. Solidarity simultaneously sustains such differences by virtue of the sentiments of mutual support that it provides, and it undermines such differences by virtue of the sentiments of shared values that it glorifies. Achieving a salutary balance is a matter of some subtlety.

The balancing of the constructive and destructive sides of solidarity is central to the idea of democratic discourse, which is given a role in an institutional perspective that is substantially broader than the information role imagined within an exchange perspective. Participation in democratic discourse requires that differences be treated with respect. Disagreements are to be addressed through intelligent talk among empathetic listeners and the generation of reasons for and against proposed actions. Citizens are presumed to see conflict as best settled by an exchange of reasons, interpretations, explanations, and justifications tied to the general good. The emphasis on the linkage between individual concerns and the common good serves to further solidarity while allowing differences. By relating their particularistic interests to more general interests, political actors become united by a sense of commonality while retaining a sense of individuality.[40] This commonality is a necessary, but not sufficient, condition for fruitful democratic engagement through discourse.

The substitution of talk and persuasion for threats of physical violence and surrender is fundamental to democracy. It carries with it, however, some democratic difficulties. First, it presumes that most of the time discourse brings citizens together rather than tears them apart. Yet, it is clear that there are situations in which talk accentuates awareness of differences as well as differences themselves, thus making democracy harder to sustain. Second, discourse requires time. It must fit into the other demands on a citizen's time. As individuals make decisions with respect to their own allocations of time, there is no assurance that those for whom discourse will be attractive will be those who can best serve the collective objectives of talk. Third, discourse is not neutral with respect to the position of citizens. For example, it clearly shifts power away from those capable of credible threats of physical violence and toward those capable of persuasive talk. Even beyond such major shifts, any rules of discourse, however advantageous to the process of discussion, give advantage to some and disadvantage to others.

To control such difficulties, democratic political systems seek to impose some rules on democratic discussion, and one of the ways that schooling may contribute to democratic practice is by reinforcing norms of proper discourse that are essential to democratic institutions.[41] Future citizens with a variety of sentiments and motives engage in talk that is constrained within strong norms of politeness. Norms of polite discourse affect not only the consequences of interpersonal conflicts but also their persistence. They control the expression of negative feelings through a ritualized style of interaction that maintains a pretense of shared values and affection that becomes self-confirming.

Polite and reasoned discourse among citizens having the right values is not enough, however. Democracy requires that citizens also be endowed with capabilities to function as citizens, and this requires resources and capabilities.[42] In particular, democratic rights (e.g., freedom of expression, political equality) have to be secured, and threats to those rights from such things as physical and economic inequalities have to be contained. Capabilities for democratic organizing have to be nurtured. Competencies at interpreting the claims of history, knowledge, and data and at making decisions need to be developed and practiced.

Securing democratic rights involves exercising them and defending their exercise by others, activities that may call for enough counterintuitive heroism to require conscious modeling and patterning in school. Protecting political equality and personal dignity from the "inter-sector trading" claims of economic and physical bullies involves not only indoctrination in the moral repugnance of bribery and assault but also training in practical measures by which one can be protected from either succumbing to bullies or becoming one. "Democracy presumes an ethic of voluntary self-restraint on the part of legitimate authority, a residual rule of democratic humility. The future is protected against the imperium of the present. The weak are protected against the imperium of the strong. Strangers are protected against the imperium of the self."[43]

Molding a comprehensible and accountable political system. A democratic regime is properly accountable to its citizens. That principle of democratic accountability is well established, but enthusiasms for accountability often leave some important dimensions ill defined. This deficiency is reflected in efforts by thoughtful students of "evaluation" to specify an appropriate model for holding the political system accountable for the consequences of public policies.[44] In particular, the principle of democratic accountability requires not only knowing what has happened and why, but also finding a way to determine whether the society, taken as a whole, has been served. The latter question is made particularly difficult by the way it involves specifying the relative weights to be given to the future (in addition to the present) preferences of present political actors, to the future preferences of future actors not currently present (e.g., the unborn), and to the future interests of a wider society.

Democratic accountability is also complicated in this case by the fact that historical knowledge and traditions of accountability are potentially at odds. Accountability depends on the specification of individual and group responsibility for political outcomes. It is secured by story lines that relate historical outcomes to the actions of specific officeholders or political parties. History, however, frequently teaches that individual and group responsibilities are difficult to establish. History is the joint product of multiple actors producing outcomes reflecting considerable causal complexity and evaluated by obscure standards. Although the logic of political life seems to call for an "adequately blameworthy agent,"[45] the precise assignment of individual responsibility for collective successes and failures is difficult.

Being held accountable affects the behavior and justifications of decision makers.[46] March and Olsen list three major consequences:[47] (1) Accountability tends to increase deliberateness. It increases the amount of information sought and the care with which it is considered. The consequence is to reduce various errors of judgment (e.g., interpreting subsequent information in ways that confirm early information) but also to encourage the consideration of extraneous factors of little decision relevance. (2) Accountability tends to reduce risk taking, to make potential losses more salient than potential gains, which has the consequence of making the person held accountable more cautious and more concerned about immediate costs than possible long-run gains. (3) Accountability tends to accentuate defensiveness. This inclination has the consequence of making an individual resistant to changing a decision once made and predisposed to seek and accept information that confirms prior actions rather than questions them. Thus, in general, accountability has two-sided motivational and cognitive consequences. Making an individual accountable tightens social control, increases the likelihood of socially appropriate behavior, and strengthens the desire to be thoughtful, careful, and thorough. At the same time, it is likely to encourage excessive caution and procrastination, risk aversion, and resistance to change.

Because of the complications in its conception and its effects, democratic accountability is far from mechanical. It involves a continuous debate among citizens and politicians, a debate that creates a climate of accountability without necessarily ever specifying a formula for it. That debate seeks to ensure that citizens are properly informed about historical events and exercise intelligent control over the officials who contribute to that history. Achieving a comprehensible and accountable politics is, however, a major act of faith. The events of history are not routinely interpretable. What happened, why it happened, and who contributed to its happening are all subject to debate. Accounts are created and validated socially. Through the accounts, citizens seek to exercise control over officials. In anticipation of the accounts, officials seek to satisfy citizens and to influence accounts. At the same time, citizens and officials jointly seek both to sustain confidence in the possibility of intentional human control over history and to avoid the deleterious motivational effects of oversight.[48]

The development of accounts requires a structure of interpretive communities within which competing accounts can be developed and evaluated and an institutional and legal framework that assures freedom of association and speech. It also requires enough of a shared framework among citizens so that alternative accounts can be compared and discussed through a free exchange of argument, evidence, and worldviews.[49] Such a vision of communicative rationality is juxtaposed with the efforts of contending political actors to influence accounts and a vision of democratic accounts as the product of free competition among conflicting liars. Since political actors view account management as a significant instrument of power, a democratic polity seeks to direct that competition in a way that contributes to collective intelligence and political equality.

Schooling has a role to play in establishing the account basis of democratic accountability. On the one hand, the stories of education become the story lines of accountability. To construct the story lines for interpreting experience is a standard teaching assignment. At the same time, schooling provides training in the processes social groups use to develop stories of accountability. The stories we tell evolve through various interpretive communities, conversations among citizens, proclamations by professors, and especially treatments in the media. In order for citizens to be productively engaged in the development of accountability stories rather than simply serving as passive recipients of such stories, they need to be trained in engaging speculations with facts and in confronting claims with challenges. Every democratic citizen is a practicing historian, one who needs to be trained to adopt an intelligently skeptical stance toward conventional interpretations of history and to enter into discussions of politics not only with interests and prejudices but also with the capabilities required to join in a public discussion that ties historical facts to political conclusions in a thoughtful way.

It is clear that no modern citizen can contribute effectively to the democratic process of accountability without elements of ordinary knowledge and the capability to absorb and validate claims of new knowledge. This general responsibility of schooling is a necessity of democracy in a modern context. Effective construction of a knowledge base in citizens is, however, made more difficult by two recent developments in the social organization of knowledge. First, pressures on schools for "practical" knowledge tend to degrade their effectiveness in developing and transferring the basic knowledge base necessary to absorb new knowledge in the longer run. In the interest of immediate efficiency, schooling sacrifices longer-run adaptiveness.[50] Second, views of knowledge as a shared public good have given way increasingly to views that define knowledge as private property. From this point of view, schools are massive dealers in stolen intellectual goods, and education is a form of governmental appropriation and redistribution of private property. The privatization of knowledge threatens the contribution of schooling to political equality and democratic effectiveness.

Even if a democratic system is able to raise the average knowledge level of citizens, it still faces the problem of unevenly distributed expertise. Knowledge is a resource and thereby a basis for individual power, but at the same time it is also a basis for democratic problem solving that serves the society. No one knows everything, thus everyone is dependent on others for knowledge that can make life better. Consequently, any system of modern decision making must weave expertise and popular will together. The basic requirement of a democratic system is that ultimately the "people" (and not experts) decide what the "people" are competent to decide collectively, but such a fundamental rule is obviously self-destructive if the individuals constituting the "people" are unable to recognize their own limitations.[51] Democracy requires that individuals have the knowledge to engage in intelligent discourse about decisions in which they participate as well as the self-knowledge and self-discipline to forgo direct participation when such knowledge is lacking.

The issues and the training required are closely allied to the issues and training involved in initiating the young into knowledge more generally. Schools are simultaneously institutions reflecting the asymmetries of knowledge and experience between children and adults and institutions within which children experience realistic practice at being adults. As a result, schools are appropriate sites for gaining experience in dealing with expertise and unequally distributed knowledge. This experience provides insight into three knotty problems of expertise. The first is the *authenticity* problem, the problem of differentiating real experts from frauds. The second is the *personal experience* problem, the problem of balancing the expertise of expert knowledge with the expertise gained from a citizen's or official's own experience. The third is the *conflict* problem, the problem of using information and advice provided by agents with values and interests different from one's own.

Each of these problems is involved in thinking about schooling and democracy. On the one hand, schooling prepares individuals both to be experts and to deal with experts. With respect to the latter, schooling seeks to train individuals in the skills of identifying true expertise without necessarily having it.[52] It seeks to teach individuals how to relate the lessons gleaned from their own special experiences to the lessons generated from more general knowledge.[53] It provides clues to the advantages (and disadvantages) involved in looking for experts with values similar to the decision maker at the cost of securing experts of lesser competence.

With respect to preparing individuals to be experts in a democratic context, schooling helps to shape definitions of expert identities, particularly the obligations of experts in politics.[54] An understanding of those obligations is particularly critical in schools, not only because many students will ultimately find themselves in the position of being experts in their own fields but also because schools are built on a premise of expert knowledge. Even as schools prepare students for a life entangled in a cobweb of expertise, they themselves are institutions within which experts on schooling (teachers, administrators, educational consultants, researchers) participate with ordinary citizens in the pursuit of policies and practices that serve the community.

Making a political system adaptive. Political systems seek to learn from their experience and the experience of others. In doing so, they have to deal with three major problems of intelligent change.[55] The first problem is *ignorance*. Neither the future nor the past can be understood precisely. The second problem is *conflict*. Citizens differ in their preferences and in their definitions of appropriate behavior, which translates into varying definitions of what is desirable. The third problem is *ambiguity*. Neither interests nor identities are clear, stable, or exogenous to the political system. On the contrary, these premises of behavior are unclear, unstable, and endogenous.

Political systems are handicapped in dealing with such problems by familiar features of historical experience and of individuals and political organizations as learners.[56] Experience rarely performs effective experiments that allow clear inference. Among other things, the environment of political organizations consists in other, simultaneously adapting organizations, and this ecology of learning complicates the drawing of lessons in any one part. Even when history is not flawed as a basis for learning, human beings interpret experience in ways that introduce systematic errors. Political actors are inclined to give human intention a larger place than it deserves and to view their successes as due to their own qualities to a greater extent than is probably justified. They are likely to shape their interpretations to fit desired actions, and conflict over preferences translates easily into conflict over accounts of history.

Democratic politics addresses such problems by trying to improve both the validity of accounts and their reliability. Improving validity involves a mix of two strategies. The first consists in trying to improve the capability of the system to develop and use knowledge. The second consists in trying to devise arenas in which contending accounts can compete for approval in ways that favor more intelligent uses of knowledge over less intelligent ones. Improving reliability involves creating conditions for convergence among competing stories, for sustaining memories of interpretations, and for sharing of interpretations with others. Since many of these conditions require a certain kind of patience, they are difficult for democratic systems that are built on assumptions of political competition and frequent turnover, the replacement of one regime with another.

On a more general level, democratic political systems, like other adaptive systems, seek to balance the exploitation of what is known with the exploration of what might come to be known.[57] Exploitation involves refining known technologies, forms, and strategies. As a rule, it has a relatively high expectation and a relatively low variance in immediate returns. Exploration involves experimenting with unknown technologies, forms, or strategies. As a rule, it has a relatively low expectation and a relatively high variance in immediate returns.

An appropriate balance between exploitation and exploration is made difficult by two classical complications. First, defining the optimal mix is extraordinarily difficult. Since the costs and returns associated with exploitation and exploration are distributed across time and space in quite different ways, any specification of an optimal mix involves trade-offs across time and space that are not easily made. Second, the natural dynamics of learning tend to drive political systems to specializing in exploration or exploitation. Exploitation is driven out by the failures of new initiatives, failures induced in large part by the tendency of political systems to oversell new endeavors and for new endeavors to require experience to realize their full value.[58] The two factors produce a strong inclination toward disappointment and thus to a pattern of moving from one failure to another in an endless chain of experiments with new ideas.[59] Exploration, on the other hand, is driven out by the successes of exploiting what is known. All political systems, but particularly democratic ones, respond to signals and pressures that are current and local more easily than they respond to signals and pressures that are more distant in time or space. The returns from immediate utilization of existing competencies are more certain, closer in time and space, and less diffuse than the returns to investment in long-term exploratory development of capabilities.[60] Consequently, democracies deal relatively poorly with the needs of the future and with needs present at some spatial distance from the locus of decision.

Democratic institutions are prone to oscillate between impatient experiments with change and excessive persistence in obsolescent programs. This political myopia makes necessary the invention of political institutions and norms that buffer political institutions from current political pressures, allowing them to experiment with new ideas and to persist in such experiments long enough to discover their true values. Effective adaptiveness requires that experiments be run and that each experiment be pursued consistently for a long enough time to allow the system to develop competence in executing it and to allow experience to accumulate enough information to permit an intelligent assessment of it. It profits from both the rebelliousness and the rigidities of imagination.[61]

For example, pressures for democratic accountability, while vital to democratic functioning, make it difficult for a democratic political system to maintain a longer-run perspective. As organized political interests and individual citizens achieve the capabilities to insist on continuous political competition and accountability, each official act tends to become subject to immediate popular oversight. The result is a strengthening of control in the short run but a weakening of the capability of the system to maintain longer-run perspectives or investments. The most obvious corrective procedure is to make accountability primarily periodic and posterior rather than continuous and prior. Such arrangements are well known to democratic systems. To protect them from excessive dependence on current and local pressures, judges and officials are given special autonomy. To protect them from excessive conformity that reduces diversity and experimentation, college faculty and students are granted special immunity from the demands of current and local intelligence.

Schooling has a significant responsibility for providing some kind of counterbalance to the tendencies of political institutions to have perspectives that resist genuine and persistent experimentation in favor of short-run expedients and superficial fads. Formal education can contribute to teaching the fundamentals of political patience, delegation, and the construction and organization of trust that are essential to democratic politics.

EDUCATIONAL BOOTSTRAPPING OF DEMOCRACY

Hopes that schools can deviate significantly from the social expectations and controls that are created by the political system and thereby quickly create a dramatically different political world are probably forlorn. Schooling is not a reliable fulcrum from which to move a nondemocratic political system. In a stable political world, politics and schooling are tied together in a story of mutual support. Schooling reflects the values and policy decisions of the political and social system and supports its institutions. When the other bases of democracy are firm, it is not hard to maintain schooling as an element of a smoothly functioning democratic system. Political institutions sustain schooling; schooling sustains the other institutions of a political system.

Despite such plausible discouragement, bootstrapping democracy in a situation in which democracy is problematic is a traditional ambition for education. An institutional perspective is a possible frame for pursuing that ambition. In particular, an institutional perspective conjures ways of bootstrapping democracy through education that are somewhat different from those conjured by an exchange perspective.

First, an institutional perspective focuses on the necessity of socializing individuals into democratic political identities, particularly the identities of citizen and official. A democratic political system depends on individuals fulfilling and developing these identities even in situations in which explicit incentives and personal self-interest might lead them to act otherwise. The understanding of the self must be molded to a democratic mold, one that encourages many forms of individuality but makes it consistent with the obligations of political identities. In this way, it emphasizes an approach to inequalities in power that goes beyond simply advocating power equalization. A democratic political system cannot expect to eliminate differences among individuals and groups, no matter how hard it may (and should) try to do so. Intractable disparities in power are made more consistent with democracy by building identities for individuals of power that emphasize the obligations of power. The idea that being a public official or having political power involves a trusteeship for the common good and a sense of humility with respect to the relevance of one's own desires is a traditional feature of successful democracies. The socialization of the strong into a code of responsibility is as critical to democracy as is the empowerment of the weak.

Second, an institutional perspective shifts the emphasis from one that sees politics as an arena for self-interested negotiation and exchange to one that sees a central role for informed discourse and a pursuit of commonalities. Theories of negotiation emphasize processes for bargaining in which participants are likely to act strategically with respect to one another and to assume that others will do likewise. Participants are assumed to lie to one another about their preferences and beliefs when such lies serve their purposes. Information is vital, but it is hard to assure that it is valid. Theories of discourse, on the other hand, emphasize processes for developing trust, sharing knowledge, and shaping attitudes among individuals who recognize their joint involvement in a common fate. Beliefs and commitments are imagined to be malleable, and ideas are evaluated in terms that separate them from the political interests of their source.

Third, an institutional perspective embeds current political interactions in a history and a future. Political actors are not located autonomously in the present but are part of a flow of history that extends far into the past and will extend far into the future. This embeddedness is captured in rules and institutions that guide current behavior in tension with current calculation of consequences and current desires. The political process is guided by such rules and, at the same time, modifies the rules. Thus, an institutional perspective emphasizes political responsibility both for maintaining institutions and for experimenting with them, resisting willful change in well-established procedures while building structures through which possible changes are explored.

An institutional conception of politics leads not only to a somewhat different view of the democratic purposes of schools but also to a different conception of schooling itself. It is less a view of schools as an arena in which autonomous individuals pursue their preferences through negotiation and exchange and more a view of an institution with a history and a future, a structure of rules and identities to be learned and practiced, and an arena for discussion of ideas and possibilities guided by rules of reasoned inquiry. As an instrument of democracy, schooling builds the identities that citizens, officials, experts, the powerful, and the weak use to guide their behavior. Those identities moderate the free play of self-interested consequentialist action. As an institution in a democracy, schooling symbolizes the importance of reason and knowledge in a democracy. It celebrates the pursuit, accumulation, and transfer of knowledge. It honors learning and proclaims its significance to human society. From this perspective, schools are less markets than temples, students are less consumers than acolytes, and teaching is less an economic activity than a calling. Participants in education learn to define themselves and to develop their skills in such terms, conceiving themselves as trustees of those traditions.

As should be obvious from what has been said, an institutional perspective is not a set of policies or recommendations for practice. It is a way of looking at democracy and life. The extent to which components of an institutional perspective will come to affect the pursuit of democratic ambitions through schooling will depend less on conscious decisions by public authorities about specific programs for schools than on how a culture of writers, teachers, politicians, parents, and citizens comes to think about democracy and the relevance of schooling for it. If the minds and worldviews of critical actors come to be structured primarily around exchange visions of democracy, those actors will come to neglect many aspects of schooling for democracy that are vital within an institutional perspective. Given the domination of rational exchange conceptions in contemporary intellectual life, an outcome in which political and educational actors see the essence of democracy as lying in negotiation and exchange among self-interested actors is certainly possible, perhaps likely; but it is not completely foreordained. Teaching, political leadership, and educational leadership were all callings and identities before they became jobs, reflections of hopes for self more than of incentives; a political democracy built on conceptions of endogenous political selves engaging in intelligent talk with other similar citizens is particularly consistent with aspirations for education.

It is a romantic aspiration, to be sure. Any argument that the odds of success are good enough to justify the hope is an implausible one. In a political system involving hundreds of millions of citizens, tens of millions of noncitizens, a global economic, political, and demographic environment, multiple languages, religions, and ethnicities, electronic technologies of communication, and the complexities of maintaining order in a diverse and aging population, democracy is not sustained by calculating plausibilities. It is sustained by a faith in human capacities for reason, empathy, and patience, the same faith that also nurtures education in the face of its own impossibilities.

NOTES

This chapter was prepared for discussion at a seminar on the democratic purposes of education held at the Aspen Institute in Washington, D.C., July 10–14, 1996, under the auspices of RAND and the Spencer Foundation. This revised version reflects the contributions of the members of that seminar, for which we are grateful. The research has been supported in various ways by the Spencer Foundation, the Stanford Graduate School of Business, the Scandinavian Consortium for Organizational Research, the Norwegian Research Centre in Organization and Management (LOS), the Center for Advanced Study in the Behavioral Sciences at Stanford, and the ARENA (Advanced Research on the Europeanization of the Nation-State) program financed by the Norwegian Research Council.

1. John Stuart Mill, *On Liberty* (1859; reprint, Indianapolis: Bobbs-Merrill, 1956), and Jean L. Cohen and Andrew Arato, *Civil Society and Political Theory* (Cambridge, Mass.: MIT Press, 1992).

2. Carl Cohen, "The Justification of Democracy," *Monist* 55 (1971): 1–28, and Sheldon S. Wolin, "The New Public Philosophy," *Democracy* 1, 4 (1981): 23–36.

3. John Rawls, *A Theory of Justice* (Cambridge, Mass.: Harvard University Press, 1971); Jürgen Habermas, *Theorie des Kommunikativen Handels* (Frankfurt: Suhrkamp, 1981); and Habermas, "Towards a Communication-Concept of Rational Collective Will-Formation: A Thought Experiment," *Ratio Juris* 2, 2 (1989): 144–54.

4. John Locke, *Second Treatise on Civil Government*, 1690; and George Klosko, "Rawls's 'Political' Philosophy and American Democracy," *American Political Science Review* 87 (1993): 348–59.

5. James G. March and Johan P. Olsen, "The New Institutionalism: Organizational Factors in Political Life," *American Political Science Review* 78 (1984): 734–49.

6. William H. Riker, *The Theory of Political Coalitions* (New Haven: Yale University Press, 1962), and Michael Taylor, "The Theory of Collective Choice," in *Handbook of Political Science,* vol. 3, ed. Fred I. Greenstein and Nelson W. Polsby (Reading, Mass.: Addison-Wesley, 1975).

7. James G. March and Johan P. Olsen, *Rediscovering Institutions* (New York: Free Press, 1989), and March and Olsen, *Democratic Governance* (New York: Free Press, 1995).

8. James S. Coleman, "Foundations for a Theory of Collective Decisions," *American Journal of Sociology* 71 (1966): 615–27; Coleman, "The Possibility of a Social Welfare Function," *American Economic Review* 56, 5 (1966): 1105–22; Anthony Downs, *Inside Bureaucracy* (Boston: Little, Brown, 1967); and William A. Niskanen, *Bureaucracy and Representative Government* (Chicago: Rand McNally, 1971).

9. John C. Harsanyi, *Rational Behavior and Bargaining Equilibrium in Games and*

Social Situations (Cambridge: Cambridge University Press, 1977), and Ronald H. Coase, *Essays on Economics and Economists* (Chicago: University of Chicago Press, 1994).

10. William H. Riker, *Liberalism Against Populism* (San Francisco: W. H. Freeman, 1982); Riker, "The Heresthetics of Constitution-Making: The Presidency in 1787, with Comments on Determinism and Rational Choice," *American Political Science Review* 78 (1984): 1–16; and Riker, *The Art of Political Manipulation* (New Haven, Conn.: Yale University Press, 1986).

11. Richard M. Cyert and James G. March, *A Behavioral Theory of the Firm* (Englewood Cliffs, N.J.: Prentice-Hall, 1963); and James G. March, "The Evolution of Evolution," in *The Evolutionary Dynamics of Organizations*, ed. Joel A. Baum and Jitendra V. Singh (New York: Oxford University Press, 1994), 39–49.

12. John W. Kingdon, *Agendas, Alternatives, and Public Policies*, 2d ed. (New York: HarperCollins, 1995).

13. Robert O. Keohane, *After Hegemony* (Princeton, N.J.: Princeton University Press, 1984); James S. Coleman, *Foundations of Social Theory* (Cambridge, Mass.: Harvard University Press, 1990); and Terry M. Moe, "Political Institutions: The Neglected Side of the Story," *Journal of Law, Economics, and Organization* 6 (1990): 213–66.

14. Douglas C. North, *Institutions, Institutional Change, and Economic Performance* (Cambridge: Cambridge University Press, 1990); and Geoff Garrett and Barry R. Weingast, "Ideas, Interests and Institutions: Constructing the European Community's Internal Market," in *Ideas and Foreign Policy*, ed. J. Goldstein and R. O. Keohane (Ithaca, N.Y.: Cornell University Press, 1993), 173–207.

15. Robert M. Axelrod, *The Evolution of Cooperation* (New York: Basic Books, 1984); R. Sugden, *The Economics of Rights, Co-operation, and Welfare* (Oxford: Basil Blackwell, 1986); David M. Kreps, "Corporate Culture and Economic Theory," in *Perspectives on Positive Political Economy*, ed. James E. Alt and Kenneth A. Shepsle (New York: Cambridge University Press, 1990); and North, *Institutions, Institutional Change*.

16. Mathew D. McCubbins, Roger G. Noll, and Barry R. Weingast, "Administrative Procedures as Instruments of Political Control," *Journal of Law, Economics, and Organization* 3 (1987): 243–77, and Barry R. Weingast and William J. Marshall, "The Industrial Organization of Congress," *Journal of Political Economy* 96 (1988): 132–63.

17. Terry M. Moe and Michael Caldwell, "The Institutional Foundations of Democratic Government: A Comparison of Presidential and Parliamentary Systems," *Journal of Institutional and Theoretical Economics* 150 (1994): 171–95.

18. Anthony Downs, *An Economic Theory of Democracy* (New York: Harper and Row, 1957), and Kenneth A. Shepsle and Barry R. Weingast, "The Institutional Foundations of Committee Power," *American Political Science Review* 81 (1987): 85–104.

19. William H. Riker, "Implications from the Disequilibrium of Majority Rule for the Study of Institutions," *American Political Science Review* 74 (1980): 432–46; Riker, ed., *Agenda Formation* (Ann Arbor: University of Michigan Press, 1993); and Kingdon, *Agendas, Alternatives*.

20. March and Olsen, "The New Institutionalism"; March and Olsen, *Rediscovering Institutions;* and March and Olsen, *Democratic Governance.*

21. Philip Selznick, *TVA and the Grass Roots* (Berkeley: University of California Press, 1949); Samuel N. Eisenstadt, and Stein Rokkan, eds., *Building States and Nations*, 2 vols. (Beverly Hills, Calif.: Sage, 1973); John W. Meyer and Brian Rowan, "Institu-

tionalized Organizations: Formal Structure as Myth and Ceremony," *American Journal of Sociology* 83 (1977): 340–63; and Elizabeth R. Gerber and John E. Jackson, "Endogenous Preferences and the Study of Institutions," *American Political Science Review* 87 (1993): 639–56.

22. Mary Douglas, *How Institutions Think* (Syracuse, N.Y.: Syracuse University Press, 1986), and Michael Thompson, Richard Ellis, and Aaron B. Wildavsky, *Cultural Theory* (Boulder, Colo.: Westview Press, 1990).

23. Tom R. Burns and Helena Flam, *The Shaping of Social Organization: Social Rule System Theory with Applications* (Beverly Hills, Calif.: Sage, 1987), and James G. March, *Three Lectures on Efficiency and Adaptiveness in Organizations* (Helsinki: Swedish School of Economics, 1994).

24. Michael Walzer, *Spheres of Justice* (New York: Basic Books, 1983); Benjamin R. Barber, *Strong Democracy: Participatory Politics for a New Age* (Berkeley: University of California Press, 1984); and Chantal Mouffe, ed., *Dimensions of Radical Democracy* (London: Verso, 1992).

25. George H. Sabine, "The Two Democratic Traditions," *Philosophical Review* (1952): 493–511; Johan P. Olsen, *Demokrati på svenska* (Stockholm: Carlssons, 1990); and Jon Elster, *The Cement of Society* (Cambridge: Cambridge University Press, 1989).

26. Stephen D. Krasner, "Sovereignty: An Institutional Perspective," *Comparative Political Studies* 21 (1988): 66–94; March and Olsen, *Rediscovering Institutions;* and March and Olsen, *Democratic Governance.*

27. Glen R. Carroll and J. Richard Harrison, "Historical Efficiency of Competition Between Organizational Populations," *American Journal of Sociology* 100 (1994): 720–49.

28. March, "The Evolution of Evolution."

29. David W. Brady, *Critical Elections and Congressional Policy Making* (Stanford, Calif.: Stanford University Press, 1988), and Seymour Martin Lipset, *Continental Divide* (New York: Routledge, 1990).

30. Ernest Barker, *Greek Political Theory* (London: Methuen, 1947).

31. James G. March, "Preferences, Power, and Democracy," in *Power, Inequality, and Democratic Politics,* ed. Ian Shapiro and Grant Reeder (Boulder, Colo.: Westview Press, 1988), 50–66.

32. Aaron B. Wildavsky, "Choosing Preferences by Constructing Institutions: A Cultural Theory of Preference Formation," *American Political Science Review* 81 (1987): 3–22.

33. Peter A. Hall, *The Political Power of Economic Ideas* (Princeton, N.J.: Princeton University Press, 1989), and Judith Goldstein and Robert O. Keohane, eds., *Ideas and Foreign Policy* (Ithaca, N.Y.: Cornell University Press, 1993).

34. Peter Bachrach and Morton S. Baratz, "The Two Faces of Power," *American Political Science Review* 56 (1962): 947–52; Kingdon, *Agendas, Alternatives;* and Deborah A. Stone, *Policy Paradox: The Art of Political Decision Making* (New York: Norton, 1997).

35. E. E. Schattschneider, *The Semi-Sovereign People* (New York: Holt, Rinehart and Winston, 1960).

36. James G. March, "Politics and the City," in *Urban Processes as Viewed by the Social Sciences,* ed. Kenneth J. Arrow, James S. Coleman, Anthony Downs, and James G.

March (Washington, D.C.: Urban Institute Press, 1970), 23–37; March and Olsen, *Democratic Governance.*

37. Dennis W. Organ, *Organizational Citizenship Behavior: The Good Soldier Syndrome* (Lexington, Mass.: D. C. Heath, 1988), and R. M. Kramer, "Cooperation and Organizational Identification," in *Social Psychology in Organizations: Advances in Theory and Research,* ed. J. Keith Murnighan (Englewood Cliffs, N.J.: Prentice Hall, 1993), 244–68.

38. Giovani Sartori, *The Theory of Democracy Revisited,* 2 vols. Chatham, N.J.: Chatham House, 1987), and Robert A. Dahl, *Democracy and Its Critics* (New Haven, Conn.: Yale University Press, 1989).

39. Giuseppe Di Palma, *To Craft Democracies* (Berkeley: University of California Press, 1990), and Anthony D. Smith, *National Identity* (London: Penguin, 1991).

40. Olsen, *Demokrati på svenska,* and Melissa A. Orlie, "Thoughtless Assertion and Political Deliberation," *American Political Science Review* 88 (1994): 684–95.

41. Habermas, *Theorie des Kommunikativen Handels,* and Robert B. Reich, ed., *The Power of Public Ideas* (Cambridge, Mass.: Ballinger, 1988).

42. Amartya Sen, *Inequality Reexamined* (Cambridge, Mass.: Harvard University Press, 1992).

43. March and Olsen, *Democratic Governance,* 127.

44. Lee J. Cronbach, *Designing Evaluations of Educational and Social Programs* (San Francisco: Jossey-Bass, 1982).

45. Judith N. Shklar, *The Faces of Injustice* (New Haven, Conn.: Yale University Press, 1990), 62.

46. Phillip E. Tetlock, "The Impact of Accountability on Judgment and Choice: Toward a Social Contingency Model," *Advances in Experimental Social Psychology* 25 (1992): 331–76.

47. March and Olsen, *Democratic Governance,* 143–46.

48. Marvin B. Scott and Stanford M. Lyman, "Accounts," *American Sociological Review* 33, 1 (1968): 46–62, and John W. Meyer, "Social Environments and Organizational Accounting," *Accounting, Organizations, and Society* 11, 4/5 (1986): 345–56.

49. Habermas, "Towards a Communication."

50. March, *Three Lectures on Efficiency.*

51. George E. Marcus and Russell L. Hanson, *Reconsidering the Democratic Republic* (University Park: Pennsylvania State University Press, 1993).

52. James G. March, "Analytical Skills and the University Training of Educational Administrators," *Journal of Educational Administration* 7 (1974): 17–44.

53. James G. March, "Organizational Consultants and Organizational Research," *Journal of Applied Communications Research* 19 (1991): 20–31.

54. James G. March, "Science, Politics, and Mrs. Gruenberg," in *National Research Council in 1979* (Washington, D.C.: National Academy of Sciences, 1980).

55. D. A. Levinthal and James G. March, "The Myopia of Learning," *Strategic Management Journal* 14 (1993): 95–112.

56. Ibid., and Barbara Levitt and James G. March, "Organizational Learning," *Annual Review of Sociology* 14 (1988): 319–40.

57. James G. March, "Exploration and Exploitation in Organizational Learning," *Organization Science* 2 (1991): 71–87.

58. James G. March, *A Primer on Decision Making: How Decisions Happen* (New York: Free Press, 1994).

59. J. Richard Harrison and James G. March, "Decision Making and Post-Decision Surprises," *Administrative Science Quarterly* 29 (1984): 26–42.

60. March, "Exploration and Exploitation."

61. James G. March, "The Future, Disposable Organizations, and the Rigidities of Imagination," *Organization* 2 (1995): 427–40.

8

Seeking a New Politics of Education

Lorraine M. McDonnell and M. Stephen Weatherford

Over the past twenty years, research on the politics of education has become synonymous with policy analysis, as scholars have concentrated on determining how political variables shape policy outcomes. From this perspective, the institutions, values, and interests that define politics are significant only as they are manifested through discrete policies.[1] Framing the research agenda in this way has had a dramatic effect. It has, to be sure, brought more coherence to a disparate field, but it has had the unintended consequence of ignoring important intellectual and practical questions. This neglect has become especially obvious as education's political boundaries have expanded to include significant roles for every level of government, each with its own constituencies and views about the goals and criteria that define good educational practice, and as the roster of legitimate citizen participants in school politics has expanded in number and diversity. The impact of these changes cannot be understood without shifting our focus from policy outputs to devote more attention to the underlying political processes.

These changes in the politics of education have occurred in response to changes in the social and political context of public education as American society has become more deeply pluralistic. Indeed, at the beginning of a new century, the social context of education more closely resembles the situation urban districts faced a hundred years ago when they were challenged to integrate and educate millions of immigrants than the seeming homogeneity of the 1950s. But it is different in one critical way: along with virtually every other political institution, education politics is more open to participation by a wide and disparate range of claimants than were American governmental processes even a few decades ago. To understand these changes and the new forms of politics that are emerging to cope with them, a new perspective is needed, one that views "politics" not only as a production function for delivering policies but as a process important in its own right, with particular normative and practical outcomes.

The preceding two chapters present sharply contrasting models of politics, one in which political institutions largely reflect the interests of dominant groups and another in which those same institutions embody rules and norms encouraging the development of shared identities that extend beyond self-interest. Underlying each model are different assumptions about the way politics ought to work, how it currently operates, and about the conceptual frameworks scholars should use in studying politics. To a great extent, the contrast between the two approaches captures the key distinctions of tone and orientation that animate the debate over the democratic purposes of education. There is no question that at the level of fundamental theoretical assumptions, these models belong in different camps, and it is as yet an open question whether theorists will eventually succeed in combining their insights into a single logical structure. These chapters depict the models at a high level of generality that emphasizes their theoretical differences, and yet they both bring potential insights into the practical problems of understanding current education politics and outlining promising reforms. Although we attempt to build on these two chapters, our goal is less grand than the construction of a new theoretical model. We seek to develop the insights of these approaches by specifying their generalizations in two areas, the current structures and dynamics of education politics, and the practical requisites of a more deliberative political arena.

Terry M. Moe, for instance, describes education politics as hierarchical and bureaucratized, and at a general level this seems a fair depiction. But to understand actual policy-making, we need a more detailed picture of the complexities of overlapping authority and the dynamics of competing structures and interests. In the first part of this chapter, we outline the current state of knowledge on the politics of education, providing a sense of the territory that needs to be understood better. Although education garners considerable media attention and is a frequent subject of political speeches, talk shows, and informal conversations, attempts are rare to place individual events and issues into a broader perspective. We try to do that in our overview by focusing on the underlying values that define the politics of education, popular attitudes toward the schools, and the institutions that govern education. In doing so, we look across governmental levels and over the past thirty years, focusing particularly on the past decade.

Similarly, Moe proposes that the current system would benefit from revitalizing local school politics, and this is surely a promising generalization. But its silence on specifics calls for reformers to address the question of how local political participation might be structured so as to avoid replicating the deficiencies Moe decries. The ideas of deliberative theorists offer promising images of an alternative way to organize participatory institutions. We focus most of our attention on the kinds of institutional and deliberative approaches outlined by Amy Gutmann and by James G. March and Johan P. Olsen in their chapters in this book, for we believe that these approaches can help explain aspects of education politics not well accounted for by the dominant exchange model. But these chapters share

Moe's abstract and theoretical orientation, and their insights will need to be developed in order to realize their practical potential. Elaborating these theoretical ideas will inevitably entail further work at developing concepts and logics of causation, and in the second part of this chapter, we draw on the theoretical literature to outline several ideas for strengthening deliberative participation in education politics. At the same time, we are skeptical that theorizing can do the whole job of strengthing schools, and we believe that empirical research is needed on the wide range of promising—but resolutely practical—initiatives in education that are currently emerging in states and localities. We conclude the chapter with suggestions for a research approach that will focus on these new practical developments while drawing on both the general models of education politics depicted in earlier chapters.

EDUCATION POLITICS: CONTEMPORARY THEMES AND TRENDS

Little research on the politics of local school districts has been conducted for the past two decades because states, and secondarily the federal government, have been the loci of policy activity. Few analyses, for instance, tell how local school boards conceive of their role and make decisions, which topics dominate district agendas and the extent of public mobilization over those issues, or how education issues fit into the broader politics of local communities.[2] Not only do we lack good descriptive studies, but the theoretical frameworks that lend insight and context to data have atrophied, because little attention has been paid to how newer theories from relevant disciplines such as political science and organizational sociology might deepen our understanding of education politics. Consequently, the few studies and textbooks on the topic are either descriptive or rely on outmoded theories.[3] On the practical side, this gap in scholarship has consequences for how well prepared professional educators are to work in a public and intrinsically political institution. School administrators now being trained in schools of education learn about federal and state education policies but receive little coursework on the political institutions closest to their daily work lives.

Thus, the arguments in favor of focusing more scholarly attention on the politics of education take a variety of forms. More complete information about the political values that shape popular attitudes and the interests that constrain policy choices would help in understanding such pressing issues as recent opposition to curriculum policies by religious conservatives or the growing political fragmentation of urban school systems. At a practical level, teachers and administrators might be more responsive to parental and public concerns if they had a deeper understanding of what it means to work in a public institution that not only must be accountable to the electorate but also must reflect community values and interests.

Another, and perhaps stronger, argument relates to the way theoretical models of the politics of education are both shaped by and reinforce particular images and ideas about the purposes of schooling. Education for citizenship is one of the primary goals of public schooling; we expect schools to give students "the capacity to deliberate and participate in democratic politics" to instill norms of civic engagement.⁴ The way in which individual schools are organized and the curriculum they offer shape the deliberative skills that students develop and influence how young citizens view themselves in relation to the larger community. At the same time, the politics of the broader community constitutes the real-world context that gives practical meaning to the lessons of civic education: Does the community work to ensure that schools have the capacity to cultivate civic values in their students, and is the political process that governs schools one that fosters effective participation in decisions about which values are conveyed?⁵

Education politics does more than allocate resources and decide which curricular values will prevail. It also stands as the most immediately visible object of students' civic learning. Although the media may give national politics more prominence, local education politics is likely to be more relevant to students' own lives and one of the political arenas in which they and their parents have the greatest opportunity to participate. The opportunities that citizens have for meaningful political participation, the norms and structures for resolving political conflict, and the weight accorded different interests in the political process define the polity to which students are being socialized, and these characteristics are all clearly manifested in the politics of education. To what extent does this most accessible arena of real-world politics support or undermine the standards of democratic citizenship that schools are expected to instill in their students?⁶

One cannot help being struck by the mix of fluctuation and constancy that defines current education politics. Public attitudes toward the schools seem inconsistent and at times even confused. Commentators talk about growing public disengagement from the schools,⁷ but support indicators such as voter turnout and judgments about school quality have remained steady for at least a decade. The public expresses strong support for national standards and testing, but well over half of a recent national sample reported having little or no trust in elected officials in Washington.⁸ On the other hand, contemporary education politics is replete with examples of the path-dependency of institutions and policies. Many of today's most compelling value conflicts have their roots in unresolved historical debates about educational philosophy, and the structures now subject to scrutiny and reform are the product of earlier choices about appropriate designs for educational institutions. These and other seeming anomalies reinforce the need for more systematic research on education politics and for a more nuanced model of the relationship between the public and the schools.

This overview of recent trends in education politics is necessarily selective, but it illustrates both the need for better research and the extent to which current politics have been shaped by historical choices about prevailing values and institutional arrangements. We highlight three themes:

- Since the beginning of the republic, the schools have been a focal point for contested social values, and those disputes continue today.
- The students who are the direct beneficiaries of public schooling differ in important ways from the voters who must support the educational enterprise.
- Although the myriad political institutions that govern public education are fragmented, they continue to shape each other's politics, even as their own roles evolve.

Core Values and Persistent Tensions in the Politics of Education

In his essay "Education as Politics," Lawrence A. Cremin reminds us of Aristotle's dictum: "It is impossible to talk about education apart from a conception of the good life; people will inevitably differ in their conceptions of the good life, and hence they will inevitably differ on matters of education; therefore the discussion of education falls squarely within the domain of politics."[9]

In contemporary education politics, competing conceptions of the good life have been evident in debates over such basic principles as whether access to education is a fundamental right, what constitutes equal learning opportunities, and the extent to which families' control over the education of their children should be abridged in the name of state interests. Specific policy issues reflecting these disputes have ranged from school finance reform to sex education. As many historians and philosophers of education have noted, these tensions are not new. The civic mission of education was clear for the American Founders, but their writings are filled with harbingers of themes that would later become subjects of dispute.[10]

A major focal point for contested views about the purpose of education has been the continuing debate over what curriculum should be taught. With recent controversies over outcomes-based education, multiculturalism, and new proposals for standards and assessments, these value disputes have once again moved to the forefront of education politics. Although groups representing religious conservatives have been the most visible opponents of recent curricular innovations and new forms of assessment, national public opinion data indicate that some of the questions these groups are raising reflect broadly shared concerns.[11] For example, recent surveys about the teaching of mathematics and language arts point to fundamental differences between the curricular values of education reformers and large segments of the public, ranging from the selection of texts and the relative importance of grammar and spelling, to the value of teaching students in heterogenous ability groups, to the use of calculators.[12] Even as the arenas for conflict have expanded beyond local school districts and the courts, where such disputes have traditionally been aired, to state legislatures and

Congress, the issues remain the same.[13] The contention over whose values should be taught in the public schools cannot but reflect the debate over how we define the good society.

Students, Voters, and Public Support for Education

In spite of much media attention, the exact level and nature of public support for education is not well understood. Here, new research on opinion formation would not only contribute to officials' and administrators' appreciation of current public attitudes but also to their understanding of how support might be built for future initiatives.

Overall support for the schools appears to be quite high. For the past decade, slightly over 40 percent of Americans have given the quality of their local public schools a grade of A or B.[14] Willingness to support schools goes along with approval: for example, in 1993, 81 percent indicated that they consider improvement of the nation's inner-city schools to be very important, and 60 percent said they would be willing to pay more federal taxes to improve the quality of those schools.[15] And an overwhelming majority favors having local schools conform to a set of national achievement goals and standards and requiring that standardized tests be used to measure student achievement.[16] A majority also sees higher standards as a way to encourage students, including ones from low-income backgrounds, to do better in school.[17] Even on the controversial question of whether communities can agree on a set of basic values that schools should teach, over two-thirds of the general public believe that such a consensus can emerge, and huge majorities hold that schools should teach about honesty, citizenship, tolerance of those with different beliefs, and moral courage.[18]

Public judgments about the institutional performance of schools is all the more notable when placed against the twenty-year trend of declining trust in all manner of public and private institutions. For instance, the proportion of Americans who trust the government to do the right thing most or all of the time has diminished from approximately 75 percent in the mid-1960s to about 35 percent just after Watergate and to around 25 percent in the early 1990s. Similar trends are apparent in the feeling that government is "run by a few big interests" rather than "for the benefit of all." Other large institutions, from corporations and unions to churches, have also declined in the public's esteem.[19] Even allowing for methodological differences among surveys, the favorable rating for local schools is roughly equivalent to that for the Supreme Court, about twice that for the media and large corporations, and nearly three times that for Congress.

These and similar data suggest that the public is satisfied with the schools' performance, and that there is a consensus around what schools should teach. Other data, however, imply that support may not be as solid as it appears. The high ratings Americans give their local schools, for instance, coexist with a much more skeptical assessment of the nation's public schools as a whole. About half give the public schools nationally a grade of C, and only 18 percent give them an A or B.[20] In addition, the public is now evenly split on the question of whether students should be allowed to attend private schools at government expense.[21] Public schools are viewed as providing a better education for students with special needs and as offering an environment that better teaches students to deal with diversity, but private schools are seen as having higher academic standards, employing better teachers, encouraging better work habits, and providing better preparation for college.[22] If the data on public attitudes leave some questions unanswered, our information about the public's actual involvement is even less complete. There is, for instance, no single, reliable source that reports voter turnout for school board and school bond elections—a key indicator of public involvement and support for public education—although we do know that voter turnout has historically been low and continues to be so in local school elections.[23]

Demographic and other data shed some light on underlying trends. The proportion of adults with school-age children has declined significantly over the past twenty years from about 56 percent to 41 percent. However, the proportion of voters who have children in school is estimated to be only 25 to 30 percent. As a result, most adults (and most voters) have little firsthand knowledge of the schools and are only loosely connected to the ones in their local communities. These weak ties may help explain what appears to be a broad but shallow consensus about the quality of public schooling and about how students should be educated. Nevertheless, in a national survey, close to half the respondents with no children in the public schools reported attending a school play, concert, or athletic event in a local public school within the past year. Only 10 percent, however, had attended a school board meeting, and an even lower proportion had served as a member of a public school–related committee. In most cases, reported rates of participation in school activities by respondents without school-age children were about half that reported by public school parents.[24]

In a recent Gallup/Phi Delta Kappa poll, 65 percent of the respondents with no children in school said that if asked, they would be willing to work as an unpaid volunteer in any of the public schools in their community.[25] This disjunction between reported willingness to participate in the schools and chronic low voter turnout can be interpreted in a variety of ways, from respondents giving what they perceive to be socially desirable answers, to citizens judging that voting is less efficacious than actually assisting in the schools. In any event, these data do suggest that educational leaders have failed to mobilize a willing public on behalf of local schools.

The lack of connection between public intentions and actions, just like seemingly inconsistent attitudes toward the schools, suggests that we do not fully understand how those without school-age children regard the educational enterprise. In fact, because the analysis of public attitudes toward the schools has not been a topic of educational research, we lack sophisticated studies of how parents and nonparents alike view the schools. We know little about how they form their attitudes; what role information plays, as compared with other influences such as that of friends, neighbors, and elites; how attitudes are related to each other; and how attitudes change or why they are stable over time.

We do know, however, that many adults live in very different circumstances than a significant proportion of public school students, thus compounding their lack of direct experience with schools. As a group, school-age children are more likely than the adult population to be poor. In 1990, the proportion of youth younger than eighteen years old living in poverty was 20 percent compared with only 11 percent for those eighteen to sixty-four.[26] Furthermore, there are significant differences in the demographic characteristics of students attending urban schools compared with their counterparts in suburban and rural areas. In 1995, African-American students represented 17 percent of all public school students, but 32 percent of those in central-city schools; Hispanic students constituted 14 percent of all students and 24 percent of those in central-city schools.[27] In addition, the proportion of children living in poverty is almost three times higher for African-American children and two-and-a-half times higher for Hispanic youth than for white children.[28]

This student profile, and particularly the demographics of large urban schools, contrasts sharply with the adult electorate. Data are not available on the characteristics of voters in local school elections, but survey data on national elections are suggestive. For example, in the 1994 midterm elections, 69 percent of those who reported voting had no school-age children. In addition, in that same election, the reported turnout differed significantly among ethnic groups, with 60 percent of white registered voters reporting that they voted compared with 49 percent of African Americans and 43 percent of Hispanics, resulting in significant overrepresentation of whites in the electorate.[29] The composition of the electorate varies, of course, depending on the nature of individual elections and the issues they raise, but it is reasonable to infer from available data that voters differ significantly from the families of public school students in ethnicity and social class.

The contrast between students and voters does not necessarily imply diminished engagement in public schooling. However, it does suggest that active support for even the concept of public education, much less its day-to-day operations, depends on a politics broader than that of self-interest. That politics may be based on a moral commitment to meet society's responsibility to children or a belief that schools serve a common purpose extending beyond just the students currently in attendance. Public involvement need not always be supportive of current school politics or practices; indeed, public judgments may at times be quite critical of the direction that schools are taking or of their performance. What is important is that the demographic and economic differences between students and voters do not translate into a participation gap that, by fostering a politics of difference between parents and other voters, either undermines the legitimacy of parents' claim to a special relation with the schools or implies that the community as a whole relinquishes its interest in articulating schooling's larger purposes.

FRAGMENTED POLITICAL INSTITUTIONS, EVOLVING ROLES AND RESPONSIBILITIES

More than in perhaps any other policy area, Americans' characteristic suspicion of concentrated power and our sometimes nostalgic longing for local control have combined to complicate the politics of education and undermine the hopes of reformers that equality and efficiency could be achieved via uniform policies. The roots of institutional fragmentation in education are both constitutional and cultural. Madison's notion that the Constitution is "neither national nor federal . . . , but a composition of both" captures the Founders' intentions.[30] Over the next century, the spread of schooling in the United States reflected this design, as government sought to foster and support education through federal land grants, state constitutional provisions, and the oversight of locally elected school trustees, all reinforced by voluntary networks and direct citizen participation in the establishment of common schools.[31] Intertwined with these constitutional and historical factors is a cultural trait that James A. Morone has called the "democratic wish": a "dread" of public power as a threat to liberty, coupled with a "yearning" for direct, communal democracy. The upshot is a government "weak and fragmented, designed to prevent action more easily than to produce it."[32]

The history of American education is replete with instances of attempts to finesse the dilemma. David Tyack recounts how the response of the education establishment to demands for social justice that came from outside the system resulted in greater institutional fragmentation. As a result of the Progressives' efforts to make the organization of schooling more like that of the corporation, education had largely operated as a closed system for the first half of the century. However, as activists sought change at all levels of school politics

> One way in which school districts and state and federal agencies responded to dissent was to bureaucratize it. New problems became identified, and new district administrators were appointed to deal with them and to coordinate outside funding and accounting for new programs. As Meyer has noted, this produced a fragmented form of centralization. In addition, the establishment sometimes responded to the demand for community control by adding new layers of decentralized governance, or new forms of "community participation." The result of all of this, more often than not, was a more elaborate and less coordinated bureaucracy—more the appearance than the reality of democracy.[33]

Contemporary policy and institutions reflect and reinforce these historical trends. Consider, for instance, the institutional fragmentation associated with the pattern of categorical funding that has characterized the federal role over the past thirty years. In responding to the needs and interests of various student populations, from the disabled to those enrolled in vocational education, Congress has fostered the establishment of federal, state, and local bureaucracies to administer these programs and deliver services to students. In addition, the enabling legislation has often created formal roles for groups representing these students, their parents, and the professionals who serve them.[34] Once such a multiplicity of governance structures is in place, moreover, the institutions themselves hamper coherent policy, as each agency's autonomy hinges to some extent on resisting coordination; this dynamic frequently undermines the intention to promote equal resources and opportunities across schools and classrooms.[35] Although efforts have been made over the past few years to integrate federal and state categorical programs, their politics and service delivery still operate quite independently.

Public attitudes reflect similar ambivalence toward policy and institutions. Recent polls show that large majorities favor efforts by the federal government to assist students with college expenses in exchange for public service, to provide more money for work-study vocational programs, to increase significantly the level of funding for early childhood education for poor children, and to work toward agreement on academic achievement goals. But two-thirds of respondents also hold that the federal government should have less influence in determining the education programs of local public schools, and only 28 percent express a great deal of trust in local elected officials to make decisions about the schools, with an even smaller proportion (14 percent) expressing significant trust in elected officials in Washington.[36]

The interplay of contradictory public demands and fragmented institutions has produced an educational policy system that appears to some critics to be nothing more than an overly bureaucratized monolith,[37] but the real problem is more complex and may be just the opposite. David K. Cohen and James P. Spillane argue that reformers' ambitious attempts at strong policy have inevitably been implemented through a large and loosely jointed governance system: "While the design of American government incarnates a deep mistrust of state power, the design of most education policy expressed an abiding hope for the power of government and a wish to harness it to social problem solving. . . . The collisions between rapidly expanded policy-making and fragmented governance are a hallmark of U.S. education."[38]

Rather than an unresponsive and centralized system, American education politics is better described as a multiplicity of loosely connected institutions that are in fact highly responsive to narrowly defined functional and geographic constituencies. Not only the design and implementation of policy but also the complex and shifting politics of education are shaped by this context of competing demands and ideals. The result is a continuing and vigorous debate: first over the roles and responsibilities of different branches and levels of government and second over how to develop the nexus of negotiated rules and expectations that would allow separate institutions to share authority.

Over the past several decades, the judiciary has played an increasingly central role, not only in shaping education policy but also in structuring relations among other political institutions. The courts have recognized claims for equal treatment and due process that affect broad classes of students and parents and whose implementation has required fundamental changes in the operations of educational institutions. The reliance on the courts as a counterweight to majoritarian institutions such as legislatures and school boards and to the professional judgment of educators is due to several factors unique to the United States, including the constitutional role of U.S. courts in reconciling majoritarianism with individual rights; the role of interest groups such as the NAACP that use litigation as a major strategy in asserting their constituents' claims; and the effect of landmark cases such as *Brown v. Board of Education* in fostering the assertion of group rights through the use of the class action lawsuit.[39]

Judicial decisions, particularly in school finance, desegregation, and the education of disabled students and those with limited English proficiency, have forged major new policy directions. The courts have influenced education politics both directly and by constraining other political actors. For example, elective bodies are often in the position of reacting to an agenda set by the courts and of having to legislate the specifics of a general policy direction established by judicial fiat. A group with a rights-based claim pursues it through the judiciary, often after determining that legislative majorities are unlikely to be responsive. A decision in the group's favor commands the legislature's attention at the same time that it circumscribes how elected officials balance this claim against those of other interests.[40] Although the courts' influence has been concentrated in only a few critical areas, some analysts have suggested that the growing judicial role is part of a larger "antipolitical" trend, where reform advocates "seek to spare themselves the rigors and uncertainties of interest mobilization and coalition-building by shifting consideration of key issues from legislatures and school boards to institutions that are less 'political' and more authoritative, such as courts and markets."[41]

Education politics in the United States is also distinguished by the ubiquity of reciprocal influence among the three governmental levels. Congress and the presidency have, for instance, influenced state and local education politics and policy to a greater extent than the relative size of the federal fiscal contribution would suggest. But thirty years of federal program implementation have shown the limits of that level's influence, and the priorities and practices of local communities have in recent years significantly shaped the reauthorization of federal legislation, from Title I to special education.[42] Recently, the federal government appears to be moving away from a regulatory role to one that emphasizes its potential as a "bully pulpit" from which officials can use persuasion to lead schools in particular directions. The initiatives of the Bush and Clinton administrations, stressing the voluntary formulation and adoption of academic performance standards, are examples of hortatory policies that seek to influence state and local behavior by invoking a sense of shared values (e.g., "world class standards," "all children can learn to high standards") rather than primarily through tangible incentives such as rules and money.[43]

State governments have greatly enlarged the scope of their direction over local districts and schools, expanding their purview from governance and finance to the specification of what is taught, how, and by whom. Nevertheless, the expansion of state authority has not necessarily come at the expense of local authority. Rather, research on the effects of the expanded state role during the 1980s found that many local districts used state policies as leverage to promote their own priorities, and that state influence varied depending on the clarity of its policy goals and on local will and capacity to respond to state incentives.[44] With their own independent constitutional grounds for exercising authority, state and local governments are related less like principal and agent than like bargainers in a game involving both cooperative and competitive incentives.

Influence across levels and institutions is not confined to formal governmental bodies. Education politics and policies at all levels have been heavily influenced by a variety of voluntary networks composed of groups representing elected officials (e.g., National Governors' Association, National Conference of State Legislatures), corporations (Business Roundtable, National Alliance of Business), teacher unions (American Federation of Teachers, National Education Association), professional organizations (National Council of Teachers of Mathematics), education reformers (Carnegie Forum on Education and the Economy, National Board for Professional Teaching Standards), foundations (Annie E. Casey, Carnegie Corporation, Ford, McArthur, Pew), and groups advocating broad ideological positions (Eagle Forum, People for the American Way). The agendas and strategies of these organizations vary considerably, but all have influenced the array of education policy alternatives and have made the political environment much denser. The overall effect has been to make the range of policy choices richer but also to make it more difficult for any one institution or level to act authoritatively.

Behind the argument that education institutions are fragmented is a complex picture of influence patterns that run in multiple directions and of a politics that seeks to divide power and resources as much as to consolidate them. Although disagreement between national, state, and local levels is inevitable, the relative autonomy of state and local governmental entities in American federalism gives these disagreements a complex and multifaceted nature that has alternately fostered innovation and contributed to conflict. The picture is further complicated because the roles and responsibilities of these institutions are in flux. The change can be seen clearly in the states, where the adoption of academic content standards and new forms of assessment have brought deep, new conflicts over values and social goals. By raising the question of which knowledge and skills are most worthwhile for students to learn, these initiatives have brought intense political scrutiny to proposals that most education reformers imagined as the mere translation of technical, professional knowledge into practice. Although these debates have actively engaged only a small minority of parents and the public, media attention and the emergence of whole language versus phonics, new mathematics textbooks, and the content of state assessments as electoral campaign issues represents a major shift in the politics of education. Not only has the circle of participants expanded beyond the traditional one of professional educators and the groups representing them, but also the scope of deliberation has broadened beyond the traditional state focus on the allocation of financial resources.

The broadening and invigoration of state education politics began even before recent moves to standards-based reforms. For instance, the more active role in education policy taken by governors during the 1980s and the increased participation of business leaders in shaping state education policy agendas had an unmistakable impact on policy, but they also had a lasting effect on education politics, opening up the policy system and making the politics less predictable and more fluid.[45] An extreme example has been the recent politics of student testing in California, resulting in an abrupt change in policy only a few years into the implementation of a major new state assessment.[46]

At the state and federal levels, we can see the general trend of change, even if we cannot predict its precise effects, but in local education politics, at the grass roots where it is most accessible to citizen participation, the overall pattern is less clear. In many of the largest cities, local district politics are mired in divisiveness, and policy appears powerless to improve schools' performance. As states have assumed more responsibility for defining curriculum; as parents have greater choice in selecting a school for their children; and as individual school sites have been given increased discretion over their budgets, personnel, and the implementation of state curricular standards, districts are scrambling to redefine their own responsibilities and to reassert their authority. At the same time, district politics has become more fragmented. Broad-based political participation is low to nonexistent. Instead, active involvement is often limited to those with a direct stake in the schools, while sharp divisions persist along ethnic, union-management, and partisan ideological lines. A telling indicator of the deadlock caused by such politics is the shortened tenure of urban superintendents. Barbara L. Jackson and James G. Cibulka note that "the average tenure of urban superintendents is now 2.5 years, coupled with a shortage of applicants for vacant superintendencies, indicating a crisis of legitimacy for many urban school systems."[47] A recent case study of school reform politics in four communities with good school systems found that "in all four communities, groups that should work together—groups that must work together if there is to be progress—seemed continually pulled apart by suspicion, by prejudice, and by fear of losing hard-won gains."[48] Local education politics are notable for their increasingly antagonistic and narrow conflicts: the formal structures of education politics in cities and towns appear to serve more as gladiatorial arenas than deliberative spaces.

But the status of local politics is not altogether grim. As it approached its one-hundredth birthday, the Parent Teacher Association (PTA) was remaking itself, with its membership, activities, and political positions now more accurately reflecting the diversity of American schools.[49] What is perhaps most striking about efforts to revitalize the PTA is its grassroots, voluntary, problem-solving approach—all characteristics of the kinds of associations that nurture norms of civic engagement.[50] Similarly, a four-year study of the implementation of local site councils (LSCs) in Chicago found that few are characterized by divisive politics, and that a quarter to a third of the LSCs in Chicago elementary schools are models of strong democracy where parental and community involvement is strong and LSC members are actively engaged in school improvement planning.[51] It is too early to judge either the educational or political success of the devolution of greater authority to the school level in Chicago or in most other districts. Certainly the mixed record of past attempts at decentralization and the difficulties inherent in linking changes in governance to substantive changes in teaching and learning suggest that altering the balance of authority within school districts may produce only modest results.[52] Nevertheless, the growing interest in charter schools, site-based management, and other governance options that broaden and intensify participation suggests that at least the seeds have been sown for a school politics that is both more integrative and more focused on the substance of schooling.

The current state of local education politics provides unambiguous grounds for neither hope nor despair. We can be pessimistic about the level of apathy among many parents and the general public and about the gridlock that has resulted from a narrow, interest-based politics. Or we can be optimistic about the PTA with its 6.5 million local members and about thousands of other local associations involved with the schools; about 95,000 local school board members, most of whom serve with little or no financial compensation; and about the thousands of letters to the editor, op-ed articles, and informal conversations that occur daily about the state of public schools and the different ways to make them better. Even the struggles over curriculum and bilingual education that have been waged in many communities recently can be viewed as either painful signs of a withering consensus or as evidence that Americans are now willing to engage in the hard task of deciding what is most important for students to know and be able to do.

It is perhaps fitting that we end this overview of themes and trends in education politics with an equivocal conclusion, for the available literature provides neither the empirical information nor the theoretical and normative criteria needed to ground a full assessment. Two decades of research neglect have left huge gaps in our knowledge of education politics, particularly at the local level. We simply do not know, for example, the proportion of communities characterized by gridlock and dysfunctional education politics compared with those where public engagement is strong and political decision making is effective. We have few case studies that would help in interpreting the public's complex, and sometimes inconsistent, attitudes about public education and its governance. In addition, viewing politics as one of several variables in a model of policy has stunted the development of approaches that take politics and participation as proper subjects of study in themselves, not to mention the lack of theoretically based standards on which to evaluate the performance of the political system as it affects education. How should performance be measured, and what theory or approach would foster more openness on the part of researchers to emerging patterns of education politics?

DELIBERATIVE DEMOCRACY AND THE STUDY OF SCHOOL POLITICS

The kaleidoscopic array of institutions, actors, and interests that define contemporary education politics can easily lead to Balkanization and hostility, as different camps fight to secure privileged access to policy. Indeed, the renewed interest in deliberative models of politics, not only in education but across the policy spectrum, is motivated in part by the challenge of accommodating a polity growing in diversity. The practical question is whether the turn toward a more deliberative, collectively oriented process is politically feasible. This section takes up that question in two parts. We first discuss several questions confronting the translation of the normative ideal to what we might think of as "practical deliberation." Here we focus on three issues: the claimed advantages of deliberation over more adversarial processes, the question of which issues are appropriate for deliberation and which better left to marketlike processes (including majority rule) or bureaucracies, and the challenge of structuring the deliberative arena so as to include as wide a range of interests as possible. Second, we outline key elements of a research agenda appropriate to studying actual instances of community deliberation over education policy.

In elaborating the deliberative approach, we do not intend that exchange models of the political process should be supplanted. Both clearly have an important, and large, place in policy-making and in the study of politics. On the other hand, deliberative models appear to hold great potential for improving the political process in at least some venues, and they have not been extensively tested in either research or practice. In striving to strengthen research on deliberation and to disseminate information about the successes and shortfalls of deliberative experiments, we seek to broaden the range of participatory and decision modes available to citizens as well as the approaches that scholars use to understand political actions and their consequences.

Defining "Practical Deliberation"

Why deliberate? The advocates of deliberative politics emphasize the potentially transformative effect of deliberative participation. March and Olsen, for instance, describe the way in which participation contributes both to creating the individual's identity as a member of a community and to creating understandings of the expectations and responsibilities of participants in particular situations. Correspondingly, the discursive interaction of individuals in collective choice situations helps to mold political processes that are comprehensible and accountable. Unlike the competitive pursuit of individual self-interest, then, deliberative participation both fosters the most valuable traits and capacities of citizens and strengthens the accountability and legitimacy of governance and policy-making. March and Olsen are frank about the idealistic impulse, describing as "romantic" the conception of governance as contributing to the commonweal and shared aspirations for a good life.[53] If March and Olsen focus on current participants, Gutmann's view is from the perspective of the civic education of students. The political practices of the adults who govern schools inevitably serve as models for students; to the extent that deliberation entails a more elevated and civil ideal, it will more effectively inculcate the values and skills needed to live by proceduralism and constitutionalism in the future.

Two additional advantages might be adduced for deliberative processes, these relying less on the potential for transforming individuals than on improving the capacity of the policy-making process to generate workable solutions to difficult collective problems. First, deliberative processes are likely to be better at problem-solving than more competitive arrangements. Deliberation is more open to diverse interests and ideas; where participants actually engage in dialogue about how to solve some common problem rather than simply taking opposed stands or splitting the difference between their initial positions, the probability is increased that they will perceive a resolution that draws on the strengths of both sides.[54] In addition, deliberation, epitomized in Albert O. Hirschman's notion of "voice," may make it easier for governments to learn from their mistakes; where citizens voice complaints rather than simply withdrawing their support when they detect poor performance, the potential is available for government to maintain public involvement while initiating adjustments to correct the problem. Second, deliberation should be less susceptible to stalemate and gridlock than adversarial processes. Theorists such as Sheldon S. Wolin or John Rawls argue that governments relying only on balancing competing interests, in which citizens feel no responsibility to deliberate together on the basis of a sense of shared community, will eventually be immobilized by the gridlock resulting from the unchecked pursuit of interests.[55]

These are strong claims, and the logic behind them is sound, provided one subscribes initially to the presupposition that individuals' identities, preferences, and capacities can develop in response to changes in situation and institutional context. Several of the authors in this book argue persuasively for that view, but the cold water poured on it by Moe's skepticism reminds us that there are persuasive analogies and anecdotes on both sides but little direct empirical evidence to show that deliberative institutions work differently. It is unlikely that a clear comparison between exchange and deliberative models will come anytime soon, but setting the stage for that comparison requires that deliberative institutions be set up and allowed to run long enough to accumulate a track record.

In the balance of this section we focus on the prospects for establishing deliberative processes. Our argument is that the arena of education politics is unusually hospitable to reforms that move toward more deliberation. We concentrate on two sorts of stumbling blocks in the path toward deliberative institutions, stringent requirements that raise the question whether deliberation is a realistic aspiration. In both these areas—the capacity to focus scarce deliberative resources on the most appropriate issues and the capacity to design institutions that are genuinely inclusive of interests—the experience of education politics justifies optimism for the prospects of deliberative reforms.

Which Issues? Deliberation requires the commitment of more time, energy, and intellectual involvement than other forms of political decision making. Although the experience of deliberating over important issues may in time build participatory skills and knowledge, deliberative resources will always be scarce: ordinary citizens, even in the ideal situation, do not have the time, attentiveness, or expertise to support deliberative participation in collective decisions about all the issues that affect their lives.[56] At the same time, the promise of deliberation is typically seen in such rosy hues that the inclination of reformers is to push toward its universal application. We suggest two criteria that distinguish those issues for which deliberation is likely to be appropriate: the problem should involve goods or values that are produced and consumed collectively rather than individually, and the issue should be a "contested" rather than "settled" one.

Because deliberation calls into being a social process, it is appropriate to utilize it for resolving disputes over collective rather than private goods. Collective goods are ones whose provision requires social cooperation (e.g., libraries, roads, clean air, public schools) or which carry symbolic meaning that makes their value hinge on social consumption (e.g., group identities based on religion, language, or culture). Decisions about their allocation raise the salience of collective membership and common experience, and the process of discursive politics offers the occasion for individuals to consider their own identities and their conceptions of their interests in relation to the collectivity. In contrast, deliberative processes are less appropriate for goods that can be allocated adequately by market mechanisms: "economic goods" such as food, clothing, or shelter that are excludable and consumed individually.[57]

By "settled" issues, we have in mind those that are best resolved by authority, or any process in which there is little or no deliberative participation but whose decisions are not normally challenged. Legitimate claims to authority can be made on many grounds, but three are especially relevant to school politics: bureaucracies, which claim authority over routine decisions; professionals, who claim authority on the basis of specialized knowledge; and markets, which claim authority on the basis of efficiency in allocating divisible, material goods. Turning over decisions to legitimate authorities economizes on deliberative resources, allowing them to be focused on "contested" problems where deliberative institutions need to be brought to bear in order to discover a legitimate resolution. If the use of authority to resolve some issues is a rational response to complexity, "over-bureaucratization" of the sort Terry Moe indicts occurs when either markets or democratic participation would be more appropriate mechanisms. While Moe is concerned with carving out a larger role for markets, our interest in deliberation leads us to focus on the challenge for maintaining vigorous democratic control—knowing when to remove an issue from the experts.

To keep authority from supplanting the political judgment of citizens, institutions should foster opportunities for challenge and voicing complaints, and the larger political culture should nurture the sort of critical skepticism that will allow and stimulate ordinary citizens and interest groups to take up these opportunities.[58] To the extent that citizens' deliberative resources are focused on such issues, the likelihood is increased that participation will test the predictions of deliberative democrats. Deliberative theories hold that participation can contribute to socially regarding political values and the skills appropriate to deliberative reasoning, but only certain types of participation promote the transformation of interests and competitive impulses. To the extent that political institutions foster the creativity of deliberative dialogue in which novel options can be devised and debated, in contrast to limiting citizen input to conventional problems or self-interested choices among given possibilities, individual autonomy and self-development are nurtured, and citizenship values are strengthened.

Reforms that seek to move public choice processes toward more deliberation are likely to work better in those political arenas where citizens in the past have shown their adeptness at tackling problems of allocating collective goods or at moving previously settled issues onto the agenda, once valid questions have been raised about the performance of authorities. On both counts, the prospects for deliberation in education politics would appear to be positive. Despite the dearth of recent research on education politics, it is clear that many salient aspects of school politics and citizen participation over educational issues revolve around the sort of collective goods that have the greatest potential for nurturing deliberative values and skills. It is certainly true that the involvement of many parents centers on the quality of their children's education, and yet both parents and other participants in education politics move readily between claims in terms of self-interest and the public interest. And when issues such as bilingual education, charter schools, or funding class size reduction have been politicized over the last few years in California and other states, popular debates over them—whether we agree with the values espoused or not—have reflected at least as well on the reasoning skills of the public as on those of the legislature.

If we consider the place of "authority" in the relations between policymakers and constituents in education politics, the degree of healthy, competent skepticism is striking. Citizens and parents accept the special place of expertise (especially that of teachers) in deciding educational issues, but part and parcel of the tradition of school politics has been the confidence and willingness of community members to challenge bureaucrats and experts when they have overstepped their authority or failed to take community sentiments into account. Not only is the distinction between settled and contested issues apparently well understood, but groups in many districts show a canny appreciation—sometimes to the surprise and chagrin of administrators—for the processes involved in moving issues from settled to contested. Although unsystematic and spotty, the literature on local school politics is rich with occasions when democratic inputs from the community have challenged authority for poor performance; for exceeding the legitimate sphere in terms of function, expertise, or particular goods; and for violating the norm that authorities and citizens should share equally in the risks and burdens of decisions.

Whose Voice? Deliberation is a demanding form of decision making not only because it entails more time and greater involvement with the issues but also because it calls on participants to treat others—especially those with whom they disagree—with genuine respect. As Gutmann points out, the norm of equal political standing is used in deliberative theory to emphasize going beyond tolerance or noninterference (as might characterize the relationship of parties engaged in bargaining) to a process that expresses positive mutual respect. If deliberation is defined by the primacy of talk, honoring in practice the voices and claims of people with different interests, ethnicities, religions, and cultures is a crucial indicator of its successful implementation.

In a world in which different individuals and groups assemble and rank goods in different ways, it is critical that no one group's values define a single authoritative hierarchy. This requirement points toward the importance of bracketing off status hierarchies or significant disparities of resources. The notion of voice emphasizes the legitimate, privileged authority of individuals to express their own interests and experiences rather than depend on representatives to speak for them, and to expect that others will respond with due consideration to the cognitive content of their challenges and interpretations.[59] Voice is an essential component of deliberative arrangements, because the social pressure of apparently consensual meanings can silence the expression by the powerless of complaints against the injustices of a dominant group.[60] Deliberative democrats seek to go beyond the conventional norm against translating economic power or social prestige into political influence to hold that talk should be the sole means (other than votes) for resolving conflicts. Such arrangements, "if pursued consistently and thoroughly, endow talk with an authoritative status as a medium of resolving disputes and organizing collective actions."[61] Through use, talk and the agencies and arenas in which authoritative talk takes place gain the ability to shape the narratives or "accounts" that translate the ambiguous events of real world history into comprehensible stories.[62] By interpreting the roles of individuals, groups, and governments in a less competitive and adversarial frame, such accounts influence the opportunity and capacity for governments to adapt and to shape the subjective conditions for political legitimacy.

Compared with other major social institutions, the political context of education strengthens the prospects for deliberative participation. The small size of the arena of local school politics, for one, fosters participation and the development of deliberative values and skills. Localism itself has advantages in encouraging deliberative participation: the issues are likely to be familiar, and knowledge about them obtained fairly directly, with little mediation from experts, political leaders, or the media. The entry costs for participation in school politics are low: information is relatively accessible, meetings are open, and participation by ordinary citizens and parents is common. The face-to-face nature of interactions in school politics makes it harder to objectify an opponent and more likely to come to understand the situation as one's opposite number views it. In addition to fostering meaningful participation, schools also lead other social institutions in taking positive actions to integrate different identities into a common enterprise. Over recent decades, schools have begun to establish a tradition of inclusiveness, recognizing diversity, taking different backgrounds and needs as the starting point, and working from there rather than forcing minorities and students with special needs immediately to adopt the majority culture. Notable examples include bilingual programs, those for students with disabilities, and the trend of decisions on school prayer. Finally, to be self-sustaining, political participation must ultimately offer citizens the promise of affecting policy. Because of its scale, school politics rates well on this criterion: it is typically quite easy to follow one's participatory contribution and to track its influence on policy outputs.

If the arena of school politics offers unusual potential for the development of more deliberative arrangements, how can scholars best equip themselves to observe and interpret the variety of political practices, old and new? We now turn to this question.

BUILDING A NEW RESEARCH AGENDA

Our assumption that the politics of education cannot be explained by a single conceptual model stems from its fragmentation as well as from the diversity of formal institutions and citizen groups who take an active part in school politics. As our discussion in the previous section illustrates, responsibility for public education is shared not only across the three levels of government but also within them—for example, by courts and legislatures. These arenas are characterized by different models of participation and decision making, each embodying different institutional rules and norms. Just as we have argued that a deliberative model is likely to work better for some issues than for others and in smaller venues where barriers to participation are low, we would also agree with analysts who assume that exchange models predominate in many legislatures and in other arenas characterized by the presence of well-organized interests and issues of limited concern to the general public. The challenge for scholars is to structure their research to capture this variation in modes of participation and decision making across venues. For example, an exchange model may explain the politics of many state legislatures and local school boards but not all of them, nor is it likely to explain the dynamics of decision making in most charter schools. Similarly, those who yearn for a more deliberative politics should not expect to find it in venues whose institutional rules and norms favor bargaining to settle interest-based conflicts. With such variation in mind, we compare the major premises of the exchange and deliberative models and then conclude the section by suggesting how future research might be structured so as to understand better manifestations of both models in the many arenas of education politics.

The key assumptions of the exchange model are at odds with the deliberative approach in four especially notable ways. In exchange models, actors' interests are given exogenously, they are unambiguous and easily recognized by their holders, and they remain fixed unless new information shows some goal to be infeasible. Deliberative models, on the other hand, acknowledge that citizens are frequently ambivalent about public policy questions, not necessarily indifferent but aware of reasonable claims on both sides. Deliberation is the means of gathering information and hearing arguments; participating acknowledges that one's opinion is not set and might change. Second, exchange models depict actors as maximizers of material self-interest, brought together by the potential for a mutually advantageous exchange over some particular good, calculating closely the costs and benefits of prospective bargains, and relying on explicit contracts or threats of retaliation to enforce stated agreements. The deliberative approach suggests that politics is more like a conversation, a public dialogue among participants whose different personal histories, perspectives, and claims are legitimate aspects of the conversation. The relationship among the participants has value in itself, and the goal of sustaining the dialogue makes clarifying implicit understandings a conversational process open to informal expressions of reciprocity rather than a matter for contractual agreement.[63]

Third, the motivations of actors in the exchange model are purely individualistic; membership in a community is relevant only to the extent that it gives one a bargaining advantage or presents collective action dilemmas and opportunities for free riding. Alternatively, the deliberative approach seeks to take explicit account of the way people develop identities as members of a community and act on norms of responsibility or duty that inhere in particular social situations.[64] Taking account of the way individual identity is tied into social relationships is critical to understanding deliberative democracy, for the effectiveness of deliberation hinges on the way it connects individual interest with the public realm. Actual deliberation typically calls on citizens' sense that they share some responsibility for helping to remedy widespread grievances or common problems, or on their acknowledgement of norms that sanction excessive self-interest and commend reasonable unselfishness. This communitarian connection implies two predictions for the outcome of relevant comparisons: compared with exchange models, decision making by way of deliberation is slower and more social (it involves taking the time to think and talk together to develop informed judgments that are not mere aggregations of individual preferences) and deliberative decision making strengthens the community's capacity for giving explicit consideration to the future consequences of current choices for the public as a whole.

Finally, the two approaches differ in their conceptualization of government and the public realm. In exchange models, the role of government is to contribute to efficiency, for instance by disseminating information about choices among policy alternatives and by guaranteeing the enforcement of contracts. The deliberative approach, on the other hand, alerts researchers to the potential that institutions and elites (including, for instance, business leaders and the media as well as elected officials) have a role in shaping the public realm, both as a deliberative space and as a focal point around which collective identities and narratives can develop. Because social scientists have relatively little systematic information about how deliberative decision making evolves, it is impossible to specify in detail what a deliberative public realm entails, but researchers clearly need to be aware of both its procedural aspects (for instance, those provisions that ensure inclusiveness, voice, and political standing for subpublics) and its emergent properties (for instance, norms fostering reflective consideration by discouraging narratives built around themes of conflict and sensationalism or norms protecting the civility of discourse by rewarding careful listening and evidence of honest attempts to understand the validity of others' claims).

Turning to suggestions for future research, three themes that run through this chapter suggest possible research agendas. First, education politics needs to be viewed as more than just a variable explaining policy outcomes. Rather, education should be seen as a major political institution in which core societal values are shaped and transmitted and, as the governmental unit spatially and psychologically closest to citizens, the source of many of their images of politics. As a practical matter, this shift in perspective should lead researchers to focus on topics and venues that have been ignored in recent research: education politics at the local level, including formal and informal modes of participation and decision making; a greater emphasis on the study of political processes rather than just policy outcomes; and theoretically grounded examinations of how the public forms its opinions about the schools, including the sources of what may seem to be contradictory attitudes and beliefs.

A second direction suggested by our analysis is the need to examine the relationships among the multiple arenas in which education politics occurs. Despite reformers' attempts over the past century to make the education governance system more coherent, with policies ranging from school district consolidation to systemic reform and state standards setting, it remains both vertically and horizontally fragmented. Yet, as the discussion in the previous section indicated, that fragmentation persists because its roots are deeply ingrained in American culture and in the design of our institutions. Whether one views

fragmentation in education governance as a weakness that inhibits coherent policy or a strength that promotes citizen access and governmental responsiveness,
it is likely to remain an enduring feature of public education. Consequently, the
nature of that fragmentation needs to be understood, not only in order to design
more effective policy but also to develop credible participatory opportunities and
thus strengthen the public's connection to the schools.

Several implications for designing research follow from this perspective.
First, research on the politics of education needs to be explicitly comparative
across institutional venues. Differences in how they each deal with the broad political functions of participation and decision making are likely to be explained
by such factors as the size of an arena, the scope of its authority, the modes of
access, and the rules governing time lines for decision making. These and other
institutional factors, including patterns of historical development, need to be examined systematically across different political arenas.

Second, one aim of such research should be to determine what effect variation across venues has on patterns of citizen participation, policy outcomes, and
capacity to govern the educational system. The level and direction of those effects are likely to depend, at least partly, on the extent to which dominant modes
of participation and decision making are consistent across arenas. For example,
decisions about which curricular values should be reflected in classroom instruction are often shared by a variety of state level actors, including the legislature and state board of education, and by the school board and school site
councils at the local level. In such cases, school site decisions may result from
deliberation among parents and teachers with fairly open access for all interested
participants. However, if such decisions must be ratified at higher levels where
access is more limited, participation structured through more rigid rules, or decisions reached through bargaining among well-organized groups, differences
across venues may not only make it difficult for the local school perspective to
be heard, but they also may lead to incoherent policies. For that reason, a comparative perspective, focused on the institutional rules and norms of each arena,
is needed.

A third implication is that researchers should be open to the possibility that
several different models are needed to explain different aspects of education politics. The exchange perspective has been the dominant model in studies of U.S.
politics, including education, and it is likely to continue to explain much of what
happens. Yet there is sufficient evidence to suggest that other models better explain some dimensions of education politics. Several authors in this book have
presented the deliberative model as a prime alternative because of its normative
appeal and its consistency with the traditional aims of civic education. Clearly,
there are other models that might be considered, but the deliberative approach
represents a strong case for taking a broader theoretical perspective. If scholars
employ a model, such as rational choice or game theory, that is blind to deliberation, they will miss potentially beneficial knowledge. On the other hand, if they

watch carefully for deliberative processes but find none, they will lose nothing in their ability to track competition among self-interested individuals and groups.

Our focus on deliberation as one mode of political interaction suggests a final direction for future research. Scholarly understanding of the exchange model is well developed, both theoretically and empirically. The deliberative approach, in contrast, is fairly well specified as a normative model but has not been tested extensively through empirical research. Therefore, we would argue that developing a better understanding of the conditions under which deliberation is likely to occur and the extent to which the assumptions of the normative model hold up in practice represents two areas for fruitful inquiry.

The discursive nature of deliberation dictates an approach to data collection and analysis that focuses on process and interpretation. Unlike research on exchange models, which often compare conditions before and after some intervention or weigh inputs against outputs, the essentials of deliberation are in the intervening process. Unlike voting models or theoretical social welfare functions, for instance, which aggregate preferences in various stylized and easily replicated ways, deliberative outcomes depend on the specific participants and the sequence and content of the conversation. For instance, a before/after comparison of, say, school district expenditures on music programs does reveal information about priorities, but it gives little insight into how parents and administrators weighed the trade-offs of a vocational versus a nonvocational curriculum or of music versus athletics. The outcome alone tells little about how deliberation works or what difference it makes to the participants. These reflections suggest that research on deliberation would rely heavily on case study techniques, process tracing, and relatively unstructured interviews with multiple participants who come to the deliberative process from a variety of backgrounds and standpoints. If the nature of public deliberation points to the "how" of research, it also suggests the "where": established legislative bodies or relatively small-scale local communities, where familiarity with local issues will strengthen people's sense of efficacy and where the prospect of future face-to-face encounters will help undergird norms of civility and reciprocity.[65]

CONCLUSIONS

At a time when a large majority of Americans feel that they cannot rely on the national government or other large institutions to tackle a problem and get it right—and the ratings for state and local governments are not much better—almost equally large majorities praise the performance of their local schools. Indeed, the comparatively high ratings for public education have persisted over a period during which the schools have been called on to help solve some of the most trying of social problems—racial equality, the rights of religious minorities, caring for the children of poor and dysfunctional families—and when they have become the battleground for social issues that are only tangentially related to the process of teaching and learning—the treatment of immigrants, the role of religion in society. The public surveys a similar onslaught of challenges for the federal government and sees a system tied in knots as partisan and interest group demands gridlock the policy process, and yet the schools seem to plod resolutely along while coping with a mounting list of challenges. Political scientists have a fairly clear idea of how events in national politics influence the beliefs and actions of citizens, and yet we know surprisingly little about the citizen politics of education, particularly at the local level.

This chapter has highlighted two reasons for rethinking research on the politics of education. One is that school politics has been one of the great lacunae of research by both scholars of education and political scientists. We have little beyond a few insightful but narrow case studies, framed around the theoretical models of twenty-five years ago, to help us understand why the electorate's view of public schools is more robust than that of other governmental units or large private sector institutions. We know a good deal about how federal and state mandates were implemented to expand and reshape the functions that local schools serve, but we have missed the political process of adjustment, consultation, doubt, and support through which those schools and their local communities have met the challenge. It is not only the lack of information about an important aspect of society and politics but also the value of observing schools as a critical comparison case in our attempt to understand how citizens relate to government and public endeavors that makes this rationale a strong one.

The other reason does not look first to schools but to ideas about politics, ideas that are deeply influenced by the notions of active, skeptical citizenship that the best schools seek to nurture in their students. Here we have argued that the ideas of deliberative democrats are compelling enough that they deserve to be treated as theories of politics—translated into usable research designs and concepts, not simply issued as abstract normative exhortations toward better citizenship. For a number of reasons, one of the best research sites for observing deliberative politics is the context of the local school and its community. In fact, we argue that just as the educational performance of schools is routinely judged by such indicators as student achievement on standardized tests and students' postschool prospects, so should the political performance of the education system be judged by the standards of deliberative democracy—i.e., access, contribution to a civic identity, equality of political standing, opportunities for considering the merits of policy options, and policy choices broadly perceived as legitimate by the public.

At the same time, we acknowledge that researchers' spotty empirical knowledge about education politics and our limited understanding of how deliberative models might work in practice mean that we cannot predict with any certainty how a more deliberative politics would differ from the political landscape we have outlined in this chapter. Our survey of the current state of education politics indicates that public support for the schools is stable and moderately strong, but also diffuse and not readily translated into active, broad-based participation. Value conflicts over the purposes of education persist and the institutions that govern schools are fragmented. We do not really know whether these conditions differ across local communities depending on how deliberative their institutions are. Nor can we be assured, without a good deal of additional research, of the accuracy of deliberative theorists' prediction that deliberation will lead to participants having a greater understanding of each other's positions and that this understanding will result in more consensual decisions. Indeed, in the short or medium term, deliberation might only exacerbate differences, as people who do not ordinarily talk with one another clarify the true extent of their differences. And yet both the promise of a more deliberative politics and strong evidence suggesting that it already exists in a number of venues are sufficient reasons for researchers to take its possibility into account as they seek a fuller understanding of the political values and institutions shaping public education.

NOTES

1. Gerald E. Sroufe, "Politics of Education at the Federal Level," in *The Study of Educational Politics*, ed. John D. Scribner and Donald H. Layton (Bristol, Pa.: Falmer Press, 1995), 75–88, argues that even in education policy research focused on the federal level, politics has been ignored. In these studies, political variables have often been accorded insufficient attention, causing researchers to underestimate their role in explaining policy outcomes and to reach invalid conclusions.

2. There are some exceptions to this scholarly neglect of local education politics. For example, a number of analysts have focused on the ongoing implementation of the Chicago school reforms which have delegated greater authority to the elected members of local school councils and have altered the relationship between the school district and city government. See G. Alfred Hess, *Restructuring Urban Schools: A Chicago Perspective* (New York: Teachers College Press, 1995), and Anthony S. Bryk et al., "The State of Chicago School Reform," *Phi Delta Kappan* 76, 1 (1994): 74–78. Several recent studies have also looked comparatively at education politics in the nation's largest urban school districts. See Jeffrey R. Henig, Richard C. Hula, Marion Orr, and Desiree S. Pedescleaux, *The Color of School Reform: Race, Politics, and the Challenge of Urban Education* (Princeton, N.J.: Princeton University Press, 1999); Marion Orr, *Black Social Capital: The Politics of School Reform in Baltimore, 1986–1998* (Lawrence: University Press of Kansas, 1999); John Portz, Lana Stein, and Robin R. Jones, *City Schools and City Politics: Institutions and Leadership in Pittsburgh, Boston, and St. Louis* (Lawrence: University Press of Kansas, 1999); Clarence N. Stone, ed., *Changing Urban Education* (Lawrence: University Press of Kansas, 1998); and Wilbur C. Rich, *Black Mayors and School Politics* (New York: Garland, 1996). However, a review of the most recent edition of the major politics of education textbook, Frederick M. Wirt and Michael W. Kirst, *The Political Dynamics of American Education* (Berkeley, Calif.: McCutchan, 1997), indicates that more than 50 percent of the studies of local education politics cited were conducted

prior to 1980, and almost no research has been conducted on education politics in any communities other than large cities.

3. For example, Wirt and Kirst, *Political Dynamics,* 1997, use David Easton's notion of political systems analysis, first presented over thirty years ago, as a heuristic for organizing their concepts and data. Another widely used politics of education textbook by Joel H. Spring, *Conflict of Interests: The Politics of American Education* (New York: Longman, 1993), organizes its arguments around a popularized version of elite theory. Even a recent review article on the politics of education at the federal level suggested an eclectic approach that draws on conceptual work on interest groups, federalism, and symbolic politics that is over thirty years old without considering how these frameworks have been modified as a result of subsequent research (Sroufe, "Politics of Education"). Work drawing on newer theories has been limited. A few authors have suggested that rational choice theory might be used to study the politics of education and have explicated the relevant concepts for education researchers, but this framework has rarely been used to examine political questions in education (William Lowe Boyd, Robert L. Crowson, and Tyll van Geel, "Rational Choice Theory and the Politics of Education: Promise and Limits," in *The Study of Educational Politics,* ed. Jay D. Scribner and Donald H. Layton [Bristol, Pa.: Falmer Press, 1995], 127–45). Although some of the theoretical work that served as a precursor to the "new institutionalism" in sociology (e.g., John W. Meyer and Brian Rowan, "Institutionalized Organizations: Formal Structure as Myth and Ceremony," *American Journal of Sociology* 83 (1977): 340–63), was based on research on schools, little subsequent research has drawn on this theoretical perspective.

4. Amy Gutmann, *Democratic Education* (Princeton, N.J.: Princeton University Press, 1987), 153, makes an especially thoughtful and wide-ranging case for civic education, and her chapter in this book integrates recent research, building on the logic of her earlier work. See also Robert D. Putnam, *Making Democracy Work: Civic Traditions in Modern Italy* (Princeton, N.J.: Princeton University Press, 1993).

5. Pamela Johnston Conover, "Political Socialization: Where's the Politics?" in *Political Behavior,* vol. 3. of *Political Science: Looking to the Future,* ed. William Crotty (Evanston, Ill.: Northwestern University Press, 1991), 125–52, makes a similar argument in noting that past socialization research neglected the politics of socialization by losing "sight both of the state as a controller of socialization, and of social institutions as agents of socialization. We lost sight of the fact that the political system's components are related, that there is a connection between the state and those social institutions that most directly shape the character of future citizens. In this way, we also lost sight of socialization as a political process through which rulers seek to ensure their rule" (140).

6. Robert B. Westbrook, "Public Schooling and American Democracy," in *Democracy, Education, and the Schools,* ed. Roger Soder (San Francisco: Jossey-Bass, 1996), 125–50, states more bluntly the link between the nature of politics and civic education: "Even if one could make American public schools more effective vehicles of civic education; it would not be worth doing as long as American public life remains as anemic as it is today. As the neo-Hamiltonians contend, there is no point to educating children for a citizenship that will not be there to practice when they become adults" (141).

7. David Mathews, *Is There a Public for Public Schools?* (Dayton, Ohio: Kettering Foundation Press, 1996).

8. Jean Johnson and John Immerwahr, *First Things First: What Americans Expect from the Public Schools* (New York: Public Agenda, 1994).

9. Lawrence A. Cremin, *Popular Education and Its Discontents* (New York: Harper and Row, 1990), 103–4.

10. Lorraine Smith Pangle and Thomas L. Pangle, *The Learning of Liberty: The Educational Ideas of the American Founders* (Lawrence: University Press of Kansas, 1993), 188, for instance, note the persistence of "competing conceptions of the scope and importance of religion as a source of civic and moral education," reflected in the differing views of Madison, Jefferson, and Benjamin Rush.

11. Lorraine M. McDonnell, *The Politics of State Testing: Implementing New Student Assessments* (Los Angeles: UCLA/National Center for Research on Evaluation, Standards, and Student Testing, 1997); Martha M. McCarthy, "People of Faith as Political Activists in Public Schools," *Education and Urban Society* 28, 3 (1996): 308–26; and William Lowe Boyd et al., "Social Traditionalists, Religious Conservatives, and the Politics of Outcomes-Based Education: Pennsylvania and Beyond," *Education and Urban Society* 28, 3 (1996): 347–65.

12. Johnson and Immerwahr, *First Things First.*

13. During the 1974 crisis in Kanawha County, West Virginia, for example, Christian fundamentalists argued that language arts textbooks subverted traditional morality. In this case, the schools were actually closed for a time in order to ensure students' safety in the wake of shootings and firebombings; see Ann L. Page and Donald A. Clelland, "The Kanawha County Textbook Controversy: A Study of the Politics of Life Style Concern," *Social Forces* 57 (1978): 265–81. More recent challenges to textbook adoptions in California have been more peaceful but equally vigorous; see Louise Adler, "Institutional Responses: Public School Curriculum and Religious Conservatives in California," *Education and Urban Society* 28, 3 (1996): 327–46. The court case that exemplifies the tension between religious and secular values in textbook decisions is *Mozert* v. *Hawkins Public Schools,* in which the court required the schools to provide the plaintiffs' children with alternative reading material because it determined that the plaintiffs were arguing from a sincere religious position and that the government's interest in maintaining consistency in textbooks did not warrant interference with the plaintiffs' free exercise of religion. Political theorists have argued that "a civic education that satisfies the *Mozert* parents' objections . . . would interfere with teaching the virtues and skills of liberal democratic citizenship" (Amy Gutmann, "Civic Education and Social Diversity," *Ethics* 105 [1995]: 557–79); see also Stephen Macedo, "Liberal Civic Education and Religious Fundamentalism: The Case of God v. John Rawls?" *Ethics* 105 (1995): 468–96.

14. Lowell C. Rose and Alec M. Gallup, "The 30th Annual Phi Delta Kappa/Gallup Poll of the Public's Attitudes Toward the Public Schools," *Phi Delta Kappan,* 80, 1 (1998): 41–56. Another national poll found that over 50 percent of the public rated the public schools in their community as either excellent (16 percent) or good (39 percent). As with other polls, this one also indicated that parents of school-age children rate the schools in their community even higher, with 71 percent judging them to be good or excellent; see Jean Johnson et al., *Assignment Incomplete: The Unfinished Business of Education Reform* (New York: Public Agenda Foundation, 1995).

15. Stanley M. Elam, Lowell C. Rose, and Alec M. Gallup, "The 25th Annual Phi

Delta Kappa/Gallup Poll of the Public's Attitudes Toward the Public Schools," *Phi Delta Kappan* 75, 2 (1993): 137–52.

16. Stanley M. Elam, Lowell C. Rose, and Alec M. Gallup, "The 24th Annual Gallup/Phi Delta Kappa Poll of the Public's Attitudes Toward the Public Schools," *Phi Delta Kappan* 74, 1 (1992): 41–53.

17. Stanley M. Elam and Lowell C. Rose, "The 27th Annual Phi Delta Kappa/Gallup Poll of the Public's Attitudes Toward the Public Schools," *Phi Delta Kappan* 77, 1 (1995): 41–56.

18. Elam, Rose, and Gallup, "The 25th Annual Phi Delta Kappa/Gallup Poll," and Johnson et al., *Assignment Incomplete.*

19. *Washington Post*/Kaiser Family Foundation/Harvard University Survey Project, *Why Don't Americans Trust the Government?* (Washington, D.C.: Author, 1996).

20. Rose and Gallup, "The 30th Annual Phi Delta Kappa/Gallup Poll."

21. When respondents were asked whether they "favor or oppose allowing students and parents to choose a private school to attend at government expense," they split evenly, with 48 percent supporting the idea and the same proportion opposing it. When they were asked the same question with the word "public" substituted for "government," the proportion supporting the idea dropped to 44 percent, and those opposed rose to 52 percent. However, the 44 percent supporting the concept represents a significant, steady increase over four years from only 24 percent supporting it in 1993; see Stanley M. Elam, Lowell C. Rose, and Alec M. Gallup, "The 29th Annual Phi Delta Kappa/Gallup Poll of the Public's Attitudes Toward the Public Schools," *Phi Delta Kappan* 79, 1 (1997): 41–56.

22. Johnson et al., *Assignment Incomplete.*

23. For example, in a 1988 survey of school board members from across the country, these local officials reported that about 25 percent of the registered voters in their community typically voted in school elections; see Beatrice H. Cameron, Keith E. Underwood and Jim C. Fortune, "Politics and Power: How You're Selected and Elected to Lead this Nation's Schools," *American School Board Journal* (1988): 17–19. Turnout is often lower than this, particularly in large city districts when school elections do not coincide with national or state ones. In a recent election for seats on the Los Angeles Unified School District board, for example, turnout was only 11 percent; Amy Pyle, "L.A. Elections 5th District School Board: Every Vote Counts Now in Tight Runoff Race," *Los Angeles Times,* 8 June 1995. Similarly, the New York Board of Elections estimated turnout for a recent community board election to be about 8 to 10 percent of the registered voters; Jacques Steinberg, "In Tallying School Board Election Results, Time Is No Object," *New York Times,* 9 May 1996.

24. Stanley M. Elam, Lowell C. Rose, and Alec M. Gallup, "The 26th Annual Phi Delta Kappa/Gallup Poll of the Public's Attitudes Toward the Public Schools," *Phi Delta Kappan* 76, 1 (1994): 41–64. Those without children in the schools tend to judge the schools more negatively than parents of school-age children (e.g., 42 percent of those with no children in school rated their local schools as either an A or B in 1997 compared with 56 percent of public school parents). However, on almost every proposed policy solution asked about on national opinion surveys, the responses of the two groups are not significantly different (e.g., on high school graduation tests, curriculum standards, school uniforms, and community service).

25. Rose, Gallup, and Elam, "The 29th Annual Phi Delta Kappa/Gallup Poll."

26. National Center for Education Statistics, *Digest of Education Statistics 1993,* NCES 93-292 (Washington, D.C.: U.S. Department of Education, 1993), Table 20.

27. National Center for Education Statistics, *The Condition of Education 1998,* NCES 98-013 (Washington, D.C.: U.S. Department of Education, 1998), 134.

28. National Center for Education Statistics, *Digest of Education Statistics, 1997,* NCES 98-015 (Washington, D.C.: U.S. Department of Education, 1997), Table 21. Poverty rates are 42 percent, 39 percent, and 16 percent, respectively. Not only are ethnic minority students concentrated in large city districts, but they also attend segregated schools. Between 1972 and 1986, the percentage of African-American students in predominantly minority schools remained at 63 percent. In large city schools such as those in Chicago, the degree of racial isolation is significantly greater than the national average. In 1990, 98 percent of African-American and Hispanic students attending Chicago public schools were enrolled in schools whose student bodies were more than 50 percent minority; see Kenneth K. Wong and Paul E. Peterson, "Can Big-City School Systems Be Governed?" Paper presented at the 1992 Annual Meeting of the American Political Science Association, Chicago, 1992.

29. Virginia Sapiro, Steven J. Rosenstone, Warren E. Miller, and the National Election Studies, *American National Election Studies, 1948–1997* (CD-ROM), ICPSR ed. (Ann Arbor, Mich.: Inter-University Consortium for Political and Social Research, 1998). These proportions are roughly typical of recent midterm elections. They differ slightly from those for presidential elections, when overall turnout is higher, but the lower turnout of midterm contests resembles school board and local bond elections.

30. James Madison, Alexander Hamilton, and John Jay, *The Federalist Papers*, ed. C. Rossiter (New York: New American Library, 1961), no. 39, 240–46.

31. Thomas James, "State Authority and the Politics of Educational Change," *Review of Research in Education* 17 (1991): 169–224.

32. James A. Morone, *The Democratic Wish: Popular Participation and the Limits of American Government* (New York: Basic Books, 1990), 1.

33. David B. Tyack, "School Governance in the United States: Historical Puzzles and Anomalies," in *Decentralization and School Improvement: Can We Fulfill the Promise?* ed. Jane Hannaway and Martin Carnoy (San Francisco: Jossey-Bass, 1993), 17–18 (internal citations omitted). Richard F. Elmore, "School Decentralization: Who Gains? Who Loses?" in *Decentralization and School Improvement*, 33–54, notes that reform cycles in American education have alternated between centralization and decentralization. He cites the formation of the early common schools as a way to put education in the hands of the people, the Progressive reforms that centralized school governance in the hopes of making it more broadly accountable and efficient, the 1960s movement to decentralize urban schools as a way to address racial injustices, the centralizing reforms of the early 1980s to improve school performance and make it more consistent across jurisdictions, and the school-site management and parental choice initiatives in the late 1990s to move school governance closer to those most affected by it.

34. Prominent examples include advisory groups, such as those for the federal Title I program that provides assistance to poor and low-achieving students, or service providers, such as community groups working under Job Training Partnership Act (JTPA) contracts.

35. Kenneth K. Wong, "Governance Structure, Resource Allocation, and Equity Policy," *Review of Research in Education* 20 (1994): 257–89.

36. Quite interestingly, respondents expressed as much trust in teachers' union representatives and the state's governor as in local elected officials (28 percent for all these groups). Their greatest trust rests with parents and teachers; over two-thirds expressed significant trust in these two groups. See Elam, Rose, and Gallup, "The 26th Annual Phi Delta Kappa/Gallup Poll"; Johnson and Immerwahr, *First Things First;* Elam and Rose, "The 27th Annual Phi Delta Kappa/Gallup Poll."

37. Terry M. Moe, "Political Institutions: The Neglected Side of the Story, " *Journal of Law, Economics, and Organization* 6 (1990): 213–53.

38. David K. Cohen and James P. Spillane, "Policy and Practice: The Relations Between Governance and Instruction," *Review of Research in Education* 18 (1992): 7, 11.

39. David J. Jung and David L. Kirp, "Law as an Instrument of Educational Policy-Making," *American Journal of Comparative Law* 32 (1984): 625–78.

40. From the perspective of democratic deliberation, then, the role of the courts in education policy is ambiguous. Theorists such as Rawls and Habermas envision the discursive context of the courtroom as paradigmatic of deliberative arrangements: claims enter the legal domain clothed in elaborate reasons and justifications, and they are adjudicated in a framework of accepted rules of argument, evidence and inference that encourages reflection. Irrespective of whether any actual proceeding measures up to this ideal, however, the experience of judicial intervention in education policy has more often polarized and solidified adversarial positions than encouraged dialogue aimed at sympathetic understanding of opposed claims in a context of common membership.

41. David N. Plank and William L. Boyd, "Antipolitics, Education, and Institutional Choice: The Flight from Democracy," *American Educational Research Journal* 31, 2 (1994): 264.

42. Richard F. Elmore and Milbrey W. McLaughlin, *Steady Work: Policy, Practice, and the Reform of American Education* (Santa Monica, Calif.: RAND, 1988).

43. Lorraine M. McDonnell, "Assessment Policy as Persuasion and Regulation," *American Journal of Education* 102, 4 (1994): 394–420.

44. Susan H. Fuhrman and Richard F. Elmore, "Understanding Local Control in the Wake of State Education Reform," *Educational Evaluation and Policy Analysis* 12, 1 (1990): 82–96.

45. Tim L. Mazzoni, "State Policy-Making and School Reform: Influences and Influentials," in *The Study of Educational Politics*, ed. Jay D. Scribner and Donald H. Layton (Bristol, Pa.: Falmer Press, 1994), 53–73.

46. McDonnell, *The Politics of State Testing.*

47. Barbara L. Jackson and James G. Cibulka, "Leadership Turnover and Business Mobilization: The Changing Political Ecology of Urban School Systems," in *The Politics of Urban Education in the United States*, ed. James G. Cibulka, Rodney J. Reed, and Kenneth K. Wong (Bristol, Pa.: Falmer Press, 1992), 71.

48. Steve Farkas, *Divided Within, Besieged Without: The Politics of Education in Four American School Districts* (New York: Public Agenda Foundation, 1993), 28.

49. Nancy Wride, "Beyond the Bake Sale: Building a New PTA," *Los Angeles Times,* 22 June 1996.

50. Robert D. Putnam, "Tuning In, Tuning Out: The Strange Disappearance of Social Capital in America," *PS: Political Science and Politics* 28, 4 (1995): 664–83.

51. Hess, *Restructuring Urban Schools.* In contrast with these promising results,

however, Kenneth K. Wong, Robert Dreeben, Lawrence Lynn, Robert Meyer, and Gail Sunderman, *System-Wide Governance in the Chicago Public Schools: Findings and Recommendations for Institutional Redesign* (Chicago: Department of Education and Irving B. Harris Graduate School of Public Policy Studies, University of Chicago, 1995), found that over the four-year period between 1989 and 1993, voter turnout in Chicago LSC elections declined by 55 percent, from an average of 588 votes per school to 264.

52. Elmore, *School Decentralization,* 33–54; Susan A. Mohrman and Priscilla Wohlstetter, *School-Based Management: Organizing for High Performance* (San Francisco: Jossey-Bass, 1994); and Carol H. Weiss, "The Four 'I's' of School Reform: How Interests, Ideology, Information, and Institution Affect Teachers and Principals," *Harvard Educational Review* 65, 4 (1995): 571–92.

53. James G. March and Johan P. Olsen, *Democratic Governance* (New York: Free Press, 1995), 6.

54. Jane J. Mansbridge, "A Deliberative Theory of Interest Representation," in *The Politics of Interests: Interest Groups Transformed,* ed. Mark P. Petracca (Boulder, Colo.: Westview Press, 1992), 32–57.

55. Albert O. Hirschman, *Exit, Voice, and Loyalty* (Cambridge, Mass.: Harvard University Press, 1970); Sheldon S. Wolin, *Politics and Vision: Continuity and Innovation in Western Political Thought* (Boston: Little, Brown, 1960); John Rawls, "The Idea of an Overlapping Consensus," *Oxford Journal of Legal Studies* 7 (1987): 1–25; Theodore Lowi, *The End of Liberalism* (New York: Norton, 1969); and Michael J. Sandel, "The Procedural Republic and the Unencumbered Self," *Political Theory* 12, 1 (1984): 81–96.

56. Robert Dahl, *After the Revolution? Authority in a Good Society* (New Haven, Conn.: Yale University Press, 1970), 40–56.

57. Mark Warren, "Deliberative Democracy and Authority," *American Political Science Review* 90, 1 (1996): 46–60, and Amy Gutmann and Dennis Thompson, *Democracy and Disagreement* (Cambridge, Mass.: Belknap Press of Harvard University Press, 1996).

58. Richard E. Flathman, *The Practice of Political Authority* (Chicago: University of Chicago Press, 1980); Warren, "Deliberative Democracy and Authority"; and Jane J. Mansbridge, *Beyond Adversary Democracy* (Chicago: University of Chicago Press, 1983).

59. Susan Bickford, *The Dissonance of Democracy: Listening, Conflict, and Citizenship* (Ithaca, N.Y.: Cornell University Press, 1996); Warren, "Deliberative Democracy and Authority"; Simone Chambers, *Reasonable Democracy: Jürgen Habermas and the Politics of Discourse* (Ithaca, N.Y.: Cornell University Press, 1996); and James Bohman, *Public Deliberation: Pluralism, Complexity, and Democracy* (Cambridge, Mass.: MIT Press, 1996). Deliberative participation, moreover, should not be conceived as being conducted only by individuals. Indeed, interest groups and issue organizations are not only the prime means by which individuals compensate for shortages and inequalities of deliberative resources but also the centers around which individuals develop their political identities and conceptions of their interests. Challenges to the status quo in terms of inclusiveness are typically brought by dissenting groups or subpublics, "communities of interpretation" who share meanings and among whom the accumulation of common experience and the development of norms are likely; cf. Seyla Benhabib, *Situating the Self* (New York: Routledge, 1991), and Iris Marion Young, "Asymmetrical Reciprocity: On Moral Respect, Wonder, and Enlarged Thought," *Constellations* 3, 3 (1997): 340–63.

60. Our emphasis on the importance of establishing and protecting the participation

of diverse, legitimate voices explains our rejection of Richard Rorty's notion of a "liberal utopia" with a "public sphere" consisting of a small core of "consensual beliefs" (*Contingency, Irony, and Solidarity* [New York: Cambridge University Press, 1989]; cf. Keith Topper, "Richard Rorty, Liberalism, and the Politics of Redescription," *American Political Science Review* 89, 4 [1995]: 954–65). In a general way, one can imagine two approaches to the problem of the scarcity of deliberative resources: (1) to constrict and simplify the public space until ordinary citizens could be expected to have sufficient resources to participate in most or all of the issues that were relevant to them, or (2) to arrange deliberative institutions and processes in such a way that deliberative resources were directed toward those issues where they would have the most significant effect (contested issues rather than settled issues, issues with good prospects for participation to foster self-transformation rather than stimulate individualistic competition). The second route is more difficult and messier for institutional design, but it is less likely than the first to allow significant inequalities and diverse needs to be missed in the "silence" of shared meanings.

61. Warren, "Deliberative Democracy and Authority," 50. It is not necessary that deliberation be so effective as to create its own ethical commitments, as Jürgen Habermas, *Moral Consciousness and Communicative Action*, trans. Christian Lehnardt and Sherry Weber Nicholsen (Cambridge, Mass.: MIT Press, 1990), argues, but only that individuals become convinced, as Warren argues, that "talk is better than the alternatives, such as fighting or coercive imposition, and design institutions in such a way that recourse to these alternatives is difficult" (50).

62. March and Olsen, *Democratic Governance,* chap. 5.

63. Gary J. Miller, "Managerial Dilemmas: Political Leadership in Hierarchies," in *The Limits of Rationality,* ed. Karen S. Cook and Margaret Levi (Chicago: University of Chicago Press, 1990), 324–48, shows the limited role of contract and calculation even in situations that appear to be paradigmatic for rational contracting—as in the employment relation, where effective leadership in corporate hierarchies depends more on intangible relations than on job specifications.

64. As Jon Elster, *Nuts and Bolts for the Social Sciences* (Cambridge: Cambridge University Press, 1988), points out, norms regulate individuals' behavior, but individuals do not choose to obey them because they serve self-interest. Norms enter the explanation in helping to account for individuals' identities, their self-images as particular sorts of persons with particular goals and commitments (Amartya Sen, *On Ethics and Economics* [Oxford: Blackwell, 1990]), but they also enter into accounting for the actions of governments and for citizens' expectations for what governments should do, for instance regarding the redistribution of wealth from the rich to the poor or from the present generation to future ones (Robert E. Goodin, "Institutionalizing the Public Interest: The Defense of Deadlock and Beyond," *American Political Science Review* 90, 2 [1996]: 331–43).

65. In our current research, we are examining the extent to which the setting of academic standards by state commissions reflects deliberative norms as they have been specified in the theoretical literature. We are also tracking a series of local experiments, designed to be intentionally deliberative, that are occurring in four South Carolina communities.

PART III
Focusing on Democratic Purposes: Implications for Education Policy

9

Democratic Education
and the American Dream

Jennifer L. Hochschild and Nathan Scovronick

> *Nothing can more effectually contribute to the Cultivation and Improvement of a Country, the Wisdom, Riches, and Strength, Virtue and Piety, the Welfare and Happiness of a People, than a proper Education of youth, by forming their Manners, imbuing their tender Minds with Principles of Rectitude and Morality, [and] instructing them in . . . all useful Branches of liberal Arts and Science.*
>
> —Benjamin Franklin, 1749[1]

As Franklin believed it should be, the education of children is the United States' most important social policy. Public schooling involves more people, both as providers and as recipients, than any other government program for social welfare. Its provision absorbs a larger share of the gross domestic product than almost any other social program.[2] It is the main governmental activity, both financially and operationally, at the local level and a central activity of all state governments.[3] It is America's answer to the European social welfare state,[4] to massive waves of immigration, and to demands for the abolition of structures of immobility based on race, class, or gender.

THE GOALS OF PUBLIC EDUCATION

As the epigraph from Franklin also implies, this massive effort devoted to public education is intended to accomplish a variety of purposes. Virtually all Americans hold two broad goals for schooling that shape most choices for educational policy and practice.[5] First, education plays a key role in the ideology of the American dream—Franklin's "Wisdom, Riches, and Strength, Virtue and Piety, the Welfare and Happiness of a People." Most briefly, the American dream is the promise that all residents of the United States have a reasonable chance to achieve success as they define it (material or otherwise) through their own efforts and resources and to attain virtue and fulfillment through that success.[6] Equality of opportunity to become legitimately unequal is an essential part, though not the whole, of the American dream. From this perspective, publicly provided education is intended to enable individuals to succeed.

The second core value, Franklin's "Cultivation and Improvement of a Country," is a commitment to democracy or the collective good, broadly defined. By democracy we mean a governance system in which control over policy choices is chiefly vested in elected officials chosen through fair and frequent elections in which virtually all adult citizens may participate. Alternatively, citizens may choose policies directly through some fair and frequent electoral mechanism. In either case, the practice of democracy presumes a degree of civility, shared knowledge, the ability to communicate beyond face-to-face encounters, a willingness to play in accord with the rules of the voting game, tolerance or even respect for disparate views, equal opportunity to attain full citizenship, a common culture, and commitment to the polity even if one's electoral choice loses. From this perspective, publicly provided education is intended to provide benefits for the society as a whole.

Surveys, campaign platforms, Fourth of July speeches, and other indicators of popular culture show that most Americans ascribe to the ideology of the American dream and believe that democracy is the best form of government.[7] Similarly, the vast majority of Americans agree that schools should both enhance the chances for individual students to succeed in life and provide the skills and viewpoints necessary for engaging in democratic politics.

At various points in American history, and especially during the past decade, some Americans have also demanded that schools fulfill a third goal—responding to the claims of particular groups. This goal is based on the belief that members of marked racial, ethnic, religious, sexual, or other disadvantaged groups cannot have the same chance to succeed or be full participants in the American democratic polity unless their group identity is recognized, publicly respected, and treated differently from that of unmarked citizens. Thus, public education must provide distinctive benefits for children in particular groups, different from and perhaps at the expense of benefits to other groups, individual students, or the collectivity as a whole. This claim on behalf of "some" is different from the focus on the "one" of the American dream or the "all" of democracy, but it shares features of both of the core claims. It can appeal to those who seek success for their children, and it can resonate with those who seek democratic participation and the collective good. Nevertheless, it has very different implications and demands and uses different means from the individual or collective goals of education. Americans show least support for this goal, and it is the most controversial in practice.

In principle, Americans want schools to help individuals as well as to strengthen the collectivity, and some also support group differentiation. But in practice, anyone who reads the newspaper knows that endorsement of general goals does not translate into comity on when or how to pursue them. Let us examine the three values in a bit more detail before exploring the ways in which disputes among them play out in choices of education policies.[8]

The Role of Schools in the Dream of Individual Attainment

Good schools should and can help individuals attain success. Virtually all Americans share that belief. That shared belief does not, however, resolve all difficulties, because "success" can have several meanings with different pedagogical implications.[9] One form of success is *absolute*—reaching some threshold of well-being higher than where one started. Absolute success is, in principle, available to everyone. In schooling it would consist in teaching all students the skills they need to live satisfactory adult lives, such as literacy and numeracy, the ability to find and use desired information, the ability to plan and discipline oneself, and the pleasure of exercising one's mind. As that list suggests, enabling all individuals to achieve absolute success would be a triumph indeed; no society has attained it. The serious pursuit of this goal can be controversial because it can imply the provision of more educational resources to some students than to others so that all may have a chance of success regardless of their initial endowments or family context.

For most parents, absolute success is a threshold that they want their children to move beyond. This desire comports with a second, *relative* definition of success—attaining more than a comparison point such as one's parents or classmates. Relative success is egalitarian if it applies an equal standard of measurement to all, but it is inegalitarian in the sense that some individuals will do better than others. Most Americans assume that in a properly functioning system of relative success in schooling, some—but not all—children will achieve permanent upward mobility or in some other way be better off than their parents (they seldom consider the possibility of corresponding downward mobility or declines in satisfaction).

Some parents go even further and expect schools to provide their children with an advantage over other children. That is the third form of success—*competitive*—in which my success implies your failure. A system of district boundaries and a method of school finance based on local wealth can, for example, create or maintain a privileged competitive position for some children. Competitive success might (but need not) imply initial equality of opportunity to seek victory, but beyond that starting point opportunities are to be taken and advantages used, not redistributed to those with fewer.

The pursuit of success for individual students is further complicated by different visions of the American dream and thus disagreement over what schools should teach. Some share the Puritans' view: "The mind of man is a vast thing, it can take in, and swallow down Heaps of Knowledge, and yet is greedy after more; it can grasp the World in its conception."[10] Children thirst for knowledge, and schools should nurture that thirst while teaching students how to slake it. Some are more instrumental, along with Benjamin Franklin: "In Europe, the Encouragements to Learning are . . . great. . . . A poor Man's Son has a chance, if he studies hard, to rise . . . to gainful Offices or Benefices; to an extraordinary Pitch of Grandeur; . . . and even to mix his Blood with Princes."[11] In this view, children thirst for wealth or power rather than for knowledge, and schools should give them the tools they need to improve their status. The ideology of the American dream is itself agnostic on what counts as success, but its liberal neutrality can lead to disputes over whether teachers should be drilling students in the basics or encouraging them to follow their imaginations and let the correct spelling come later.

The Role of Schools in Promoting Democracy

Just as most Americans endorse some variant of the American dream, most agree that schools are a crucial locus for training children to become democratic citizens. "Democracy" is usually conceived very broadly to encompass everything from republican virtue to participation in elections to neighborliness.[12] Thus, schools are supposed to provide at least six collective outcomes.

The first is a *common core of knowledge*. Americans abhor the perhaps apocryphal boast of the French administrator that at 10 A.M. he knew just which page of Virgil all students of a certain age were reading throughout the nation. But they do generally agree that all students in the United States should end their schooling with some shared learning. They should know the rudiments of American history; they should be able to communicate in English; they should have basic literacy and numeracy; and they should understand basic rules of politics and society such as the purpose of elections and the meaning of the rule of law.

Closely allied with the goal of a common core of knowledge is the desire for students to graduate with a *common set of values*. Those values include loyalty to the nation, acceptance of the Declaration of Independence and Constitution as venerable founding documents, appreciation that in American constitutionalism rights sometimes trump majority rule and majority rule is supposed to trump intense desire, belief in the rule of law as the proper grounding for a legal system, belief in equal opportunity as the proper grounding for a social system, willingness to adhere to the discipline implied by rotation in office through an electoral system, and so on. They also include economic and social values such as the work ethic, self-reliance, and trustworthiness.

The *ability to deal with, if not warm to, diverse others* is a third collective value that Americans want schools to inculcate. At the time of the founding, the most volatile dimensions of diversity were varying Christian faiths and different views of monarchical governance. In subsequent generations, the list of things we expect students to learn to tolerate and cope with has lengthened to include differences by political and social ideology, class, region, race, ethnicity, gender, sexual orientation, and disability. Most people agree that the best way to teach mutual tolerance is to have students learn in casual contact with others unlike themselves; that is why public schools have always been under great pressure to admit all students within their duly designated district. Private schools were permitted to be parochial, but public schools were not. (The greatest exception to this point, of course, was racial segregation, which we address below.) Schools are increasingly expected to teach through a multicultural curriculum so that children will understand and appreciate each other's racial or cultural background as well as their own.

A fourth collective goal of schooling is *teaching democratic practices*. These include following properly designated procedures, negotiating rather than using violence to secure what you want, respecting those who disagree, taking turns, expressing your own views persuasively, organizing with others for change, competing fairly, and winning (or losing) gracefully. There is, of course, always tension between maintaining educators' authority and teaching democratic practices through actually permitting students to make decisions. Schools and teachers negotiate this tension differently, depending mostly on the age and social class of their students, although they can never resolve it.

Fifth, Americans expect schools to participate in the broad social goal of *providing equal opportunity* for all children. Equality of opportunity is a protean goal—it is as important in the American dream of individual success described above as in democratic governance. We discuss it here because its collective implications require more change in schooling policy than do its individual implications.[13] Most Americans now agree, at least in principle, that schools should offset some unfair disadvantages (such as disability) and should provide at least equal treatment to those with other social disadvantages (such as those occasioned by racial minority status, poverty, or lack of facility in English). After all, if unfair disadvantages into which one is born persist into adulthood, one is unlikely to be able to participate fully in public affairs. For some people, that is a matter of simple injustice that should be rectified if it can be. Others calculate, more instrumentally, that even if they themselves do not suffer these disadvantages, they do not want their children to have to confront the specter of second-class citizens and to compensate for their social, economic, and political drawbacks. Thus, it is in the interests of everyone for schools to do what they can to transform inequalities of birth into equality of adult citizenship.[14]

As with the American dream, the more specific goals within Americans' broad democratic commitment have never been fully achieved for all, or even most, students. And strong efforts to promote one or several of these specific goals are likely to conflict with strong efforts to promote others of them. But the deepest dilemmas for public schools lie not within each of these two values but between them, and among them and the third, most contentious, one.

The Role of Schools in Respecting Groups

Claims to distinctive treatment for particular groups have two roots. One origin is the demand for respect of the educational rights of individual children who were treated unjustly because of some ascriptive characteristic. In the nineteenth century, for example, reformers insisted that girls deserved access to public schooling just as much as boys did. In the twentieth century, *Brown v. Board of Education* held that once a state committed itself to a system of public education, black children were unconstitutionally deprived if they could not participate in that system on the same terms as white children. In some cases, such claims to individual rights have been broadened into an insistence that the child cannot attain an equal education unless the child's group is treated distinctively—for example, the claim that blacks would be better off if members of their own race controlled their educational system. Only that arrangement, in this view, can provide the same autonomy, respect, and cultural self-definition that whites have always enjoyed.[15]

The second root of group-based claims is itself based on group identity rather than individual treatment. In the mid-nineteenth century, Catholic leaders vigorously opposed the Protestant pedagogy of the new public schools. They proposed either that schools be religiously neutral, that they teach Catholic doctrine to Catholic children,[16] or that the state should provide public funds for a system of Catholic schools parallel to that of the Protestant "public" schools.[17] A century later, some proponents of bilingual education argue that helping to maintain a foreign student's culture is just as important as teaching that student to study and speak in English.[18] These are examples of a more general claim: schools must not only include students with particular characteristics, provide for their needs, and teach other students to accept their presence, but also either change their practices in deference to the distinctive group or enable its members to be taught separately in accord with their own distinctive values.[19]

Demands for respect for group identities are highly volatile. They emerge from an unstable mix of the desire for inclusion but on terms distinctive of and specified by that group, the desire to use public resources to be educated outside the mainstream, the desire to change the educational mainstream to accommodate the group, and the desire to be left alone or to remove one's children from the mainstream.

Some of these desires affect schooling practices but do not speak to the purposes of education. Teachers may be asked to change their pedagogical techniques to accommodate the more cooperative style of girls or the more physically oriented learning preferences of young African-American boys. Other proposals for accommodating group distinctiveness do, however, affect the purposes of schooling. Educators may be asked to change the curriculum, to teach in more than one language, to describe American history as a story of oppression rather than unbridled progress, or to teach all subjects from an Afrocentric rather than a Eurocentric perspective.[20] In its most drastic (and rare) form, policymakers may be asked to provide a separate education for particular groups, as they tried to do in Detroit when the school district adopted a plan to establish all-male Afrocentric schools.[21]

Group advocates' points of intersection or conflict with proponents of individual success or democratic training are not always predictable. What is predictable is that all of these efforts can expect sooner or later (probably sooner) to be discordant with the highest priorities of those focused on other groups and with the priorities of educators and parents focused on the two most basic values.

PUTTING THE CORE VALUES INTO PRACTICE

Many of those who have thought most carefully about the purposes of public education have insisted with Benjamin Franklin that the core goals of individual success and democratic governance must be united and that neither may supercede the other. Thomas Jefferson, for example, offered six "objects of primary education" in order "to instruct the mass of our citizens in these, their rights, interests, and duties, as men and citizens":[22]

- To give to every citizen the information he needs for the transaction of his own business;
- To enable him to calculate for himself, and to express and preserve his ideas, his contracts and accounts, in writing;
- To improve, by reading, his morals and faculties;
- To understand his duties to his neighbors and country, and to discharge with competence the functions confided to him by either;
- To know his rights; to exercise with order and justice those he retains; to choose with discretion the fiduciary of those he delegates; and to notice their conduct with diligence, with candor, and judgment;
- And, in general, to observe with intelligence and faithfulness all the social relations under which he shall be placed.[23]

The first three focus on varied forms of individual success. The fourth and sixth focus on participation in the public arena. The fifth combines both goals. Based on these principles, Jefferson designed an elaborate system of public elementary and secondary education for all (white) children of Virginia, to be publicly subsidized for those who could not afford it.

Almost two hundred years later, the Supreme Court echoed the Framers' assumption that both individual and collective goals jointly and equally constitute the purpose of public schooling: "The 'American people . . .' have recognized 'the public schools as a most vital civic institution for the preservation of a democratic form of government,' and as the primary vehicle for transmitting 'the values on which our society rests' . . . In addition, education provides the basic tools by which individuals might lead economically productive lives."[24]

Public opinion surveys similarly demonstrate Americans' commitment to using the schools simultaneously to promote individual success and democratic engagement. Almost everyone supports the mastery of basic skills, endorses teachers and principals who will "push students to . . . excel," and wants every student to be given a chance to successfully complete a high school curriculum.[25] Over eight in ten also agree that schools must "teach values such as honesty, respect, and civility" and believe that "the percentage of students practicing good citizenship" is a very important measure of schools' success.[26] Most want textbooks and lesson plans to teach racial and ethnic respect as well as gender equality; 70 percent want schools to teach that "democracy is the best form of government."[27] Between one-half and three-quarters of Americans endorse teaching "the diverse cultural traditions of the different population groups in America" even when that implies "decreas[ing] the amount of information on traditional subjects in U.S. . . . history."[28]

Finally, Americans occasionally endorse schooling claims of particular groups in ways that are inconsistent with their general verbal support for the goal of democratic inclusiveness. Thus, on several surveys a majority think that "special public schools for young black males should be allowed." Similarly, on one survey almost nine out of ten women favor single-sex education for part of a student's career in school.[29]

Some school practices can in fact foster the two basic values, or even all three values, simultaneously. Enabling the brightest students to learn as much as they can not only bolsters them as individuals but also increases the possibility that they benefit the nation through discoveries, insights, or leadership. Ensuring that all students are verbally and mathematically competent helps them to live satisfying lives at the same time that it makes them better democratic citizens. Teaching foreign students to speak English makes their transition into the American workplace easier as well as reinforcing the cultural core so essential to a huge and diverse democracy. Showing respect for the identity of students who are outside the racial or cultural mainstream encourages them to achieve while teaching all students to be mutually tolerant. Allowing some children to be educated separately might enhance their individual success as well as respecting their distinctiveness.

However, amity and balance do not usually reign. In the actual practice of schooling, fostering what is good for all may divert resources from one or some; what shows respect for the identity of some may violate the convictions of others or distort democratic practices; what encourages success for the brightest or luckiest may deny opportunity for the weakest or unluckiest. When choices must be made and priorities determined—under pressure from demographic change, political demands, fiscal limits, global competition, competing values, or fear—one goal or another is likely to take precedence.

The history of previous trade-offs among goals itself shapes the context within which new choices must be made. In the first decades of this century, for example, many citizens saw immigration as a frightening challenge to democracy and demanded that schools be transformed in order to "Americanize" these future citizens. In the 1980s, with many people fearing economic challenges from abroad and reduced opportunities for success at home, the emphasis shifted even more to individual achievement, and parents engaged in an intense competition for advantage in educational or fiscal resources. Most recently, demands for group respect that started as a drive for integration in the 1960s have sometimes been transformed into advocacy for separate schools or distinct treatment within common schools.

Over time, the combination of multiple goals, competing interests, and a fragmented governance structure has created considerable incoherence in policy and instability in decision making. As one goal takes precedence and then is replaced by another, some policies, institutions, and practices continue to function well in the new environment. Others, however, become relics that create an inappropriate policy emphasis, use a disproportionate amount of resources, or otherwise distort the system. Too much bureaucracy may remain from Progressive era attempts to deal with demographic change; too much willingness to accept an unequal educational system or to jettison public schooling entirely may be the legacy of fear from the 1980s; too much separatism may be the consequence of the newest demand for group rights and respect.

INTERACTION AMONG GOALS IN EDUCATIONAL POLICY AND PRACTICE

We cannot in this chapter analyze the layers remaining from previous emphases on one goal or another, or sort out the many ways in which the values combine, coincide, or conflict. We will instead look briefly at several major policy disputes in which the interaction among values has crucially shaped schooling policy, practice, and outcomes.

School Desegregation

The elimination of de jure segregation was essential to permit equal educational opportunity for all children. In principle, it provided a greater chance for children of all races to attain success, enhanced the ability of the United States to become a fully democratic community, and ensured that African Americans would be recognized as full citizens. Thus, the elimination of de jure segregation reinforced both of the values central to American public education.

Most Americans concur on the necessity and even desirability of desegregated schooling. In the two decades after 1964, the proportion who agreed that black and white children should attend the same schools rose from fewer than two-thirds to over 90 percent. Over 40 percent of whites were unwilling to send their child to a school in which half or more of the students were black in 1964; that figure has since declined to fewer than 20 percent.[30]

In one important sense the practice of school desegregation did in fact promote the two basic values. The most careful studies of desegregated schools indicate that when properly implemented, the African-American children involved showed improved achievement scores, more attainment of schooling, greater college attendance, and more adult participation in integrated jobs and neighborhoods. There is no systematic evidence that desegregation hurt the achievement of white children and arguably it made them more inclined to respect and live among African Americans as adults.[31] Most Americans now recognize the gains for blacks, and a plurality perceive gains for whites as well. In 1971, four in ten Americans thought desegregated schools had improved the quality of education for blacks; by 1996, six in ten did. The proportion who thought desegregated schools had improved the quality of education for whites increased over the same period from one-quarter to almost one-half. Similarly, in 1971, four in ten thought that desegregated schools had improved the quality of race relations (though almost as many thought it had "worked against better relations"). By 1994, two-thirds saw improvement, and fewer than three in ten saw worsening.[32]

School desegregation has, of course, been tried only in a limited way and was often implemented in a fashion that seemed designed to ensure its academic and political failure.[33] It has rarely been used to remedy de facto segregation or racial separation across district lines, even though cross-district remedies have in many ways been the most successful of all.[34] Too often it has been imposed without sensitivity to the real allegiance of both blacks and whites to local governance, neighborhood schools, or well-known teachers and administrators. Frequently it did not sufficiently recognize that parents were worried that their children would be uncomfortable, unable to learn, or even physically endangered if they were in the minority in a tense situation. Legitimate opposition occurred for all of these reasons, among others.

Thus, in a different and larger sense the policy of mandated school desegregation has not succeeded in fostering the basic goals of education. White opponents argued that individual white children would suffer, and that the pursuit of collective goals could not be allowed to outweigh the pursuit of individual success. More recently, black opponents have argued that individual black children also are harmed, or at least that they are not benefited enough to offset the costs imposed on individuals or the damage that desegregation does to the racial identity of children and the black community.[35] Despite support for desegregation in principle, the opposition to its vigorous pursuit, especially through busing, is as strong as ever. In 1988, three-quarters of Americans rejected busing even if "white children were bused to top quality schools in the inner city and black children were bused to equally good schools outside of where they live."[36] A decade later, four in ten black parents and twice as many white parents were opposed to "busing children to achieve a better racial balance in schools."[37]

By the mid-1990s, about one-third of black children were educated in majority white schools, but another third continued to attend schools that approach 100 percent minority (black and Hispanic) population. For the typical Anglo student in the mid-1990s, the population of his or her school was between 5 percent and 20 percent black, depending on how urban the community was.[38] African Americans' and whites' achievement test scores converged somewhat in the 1970s and 1980s (largely because blacks' scores rose more than whites' scores did). But the convergence has been arrested in the 1990s.[39]

Thus, school desegregation brought Americans part but not all of the way toward putting into practice their ideals of using schools to enable individual success and prepare for democratic governance. Mandated desegregated schooling may be the right policy for a democratic society; it may be the best way to guarantee the same educational opportunities for children of all races; and it may have been a successful method to enhance the chances of individual success. It is not, however, a viable policy option, because individual fears as well as concerns about group identities have overwhelmed broader, collective values.

Equitable School Funding

Once it became clear that opposition to mandated racial desegregation would prevent most further efforts, reformers shifted their focus from the redistribution of students to the redistribution of resources. They argued that equal school funding—or at least funding at a level to permit absolute and relative success for most students—was essential for the American dream to be something other than a hypocritical cover for maintaining class privilege. If education had to be separate for most poor, often black, children, they wanted it at least to be equal. They believed that these children warranted the same training to enable them to pursue success as better-off children, and that poor communities have the same claim to public respect as wealthy ones.

As with school desegregation, most Americans agree, in theory. Since 1990, between 70 and 90 percent of Americans have endorsed an equal allocation of public education funds to all students regardless of their wealth. Results are similar in state-level polls that ask about support for particular measures to equalize funding. As with school desegregation, however, many politicians who have tried to redistribute funds have been punished in the next election. Legislatures have found it very difficult politically to redistribute schools funds except under threat of court order. Again, as in the case of school desegregation, the courts moved into the void; of the state supreme courts that have considered this issue, half have found grounds in their state constitutions to require greater equality in funding school districts. Some (e.g., in New Jersey and Texas) have made such a finding several times or more or have ordered legislatures back to the drawing board in order to see their orders carried out. Even when the public has approved new funding formulas, the new ratios of funding have often proved difficult to sustain.

In short, although a great deal more money is now available for education, and some places have achieved much greater equity, there has been an acrimonious debate for twenty-five years about the level of funding to which all children should be entitled and particularly about the obligation of all citizens to pay for the schooling of poor children. Like the controversy over school desegregation, the debate over funding equality has involved other issues, such as corruption, management efficiency, program impact, and especially the relationship between financial reform and achievement outcomes.[40] But underlying particular disputes over school funding has been the conflict between enabling one's own child to achieve the American dream, defined competitively, and enhancing democratic outcomes for all Americans. Many parents, particularly those who worked hard to move to a district with better schools, see little reason to subsidize the districts they left. Many parents, anxious for the success of their children, have little desire to use their resources to level the playing field; privileged parents naturally want to pass on their privileges to their children. Thus, while all adults accept responsibility to finance a basic education for everyone, there is little consensus beyond that on the proper relationship between the pursuit or maintenance of competitive advantage and the goal of equal opportunity.[41]

Distinctive Group Treatment

As most commonly understood, multicultural education seeks to be inclusionary and mutually respectful by exposing all students to the array of cultural heritages represented in the school, district, state, or nation. It is an attempt to redefine American culture away from that of the culturally dominant Anglo-Saxon Protestant majority and thereby to enrich it. During the 1990s, most Americans came to endorse this understanding of multiculturalism. Typically, more than seven in ten respondents agree with survey questions asking if schools should "increase the amount of coursework, counseling, and school activities . . . to promote understanding and tolerance among students of different races and ethnic backgrounds," to quote one unusually specific question.[42] This is a fairly new conviction for most Americans; the rapidity of its acceptance is a testament to Americans' belief in the need for mutual tolerance and respect in order to promote democracy.

Even thus understood, multicultural education is difficult to implement well. At a minimum, schools do not have time to do everything; if they teach the history of African Americans and Hispanics as well as that of European immigrants, they are leaving out Asian Americans and Native Americans (not to speak of variations within each category). The more inclusive school curricula and activities become, the sharper the exclusion of those remaining outside the fold. And absent a lot of thorny intellectual work, the more inclusive the curriculum becomes, the more superficially it treats all subjects. Finally, the more inclusive it becomes, in the usual sense of adding another cultural dimension to those already taught, the more difficult it is for teachers and students to retain any focus on the culture that was traditionally considered American—or any other common core.

But there is a deeper complexity, which moves the concept of multicultural-ism away from promoting the good of "all" into promoting the good of "some." Some advocates have altered their position from a call for inclusion and respect to a demand for separate and distinctive schooling appropriate to the particular-ity of their group. They often begin from a perception of power imbalance: "The nation's predominantly white educators have been slow to recognize that their own backgrounds—and the culture of the school—have a bearing on learning. And, rather than think of minority students as having a culture that is valid and distinct from theirs, they sometimes think of the youngsters as deficient."[43] To that perspective they add a distinct pedagogical philosophy, claiming that peda-gogy must change to fit the cultural context of particular types of children, preferably by having a teacher from the same culture.[44]

The most assertive advocates of, for example, cultural maintenance pro-grams for bilingual education, Afrocentrism, or fundamentalist Christianity may insist on the unique merit of their group's heritage and identity, and implicitly or explicitly reject the value of other cultures or the idea of a common culture. "Pub-lic school integration and the associated demolition of the black school has had a devastating impact on African American children—their self-esteem, motivation to succeed, conceptions of heroes or role models, respect for adults, and academic performance. Unless rational alternatives are devised that take into account the uniqueness of the African American heritage, . . . compulsory school integration will become even more destructive, . . . ultimately to the nation as a whole."[45]

Most African Americans do not share that view (nor do most whites, not sur-prisingly). But almost half agree that African-American students are not doing as well as white students because "schools are often too quick to label black kids as having behavior or learning problems," and in most surveys blacks no longer place a high priority on racial integration in schooling. Their priorities instead lie in higher achievement, safety and discipline, and sometimes political control of black schools by members of their own race.[46] About one-fifth of whites also blame schools' behavior for black students' problems.[47] Thus, a significant seg-ment of the population is available to be mobilized by advocates who value group differentiation more strongly than they do but are concerned about cultural loss and frustrated by the failures or the discriminatory practices of some public schooling.

Other programs for separating students focus less on group identity and more on satisfying particular needs. Advocates of these programs typically begin with an emphasis on the core values of promoting individual success or enabling full participation in the democratic community. But they sometimes end up seek-ing distinctive treatment for a particular group of students if they come to believe that conventional educational practices cannot satisfy those students' needs. Thus, for example, some advocates for children with disabilities fight to get many more disabled children into a regular classroom on the grounds that "individuals of varying achievement levels and competency and behavioral patterns can learn together. Although they may learn different things at different times, their learning is enhanced by contact and interaction."[48] But others argue that the goal of promoting the good of some requires their separation from all. Thus, the Learning Disabilities Association of America

> does not support "full inclusion" or any policies that mandate same placement, instruction, or treatment for all students. . . . The regular education classroom is not the appropriate placement for a number of students with learning disabilities who may need alternative instructional environments, teaching strategies, and/or materials that cannot or will not be provided within the context of a regular classroom environment. . . . The placement of all children with disabilities in the regular classroom is as great a violation of IDEA as the placement of all children in separate classrooms on the basis of their type of disability.[49]

Contests over whether and how to provide distinctive group recognition are played out at all levels of government. The federal Department of Education issues regulations on special education and bilingual education, and the Supreme Court rules on religion in the schools; state legislatures and local school boards debate the use of particular books in classrooms; principals and teachers contend over appropriate pedagogy and student placement; some parents demand to have their child included in all-black classes, and others demand to have their children removed from them. All of these disputes take place without regard to the bits of compelling evidence about the actual educational benefits of various programs and sometimes in the absence of any achievement data at all.

There is, in fact, almost no evidence on the outcomes of some forms of group-distinctive schooling such as Afrocentric schools or schools for gay and lesbian students. The lack of evidence is unfortunate but not surprising; few advocates or opponents seek systematic evaluations that might turn up distressing results. Even when researchers do seek dispassionate measures of outcomes of distinctive group treatment, many programs are too variable in quality or design to be compared, or the desired outcomes are too subtle to be clearly measured. Thus, for example, the evidence for sustaining many bilingual programs beyond the point of basic English proficiency is not clear, since "the major national-level evaluations suffer from design limitations; lack of documentation of study objectives; conceptual details and procedures followed; poorly articulated goals; lack of fit between goals and research design; and excessive use of elaborate statistical designs to overcome shortcomings in research designs."[50] For similar reasons, scholars produce contradictory conclusions on the benefits of separate classes for children with learning disabilities or emotional disturbances.[51] Pullout programs for disadvantaged children apparently do little to help them although supporters continue to promote them.[52]

Although there are relatively few advocates of group-distinctive education in the American population as a whole and relatively little evidence about their claims, they have a disproportionate impact on debates over educational policy for several reasons. First, their claims are sufficiently close to the core values that they cannot be dismissed as illegitimate, but they are sufficiently antagonistic that they do not fit well into most reform efforts. Second, their claims do not sort neatly into a consistent liberal or conservative framework[53] or into a consistent demand for inclusion or separation, so the advocates of "some" must usually be dealt with one group or even one school at a time. Finally, a substantial part of the American public can sometimes be mobilized into support for distinctive treatment for some students, usually because they are frustrated with schools' efforts to promote individual success or the collective good.

School Reform and School Choice

The field of public education has been full of reformers since it was first conceived—by reformers. From the mid-nineteenth century onward, the American public has devoted considerable effort to building and improving the public school system. In the last few decades, the public has demonstrated its willingness to spend an enormous amount of money on the schools;[54] at the same time, reform activity has been particularly intense. This activity has been driven to a great extent by serious failures in some poor urban school districts. It also results from economic changes that have made education even more important to individual success as well as from demographic and social changes that have placed additional demands on the public schools. In all its forms, however, these efforts to improve the system represent a serious national commitment to public education and its multiple goals.

The past few decades have seen several waves of school reform. Although they have been characterized differently in different places, most studies identify four distinct stages. The first can be broadly characterized as an attempt to fix various parts of the system through research and development. The second focused on fixing the people, that is, on improving the knowledge and skills of educational professionals, preparing them for innovation, and helping them improve classroom practice. The third emphasized fixing the schools by restructuring the organization, changing the culture, or adopting a schoolwide pedagogical approach. The most recent wave of reform is in a real sense an effort to fix everything in a coherent way—by setting high standards, changing the curriculum to be consistent with the standards, developing appropriate tests to measure student progress, and improving teachers' capacity to help students take advantage of more demanding material.[55] Many of the previous reform efforts have continued and are thriving within the framework of this new, systemic reform.

The public broadly supports the idea of school reform, the implementation of high standards, and many of these individual reform initiatives.[56] There is evidence of positive achievement effects from the implementation of standards[57] and from some initiatives such as substantive teacher education and professional development;[58] some whole school and curricular reform models;[59] quality preschool programs;[60] and small classes in the early grades.[61]

Systemic reformers in many ways have attempted to learn from the mistakes of the past and respond to a public system that they believe had become too fragmented, bureaucratic, and focused on unchallenging, short-term, quantifiable results. These problems resulted partly from the layering of previous reforms,[62] partly from the multiple demands coming from an array of stakeholders,[63] and partly from the variety of children who come through the doors of public schools. Although they disagree somewhat on explanations and prescriptions, the reformers believe that the problems with public schools can be remedied within them.

During this entire recent history of school reform, there has been a parallel movement promoting a very different type of educational change based on a market approach. Advocates of school choice see many of the same problems as school reformers but no longer believe that reform is possible or think it is preferable. Thus, they seek to drastically modify or even eliminate the present structure of public schooling. A few share with the reformers a belief in the multiple goals of education, but most hold this view because they do not. Either they are almost entirely focused on relative or competitive individual success and think it will be best achieved in a fairly unregulated market, or they seek the validation of group identities and think it will be best achieved in a system where distinct groups can choose to school their children together.

In its strongest form, market proponents advocate a system of vouchers that would permit students to make publicly funded choices among public, private, and parochial schools. A libertarian economist first promoted vouchers in the 1950s as an alternative to the heavy hand of government implied by geographically based school districting and assignment.[64] In the late 1960s, progressive reformers, with a particular interest in improving education for poor and minority children, adopted the idea as a variant of "alternative schooling."[65] In the 1980s, proponents of deregulation and market-based solutions to a range of problems once again revived the idea, generally to the dismay of liberals.[66] In the 1990s, two new groups of voucher supporters emerged: advocates of private schools devoted to maintaining group identity through association and distinctive forms of teaching,[67] and parents of children in atrocious inner-city schools who often support vouchers along with any other reform idea offered to them.[68] The evidence is mixed and deeply controversial on the achievement effects of voucher programs for private schools; the main point that can be made at present is that parents whose children participate are more satisfied with the choice.[69]

Although Americans broadly support greater choice within the public system, in general they are ambivalent about the desirability of vouchers for private and parochial schools. Several surveys in the 1990s asked Americans to choose among voucher proposals; in each case, respondents split evenly regardless of the number or type of options. That is, when asked to choose between vouchers restricted to public schools and those that could be used in private schools as well, roughly one-half chose each; when asked to choose between the current system, public vouchers, and private vouchers, roughly one-third chose each. If schools in their community were failing, identical proportions of the public (28 percent) would want private school vouchers or to have the public schools over-hauled.[70] Nevertheless, Americans consistently and strongly prefer spending more money to fix the public schools than providing alternatives to it.[71]

Charter schools represent a compromise position: they are quasi-public schools financed by public funds and subject to periodic public scrutiny, but they are run by private trustees and compete in a market. Charters are supported by those trying to move toward vouchers as well as by those trying to stop them; they have been seen as a drain on the public system and an attempt to strengthen it. After considerable controversy, they have been authorized in a majority of states and appear in various forms: limited in number or quite widespread; held tightly accountable or left largely alone; exclusive or inclusive; espousing single or multiple goals; pedagogically innovative or traditional. They are too new and too varied to permit any conclusions about whether they have any impact on student performance or on the vast majority of schools remaining within the regular public system.

At the root of the controversy over private school choice is the issue of whether to risk the public system to allow a focus on individual achievement or group identity alone, or try to preserve the public system as a central democratic institution with multiple individual and collective goals. At the heart of this serious, unresolved, public policy debate is, again, this conflict of values.

TRACKING

Tracking is in a real sense the issue that brings all these themes together. Sorting students by ability group is almost universal, and children who are white or come from upper-class, middle-class, or professional families almost always dominate the high tracks.[72] In many places, therefore, it is a race issue, like desegregation, or a class issue, like funding; it is by definition about the separation of students. Tracking may be the price paid for desegregation; in many districts, white students attend school with black students but rarely go to class with them. Tracking may also be the price paid to keep the children of the elite in the public schools; many wealthy parents will forgo private schools as long as their children are educated separately in the high track and have access to the best teachers and the most resources. Finally, while bilingual education is about students whose language ability may affect their ability to learn with others, and special education is about students whose disability may affect their ability to learn with others, tracking is actually about all students whose ability to learn affects their ability to learn with others. In this way, it is a more fundamental issue than all of those we have discussed so far.

Tracking is different from most of the other controversies because it is also a matter of pedagogical practice and, for that reason, rarely the subject of action by the legislatures or the courts except as part of a desegregation case. People genuinely disagree about the educational benefits or costs of tracking. According to much of the academic literature, however, the chief impact of ability grouping seems to be the educational disadvantage at which it puts those in the low tracks. Being in the high track is certainly preferable when the best teachers, the smallest classes, and the most resources are available there, but this advantage means that everyone would be better off in the high track, and there is evidence that this premise is true.[73] In the same way, being in the lower track when resources and expectations are low is not a prescription for success, and we have evidence that this, too, is the case.[74] In general, when studies of tracking are fairly evaluated, and the number of cases is large enough to deal with the impact of resources and other factors, much of the evidence indicates that tracking *per se* may not help anyone.[75] With some exceptions, even the best students will be just as well off in properly taught, heterogeneous classrooms.

Yet we have witnessed not only generalized policy debates about tracking but also school by school warfare every time someone tries to eliminate it. It is difficult to eliminate for several reasons. First, tracking is compatible with the way many teachers have been trained, and it is very hard to teach well in heterogeneous classrooms without the proper preparation. Second, many parents were themselves taught in tracked classrooms and sincerely believe, despite the evidence, that it is the only proper way for children to learn.[76] As we know, it is very hard to change schools in any manner that is a dramatic departure from the adult image of how they should look.[77] Third and perhaps most important, tracking is often supported by elite or politically powerful parents whose children occupy the high tracks and who seek to maintain an advantage for them.[78]

Like the other issues discussed here, this one is complicated, involving matters of policy as well as of implementation. Tracking is more questionable when it is mandatory and begins in the primary grades than when it is voluntary and occurs late in high school. At root, however, the tracking debate usually represents a conflict between a policy that is believed to be good for individual achievement, at least for those at the top,and one that is better for equal opportunity.

Although it is so embedded in practice, some districts have been at least partly successful in detracking.[79] And on all the other policy issues discussed here, real changes have been made in the last fifty years. There is a much higher level of integration than before *Brown* as well as a striking transformation in the way schooling is organized in the South.[80] In part because of desegregation, there has been a substantial growth in the black middle class. School funding, similarly, is at a much higher level than before 1974, and in many states it is much more equitable.[81] Children with disabilities have been brought much more into the mainstream, and parents continue to challenge the separation of disabled and other students when they believe justification for it is weak. National Assessment of Educational Progress (NAEP) scores, although uneven, have shown improvement for most age groups in most subjects over the last thirty years despite many more children with language and other problems. And black students have in fact made the greatest gains.[82] Through it all, Americans have sustained a remarkable commitment to the public schools. The conflicts over education policy are clearly serious and intractable, but movement on these issues is clearly not impossible.

These changes have, to be sure, taken place in the context of a sustained prosperity that has made it much easier to dedicate more resources to education and to broaden opportunity. They have also been driven in part by wider political and demographic developments. Yet in part they can be explained by the fact that Americans truly believe in the promise of equal opportunity that is inherent in the American dream. Cumulatively, the changes have been remarkable.

POLICY IMPLICATIONS

To discuss the future policy implications of all these developments is both daunting and appealing. However complicated, it is easier to document the conflicts created by the multiple goals of education or to identify the dominant role of one or another of them in the past than to try to determine the direction of future policy. In part this is because the context for policy-making will certainly change; developments in education will continue to be affected by electoral shifts, economic trends, and international challenges, and these are extremely difficult to anticipate.

On the other side, we can predict future policy developments without fear of authoritative contradiction and can base them upon our own views of these matters with the knowledge that the foundation is as solid as any other in such circumstances. We believe that both core values—success for each one and the collective good of all—are appropriate goals of the American educational system. We do *not* believe that either core value should be completely dominant: too much attention to individual success leads to atomistic selfishness, and too much attention to the collective good leads to populist despotism. In the same way, too much attention to group identity leads to fragmentation and mutual antagonism.

Except in a few tragic cases, parents can be trusted to work energetically on behalf of their own children. Some parents (and students) will be more successful than others, fairly or not, but we do not fear that the value of individual success will lose its motivating force. Similarly, advocates can be trusted to work energetically on behalf of their group, whether they seek fuller incorporation of "their" students into or treatment separate from the mainstream. In contrast, there are few besides policymakers and public officials who will persistently focus on efforts to attain the collective good;[83] that is their job and their job alone. In short, if one supports the two core values equally or even group values as well, then we believe that public officials should place a priority on the value of "all"; otherwise, it will be submerged under pressures for "one" and "some."[84] Specifically, public policy should promote inclusion, tolerance, equal opportunity, and democratic knowledge and commitments.

Furthermore, we believe that this position may in the future be good politics as well as good policy. Despite all the political pressures in the other direction, despite the fact that policymakers will have mixed incentives and will hold other, competing values, a new political context will permit a sustained focus on the public good.

The Changing Demography

While many future developments cannot be easily predicted, demographic projections for the United States are relatively clear as well as dramatic. The evidence points to another era, like that at the turn of twentieth century, when population trends will again drive decision making.

The outstanding demographic impact for the next few decades will come from the aging of the baby boomers and, absent a major change in immigration laws, from the increased diversity of the population. The first of the baby boomers will reach age sixty-five shortly after 2010. They will still be a substantial part of the total U.S. population—roughly 20 percent, or 70 million people—in 2025. Only Florida now has an elderly population of more than 15 percent, but virtually all states[85] are expected to exceed that figure by then.

Over the same period, the Anglo population of the country is projected to become a smaller proportion of the total, decreasing from 77 percent in 1990 to about 60 percent in 2025. The black population, about 12 percent of the population in 1990, is expected to grow slowly during the same period, but the percentages of Latinos (8 percent in 1990) and Asian Americans (3 percent) are both projected to more than double by 2025.[86] These trends will be felt most powerfully in California, where the Latino population could exceed the white population well before 2025.[87] By that time there are expected to be 21 million Latinos, 17 million Anglos, and 9 million Asian Americans in California. Other states will see major changes as well.[88] Nationally, because of the growth in the (mostly Anglo) elderly population and the size of the (increasingly minority) school-aged population, the dependency ratio (that is, the ratio of those of working age to the young and old) is expected to become much worse.[89]

A larger and more diverse school population, combined with a larger and relatively homogeneous elderly population, could create a series of difficult policy dilemmas. The need for schooling for the young will be great at the same time that the demand for health care and social services for the elderly will peak. At the least, a severe competition for scarce public resources is likely. Furthermore, communities with large numbers of senior citizens already demonstrate some resistance to proposals for increased spending on school buildings or operations, and this opposition is also likely to get worse.[90]

The potential for social division will be very high. In addition to polarization between young and old, we may see increased divisions between wealthy and poor, white and nonwhite populations, immigrants and nonimmigrants, and among communities of immigrants themselves. We saw some of this in the early 1990s in California, where it could be expected.[91]

Politics and Policy

Many policymakers, particularly elected officials, do not think much about the long run; the horizon until the next election is too short and the rewards for small, symbolic actions too great. Some will no doubt yield to the temptation to practice the politics of division or exclusion in the face of the coming demographic changes, especially in situations of volatile transition. In some contexts, at some times, that approach will succeed politically, as it did for the Republicans in California in 1994 with Proposition 187. But the old demagoguery will not work the same way where there is a new majority or even a substantial voting bloc of non-whites, once those new citizens begin to participate in politics. In jurisdictions like California and Texas, it will be risky for white politicians to try to play on racial or ethnic divisions; the backlash against Republicans in the 1998 California gubernatorial and senatorial elections provides some evidence for that.[92] Even in places where the changes in racial proportions will be less dramatic, the demagogic approach will offer substantial risks for politicians. Divisiveness and reaction never worked with some segments of the white population and are likely to be opposed by identity-based groups who will have more political power than ever before and may be prepared to exercise it.

In this new world, a message that focuses on democratic values, national unity, mutual respect, and evenhanded treatment could be politically very attractive. It will be important, as always, to provide special services when students' educational progress depends on it, but controversial to use resources to benefit any group when it does not. Groups seeking extra resources to foster inclusion may be treated differently from groups seeking resources to foster separate or oppositional identities. It is likely to be crucial for everyone to perceive that they have an equal chance to pursue success, and more difficult for anyone to defend special privileges. Individuals seeking extra resources to maintain their inherited advantages may find less sympathy than individuals seeking resources to overcome their inherited disadvantages. In short, with the coming set of demographic changes, inclusive policies could work better than divisive politics in many places, even in the short term. In the long run, with the potential for political chaos so great, more people in the next generation of Americans could want to find their leaders on the high road rather than in the swamp.

Good Education for All Students

If our claim about the political advantages of the high road is correct, it means that policies that separate distinct categories of students or that provide unusual opportunities to well-off children are likely to be called into question. Absent better proof than we now have that they are worth their educational costs, policies on extended bilingual education, pull-out classes for poor children, curricula keyed to particular groups, and separate education for many children with disabilities will come under even greater scrutiny. It may become difficult to argue that the collective good should give way to group needs if the expression of group needs does not provide clear educational benefit to individual students or clear support for democratic politics. It may become similarly difficult to argue that children in wealthy school districts should retain the advantages that high levels of funding bring if other children lack them.

This does not mean that changing these policies will be easy. The new ways may not always save money. Reducing the number of students inappropriately labeled "disabled" may provide savings, for example, but properly mainstreaming more of the disabled could cost just as much as separation. Furthermore, schooling is very difficult to change for reasons having little to do with finances: parents are used to particular forms of organization and methods of teaching; the essential retraining of teachers will be personally and politically painful; the radical decentralization of American schooling means that all reform will be incremental and uneven across districts; and elites will continue to resist changes that threaten their status. Nevertheless, as the evidence about the ineffectiveness of some current practices is circulated more widely, as teacher preparation changes, and especially as special privileges become politically more difficult to defend, these issues should become more amenable to compromise and change.

Some courts are in fact currently developing a set of standards on special education that may in the future be broadly appropriate beyond it.[93] These standards clearly put the burden of proof on school districts to show that a child has been mainstreamed "to the maximum extent appropriate." This approach requires a greater level of inclusion than at present, absent clear evidence that the child's achievement would substantially suffer, that the child's presence would be very disruptive for the other students, or that a more inclusive placement would be much more expensive. Although there have been plenty of problems in implementing special education policy, variations on this general standard may in the new context be applied to a range of issues involving the separation of students.

If the playing field levels, elite parents are likely to provide a new and stronger set of advocates for public-private choice programs. Those who would like voters to think of themselves more as individual consumers in a marketplace and less as citizens in democracy will support them. The schools in elite communities, however, are unlikely to be in sufficient trouble that the wider public will be willing to replace the public system to improve them. If their schools are not as good as they should be, elite parents and their neighbors will continue to have the capacity to fix them. Endangering a democratic institution as central as the public schools by draining resources from public education is likely to be too high a price for most people to pay in order to permit elite parents to pursue individual competitive advantage for their children. Elite parents may have to settle for the continued benefits of residential separation or pay for private schooling.[94]

The case will be stronger for vouchers for poor children who attend public schools that fail to achieve any of the goals of education. A public-private system for all children has the potential to further fragment or stratify educational settings and arguably will leave urban children even more isolated than they are now. Public school choice programs that move across district lines and inclusive charter schools, however, could decrease the racial and class isolation of urban children, since these programs could make it easier for them to attend suburban schools. These mechanisms could therefore be increasingly attractive in the new demographic and political context. They may also improve the quality of teaching for poor children, if arguments about the salutary effects of competition are at all correct.

In general, improving terrible urban and rural schools will continue to be the most important and difficult policy challenge for public schooling over the next few decades.[95] Current attention to high standards and high expectations and the recent focus on the professionalization of teachers have begun to show effects. Politicians may have supported these changes for the wrong reasons—for the pleasure of challenging their opponents to come out in favor of low standards and incoherence—but the reforms themselves are based on lessons learned over time, are consistent with reliable, though scarce, research, and correctly place the focus of change on quality of instruction. They provide an appropriate framework for securing the right to a good school for all students.[96]

However, meeting high standards, developing knowledgeable teachers, acquiring good materials, and ensuring adequate buildings cost tax money; here the politics of one versus all has been and will continue to be most difficult. It is of course hypocrisy to endorse high standards, comprehensive reform, and quality instruction without providing sufficient funding for everyone, but hypocrisy is not unusual where taxes are involved. In the future it may become easier to secure adequate funding for regular education in all districts if the dramatic growth in some special programs can be brought under control; both changes can be made and justified in the name of equal treatment.[97] Court decisions may, however, still be necessary to make the hard financial reforms possible.

To resolve all the issues raised in this chapter, there will in fact be no substitute for democratic decision making of all possible types; executive leadership, legislative determination, and court intervention will no doubt all be necessary, along with appeals to and persuasion of citizens. The debate on these matters will be intense, the potential for social division will be high, and the competition for public resources will be fierce. Yet the new demography will present great opportunities as well as enormous challenges. There will be a real chance to bring people together in a new way to work for the common good. Education will clearly be more important than ever, not only to enable individuals to achieve their dreams but also to enable the United States to thrive as a democracy. It could be a new America.

NOTES

Our deepest thanks go to Smriti Belbase, without whom this chapter would be much less complete, and without whom we might never have gotten past our arguments. Thanks also for excellent suggestions, some of which we accepted, to Rainer Baubock, Elaine Bonner-Tompkins, Thomas Corcoran, Jeffrey Henig, Christopher Jencks, Lorraine McDonnell, Richard Murnane, Michael Paris, Harry Stein, Clarence Stone, Michael Timpane, and the participants in the seminar series on inequality and social policy, J. F. Kennedy School, Harvard University.

1. Benjamin Franklin, "Constitutions of the Publick Academy in the City of Philadelphia," in *Benjamin Franklin on Education*, ed. John Best (1749; reprint, New York: Teachers College Press, 1962): 152–53.

2. In 1996, 2.7 million people were employed as public elementary and secondary classroom teachers. That compares with, for example, 66,314 who were employed in providing Social Security payments and approximately 1.5 million people who were employed in the armed forces. In 1996–1997, the United States spent an estimated $314 billion on elementary and secondary public education compared with $190 billion for Medicare and $365 billion for Social Security (National Center for Education Statistics, *The Digest of Education Statistics 1997* [Washington, D.C.: U.S. Department of Education, 1997], table 4; *Statistical Abstract of the United States* [Washington, D.C.: U.S. Department of Commerce, 1998], tables 251, 543, 559, and 582).

3. In 1996, local governments spent $292 billion on education (including higher education) compared with $42 billion on hospitals, $38 billion on police, and $33 billion on public welfare (http://www.census.gov/govs/estimate/96stlus.txt). A different measure shows that in 1997, 31 percent of all state expenditures went to education; the next most expensive state program was public welfare, at 23 percent (http://www.census.gov/govs/state/97stus.txt).

4. In 1994, the most recent year for which data are available, the United States spent $5,944 per student in elementary and secondary education. Among the G-7 countries, the next highest was Germany, at $5,262 per student. The lowest in this group was the United Kingdom, at $3,914 per student (U.S. Department of Education, *The Condition of Education: 1998* [Washington, D.C.: Government Printing Office, 1998], table 56-4). Arnold Heidenheimer, "The Politics of Public Education, Health and Welfare in the USA and Western Europe," *British Journal of Political Science* 3, 1 (1973): 315–40, and Heidenheimer, "Education and Social Security Entitlements in Europe and America," in *The Development of Welfare States in Europe and America*, ed. Peter Flora and Arnold Heidenheimer (New Brunswick, N.J.: Transaction Books, 1981), 269–304, analyze why the United States focused more and earlier on public education than European nations did.

5. "Education" here is elementary and secondary schooling that is universal, mandatory, and directly provided or otherwise ensured by public authorities. We are not considering college or postgraduate schooling, vocational training, preschool or after-school child care, or other programs that teach in some sense but are not a central part of the system of schooling. We do at times consider private and religious elementary and secondary schools. The "educational system" is the set of institutions that are formally and publicly granted the authority and resources to convey "education."

6. Jennifer Hochschild, *Facing Up to the American Dream: Race, Class, and the Soul of the Nation* (Princeton, N.J.: Princeton University Press, 1995), provides an extensive discussion of the meaning and practice of the American dream.

7. See ibid., chapter 1, for evidence of support for the American dream; Herbert McClosky and John Zaller, *The American Ethos: Public Attitudes Toward Capitalism and Democracy* (Cambridge, Mass.: Harvard University Press, 1984); and Sidney Verba and Gary Orren, *Equality in America: The View from the Top* (Cambridge, Mass.: Harvard University Press, 1985), provide evidence on support of democratic values. Many Americans reject claims that our values are actually practiced, but they are often those who are most committed to the values themselves; see Samuel Huntington, *American Politics: The Promise of Disharmony* (Cambridge, Mass.: Harvard University Press, 1981).

8. An increasing number of scholars share our core framing that disputes over educational pedagogy and policy are really disputes over the nature and priority of core values. Larry Cuban, "A Tale of Two Schools," *Education Week* (28 January 1998): 33, 48; David F. Labaree, *How to Succeed in School Without Really Learning* (New Haven, Conn.: Yale University Press, 1997), and David C. Paris, *Ideology and Educational Reform: Themes and Theories in Public Education* (Boulder, Colo.: Westview Press, 1995), are excellent examples.

9. Hochschild, *Facing Up to the American Dream*, 16–17, further explicates these three forms of success.

10. Perry Miller, *The New England Mind: The Seventeenth Century* (Cambridge, Mass.: Harvard University Press, 1954), 66.

11. Benjamin Franklin, "Proposals Relating to the Education of Youth in Pennsylvania," in *Writings,* ed. J. A. Lemay (1749; reprint, New York: Library of America, 1987), 326.

12. Benjamin R. Barber, *An Aristocracy of Everyone: The Politics of Education and the Future of America* (New York: Oxford University Press, 1992), and Amy Gutmann, *Democratic Education* (Princeton, N.J.: Princeton University Press, 1987), focus on the centrality of public education for a well-functioning democracy.

13. Our discussion of school desegregation in the text explains and justifies this proposition.

14. Economic purposes of education, official and unofficial, are beyond our discussion here. In this category, we would place the pursuit of national economic competitiveness as well as the desires to protect children from economic exploitation, to keep them out of economic competition with adults, and to permit adults to work without child care responsibilities for most of the day. Finally, there is the role that education plays in sorting students for their future economic roles.

15. The classic claim here is Derrick Bell, "Serving Two Masters: Integration Ideals and Client Interests in School Desegregation Litigation," *Yale Law Journal* 85, 4 (1976):

470–516. Plaintiffs in a school desegregation suit in Atlanta, for example, chose to have the school system turned over to black educators rather than to pursue desegregation with neighboring white communities partly because they valued the chance for the black community to run its own schools. By the 1990s, most local black activists endorsed black-run schools over desegregative efforts. See Paul Gewirtz, "The Triumph and Transformation of Antidiscrimination Law," in *Race, Law, and Culture,* ed. Austin Sarat (New York: Oxford University Press, 1997): 110–34, for a discussion of the spread of group-based claims from race to other ascriptive traits.

16. Steven Macedo, *Liberalism, Civic Education, and Diversity* (Cambridge, Mass.: Harvard University Press, 1999).

17. Carl F. Kaestle, *Pillars of the Republic: Common Schools and American Society, 1780–1860* (New York: Hill and Wang, 1983), 136–81, esp. 166–71, and Joseph Viteritti, "Blaine's Wake: School Choice, the First Amendment, and State Constitutional Law," *Harvard Journal of Law and Public Policy* 21, 3 (1998): 664–75.

18. "The loss of language . . . causes [children] to be cut off from their past and their heritage. . . . A sense of group belonging . . . is badly needed in today's American schools which are mainly Eurocentric, competitive, individualistic, and materialistic" (Cornel Pewewardy, "Melting Pot, Salad Bowl, Multicultural Mosaic, Crazy Quilt, or Indian Stew," *Indian Country Today* 20 [January 1997]: 2).

19. See section on "Group Rights," *The Good Society* 6, 2 (Spring 1996): 1–37.

20. See the "African-American Baseline Essays" used in school systems in Portland, Oregon. The Portland School District is developing three additional sets of essays, one for each of the remaining minority groups. The Atlanta City School District instructs its teachers to include the original essays among their resources; the essays are also used by individual teachers in Milwaukee and in Prince Georges County, Maryland. See Walter F. Rowe, "School Daze: A Critical Review of the 'African-American Baseline Essays' for Science and Mathematics," *Skeptical Inquirer* (September/October 1995): 27–32; Bernard Ortiz de Montellano, "Politically Correct Is Scientifically Fatal; Pharaoh Was No Einstein," *New York Times,* 9 July 1995; Education Week on the Web, "Oregon Summary," in *Quality Counts '98,* http://www.edweek.org/, 1998); and Amy Binder, "Friend and Foe: Boundary Work and Collective Identity in the Afrocentric and Multicultural Curriculum Movements in American Public Education," in *The Cultural Territories of Race: Black and White Boundaries,* ed. Michele Lamont (Chicago: University of Chicago Press, 1999).

21. Yancey Roy, "Eve Calls for All-Black Academies," *Times Union* (Albany, New York), 17 January 1995; James R. Campbell, "Quayle Pitches 'G.I. Bill for Kids' at Inner City Academy," report for UPI, 26 June 1992; "U.S. Judge Blocks Plan for All-Male Public Schools in Detroit," *New York Times,* 16 August 1991; and Isabel Wilkerson, "Detroit's Boys-Only Schools Facing Bias Lawsuit," *New York Times,* 14 August 1991. After a challenge by the ACLU, the schools were opened to girls, but they remain focused on a particular race and gender. A school in New York City was similarly established to provide "leadership training" for young black girls, and another there and in Los Angeles were set aside for gay teens. See Scott Baldouf, "More Schools Take Up Gay-Bias Issue," *Christian Science Monitor,* 29 September 1997.

22. Thomas Jefferson, "Report of the Commissioners Appointed to Fix the Site of the University of Virginia," in *Early History of the University of Virginia, as Contained in*

the Letters of Thomas Jefferson and Joseph Cabell (1818; reprint, Richmond Va.: J. W. Randolph, 1856, 432–47.

23. Ibid.

24. *Plyler v. Doe,* 457 U.S. 202, 221 (1982).

25. Public Agenda Foundation, "Time to Move On: An Agenda for Public Schools Survey," conducted 26 March–17 April 1998, ques. 23; Phi Delta Kappa, "Attitudes Toward the Public Schools 1998 Survey," conducted by the Gallup Organization, 5–23 June 1998, ques. 17 (accession nos. 0306952 and 0308651 in RPOLL, available through Lexis/Nexis).

26. Public Agenda Foundation, "An Agenda for Public Schools Survey," ques. 25; Phi Delat Kappa, "Attitudes Toward the Public Schools 1998 Survey," ques. 18 (accession nos. 0306954 and 0308652 in RPOLL).

Jean Johnson and John Immerwahr, *First Things First: What Americans Expect from the Public Schools* (New York: Public Agenda Foundation, 1994), ques. 43–49.

27. Jean Johnson and John Immerwahr, *First Things First: What Americans Expect from the Public Schools* (New York: Public Agenda Foundation, 1994), 46.

28. Phi Delta Kappa, "Attitudes Toward the Public Schools 1994 Survey" conducted by the Gallup Organization, 10 May–8 June 1994, ques. 55 and 56 (accession nos. 0220676 and 0253725 in RPOLL); Time/Cable News Network, poll conducted by Yankelovitch Partners, 7–8 December 1994, ques. 54 (accession no. 0226911 in RPOLL).

29. *Los Angeles Times* poll conducted 21–25 September 1991, ques. 34 (accession no. 0163132 in RPOLL); Cable News Network/*USA Today* poll conducted by the Gallup Organization, 22–24 April 1994, ques. 70 (accession no. 0234970); National Black Politics Study, Michael Dawson and Ronald Brown, principal investigators, University of Michigan, ICPSR, 1993–1994, ques. D6d (blacks only); *Redbook* poll conducted by E.D.K. Associates, 7–10 February 1994, ques. 7, 8 (accession nos. 0233559, 0233560 in RPOLL).

30. Jennifer Hochschild and Bridget Scott, "The Polls—Trends: Governance and Reform of Public Education in the United States," *Public Opinion Quarterly* 62, 1 (1998): 84.

31. For evidence on trends in students' academic achievement by race and ethnicity, see National Center for Education Statistics, *NAEP 1996 Trends in Academic Progress* (Washington, D.C.: U.S. Department of Education, 1998), 13–14, 62–63, 112–13, 160–61. On the effects of desegregation in particular see Amy Wells and Robert Crain, "Perpetuation Theory and the Long-Term Effects of School Desegregation," *Review of Educational Research,* 64, 4 (1994): 531–55; Janet Schofield, "Review of Research on School Desegregation's Impact on Elementary and Secondary School Students," in *Handbook on Multicultural Education,* ed. James Banks and Cherry McGee Banks (New York: Macmillan, 1995): 597–616; Lee Sigelman, Timothy Bledsoe, Susan Welch, and Michael Combs, "Making Contact? Black-White Social Interaction in an Urban Setting," *American Journal of Sociology* 101, 5 (1996): 1306–32; and Robert Lissitz, "Assessment of Student Performance and Attitude, Year IV–1994," report submitted to Voluntary Interdistrict Coordinating Council, St. Louis, Missouri, 1994.

32. Hochschild and Scott, "The Polls—Trends," 102.

33. William Berg and David Colton, "Budgeting for Desegregation in Urban School Systems," *Integrated Education* 20, 1–2 (1982): 40–48, provide a classic example of atrocious implementation.

34. Jennifer Hochschild, *The New American Dilemma: Liberal Democracy and School Desegregation* (New Haven, Conn.: Yale University Press, 1984): 62–70.

35. In a 1998 survey, about 50 percent of blacks and 28 percent of whites said that it was "very important" that their child's school be racially integrated. In the same survey, however, 82 percent of all respondents chose "raising academic standards and achievement" over "more diversity and integration" as their preferred priority for their children's school (Public Agenda Foundation, "An Agenda for Public Schools Survey," ques. 13, 2; accession nos. 0306942, 0306931 in RPOLL).

36. NAACP Legal Defense and Education Fund, "Unfinished Agenda on Race," survey conducted by Louis Harris and Associates, 3 June–12 September 1988), ques. 21 (accession no. 0074189 in RPOLL).

37. Public Agenda Foundation, "An Agenda for Public Schools Survey," ques. 57 (accession no. 0306986 in RPOLL).

38. Gary Orfield, Mark D. Bachmeier, David R. James, and Tamela Eitle, "Deepening Segregation in American Public Schools," paper prepared for Harvard Project on School Desegregation, 1997, 11–14, 21.

39. National Center for Education Statistics, *NAEP 1996 Trends in Academic Progress,* xiii; David Grissmer, Ann Flanagan, and Stephanie Williamson, "Why Did the Black-White Score Gap Narrow in the 1970s and 1980s?" in *The Black-White Test Score Gap,* ed. Christopher Jencks and Meredith Phillips (Washington, D.C.: Brookings Institution, 1998), 182–226.

40. Gary Burtless, ed., *Does Money Matter: The Effect of School Resources on Student Achievement and Adult Success* (Washington D.C.: Brookings Institution, 1996), and Thomas Corcoran and Nathan Scovronick, "More Than Equal: New Jersey's Quality Education Act," in *Strategies for School Equity: Creating Productive Schools in a Just Society,* ed. Marilyn Gittell (New Haven, Conn.: Yale University Press, 1998).

41. Douglas S. Reed, "Court-Ordered School Finance Equalization: Judicial Activism and Democratic Opposition," in *Developments in School Finance, 1996,* ed. William J. Fowler (Washington, D.C.: Department of Education, National Center for Education Statistics, 1997), 91–120.

42. Phi Delta Kappa, "Attitudes Toward the Public Schools, 1992" survey conducted by the Gallup Organization, 23 April–14 May 1992, ques. 41 (accession no. 0202655 in RPOLL). Typically, the less specific the query and the more generic its focus on "teaching respect for people of different racial and ethnic groups," the higher the rate of support, which sometimes reaches 90 percent or more.

43. Debra Viadero, "Culture Clash," *Education Week* (10 April 1996): 1.

44. Lisa Delpit, *Other People's Children: Cultural Conflict in the Classroom* (New York: New Press, 1995), and Deborah Prentice and Dale Miller, eds., *Cultural Divides: Understanding and Overcoming Group Conflicts* (New York: Russell Sage Foundation, 1999), chap. 20.

45. Doris Wilkinson, "Integration Dilemmas in a Racist Culture," *Society* 33, 3 (1996): 27–28.

46. Jeffrey Henig, Richard Hula, Marion Orr, and Desiree Pedesclaux, *The Color of School Reform: Race, Politics and the Challenge of Urban Education* (Princeton, N.J.: Princeton University Press, 1999).

47. Public Agenda Foundation, "An Agenda for Public Schools Survey," ques. 34,

13, 20–22, 24, 26– 28 (accession nos. 0306963, 0306942, 0306949–0306951, 0306953, 0306955–0306957 in RPOLL).

48. Ellen Branﬂinger, "Using Ideology: Cases of Nonrecognition of the Politics of Research and Practice in Special Education," *Review of Educational Research* 67, 4 (Winter 1997): 425–59.

49. Learning Disabilities Association of America, "Inclusion," position paper, 1993 (http://www.ldanatl.org/positions/inclusion.html).

50. Laurel Walters, "The Bilingual Education Debate," *Harvard Education Letter* 14, 3 (1998): 1–4, and Diane August and Kenji Hakuta, eds., *Educating Language-Minority Children* (Washington, D.C.: National Academy Press, 1988).

51. K. Heller, W. Holtzman, and Samuel Messick, *Placing Children in Special Education: A Strategy for Equity* (Washington, D.C.: National Academy of Science Press, 1982), found special education classes to be "ineffective and discriminatory." Edward Baker, Margaret Wang, and Herbert Walberg, "The Effects of Inclusion on Learning," *Educational Leadership* 52 (1994): 4; found that inclusion in regular classrooms leads to academic and social benefits for disabled and special needs children. However, Kenneth Kavale, "Effectiveness of Special Education," in *The Handbook of School Psychology*, ed. Terry B. Gutkin and Cecil R. Reynolds (New York: Wiley, 1990); Conrad Carlberg and Kenneth Kavale "The Efficacy of Special Versus Regular Class Placement for Exceptional Children: A Meta-Analysis," *Journal of Special Education* 14 (1980): 295–309; and Paul Sindelar and Stanley Deno, "The Effectiveness of Resource Programming," *Journal of Special Education* 12, 1 (1979): 149–77, find that separation improves the academic achievement of learning disabled and emotionally disturbed children.

52. Michael Puma et al., *Prospects: Final Report on Student Outcomes* (Cambridge, Mass.: Abt Associates, 1997). The evidence cited in this paragraph, however, may have little bearing on the concerns of those seeking distinctive group treatment, since it is all focused on the two primary values of individual success and the collective good. One could argue that even if separate programs do not benefit "one" or "all," they could still enhance the values behind "some."

53. Fundamentalist Christian requests for curriculum changes are on the conventionally defined right; schools for gay and lesbian students or Afrocentric schools for black boys are on the conventionally defined left. No proposal for distinctive group treatment is "liberal" as conventionally understood. In contrast, one can reasonably begin with the assumption that people concerned about individual success will be more conservative in conventional terms than will people concerned about the community as a whole. (One must be cautious here about labeling: those concerned about "one" could call for dramatic downward redistribution if they focus on absolute success, whereas a concern for "all" could take the form of strong pressure toward conformity to rules and laws, or passionate patriotism. Nevertheless, the political allegiances of advocates for particular groups are harder to predict than those for advocates of individual success or the collective good.)

54. Hochschild and Scott, "The Polls—Trends," 85–86, 103–12. Since 1960, the United States has increased its expenditures on public elementary and secondary education from less than $75 billion to over $250 billion in 1997, in constant 1997–1998 dollars (National Center for Education Statistics, *The Digest of Education Statistics 1998* [Washington, D.C.: U.S. Department of Education, 1998], fig. 8).

55. Marshall Sahskin and John Egirmeir, *School Change Models and Processes: A*

Review and Synthesis of Research and Practice (Washington, D.C.: U.S. Department of Education, 1993), and Margaret E. Goertz, Robert E. Floden, and Jennifer O'Day, *Studies of Education Reform: Systemic Reform* (Washington, D.C.: Government Printing Office, 1996).

56. Hochschild and Scott, " The Polls—Trends," 86–87, 114–16; Stanley Elam, ed. *The Gallup/Phi Delta Kappa Polls of Attitudes Toward the Public Schools, 1969–88* (Bloomington, Ind.: Phi Delta Kappa Educational Foundation, 1989); Elam, *How America Views Its Schools: The PDK/Gallup Polls, 1969–1994* (Bloomington, Ind.: Phi Delta Kappa Educational Foundation, 1995); Kathryn Doherty, "Changing Urban Education: Defining the Issues," in *Changing Urban Education*, ed. Clarence Stone (Lawrence: University Press of Kansas, 1998); Phi Delta Kappa, "Attitudes Toward the Public Schools 1998 Survey," ques. 31, 35 (accession nos. 0308665 and 0308669 in RPOLL); American Association of University Women, "American Association of University Women Survey," conducted by Lake, Snell, Perry and Associates, June 1998, ques. 45, 57 (accession nos. 0320047 and 0320059); Henry J. Kaiser Foundation/Harvard School of Public Health, "Kaiser, Harvard Post-Election Survey: Priorities for 106th Congress," conducted by Princeton Survey Research Associates, 4 November–6 December 1998, ques. 11 (accession no. 0322421).

57. David Grissmer and Ann Flanagan, "Exploring Rapid Achievement Gains in North Carolina and Texas" (Washington, D.C.: National Education Goals Panel, November 1998).

58. Linda Darling-Hammond, *What Matters Most: Teaching for America's Future* (New York: National Commission on Teaching and America's Future, 1996); also see Richard F. Elmore, *Investing in Teacher Learning: Staff Development and Instructional Improvement in Community School District #2, New York City* (New York: National Commission on Teaching and America's Future, 1997).

59. Steven W. Barnett, "Economics of School Reform: Three Promising Models," in *Holding Schools Accountable: Performance-Based Reform in Education*, ed. H. F. Ladd (Washington, D.C.: Brookings Institution, 1996).

60. Deanna S. Gomby, Mary B. Larner, Carol S. Stevenson, Eugene M. Lewit, and Richard E. Behrman, "Long-Term Outcomes of Early Childhood Programs: Analysis and Recommendations," *The Future of Children* 5, 3 (1995): 6–24; Steven W. Barnett, "Long-Term Effects of Early Childhood Programs on Cognitive and School Outcomes," *The Future of Children* 5, 3 (1995): 25–50; Arthur J. Reynolds, "The Chicago Child-Parent Center and Expansion Program: A Study of Extended Early Child Intervention," in *Social Programs That Work*, ed. Jonathan Crane (New York: Russell Sage Foundation, 1998).

61. Frederick Mosteller, "The Tennessee Study of Class Size in the Early School Grades," *Future of Children* 5, 2 (1995): 113–27; Alan B. Krueger, "Reassessing the View That American Schools Are Broken," *FRBNY Economic Policy Review* (March 1998): 29–43; and Larry Cuban, "The Myth of Failed School Reform," *Education Week* (1 November 1995).

62. See our comments in the text; for more detail, see Marshall S. Smith and Jennifer O'Day, "Systemic School Reform," *Politics of Education Yearbook* (1990): 233–67.

63. John E. Chubb and Terry M. Moe, *Politics, Markets, and America's Schools* (Washington D.C.: Brookings Institution, 1990); Clarence Stone, ed., *Changing Urban Education* (Lawrence: University Press of Kansas, 1998); and Jeffrey R. Henig, Richard

C. Hula, Marion Orr, and Desiree S. Pedescleaux, *The Color of School Reform: Race, Politics, and the Challenge of Urban Education* (Princeton, N.J.: Princeton University Press, 1999).

64. Milton Friedman, *Capitalism and Freedom* (Chicago: University of Chicago Press, 1982).

65. Christopher Jencks, "Giving Parents Money for Schools: Education Vouchers," *Phi Delta Kappan* 111, 1 (1970): 49–52.

66. Chubb and Moe, *Politics, Markets.*

67. Diane Ravitch, "Somebody's Children: Educational Opportunity for All American Children," in *Social Policies for Children*, ed. Irwin Garfinkel, Jennifer Hochschild, and Sara McLanahan (Washington D.C.: Brookings Institution, 1996), 83–111, and Jeffrey R. Henig, *Rethinking School Choice: Limits of the Market Metaphor* (Princeton, N.J.: Princeton University Press, 1994), 113–16.

68. Joint Center for Political and Economic Studies, *1996 National Opinion Poll—Political Attitudes* (Washington D.C.: Joint Center for Political and Economic Studies, 1996), table 10; *1997 Poll,* table B-3; *1998 Poll,* table 4; Public Agenda Foundation, "An Agenda for Public Schools Survey," ques. 41–48 (accession nos. 0306970–0306977); John F. Witte, *The Market Approach to Education: An Analysis of America's First Voucher Program* (Princeton, N.J.: Princeton University Press, 2000), chap. 3.

69. Jay P. Green, Paul E. Peterson, and Jiangtao Du, "The Effectiveness of School Choice in Milwaukee: A Secondary Analysis of Data from the Program's Evaluation," paper prepared for the annual meeting of the American Political Science Association, San Francisco, 28 August–1 September 1996; Witte, *Market Approach;* and Cecilia E. Rouse, "Private School Vouchers and Student Achievement: An Evaluation of the Milwaukee Parental Choice Program," *Quarterly Journal of Economics* 113, 2 (May 1998): 553–602.

70. Hochschild and Scott, "The Polls—Trends," Jean Johnson et al., *Assignment Incomplete: The Unfinished Business of Education Reform* (New York: Public Agenda Foundation, 1995), table 3; and *U.S. News and World Report* poll, conducted by the Tarrance Group and Lake Research, 3–4 September 1996.

71. NBC News/*Wall Street Journal* poll, conducted by Hart Teeter Research Companies, 10–13 September 1998, ques. 74 (accession no. 0310011); Democratic Leadership Council, "Active Center Holds Survey," conducted by Penn, Schoen, and Berland Associates, 30 July–2 August 1998, ques. 76 (accession no. 0314686); American Association of University Women, 1998 Survey, ques. 27, 62, 63 (accession nos. 0320029, 0320064, and 0320065); and Phi Delta Kappa, "Attitudes Toward the Public Schools 1999 Survey," conducted by the Gallup Organization, 18 May–11 June 1999, ques 2.

72. Samual Roundfield Lucas, *Tracking Inequality: Stratification and Mobility in American High Schools* (New York: Teachers College Press, Columbia University, 1990).

73. Adam Gamoran and Robert D. Mare, "Secondary School Tracking and Educational Inequality: Compensation, Reinforcement, or Neutrality?" *American Journal of Sociology* 94, 5 (1989): 1146–83.

74. Jeannie Oakes, *Keeping Track: How Schools Structure Inequality* (New Haven, Conn.: Yale University Press, 1985).

75. Robert E. Slavin, "Achievement Effects of Ability Grouping in Secondary Schools: A Best-Evidence Synthesis," paper prepared for the National Center on Effective Secondary Schools, Wisconsin Center for Education Research, University of Wisconsin–Madison,

1990). One recent review finds evidence that, when properly done, tracking can help low—as well as high—achievers. See Ronald Ferguson, "Can Schools Narrow the Black-White Test Score Gap?" in Jencks and Phillips, *The Black-White Test Score Gap*, 318–74.

76. Johnson and Immerwahr, *First Things First*, 19.

77. David Tyack and Larry Cuban, *Tinkering Toward Utopia: A Century of Public School Reform* (Cambridge, Mass.: Harvard University Press, 1995).

78. See Michelle Fine, "Communities of Difference: A Critical Look at Desegregated Spaces Created for and by Youth," *Harvard Educational Review* 67, 2 (1997): 247–84.

79. Amy Stuart Wells and Irene Serna, "The Politics of Culture: Understanding Local Political Resistance to Detracking in Racially Mixed Schools," *Harvard Educational Review* 66, 1 (1996): 93–118, and Alexa J. Shore, "Detracking: The Politics of Creating Heterogeneous Ability Classrooms" (Thesis, Woodrow Wilson School of Public and International Affairs, Princeton University, 1996).

80. Gary Orfield and John T. Yun, "Resegregation in American Schools," paper prepared for the Civil Rights Project, Harvard University, 1999, 13–15; paper available at http://www.law.harvard.edu/civilrights.

81. Sheila E. Murray, William N. Evans, and Robert M. Schwab, "Education-Finance Reform and the Distribution of Education Resources," *American Economic Review* 88, 4 (1998): 789–812.

82. Krueger, "Reassessing the View," 30–31.

83. Mancur Olson, *The Logic of Collective Action* (Cambridge, Mass.: Harvard University Press, 1965).

84. Paris, *Ideology and Educational Reform*, and Labaree, *How to Succeed*.

85. Paul Campbell, "Population Projections: States, 1995–2025," paper prepared for U.S. Census Bureau, U.S. Department of Commerce, 1997.

86. U.S. Bureau of the Census website, *http://www.census.gov.;* 1996 data from website. These projections, of course, assume that the current racial and ethnic labels will remain fixed and relevant, and that intermarriage will not radically increase.

87. New Mexico is projected to follow the same pattern as California, and New York and New Jersey will probably be home to more Latinos than Anglos soon after 2025. Unless otherwise noted, the information in this paragraph comes from population projection charts on the U.S. Bureau of the Census website.

88. See, for example, Leon Bouvier and Vernon Briggs Jr., *The Population and Labor Force of New York, 1990–2050* (Washington, D.C.: Population Reference Bureau, 1988), and Leon Bouvier, *Florida in the 21st Century: The Challenge of Population Growth* (Washington D.C.: Center for Immigration Studies, 1992).

89. The dependency ratio is defined as the number of people younger than twenty and older than sixty-five for every 100 people of working age. By one prediction, the dependency ratio in the United States will increase from about 63:100 in 1992 to about 78:100 in 2030; see Jennifer C. Day, *Population Projections of the United States by Age, Sex, Race, and Hispanic Origin: 1995 to 2050*, U.S. Bureau of the Census, Current Population Reports, P25-1130 (Washington, D.C.: Government Printing Office, 1996), fig. 6 and table E.

90. Jennifer Hochschild and Deidre Kolarick, "Public Involvement in Decisions about Public Education," paper commissioned by the National Academy of Sciences

Committee on Educational Finance, 1997, 11–12, review the evidence on when the elderly do and do not oppose new spending on schools. The most recent study finds that the black elderly are more likely and the white elderly are less likely than the rest of the population to support higher school spending; see Gregory Weiher, Kent Tedin, and Richard Matland, "Age and Support for School Bonds: A Test of Voting Theories," paper presented at the annual meeting of the Midwest Political Science Association, Chicago, 1998.

91. Jennifer Hochschild and Reuel Rogers, "Race Relations in a Diversifying Nation," in *New Directions: African Americans in a Diversifying Nation*, ed. James Jackson (Washington D.C.: National Planning Association, 1999); Paula McClain and Joseph Stewart Jr., *Can We All Get Along? Racial and Ethnic Minorities in American Politics*, 2d ed. (Boulder, Colo.: Westview Press, 1998); and Michael Preston, Bruce Cain, and Sandra Bass, *Racial and Ethnic Politics in California*, vol. 2 (Berkeley, Calif.: Institute of Governmental Studies Press, 1998), discuss coalitional possibilities and tensions among racial and ethnic groups.

92. In the past few years, Hispanic immigrants to California have become naturalized citizens, registered voters, and Democratic Party supporters all at much higher rates than they did before Proposition 187. Many analysts attribute Governor Gray Davis's and other Democrats' success in the 1998 election to Hispanic support; soon after taking office, he made several high-profile Latino appointments (Robert Salladay and Zachary Coile, "Davis Takes the Helm," *San Francisco Examiner,* 4 January 1999; reduced efforts to implement Proposition 187 (Dave Lesher, "Davis Won't Follow Prop. 187 on Schools," *Los Angeles Times,* 21 May 1999; and pledged reform of public schools (Salladay and Coile, "Davis Takes the Helm"). Governor George Bush of Texas is learning the same lesson. As the composition and mood of voters in Texas change, the nationally ambitious governor increasingly emphasizes his inclusionary, pragmatic, compassionate conservatism over his former more rightist proclivities. See Richard Berke, "High in the Polls and Close to Home, Bush Navigates by the Center Line," *New York Times,* 9 April 1999.

93. *Sacramento v. Rachel Holland,* 512 U.S. 1207 (1994).

94. The best articulation of this position that we know of is Henry Levin, "Educational Choice and the Pains of Democracy," in *Public Dollars for Private Schools: The Case of Tuition Tax Credits,* ed. Thomas James and Henry M. Levin (Philadelphia: Temple University Press, 1983), 17–38. Elite parents might be reassured, although the rest of us will not be, by the fact that local communities and even whole regions are becoming increasingly, and unprecedentedly, segregated by class. See Paul Jargowsky, *Poverty and Place: Ghettos, Barrios, and the American City* (New York: Russell Sage Foundation, 1997); and William Frey, "The New Geography of Population Shifts: Trends Toward Balkanization," in *State of the Union—America in the 1990s,* vol. 2, *Social Trends,* ed. Reynolds Farley (New York: Russell Sage Foundation, 1995), 271–334.

95. Stone, *Changing Urban Education;* Richard Elmore, "Getting to Scale with Good Educational Practices," *Harvard Educational Review* 66, 1 (1996): 1–26; and Henig et al., *Color of School Reform,* all offer convincing analyses of why it will be difficult.

96. Jay P. Heubert and Robert M. Hauser, eds., *High Stakes: Testing for Tracking, Promotion, and Graduation* (Washington, D.C.: National Academy Press, 1999), and Lorraine McDonnell, Margaret McLaughlin, and Patricia Morison, eds., *Educating One and All: Students with Disabilities and Standards-Based Reform* (Washington, D.C.: National Academy Press, 1997).

97. Absent sufficient capital funding, new operating funds get diverted from instruction to buildings. Given the demographic trends, construction and renovation should be started as soon as possible so that the debt retires before the baby boomers do. Substantial state assistance, not just local bond funds, are needed, but politically this should be feasible given that public works means ribbon-cutting ceremonies.

Selected Bibliography

Ackerman, Bruce. *Social Justice in the Liberal State.* New Haven, Conn.: Yale University Press, 1980.

——. "Why Dialogue?" *Journal of Philosophy* 86 (1989): 5–22.

Adams, John. "A Dissertation on the Canon and Feudal Law." In *The Works of John Adams,* ed. Charles Francis Adams. Boston: Charles C. Little and James Brown, 1851.

Adler, Louise. "Institutional Responses: Public School Curriculum and Religious Conservatives in California." *Education and Urban Society* 28, 3 (1996): 327–46.

Alexander, Kern. "The Common School Ideal and the Limits of Legislative Authority: The Kentucky Case." *Harvard Journal on Legislation* 28, 2 (1991): 341–66.

Althschuler, Glenn, and Stuart M. Blumin. "Limits of Political Engagement in Antebellum America: A New Look at the Golden Age of Participatory Democracy." *Journal of American History* 84 (December 1997): 855–85.

American Association of University Women. "American Association of University Women Survey." Conducted by Lake, Snell, Perry, and Associates, June 1998.

Anderson, Benedict. *Imagined Communities: Reflections on the Origin and Spread of Nationalism.* Rev. ed. London: Verso, 1991.

Anderson, Christopher, Patricia G. Avery, Patricia V. Pederson, Elizabeth S. Smith, and John L. Sullivan. "Perspectives on Citizenship Education." Paper presented at the Annual Meeting of the American Educational Research Association, San Francisco, 22 April 1995.

Anderson, Lee, Lynn B. Jenkins, James Leming, Walter B. MacDonald, Ina V.S. Mullis, Mary Jane Turner, and Judith S. Wooster. *The Civics Report Card.* Princeton, N.J.: Education Testing Service, National Assessment of Educational Progress, 1990.

Appleby, Joyce. *Liberalism and Republicanism in the Historical Imagination.* Cambridge, Mass.: Harvard University Press, 1992.

Arrow, Kenneth J. *Social Choice and Individual Values.* Rev. ed. New York: Wiley, 1963.

August, Diane, and Kenji Hakuta, eds. *Educating Language-Minority Children.* Washington, D.C.: National Academy Press, 1998.

Avery, Patricia G., Karen Bird, Sandra Johnstone, John L. Sullivan, and Kristina

Thalhammer. "Exploring Political Tolerance with Adolescents." *Theory and Research in Social Education* 20, 4 (Fall 1992): 386–420.

Axelrod, Robert M. *The Evolution of Cooperation.* New York: Basic Books, 1984.

Bachrach, Peter, and Morton Baratz. "The Two Faces of Power." *American Political Science Review* 56 (1962): 947–952.

Baker, Edward, Margaret Wang, and Herbert Walberg. "The Effects of Inclusion on Learning." *Educational Leadership* 52, 4 (1994/1995): 33–35.

Barber, Benjamin R. *Strong Democracy: Participatory Politics for a New Age.* Berkeley: University of California Press, 1984.

———. *An Aristocracy of Everyone: The Politics of Education and the Future of America.* New York: Oxford University Press, 1992.

Barber, Bernard. "Some Problems in the Sociology of Professions." In *The Professions in America*, ed. K. S. Lyn. Boston: Houghton Mifflin, 1965.

Barker, Ernest. *Greek Political Theory.* London: Methuen, 1947.

Barnett, W. Steven. "Long-Term Effects of Early Childhood Programs on Cognitive and School Outcomes." *Future of Children* 5, 3 (1995): 25–50.

Bell, Derrick. "Serving Two Masters: Integration Ideals and Client Interests in School Desegregation Litigation." *Yale Law Journal* 85, 4 (1976): 470–516.

Bennett, Stephen Earl. "'Know Nothings' Revisited: The Meaning of Political Ignorance Today." *Social Science Quarterly* 69 (1988): 476–90.

———. "Trends in Americans' Political Information, 1967–1987." *American Politics Quarterly* 17 (October 1989): 422–35.

Berg, William, and David Colton. "Budgeting for Desegregation in Urban School Systems." *Integrated Education* 20, 1–2 (1982): 40–48.

Bessette, Joseph M. *The Mild Voice of Reason: Deliberative Democracy and American National Government.* Chicago: University of Chicago Press, 1994.

Bickford, Susan. *The Dissonance of Democracy: Listening, Conflict, and Citizenship.* Ithaca, N.Y.: Cornell University Press, 1996.

Binder, Amy. "Friend and Foe: Boundary Work and Collective Identity in the Afrocentric and Multicultural Curriculum Movements in American Public Education." In *The Cultural Territories of Race: Black and White Boundaries,* ed. Michele Lamont. Chicago: University of Chicago Press, 1999.

Bleyer, Willard. *Main Currents in the History of American Journalism.* Boston: Houghton Mifflin, 1927.

Bohman, James. *Public Deliberation: Pluralism, Complexity, and Democracy.* Cambridge, Mass.: MIT Press, 1996.

Bouvier, Leon, and Vernon Briggs Jr. *The Population and Labor Force of New York, 1990–2050.* Washington, D.C.: Population Reference Bureau, 1988.

———. *Florida in the 21st Century: The Challenge of Population Growth.* Washington, D.C.: Center for Immigration Studies, 1992.

Boyd, William Lowe, Robert L. Crowson, and Tyll van Geel. "Rational Choice Theory and the Politics of Education: Promise and Limits." In *The Study of Educational Politics*, ed. Jay D. Scribner and Donald H. Layton. Bristol, Pa.: Falmer Press, 1995.

Boyd, William Lowe, et al. "Social Traditionalists, Religious Conservatives, and the Politics of Outcomes-Based Education: Pennsylvania and Beyond." *Education and Urban Society* 28, 3 (1996): 247–365.

Boyer, Ernest. *High School: A Report on Secondary Education in America.* New York: Harper and Row, 1983.

Brady, David W. *Critical Elections and Congressional Policy Making.* Stanford, Calif.: Stanford University Press, 1988.

Brantlinger, Ellen. "Using Ideology: Cases of Nonrecognition of the Politics of Research and Practice in Special Education." *Review of Educational Research* 67, 4 (Winter 1997): 425–59.

Brown, Richard D. *Knowledge Is Power: The Diffusion of Information in Early America, 1700–1865.* New York: Oxford University Press, 1989.

———. *The Strength of a People: The Idea of an Informed Citizenry in America, 1650–1870.* Chapel Hill: University of North Carolina Press, 1996.

Bruner, Jerome. *The Culture of Education.* Cambridge, Mass.: Harvard University Press, 1996.

Bryk, Anthony S., et al. "The State of Chicago School Reform." *Phi Delta Kappan* 76, 1 (1994): 74–78.

Burns, Tom R., and Helena Flam. *The Shaping of Social Organization: Social Rule System Theory with Applications.* Beverly Hills, Calif.: Sage, 1987.

Burtless, Gary, ed. *Does Money Matter: The Effect of School Resources on Student Achievement and Adult Success.* Washington, D.C.: Brookings Institution, 1996.

Butts, R. Freeman. *The Civic Mission in Educational Reform: Perspectives for the Public and the Profession.* Stanford, Calif.: Hoover Institution Press, 1989.

Cabell, Nathaniel Francis, ed. *Early History of the University of Virginia as Contained in the Letters of Thomas Jefferson and Joseph Cabell.* Richmond, Va.: J. W. Randolph, 1856.

Cable News Network/*USA Today.* Poll conducted by the Gallup Organization, April 22–24, 1994.

Cameron, Beatrice H., Keith E. Underwood, and Jim C. Fortune. "Politics and Power: How You're Selected and Elected to Lead This Nation's Schools." *American School Board Journal* (1988): 17–19.

Campbell, Paul. "Population Projections: States, 1995–2025." Paper prepared for the U.S. Census Bureau, U.S. Department of Commerce, 1997.

Campbell, Roald F., et al. *The Organization and Control of American Schools.* 4th ed. Columbus, Ohio: Charles E. Merrill, 1980.

Cantor, Nancy, Hazel Marcus, Paula Niedenthal, and Paula Nurius. "On Motivation and the Self Concept." In *Handbook of Motivation and Cognition,* ed. Richard M. Sorrentino and E. Tory Higgins. New York: Guilford Press, 1986.

Cappon, Lester J., ed. *The Adams–Jefferson Letters,* 2 vols. Chapel Hill: University of North Carolina Press, 1959.

Carlberg, Conrad, and Kenneth Kavale. "The Efficacy of Special Versus Regular Class Placement for Exceptional Children: A Meta-Analysis." *Journal of Special Education* 14 (1980): 295–309.

Carroll, Glenn R., and J. Richard Harrison. "Historical Efficiency of Competition Between Organizational Populations." *American Journal of Sociology* 100 (1994): 720–49.

Chambers, Simone. *Reasonable Democracy: Jürgen Habermas and the Politics of Discourse.* Ithaca, N.Y.: Cornell University Press, 1996.

Chancellor, William Estabrook. *Our Schools: Their Administration and Supervision.* Rev. ed. Boston: D. C. Heath, 1915.

Cheney, Lynne V. *American Memory: A Report on the Humanities in the Nation's Public Schools.* Washington, D.C.: National Endowment for the Humanities, 1987.

Chubb, John E., and Terry M. Moe. *Politics, Markets, and America's Schools.* Washington, D.C.: Brookings Institution, 1990.

Coase, Ronald H. *Essays on Economics and Economists.* Chicago: University of Chicago Press, 1994.

Cohen, Carl. "The Justification of Democracy." *Monist* 55 (1971): 1–28.

Cohen, David K., and James P. Spillane. "Policy and Practice: The Relations Between Governance and Instruction." *Review of Research in Education* 18 (1992): 3–49

Cohen, Jean L., and Andrew Arato. *Civil Society and Political Theory.* Cambridge, Mass.: MIT Press, 1992.

Coleman, James S. "Foundations for a Theory of Collective Decisions." *American Journal of Sociology* 71 (1966): 615–27.

———. "The Possibility of a Social Welfare Function." *American Economic Review* 56, 5 (1966): 1105–22.

———. *Foundations of Social Theory.* Cambridge, Mass.: Harvard University Press, 1990.

Coleman, James S., et al. *Report on Equality of Educational Opportunity.* Washington, D.C.: Government Printing Office, 1966.

Committee on the Political Economy of the Good Society, *The Good Society.* College Park, Md.: Symposium on Group Rights, Spring 1996.

Conant, James B. *Slums and Suburbs.* New York: McGraw-Hill, 1961.

Connolly, William. *Identity/Difference: Democratic Negotiations of Political Paradox.* Ithaca, N.Y.: Cornell University Press, 1991.

Conover, Pamela Johnston. "Political Socialization: Where's the Politics?" In *Political Behavior,* vol. 3 of *Political Science: Looking to the Future,* ed. William Crotty, 125–52. Evanston, Ill.: Northwestern University Press, 1991.

———. "Citizen Identities and Conceptions of the Self." *Journal of Political Philosophy* 3 (1995): 133–65.

Conover, Pamela Johnston, and Barbara Hicks. "The Psychology of Overlapping Identities: Ethnic, Citizen, Nation, and Beyond." In *National Identities and Ethnic Minorities in Eastern Europe,* ed. Ray Taras. New York: Macmillan, 1998.

Conover, Pamela Johnston, and Donald Searing. "Political Discussion and the Politics of Identity." Paper presented at the 1998 Annual Meeting of the Midwest Political Science Association, Chicago, April 1998.

Cook, Timothy E. "The Bear Market in Political Socialization and the Costs of Misunderstood Psychological Theories." *American Political Science Review* 79 (1985): 1079–93.

Cooper, James Fenimore. *The American Democrat.* Indianapolis: Liberty Fund, n.d.

Coram, Robert. "Political Inquiries, to Which Is Added, a Plan for the General Establishment of Schools." In *Essays on Education in the Early Republic,* ed. Frederick Rudolph. Cambridge, Mass.: Harvard University Press, 1965.

Corcoran, Thomas, and Nathan Scovronick. "More Than Equal: New Jersey's Quality Education Act." In *Strategies for School Equity: Creating Productive Schools in a Just Society,* ed. Marilyn Gittell. New Haven, Conn.: Yale University Press, 1998.

Counts, George S. *The Social Composition of Boards of Education: A Study in the Social Control of Public Education*. Chicago: University of Chicago Press, 1927.

Cox, Gary, and Mathew D. McCubbins. *Legislative Leviathan*. Berkeley: University of California Press, 1994.

Cremin, Lawrence A. *The Genius of American Education*. Pittsburgh: University of Pittsburgh Press, 1965.

———. *Popular Education and Its Discontents*. New York: Harper and Row, 1990.

Cronbach, Lee J. *Designing Evaluations of Educational and Social Programs*. San Francisco: Jossey-Bass, 1982.

Cuban, Larry. "A Tale of Two Schools." *Education Week* (28 January 1998): 33, 48.

Cubberley, Ellwood P. *Public School Administration*. Boston: Houghton-Mifflin, 1916.

Cyert, Richard M., and James G. March. *A Behavioral Theory of the Firm*. Englewood Cliffs, N.J.: Prentice-Hall, 1963.

Dahl, Robert A. *After the Revolution? Authority in a Good Society*. New Haven, Conn.: Yale University Press, 1970.

———. *Dilemmas of Pluralist Democracy: Autonomy vs. Control*. New Haven, Conn.: Yale University Press, 1982.

———. *Democracy and Its Critics*. New Haven, Conn.: Yale University Press, 1989.

Day, Jennifer C. *Population Projections of the United States by Age, Sex, Race, and Hispanic Origin: 1995 to 2050*, U.S. Bureau of the Census, Current Population Reports, P25-1130. Washington, D.C.: Government Printing Office, 1996.

Delli Carpini, Michael X., and Scott Keeter. *What Americans Know About Politics and Why It Matters*. New Haven, Conn.: Yale University Press, 1996.

Delpit, Lisa. *Other People's Children: Cultural Conflict in the Classroom*. New York: New Press, 1995.

Democratic Leadership Council. "Active Center Holds Survey." Conducted by Penn, Schoen, and Berland Associates, July 30–August 2, 1998.

Dewey, John. *Liberalism and Social Action*. New York: G. P. Putnam's Sons, 1935.

———. *Freedom and Culture*. New York: G. P. Putnam's Sons, 1939.

———. *Introduction to the Living Thoughts of Thomas Jefferson*. New York: Longmans, Green, 1940.

———. *German Philosophy and Politics*. Rev. ed. New York: G. P. Putnam's Sons, 1942.

———. *The Public and Its Problems*. Rev. ed. Chicago: Gateway Books, 1946.

———. *Experience and Education*. New York: Collier Books, 1963.

———. *Democracy and Education*. New York: Free Press, 1966.

———. *John Dewey on Education*. Ed. Reginald D. Archambault. Chicago: University of Chicago Press, 1974.

Di Palma, Giuseppe. *To Craft Democracies*. Berkeley: University of California Press, 1990.

Doherty, Kathryn. "Changing Urban Education: Defining the Issues." In *Changing Urban Education*, ed. Clarence Stone. Lawrence: University Press of Kansas, 1998.

Douglas, Mary. *How Institutions Think*. Syracuse, N.Y.: Syracuse University Press, 1986.

Downs, Anthony. *An Economic Theory of Democracy*. New York: Harper and Row, 1957.

———. *Inside Bureaucracy*. Boston: Little, Brown, 1967.

Durkheim, Emile. *Moral Education*. Trans. E. K. Wilson and H. Schnurer. New York: Free Press, 1961.

Education Week on the Web. "Oregon Summary." In *Quality Counts '98*, *http://www.ed-week.org/*, 1998.

Eisenstadt, Samuel N., and Stein Rokkan, eds. *Building States and Nations*. 2 vols. Beverly Hills, Calif.: Sage, 1973.

Elam, Stanley. *How America Views Its Schools: The PDK/Gallup Polls, 1969–1994*. Bloomington, Ind.: Phi Delta Kappa Educational Foundation, 1995.

Elam, Stanley, ed. *The Gallup/Phi Delta Kappa Polls of Attitudes Toward the Public Schools, 1969–88*. Bloomington, Ind.: Phi Delta Kappa Educational Foundation, 1989.

Elam, Stanley M., and Lowell C. Rose. "The 27th Annual Phi Delta Kappa/Gallup Poll of the Public's Attitudes Toward the Public Schools." *Phi Delta Kappan* 77, 1 (1995): 41–56.

Elam, Stanley M., Lowell C. Rose, and Alec M. Gallup. "The 24th Annual Phi Delta Kappa/Gallup Poll of the Public's Attitudes Toward the Public Schools." *Phi Delta Kappan* 74, 1 (1992): 41–53.

———. "The 25th Annual Phi Delta Kappa/Gallup Poll of the Public's Attitudes Toward the Public Schools." *Phi Delta Kappan* 75, 2 (1993): 137–52.

———. "The 26th Annual Phi Delta Kappa/Gallup Poll of the Public's Attitudes Toward the Public Schools." *Phi Delta Kappan* 76, 1 (1994): 41–64.

———. "The 28th Annual Phi Delta Kappa/Gallup Poll of the Public's Attitudes Toward the Public Schools." *Phi Delta Kappan* 78, 1 (1996): 41–59.

———. "The 29th Annual Phi Delta Kappa/Gallup Poll of the Public's Attitudes Toward the Public Schools." *Phi Delta Kappan* 79, 1 (1997): 41–56.

Ellis, Richard E. "The Market Revolution and the Transformation of American Politics, 1801–1837." In *The Market Revolution in America: Social, Political, and Religious Expressions, 1800–1880*, ed. Melvyn Stokes and Stephen Conway. Charlottesville: University Press of Virginia, 1996.

Elmore, Richard F. "School Decentralization: Who Gains? Who Loses?" In *Decentralization and School Improvement: Can We Fulfill the Promise?* ed. Jane Hannaway and Martin Carnoy. San Francisco: Jossey-Bass, 1993.

———. "Getting to Scale with Good Educational Practices." *Harvard Educational Review* 66, 1 (1996): 1–26.

Elmore, Richard F., and Milbrey W. McLaughlin, *Steady Work: Policy, Practice, and the Reform of American Education*. Santa Monica, Calif.: RAND, 1988.

Elster, Jon. *Nuts and Bolts for the Social Sciences*. Cambridge: Cambridge University Press, 1988.

———. *The Cement of Society*. Cambridge: Cambridge University Press, 1989.

Epstein, David. *The Political Theory of* The Federalist. Chicago: University of Chicago Press, 1984.

Etzioni, Amitai. *The Spirit of Community: Rights, Responsibilities, and the Communitarian Agenda*. New York: Crown Publishers, 1993.

Factory Inspectors of Illinois. *Third Annual Report of the Factory Inspectors of Illinois*. Springfield, Ill.: H. W. Rokker, 1895.

Farkas, Steve. *Divided Within, Besieged Without: The Politics of Education in Four American School Districts*. New York: Public Agenda Foundation, 1993.

Feller, Daniel. "The Market Revolution Ate My Homework." *Reviews in American History* 25 (September 1997): 408–15.

Ferguson, Ronald. "Can Schools Narrow the Black-White Test Score Gap?" In *The Black-White Test Score Gap,* ed. Christopher Jencks and Meredith Phillips, 318–74. Washington, D.C.: Brookings Institution, 1998.

Fine, Michelle. "Communities of Difference: A Critical Look at Desegregated Spaces Created for and by Youth." *Harvard Educational Review* 67, 2 (1997): 247–84.

Fishkin, James S. *Democracy and Deliberation: New Directions for Democratic Reform* New Haven, Conn.: Yale University Press, 1991.

Flathman, Richard E. *The Practice of Political Authority.* Chicago: University of Chicago Press, 1980.

Franklin, Benjamin. "Constitutions of the Publick Academy in the City of Philadelphia." In *Benjamin Franklin on Education*, ed. John Best, 152–58. 1749. Reprint. New York: Teachers College Press, 1962.

———. *The Works of Benjamin Franklin.* 10 vols. Ed. Jared Sparks. London: B. F. Stevens, 1882.

———. *The Papers of Benjamin Franklin.* 34 vols. Ed. Leonard Labaree et al. New Haven, Conn.: Yale University Press, 1959–.

———. *The Autobiography of Benjamin Franklin.* Ed. Leonard W. Labaree. New Haven, Conn.: Yale University Press, 1964.

———. "Proposals Relating to the Education of Youth in Pennsylvania." In *Writings*, ed. J. A. Lemay. New York: Library of America, 1987.

Frazer, Elizabeth, and Nicola Lacey. "MacIntyre, Feminism, and the Concept of Practice." In *After MacIntyre: Critical Perspectives on the Work of Alasdiar MacIntyre*, ed. John Horton and Susan Mendus. Notre Dame, Ind.: University of Notre Dame Press, 1994.

Frey, William. "The New Geography of Population Shifts: Trends Toward Balkanization." In *Social Trends,* vol. 2 of *State of the Union—America in the 1990s,* ed. Reynolds Farley. New York: Russell Sage Foundation, 1995.

Friedman, Milton. *Capitalism and Freedom.* Chicago: University of Chicago Press, 1982.

Fuhrman, Susan H., and Richard F. Elmore. "Understanding Local Control in the Wake of State Education Reform." *Educational Evaluation and Policy Analysis* 12, 1 (1990): 82–96.

Galston, William A. "Liberal Virtues." *American Political Science Review* 82 (1988): 1277–92.

———. *Liberal Purposes.* New York: Cambridge University Press, 1991.

Gamoran, Adam, and Robert D. Mare. "Secondary School Tracking and Educational Inequality: Compensation, Reinforcement, or Neutrality?" *American Journal of Sociology* 94, 5 (1989): 1146–83.

Garrett, Geoff, and Barry R. Weingast. "Ideas, Interests and Institutions: Constructing the European Community's Internal Market." In *Ideas and Foreign Policy*, ed. J. Goldstein and R. O. Keohane. Ithaca, N.Y.: Cornell University Press, 1993.

Gerber, Elizabeth R., and John E. Jackson. "Endogenous Preferences and the Study of Institutions." *American Political Science Review* 87 (1993): 639–56.

Gewirtz, Paul. "The Triumph and Transformation of Antidiscrimination Law." In *Race, Law, and Culture*, ed. Austin Sarat. New York: Oxford University Press, 1997.

Glendon, Mary Ann. *Rights Talk: The Impoverishment of Political Discourse.* New York: Free Press, 1991.

Goldstein, Judith, and Robert O. Keohane, eds. *Ideas and Foreign Policy.* Ithaca, N.Y.: Cornell University Press, 1993.

Gomby, Deanna S., Mary B. Larner, Carol S. Stevenson, Eugene M. Lewit, and Richard E. Behrman. "Long-Term Outcomes of Early Childhood Programs: Analysis and Recommendations." *The Future of Children* 5, 3 (1995): 6–24.

Goode, Harry G. *Benjamin Rush and His Services to American Education.* Berne, Ind.: Witness Press, 1918.

Goodin, Robert E. "Institutionalizing the Public Interest: The Defense of Deadlock and Beyond." *American Political Science Review* 90, 2 (1996): 331–43.

Green, Donald P., and Ian Shapiro, *Pathologies of Rational Choice Theory.* New Haven, Conn.: Yale University Press, 1993.

Green, Jay P., Paul E. Peterson, and Jiangtao Du. *The Effectiveness of School Choice in Milwaukee: A Secondary Analysis of Data from the Program's Evaluation.* Paper prepared for the annual meeting of the American Political Science Association, San Francisco, 1996.

Grissmer, David, and Ann Flanagan. "Exploring Rapid Achievement Gains in North Carolina and Texas." Washington, D.C.: National Education Goals Panel, November 1998.

Gruber, Judith E. *Controlling Bureaucracies: Dilemmas in Democratic Governance.* Berkeley: University of California Press, 1987.

Gutmann, Amy. *Democratic Education.* Princeton, N.J.: Princeton University Press, 1987.

———. "Undemocratic Education." In *Liberalism and the Moral Life*, ed. Nancy L. Rosenblum. Cambridge, Mass.: Harvard University Press, 1989.

———. "Civic Education and Social Diversity." *Ethics* 105 (1995): 557–79.

———. "The Virtues of Democratic Self-Restraint." In *New Communitarian Thinking: Persons, Virtues, Institutions, and Communities*, ed. Amitai Etzioni. Charlottesville: University Press of Virginia, 1995.

———. "Challenges of Multiculturalism in Democratic Education." In *Public Education in a Multicultural Society*, ed. Robert K. Fullinwider. Cambridge: Cambridge University Press, 1996.

Gutmann, Amy, and Dennis Thompson, *Democracy and Disagreement.* Cambridge, Mass.: Belknap Press of Harvard University Press, 1996.

Habermas, Jürgen. *Theorie des Kommunikativen Handels.* Frankfurt: Suhrkamp, 1981.

———. *The Structural Transformation of the Public Sphere: An Inquiry into a Category of Bourgeois Society.* Trans. Thomas Berger. Cambridge, Mass.: MIT Press, 1989.

———. "Towards a Communication-Concept of Rational Collective Will-Formation: A Thought Experiment." *Ratio Juris* 2, 2 (1989): 144–54.

———. *Moral Consciousness and Communicative Action.* Trans. Christian Lehnardt and Sherry Weber Nicholsen. Cambridge, Mass.: MIT Press, 1990.

Hall, David D. *Worlds of Wonder, Days of Judgment: Popular Religious Belief in Early New England.* Cambridge, Mass.: Harvard University Press, 1989.

Hall, Peter A. *The Political Power of Economic Ideas.* Princeton, N.J.: Princeton University Press, 1989.

Hammond, Thomas H. "Formal Theory and the Institutions of Governance." *Governance* 9 (1996): 107–85.

Harrison, J. Richard, and James G. March. "Decision Making and Post-Decision Surprises." *Administrative Science Quarterly* 29 (1984): 26–42.

Harsanyi, John C. *Rational Behavior and Bargaining Equilibrium in Games and Social Situations.* Cambridge: Cambridge University Press, 1977.

Heidenheimer, Arnold. "The Politics of Public Education, Health, and Welfare in the USA and Western Europe." *British Journal of Political Science* 3, 1 (1973): 315–40.

———. "Education and Social Security Entitlements in Europe and America." In *The Development of Welfare States in Europe and America*, ed. Peter Flora and Arnold Heidenheimer, 269–304. New Brunswick, N.J.: Transaction Books, 1981.

Held, David. *Models of Democracy.* Oxford: Polity Press, 1987.

Heller, K., W. Holtzman, and Samuel Messick. *Placing Children in Special Education: A Strategy for Equity.* Washington, D.C.: National Academy of Science Press, 1982.

Henig, Jeffrey R. *Rethinking School Choice: Limits of the Market Metaphor.* Princeton, N.J.: Princeton University Press, 1994.

Henig, Jeffrey, Richard Hula, Marion Orr, and Desiree Pedesclaux. *The Color of School Reform: Race, Politics, and the Challenge of Urban Education.* Princeton, N.J.: Princeton University Press, 1999.

Henry J. Kaiser Foundation/Harvard School of Public Health. "Kaiser, Harvard Post-Election Survey: Priorities for 106th Congress." Conducted by Princeton Survey Research Associates, November 4–December 6, 1998.

Hess, G. Alfred. *Restructuring Urban Schools: A Chicago Perspective.* New York: Teachers College Press, 1995.

Hibbing, John R., and Elizabeth Theiss-Morse. "Civics is Not Enough: Teaching Barbarics in K–12." *PS: Political Science and Politics* 29 (1996): 57–62.

Hirschman, Albert O. *Exit, Voice, and Loyalty.* Cambridge, Mass.: Harvard University Press, 1970.

Hochschild, Jennifer L. *The New American Dilemma: Liberal Democracy and School Desegregation.* New Haven, Conn.: Yale University Press, 1984.

———. *Facing Up to the American Dream: Race, Class, and the Soul of the Nation.* Princeton, N.J.: Princeton University Press, 1995.

Hochschild, Jennifer, and Deidre Kolarick. "Public Involvement in Decisions About Public Education." Paper commissioned by the National Academy of Sciences Committee on Educational Finance, 1997.

Hochschild, Jennifer, and Reuel Rogers. "Race Relations in a Diversifying Nation." In *New Directions: African Americans in a Diversifying Nation,* ed. James Jackson. Washington, D.C.: National Planning Association, 1999.

Hochschild, Jennifer, and Bridget Scott. "The Polls—Trends: Governance and Reform of Public Education in the United States." *Public Opinion Quarterly* 62, 1 (1998): 79–120.

Horn, Murray J. *The Political Economy of Public Administration: Institutional Choice in the Public Sector.* New York: Cambridge University Press, 1995.

Howe, Daniel Walker. *The Political Culture of the American Whigs.* Chicago: University of Chicago Press, 1979.

Huntington, Samuel. *American Politics: The Promise of Disharmony.* Cambridge, Mass.: Harvard University Press, 1981.

Isenberg, Nancy. *Sex and Citizenship in Antebellum America.* Chapel Hill: University of North Carolina Press, 1998.

Jackson, Barbara L., and James G. Cibulka. "Leadership Turnover and Business Mobilization: The Changing Political Ecology of Urban School Systems." In *The Politics of Urban Education in the United States*, ed. James G. Cibulka, Rodney J. Reed, and Kenneth M. Wong. Bristol, Pa.: Falmer Press, 1992.

James, Thomas. "State Authority and the Politics of Educational Change." *Review of Research in Education* 17 (1991): 169–224.

Janowitz, Morris. *The Reconstruction of Patriotism: Education for Civic Consciousness.* Chicago: University of Chicago Press, 1983.

Jargowsky, Paul. *Poverty and Place: Ghettos, Barrios, and the American City.* New York: Russell Sage Foundation, 1997.

Jefferson, Thomas. "Report of the Commissioners Appointed to Fix the Site of the University of Virginia." In *Early History of the University of Virginia, as Contained in the Letters of Thomas Jefferson and Joseph Cabell,* 432–47. 1818. Reprint. Richmond, Va.: J. W. Randolph, 1856.

———. *The Writings of Thomas Jefferson.* 20 vols. Ed. Andrew A. Lipscomb and Albert E. Bergh. Washington, D.C.: Thomas Jefferson Memorial Association, 1903.

———. *The Works of Thomas Jefferson.* 12 vols. Ed. Paul L. Ford. New York: G. P. Putnam's Sons, 1904–1905.

———. *The Complete Jefferson.* Ed. Saul Padover. New York: Duell, Sloan, and Pearce, 1943.

———. *The Life and Selected Writings of Thomas Jefferson.* Ed. Adrienne Koch and William Peden. New York: Random House, Modern Library, 1944.

———. *The Papers of Thomas Jefferson.* 2 vols. Ed. Julian Boyd et al. Princeton, N.J.: Princeton University Press, 1950.

———. *Notes on the State of Virginia.* New York: W. W. Norton, 1972.

Jencks, Christopher. "Giving Parents Money for Schools: Education Vouchers." *Phi Delta Kappan* 111, 1 (1970): 49–52.

Jencks, Christopher, and Meredith Phillips, eds. *The Black-White Test Score Gap.* Washington, D.C.: Brookings Institution, 1998.

Johnson, Jean, and John Immerwahr. *First Things First: What Americans Expect from the Public Schools.* New York: Public Agenda Foundation, 1994.

Johnson, Jean, et al. *Assignment Incomplete: The Unfinished Business of Education Reform.* New York: Public Agenda Foundation, 1995.

Joint Center for Political and Economic Studies. *1996 National Opinion Poll—Political Attitudes.* Washington, D.C.: Joint Center for Political and Economic Studies, 1996.

———. *1997 National Opinion Poll—Children's Issues.* Washington, D.C.: Joint Center for Political and Economic Studies, 1997.

———. *1998 National Opinion Poll—Education.* Washington, D.C.: Joint Center for Political and Economic Studies, 1998.

Jung, David J., and David L. Kirp. "Law as an Instrument of Educational Policy-Making." *American Journal of Comparative Law* 32 (1984): 625–78.

Kaestle, Carl F. *Pillars of the Republic: Common Schools and American Society, 1780–1860.* New York: Hill and Wang, 1983.

Kaestle, Carl F., with Helen Damon-Moore, Lawrence C. Stedman, Katherine Tinsley, and William Vance Trollinger Jr. *Literacy in the United States: Reading and Readers Since 1880.* New Haven, Conn.: Yale University Press, 1991.

Kaestle, Carl F., and Maris A. Vinovskis. *Education and Social Change in Nineteenth-Century Massachusetts.* New York: Cambridge University Press, 1980.

Katznelson, Ira, and Margaret Weir. *Schooling for All: Class, Race, and the Decline of the Democratic Ideal.* New York: Basic Books, 1985.

Kavale, Kenneth. "Effectiveness of Special Education." In *The Handbook of School Psychology*, ed. Terry B. Gutkin and Cecil R. Reynolds. New York: Wiley, 1990.

Keohane, Robert O. *After Hegemony.* Princeton, N.J.: Princeton University Press, 1984.

Kerber, Linda K. "The Republican Ideology of the Revolutionary Generation." *American Quarterly* 37 (1985): 474–95.

———. "The Meanings of Citizenship." *Journal of American History* 84 (December 1997): 833–54.

———. *No Constitutional Right to Be Ladies: Women and the Obligations of Citizenship.* New York: Hill and Wang, 1998.

Kiewiet, D. Roderick, and Mathew D. McCubbins. *The Logic of Delegation.* Chicago: University of Chicago Press, 1991.

Kingdon, John W. *Agendas, Alternatives, and Public Policies.* 2d ed. New York: Harper-Collins, 1995.

Klosko, George. "Rawls's 'Political' Philosophy and American Democracy." *American Political Science Review* 87 (1993): 348–59.

Knight, Edgar W. *A Documentary History of Education in the South Before 1860.* 5 vols. Chapel Hill: University of North Carolina Press, 1950.

Knox, Samuel. "An Essay on the Best System of Liberal Education." In *Essays on Education in the Early Republic*, ed. Frederick Rudolph. Cambridge, Mass.: Harvard University Press, 1965.

Kramer, R. M. "Cooperation and Organizational Identification." In *Social Psychology in Organizations: Advances in Theory and Research*, ed. J. Keith Murnighan. Englewood Cliffs, N.J.: Prentice-Hall, 1993.

Krasner, Stephen D. "Sovereignty: An Institutional Perspective." *Comparative Political Studies* 21 (1988): 66–94.

Kreps, David M. "Corporate Culture and Economic Theory." In *Perspectives on Positive Political Economy*, ed. James E. Alt and Kenneth A. Shepsle. New York: Cambridge University Press, 1990.

Kurland, Philip, and Ralph Lerner, eds. *The Founders' Constitution.* 5 vols. Chicago: University of Chicago Press, 1987.

Kyle, M. J., ed. *Reaching for Excellence: An Effective Schools Sourcebook.* Washington, D.C.: National Institute of Education, 1985.

Labaree, David F. *How to Succeed in School Without Really Learning.* New Haven, Conn.: Yale University Press, 1997.

———. "Public Goods, Private Goods: The American Struggle over Educational Goals." *American Educational Research Journal* 34 (1997): 39–81.

Lafitte du Courteil, Amable-Louis-Rose de. "Proposal to Demonstrate the Necessity of a National Institution in the United States of America, for the Education of Children of Both Sexes." In *Essays on Education in the Early Republic,* ed. Frederick Rudolph. Cambridge, Mass.: Harvard University Press, 1965.

Lawrence, D. H. "Benjamin Franklin." *English Review* 27 (1918): 397–408.

———. *Studies in Classic American Literature.* New York: Viking Press, 1961.

Lazerson, Marvin, and W. Norton Grubb, eds. *American Education and Vocationalism: A Documentary History, 1870–1970.* New York: Teachers College Press, 1974.

Lee, Gordon C., ed. *Crusade Against Ignorance: Thomas Jefferson on Education.* New York: Teachers College Press, 1961.

Lerner, Ralph. "Commerce and Character: The Anglo-American as New-Model Man," *William and Mary Quarterly,* 3d ser., 36 (1979): 3–26.

Levin, Henry. "Educational Choice and the Pains of Democracy." In *Public Dollars for Private Schools: The Case of Tuition Tax Credits,* ed. Thomas James and Henry M. Levin, 17–38. Philadelphia: Temple University Press, 1983.

Levinthal, D. A., and James G. March. "The Myopia of Learning." *Strategic Management Journal* 14 (1993): 95–112.

Levitt, Barbara, and James G. March. "Organizational Learning." *Annual Review of Sociology* 14 (1988): 319–40.

Lieberman, Myron. *Public Education: An Autopsy.* Cambridge, Mass.: Harvard University Press, 1993.

———. *The Teacher Unions.* New York: Free Press, 1997.

Lipset, Seymour Martin. *Continental Divide.* New York: Routledge, 1990.

Lissitz, Robert. "Assessment of Student Performance and Attitude, Year IV—1994." Report submitted to Voluntary Interdistrict Coordinating Council, St. Louis, Missouri, 1994.

Locke, John. *Second Treatise on Civil Government,* 1690.

Los Angeles Times. Poll conducted September 21–25, 1991.

Lowi, Theodore. *The End of Liberalism.* New York: Norton, 1969.

Macedo, Stephen. "Liberal Civic Education and Religious Fundamentalism: The Case of God v. John Rawls?" *Ethics* 105 (1995), 468–96.

———. *Liberalism, Civic Education, and Diversity.* Cambridge, Mass.: Harvard University Press, 1999.

MacIntyre, Alasdair. *After Virtue.* Notre Dame, Ind.: University of Notre Dame Press, 1984.

Lee, Valerie E., and Anthony S. Bryk. "Science or Policy Argument: A Review of the Quantitative Evidence in Chubb and Moe's *Politics, Markets, and America's Schools.*" In *School Choice: Examining the Evidence,* ed. Edith Rasell and Richard Rothstein. Washington, D.C.: Economic Policy Institute, 1993.

Madison, James. *Letters and Other Writings of James Madison.* 4 vols. Philadelphia: J. B. Lippincott, 1865.

Madison, James, Alexander Hamilton, and John Jay. *The Federalist Papers.* Ed. Clinton Rossiter. New York: New American Library, 1961.

Malbin, Michael J. *Religion and Politics: The Intentions of the Authors of the First Amendment.* Washington, D.C.: American Enterprise Institute, 1978.

Mann, Horace. *Twelfth Report.* Boston: Massachusetts Legislature, 1848.

Mansbridge, Jane J. *Beyond Adversary Democracy.* Chicago: University of Chicago Press, 1983.

———. "A Deliberative Theory of Interest Representation." In *The Politics of Interests: Interest Groups Transformed,* ed. Mark P. Petracca. Boulder, Colo.: Westview Press, 1992.

March, James G. "Politics and the City." In *Urban Processes as Viewed by the Social Sciences,* ed. Kenneth J. Arrow, James S. Coleman, Anthony Downs, and James G. March, 23–37. Washington, D.C.: Urban Institute Press, 1970.

———. "The Technology of Foolishness." *Civiløkonomen* (Copenhagen) 18, 4 (1971): 4–12.

——. "Analytical Skills and the University Training of Educational Administrators." *Journal of Educational Administration* 7 (1974): 17–44.

——. "Science, Politics, and Mrs. Gruenberg." In *National Research Council in 1979*. Washington, D.C.: National Academy of Sciences, 1980.

——. "Preferences, Power, and Democracy." In *Power, Inequality, and Democratic Politics*, ed. Ian Shapiro and Grant Reeder. Boulder, Colo.: Westview Press, 1988.

——. "Exploration and Exploitation in Organizational Learning." *Organization Science* 2 (1991): 71–87.

——. "Organizational Consultants and Organizational Research." *Journal of Applied Communications Research* 19 (1991): 20–31.

——. "The Evolution of Evolution." In *The Evolutionary Dynamics of Organizations*, ed. Joel A. Baum and Jitendra V. Singh. New York: Oxford University Press, 1994.

——. *A Primer on Decision Making: How Decisions Happen*. New York: Free Press, 1994.

——. *Three Lectures on Efficiency and Adaptiveness in Organizations*. Helsinki: Swedish School of Economics, 1994.

——. "The Future, Disposable Organizations, and the Rigidities of Imagination." *Organization* 2 (1995): 427–40.

March, James G., and Johan P. Olsen. "The New Institutionalism: Organizational Factors in Political Life." *American Political Science Review* 78 (1984): 734–49.

——. *Rediscovering Institutions*. New York: Free Press, 1989.

——. *Democratic Governance*. New York: Free Press, 1995.

Marcus, George E., and Russell L. Hanson. *Reconsidering the Democratic Republic*. University Park: Pennsylvania State University Press, 1993.

Marcus, George, John L. Sullivan, Elizabeth Theiss-Moore, and Sandra L. Wood. *With Malice Toward Some: How People Make Civil Liberties Judgments*. Cambridge: Cambridge University Press, 1995.

Markus, Hazel, and Paula Nurius. "Possible Selves." *American Psychologist* 41 (1986): 954–69.

Marshall, Ray, and Marc Tucker. *Thinking for a Living: Education and the Wealth of Nations*. New York: Basic Books, 1992.

Martin, Roscoe C. *Government and the Suburban School*. Syracuse, N.Y.: Syracuse University Press, 1962.

Mathews, David. *Is There a Public for Public Schools?* Dayton, Ohio: Kettering Foundation Press, 1996.

Mayhew, David. *Congress: The Electoral Connection*. New Haven, Conn.: Yale University Press, 1974.

Mazzoni, Tim L. "State Policy-Making and School Reform: Influences and Influentials." In *The Study of Educational Politics*, ed. Jay D. Scribner and Donald H. Layton. Bristol, Pa.: Falmer Press, 1995.

McCarthy, Martha M. "People of Faith as Political Activists in Public Schools." *Education and Urban Society* 28, 3 (1996): 308–26.

McClain, Paula, and Joseph Stewart Jr. *Can We All Get Along? Racial and Ethnic Minorities in American Politics*, 2d ed. Boulder, Colo.: Westview Press, 1998.

McClosky, Herbert, and Alida Brill. *Dimensions of Tolerance: What Americans Believe About Civil Liberties*. New York: Russell Sage Foundation, 1983.

McClosky, Herbert, and John Zaller. *The American Ethos: Public Attitudes Toward Capitalism and Democracy.* Cambridge, Mass.: Harvard University Press, 1984.

McCoy, Drew. *The Elusive Republic: Political Economy in Jeffersonian America.* Chapel Hill: University of North Carolina Press, 1980.

McCubbins, Mathew D., and Thomas Schwartz. "Congressional Oversight Overlooked: Police Patrols Versus Fire Alarms." *American Journal of Political Science* 28 (1984): 165–79.

McCubbins, Mathew D., Roger G. Noll, and Barry R. Weingast. "Administrative Procedures as Instruments of Political Control." *Journal of Law, Economics, and Organization* 3 (1987): 243–77.

McDonnell, Lorraine M. "Assessment Policy as Persuasion and Regulation." *American Journal of Education* 102, 4 (1994): 394–420.

———. *The Politics of State Testing: Implementing New Student Assessments.* Los Angeles: UCLA/National Center for Research on Evaluation, Standards, and Student Testing, 1997.

McDonnell, Lorraine M., Leigh Burstein, Tor Ormseth, James M. Catterall, and David Moody. *Discovering What Schools Really Teach.* Santa Monica, Calif.: RAND, 1990.

McGerr, Michael E. *The Decline of Popular Politics: The American North, 1865–1928.* New York: Oxford University Press, 1986.

McKelvey, Richard D. "Intransitivities in Multidimensional Voting: Models and Some Implications for Agenda Control." *Journal of Economic Theory* 12 (1976): 472–82.

Meier, Deborah. *The Power of Their Ideas: Lessons for America from a Small School in Harlem.* Boston: Beacon Press, 1995.

Meyer, John W. *The Impact of the Centralization of Educational Funding and Control of State and Local Educational Governance.* Stanford, Calif.: Institute for Research on Educational Finance and Governance, Stanford University, 1980.

———. "Social Environments and Organizational Accounting." *Accounting, Organizations, and Society* 11, 4/5 (1986): 345–56.

Meyer, John W., and Brian Rowan. "Institutionalized Organizations: Formal Structure as Myth and Ceremony. " *American Journal of Sociology* 83 (1977): 340–63.

Meyer, Marvin, ed. *The Mind of the Founder.* Indianapolis: Bobbs-Merrill, 1973.

Mill, John Stuart. *On Liberty.* Indianapolis: Bobbs-Merrill, 1956.

Miller, Gary J. "Managerial Dilemmas: Political Leadership in Hierarchies." In *The Limits of Rationality,* ed. Karen S. Cook and Margaret Levi. Chicago: University of Chicago Press, 1990.

Miller, Perry. *The New England Mind: The Seventeenth Century.* Cambridge, Mass.: Harvard University Press, 1954.

Moe, Terry M. "The New Economics of Organization." *American Journal of Political Science* 28 (1984): 739–77.

———. "The Politics of Bureaucratic Structure." In *Can the Government Govern?* ed. John E. Chubb and Paul E. Peterson. Washington, D.C.: Brookings Institution, 1989.

———. "Political Institutions: The Neglected Side of the Story." *Journal of Law, Economics, and Organization* 6 (1990): 213–54.

———. "The Politics of Structural Choice: Toward a Theory of Public Bureaucracy." In *Organization Theory: From Chester Barnard to the Present and Beyond,* ed. Oliver E. Williamson. New York: Oxford University Press, 1990.

————. "The Positive Theory of Public Bureaucracy." In *Perspectives on Public Choice,* ed. Dennis R. Mueller. New York: Cambridge University Press, 1997.

Moe, Terry M., and Michael Caldwell. "The Institutional Foundations of Democratic Government: A Comparison of Presidential and Parliamentary Systems." *Journal of Institutional and Theoretical Economics* 150 (1994): 171–95.

Mohrman, Susan A., and Priscilla Wohlstetter. *School-Based Management: Organizing for High Performance.* San Francisco: Jossey-Bass, 1994.

Monaghan, E. Jennifer. *A Common Heritage: Noah Webster's Blue-Back Speller.* Hamden, Conn.: Archon Press, 1983.

Montgomery, David. *Citizen Worker: The Experience of Workers in the United States with Democracy and the Free Market During the Nineteenth Century.* Cambridge: Cambridge University Press, 1993.

Morone, James A. *The Democratic Wish: Popular Participation and the Limits of American Government.* New York: Basic Books, 1990.

Mosteller, Frederick. "The Tennessee Study of Class Size in the Early School Grades." *Future of Children* 5, 2 (1995): 113–27.

Mouffe, Chantal, ed. *Dimensions of Radical Democracy.* London: Verso, 1992.

NAACP Legal Defense and Education Fund. "Unfinished Agenda on Race [Poll]." Conducted by Louis Harris and Associates, June 3–September 12, 1988.

National Assessment of Educational Progress. *Changes in Political Knowledge and Attitudes, 1969–1976.* Washington, D.C.: U.S. Department of Education, March 1978.

National Center for Education Statistics. *Digest of Education Statistics 1993.* Washington, D.C.: U.S. Department of Education, 1993.

————. *The Condition of Education 1995.* Washington, D.C.: U.S. Department of Education, 1995.

————. *The Digest of Education Statistics 1997.* Washington, D.C.: U.S. Department of Education, 1997.

————. *The Condition of Education 1998.* Washington, D.C.: U.S. Department of Education, 1998.

————. *The Digest of Education Statistics 1998.* Washington, D.C.: U.S. Department of Education, 1998.

————. *NAEP 1996 Trends in Academic Progress.* Washington, D.C.: U.S. Department of Education, 1998.

National Commission on Excellence in Education. *A Nation at Risk: The Imperative for Educational Reform.* Washington, D.C.: U.S. Department of Education, 1983.

National Opinion Research Center. General Social Survey 1994. Data available at *http://www.icpsr.umich.edu/gss/home.htm,* 1994.

NBC News/*Wall Street Journal* Poll conducted by Hart and Teeter Research, September 10–13, 1998.

Nelson, Dana D. *National Manhood: Capitalist Citizenship and the Imagined Fraternity of White Men.* Durham, N.C.: Duke University Press, 1998.

Nie, Norman, Jane Junn, and Kenneth Stehlik-Barry. *Education and Democratic Citizenship in America.* Chicago: University of Chicago Press, 1996.

Niemi, Richard G., and Jane Junn. *Civic Education: What Makes Students Learn.* New Haven, Conn.: Yale University Press, 1998.

Niemi, Richard G., and M. A. Hepburn. "The Rebirth of Political Socialization." *Perspectives on Political Science* 24 (1995): 7–16.

Niskanen, William A. *Bureaucracy and Representative Government.* Chicago: Rand McNally, 1971.

North, Douglas C. *Institutions, Institutional Change, and Economic Performance.* Cambridge: Cambridge University Press, 1990.

North, Douglass R., and Barry R. Weingast. "Constitutions and Commitment: The Evolution of the Institutions Governing Public Choice in Seventeenth-Century England." *Journal of Economic History* 49 (1989): 803–32.

Nussbaum, Martha C. *Poetic Justice: The Literary Imagination and Public Life.* Boston: Beacon Press, 1995.

Oakes, Jeannie. *Keeping Track: How Schools Structure Inequality.* New Haven, Conn.: Yale University Press, 1985.

Okin, Susan. Review of *Democracy's Discontent* by Michael J. Sandel. *Political Theory* 91 (June 1997): 440–42.

Olsen, Johan P. *Demokrati på svenska.* Stockholm: Carlssons, 1990.

Olsen, Johan P., and B. G. Peters, eds. *Lessons from Experience: Experiential Learning in Administrative Reforms in Eight Democracies.* Oslo: Scandinavian University Press, 1995.

Olson, Mancur. *The Logic of Collective Action.* Cambridge, Mass.: Harvard University Press, 1965.

Orfield, Gary, Mark D. Bachmeier, David R. James, and Tamela Eitle. "Deepening Segregation in American Public Schools." Paper prepared for Harvard Project on School Desegregation, 1997.

Organ, Dennis W. *Organizational Citizenship Behavior: The Good Soldier Syndrome.* Lexington, Mass.: D. C. Heath, 1988.

Orlie, Melissa A. "Thoughtless Assertion and Political Deliberation." *American Political Science Review* 88 (1994): 684–95.

Ornstein, Allan C. "Centralization and Decentralization of Large Public School Systems." *Urban Education* 24 (1989): 233–35.

Orr, Marion. *Black Social Capital: The Politics of School Reform in Baltimore, 1986–1998.* Lawrence: University Press of Kansas, 1999.

Oyserman, Daphna, and Hazel Rose Markus. "Possible Selves and Delinquency." *Journal of Personality and Social Psychology* 59 (1990): 112–25.

Page, Ann L., and Donald A. Clelland. "The Kanawha County Textbook Controversy: A Study of the Politics of Life Style Concern." *Social Forces* 57 (1978): 265–81.

Pangle, Lorraine Smith, and Thomas L. Pangle. *The Learning of Liberty: The Educational Ideas of the American Founders.* Lawrence: University Press of Kansas, 1993.

Pangle, Thomas L. "The Retrieval of Civic Virtue: A Critical Appreciation of Sandel's Democracy's Discontent." In *Michael Sandel's America: Essays on Politics, Law, and Public Philosophy,* ed. Anita L. Allen and Milton Regan. Oxford: Oxford University Press, 1998.

Paris, David C. *Ideology and Educational Reform: Themes and Theories in Public Education.* Boulder, Colo.: Westview Press, 1995.

Petracca, Mark P. "The Rational Choice Approach to Politics: A Challenge to Democratic Theory." *Review of Politics* 52 (1991): 289–319.

Pewewardy, Cornel. "Melting Pot, Salad Bowl, Multicultural Mosaic, Crazy Quilt, or Indian Stew." *Indian Country Today,* 20 January 1997.

Phi Delta Kappa. "Attitudes Toward the Public Schools 1992 Survey." Conducted by the Gallup Organization, April 23–May 14, 1992.

———. "Attitudes Toward the Public Schools 1994 Survey." Conducted by the Gallup Organization, May 10–June 8, 1994.

———. "Attitudes Toward the Public Schools 1998 Survey." Conducted by the Gallup Organization, June 5–23, 1998.

———. "Attitudes Toward the Public Schools 1999 Survey." Conducted by the Gallup Organization, May 18–June 11, 1999.

Plank, David N., and William L. Boyd. "Antipolitics, Education, and Institutional Choice: The Flight from Democracy." *American Educational Research Journal* 31, 2 (1994): 263.

Popkin, Samuel L. *The Reasoning Voter: Communication and Persuasion in Presidential Campaigns.* Chicago: University of Chicago Press, 1991.

Portz, John, Lana Stein, and Robin R. Jones. *City Schools and City Politics: Institutions and Leadership in Pittsburgh, Boston, and St. Louis.* Lawrence: University Press of Kansas, 1999.

Pratt, John W., and Richard J. Zeckhauser. *Principals and Agents: The Structure of Business.* Boston: Harvard Business School Press, 1985.

Preston, Michael, Bruce Cain, and Sandra Bass. *Racial and Ethnic Politics in California.* Vol. 2. Berkeley, Calif.: Institute of Governmental Studies Press, 1998.

Public Agenda Foundation. "Time to Move On: An Agenda for Public Schools Survey." March 26–April 17, 1998.

Puma, Michael, et al. *Prospects: Final Report on Student Outcomes.* Cambridge, Mass.: Abt Associates, 1997.

Purkey, Stewart C., and Marshall S. Smith. "Effective Schools: A Review." *Elementary School Journal* 83 (March 1983): 427–52.

Purta, Judith Torney. "Links and Missing Links Between Education, Political Knowledge, and Citizenship." *American Journal of Education* 105 (August 1997): 447–57.

Putnam, Robert D. *Making Democracy Work: Civic Traditions in Modern Italy.* Princeton, N.J.: Princeton University Press, 1993.

———. "Bowling Alone: America's Declining Social Capital." *Journal of Democracy* 6 (1995): 65–78.

———. "Tuning In, Tuning Out: The Strange Disappearance of Social Capital in the United States." *PS: Political Science and Politics* 28, 4 (1995): 664–83.

Ravitch, Diane. "The Precarious State of History." *American Educator* 9 (Spring 1985): 11–17.

———. *The Schools We Deserve: Reflections on the Educational Crises of Our Times.* New York: Basic Books, 1985.

———. "Somebody's Children: Educational Opportunity for All American Children." In *Social Policies for Children,* ed. Irwin Garfinkel, Jennifer Hochschild, and Sara McLanahan, 83–111. Washington, D.C.: Brookings Institution, 1996.

Ravitch, Diane, and Chester E. Finn Jr. *What Do Our 17-Year-Olds Know?* New York: Harper and Row, 1987.

Rawls, John. *A Theory of Justice.* Cambridge, Mass.: Harvard University Press, 1971.

———. "The Idea of an Overlapping Consensus." *Oxford Journal of Legal Studies* 7 (1987): 1–25.

Redbook. Poll conducted by EDK Associates, February 7–10, 1994.

Reed, Douglas S. "Court-Ordered School Finance Equalization: Judicial Activism and Democratic Opposition." In *Developments in School Finance, 1996,* ed. William J. Fowler, 91–120. Washington, D.C.: Department of Education, National Center for Education Statistics, 1997.

Reich, Robert B., ed. *The Power of Public Ideas.* Cambridge, Mass.: Ballinger, 1988.

Resnick, Lauren. "Learning in School and Out." *Educational Researcher* 16 (December 1987): 13–20.

Reuben, Julie A. "Beyond Politics: Community Civics and the Redefinition of Citizenship in the Progressive Era." *History of Education Quarterly* 37 (Winter 1997): 399–420.

Rich, Wilbur C. *Black Mayors and School Politics.* New York: Garland, 1996.

Riker, William H. *The Theory of Political Coalitions.* New Haven, Conn.: Yale University Press, 1962.

———. "Implications from the Disequilibrium of Majority Rule for the Study of Institutions." *American Political Science Review* 74 (1980): 432–46.

———. *Liberalism Against Populism.* San Francisco: W. H. Freeman, 1982.

———. "The Heresthetics of Constitution-Making: The Presidency in 1787, with Comments on Determinism and Rational Choice." *American Political Science Review* 78 (1984): 1–16.

———. *The Art of Political Manipulation.* New Haven, Conn.: Yale University Press, 1986.

Riker, William H., ed. *Agenda Formation.* Ann Arbor: University of Michigan Press, 1993.

Rodgers, Daniel T. *The Work Ethic in Industrial America, 1850–1920.* Chicago: University of Chicago Press, 1978.

Rorty, Richard. *Contingency, Irony, and Solidarity.* New York: Cambridge University Press, 1989.

Rose, Lowell C., and Alec M. Gallup. "The 30th Annual Phi Delta Kappa/Gallup Poll of the Public's Attitudes Toward the Public Schools." *Phi Delta Kappan* 80, 1 (1998): 41–56.

Rosenberg, Alexander. *Philosophy of Social Science.* Oxford: Oxford University Press, 1988.

Rouse, Cecilia E. "Private School Vouchers and Student Achievement: An Evaluation of the Milwaukee Parental Choice Program." *Quarterly Journal of Economics* 113, 2 (May 1998): 553–602.

Rowe, Walter F. "School Daze: A Critical Review of the 'African-American Baseline Essays' for Science and Mathematics." *Skeptical Inquirer* (September/October 1995): 27–32.

Rush, Benjamin. "A Plan for the Establishment of Public Schools and the Diffusion of Knowledge in Pennsylvania." In *Essays on Education in the Early Republic,* ed. Frederick Rudolph. Cambridge, Mass.: Harvard University Press, 1965.

———. "Thoughts Upon Female Education, Accommodated to the Present State of Society, Manners, and Government in the United States of America." In *Essays on Education in the Early Republic,* ed. Frederick Rudolph. Cambridge, Mass.: Harvard University Press, 1965.

Rutter, Michael, et al. *Fifteen Thousand Hours: Secondary Schools and Their Effects on Children.* Cambridge, Mass.: Harvard University Press, 1979.

Sabine, George H. "The Two Democratic Traditions." *Philosophical Review* (1952): 493–511.

Sahskin, Marshall, and John Egirmeir. *School Change Models and Processes: A Review and Synthesis of Research and Practice.* Washington, D.C.: U.S. Department of Education, 1993.

Salomone, Rosemary C. *Equal Education Under Law: Legal Rights and Federal Policy* New York: St. Martin's Press, 1986.

Sandel, Michael J. *Liberalism and the Limits of Justice.* Cambridge: Cambridge University Press, 1982.

———. "The Procedural Republic and the Unencumbered Self." *Political Theory* 12, 1 (1984): 81–96.

———. *Democracy's Discontent: America in Search of a Public Philosophy.* Cambridge, Mass.: Belknap Press of Harvard University Press, 1996.

Sapiro, Virginia, Steven J. Rosenstone, Warren E. Miller, and the National Election Studies. *American National Election Studies, 1948–1997.* CD-ROM, ICPSR ed. Ann Arbor, Mich.: Inter-University Consortium for Political and Social Research (producer and distributor), 1998.

Sartori, Giovani. *The Theory of Democracy Revisited.* 2 vols. Chatham, N.J.: Chatham House, 1987.

Schattschneider, E. E. *The Semi-Sovereign People.* New York: Holt, Rinehart and Winston, 1960.

Schlesinger, Jr., Arthur M. *The Disuniting of America: Reflections on a Multicultural Society.* New York: W. W. Norton, 1992.

Schofield, Janet. "Review of Research on School Desegregation's Impact on Elementary and Secondary School Students." In *Handbook on Multicultural Education*, ed. James Banks and Cherry McGee Banks. New York: Macmillan, 1995.

Schrag, Francis. *Thinking in School and Society.* New York: Routledge, 1988.

Schudson, Michael. "Was There Ever a Public Sphere? If So, When? Reflections on the American Case." In *Habermas and the Public Sphere*, ed. Craig Calhoun. Cambridge, Mass.: MIT Press, 1992.

———. *The Good Citizen: A History of American Civic Life.* New York: Free Press, 1998.

Scott, Marvin B., and Stanford M. Lyman. "Accounts." *American Sociological Review* 33, 1 (1968): 46–62.

Secretary's Commission on Achieving Necessary Skills. *What Work Requires of Schools.* Washington, D.C.: U.S. Department of Labor, June 1991.

———. *Learning a Living: A Blueprint for High Performance.* Washington, D.C., U.S. Department of Labor, April 1992.

Sellers, Charles. *The Market Revolution: Jacksonian America, 1815–1846.* New York: Oxford University Press, 1991.

Selznick, Philip. *TVA and the Grass Roots.* Berkeley: University of California Press, 1949.

Sen, Amartya. *On Ethics and Economics.* Oxford: Blackwell, 1990.

———. *Inequality Reexamined.* Cambridge: Harvard University Press, 1992.

SenGupta, Gunja. *For God and Mammon: Evangelicals and Entrepreneurs, Masters and Slaves in Territorial Kansas, 1854–1860.* Athens: University of Georgia Press, 1996.

Shepsle, Kenneth A. "Institutional Equilibrium and Equilibrium Institutions." In *Political Science: The Science of Politics*, ed. Herbert F. Weisberg. New York: Agathon Press, 1986.

Shepsle, Kenneth A., and Barry R. Weingast. "The Institutional Foundations of Committee Power." *American Political Science Review* 81 (1987): 85–104.

Shklar, Judith N. *The Faces of Injustice.* New Haven, Conn.: Yale University Press, 1990.

———. *American Citizenship: The Quest for Inclusion.* Cambridge, Mass.: Harvard University Press, 1991.

Sigelman, Lee, Timothy Bledsoe, Susan Welch, and Michael Combs. "Making Contact? Black-White Social Interaction in an Urban Setting." *American Journal of Sociology* 101, 5 (1996): 1306–32.

Simon, Ken A., and W. V. Grant. *Digest of Educational Statistics.* Washington, D.C.: U.S. Department of Education, 1970.

Sindelar, Paul, and Stanley Deno. "The Effectiveness of Resource Programming." *Journal of Special Education* 12, 1 (1979): 149–77.

Sizer, Theodore. *Horace's School: Redesigning the American High School.* Boston: Houghton Mifflin, 1992.

Slavin, Robert E. "Achievement Effects of Ability Grouping in Secondary Schools: A Best-Evidence Synthesis." Paper prepared for the National Center on Effective Secondary Schools, Wisconsin Center for Education Research, University of Wisconsin–Madison, 1990.

Smith, Anthony D. *National Identity.* London: Penguin, 1991.

Smith, Rogers M. *Civic Ideals: Conflicting Visions of Citizenship in U.S. History.* New Haven, Conn.: Yale University Press, 1997.

Smith, Samuel Harrison. "Remarks on Education, Illustrating the Close Connection between Virtue and Wisdom." In *Essays on Education in the Early Republic,* ed. Frederick Rudolph. Cambridge, Mass.: Harvard University Press, 1965.

Spragens, Thomas A. *Reason and Democracy.* Durham, N.C.: Duke University Press, 1990.

Spring, Joel H. *Conflict of Interests: The Politics of American Education.* New York: Longman, 1993.

Sroufe, Gerald E. "Politics of Education at the Federal Level." In *The Study of Educational Politics*, ed. John D. Scribner and Donald H. Layton, 75–88. Bristol, Pa.: The Falmer Press, 1995.

Statistical Abstract of the United States. Washington, D.C.: U.S. Department of Commerce, 1998.

Stedman, Lawrence C. "International Achievement Differences: An Assessment of a New Perspective." *Educational Researcher 26* (April 1997): 4–15.

Stille, Alexander. "The Betrayal of History." *New York Review of Books* 15–16 (11 June 1998): 15–20.

Stone, Clarence, ed. *Changing Urban Education.* Lawrence: University Press of Kansas, 1998.

Stone, Deborah A. *Policy Paradox: The Art of Political Decision Making.* New York: Norton, 1997.

Storing, Herbert, ed. *The Complete Anti-Federalist.* Chicago: University of Chicago Press, 1981.

Sugden, R., *The Economics of Rights, Co-operation and Welfare*. Oxford: Basil Blackwell, 1986.

Sullivan, John L., James Piereson, and George Marcus. *Political Tolerance and American Democracy*. Chicago: University of Chicago Press, 1982.

Sunstein, Cass R. *After the Rights Revolution*. Cambridge, Mass.: Harvard University Press, 1990.

Tamir, Yael, ed. *Democratic Education in a Multicultural State*. Oxford: Blackwell Publishers, 1995.

Tarcov, Nathan. "The Meanings of Democracy." In *Democracy, Education, and the Schools*, ed. Roger Soder. San Francisco: Jossey-Bass, 1996.

Taylor, Charles. "The Politics of Recognition." In *Multiculturalism*, ed. Amy Gutmann Princeton, N.J.: Princeton University Press, 1994.

Taylor, Michael. "The Theory of Collective Choice." In *Handbook of Political Science*. Vol. 3. Ed. Fred I. Greenstein and Nelson W. Polsby. Reading, Mass.: Addison-Wesley, 1975.

Tetlock, Phillip E. "The Impact of Accountability on Judgment and Choice: Toward a Social Contingency Model." *Advances in Experimental Social Psychology* 25 (1992): 331–76.

Thompson, Dennis F. "Mediated Corruption: The Case of the Keating Five," *American Political Science Review* 87, 2 (1993): 369–81.

Thompson, Michael, Richard Ellis, and Aaron B. Wildavsky. *Cultural Theory*. Boulder, Colo.: Westview Press, 1990.

Time/Cable News Network. Poll conducted by Yankelovitch Partners, December 7–8, 1994.

Tocqueville, Alexis de. *De la Démocratie en Amérique*. Vol. 2. Ed. Eduardo Nolla. Paris: J. Vrin, 1990.

Topper, Keith. "Richard Rorty, Liberalism, and the Politics of Redescription," *American Political Science Review* 89, 4 (1995): 954–65.

Turner, Stephen. *The Social Theory of Practices*. Chicago: University of Chicago Press, 1994.

Tyack, David B. *The One Best System: A History of American Urban Education*. Cambridge, Mass.: Harvard University Press, 1974.

———. "School Governance in the United States: Historical Puzzles and Anomalies." In *Decentralization and School Improvement: Can We Fulfill the Promise?* ed. Jane Hannaway and Martin Carnoy. San Francisco: Jossey-Bass, 1993.

Tyack, David B., and Larry Cuban. *Tinkering Toward Utopia: A Century of Public School Reform*. Cambridge, Mass.: Harvard University Press, 1995.

Tyack, David B., and Elisabeth Hansot. *Managers of Virtue*. New York: Basic Books, 1982.

U.S. Bureau of the Census website, *http://www.census.gov*.

U.S. Department of Education, *The Condition of Education: 1998*. Washington, D.C.: Government Printing Office, 1998.

Verba, Sidney, and Gary Orren. *Equality in America: The View from the Top*. Cambridge, Mass.: Harvard University Press, 1985.

Verba, Sidney, Kay Lehman Schlozman, and Henry E. Brady. *Voice and Equality*. Cambridge, Mass.: Harvard University Press, 1995.

Viadero, Debra. "Culture Clash." *Education Week* (10 April 1996): 1.

Vinovskis, Maris A. "Horace Mann on the Economic Productivity of Education." *New England Quarterly* 43 (December 1970): 571.

Viteritti, Joseph. "Blaine's Wake: School Choice, the First Amendment, and State Constitutional Law." *Harvard Journal of Law and Public Policy* 21, 3 (1998): 657–718.

Walters, Laurel. "The Bilingual Education Debate." *Harvard Education Letter* 14, 3 (1998): 1–4.

Walzer, Michael. *Spheres of Justice.* New York: Basic Books, 1983.

Warfel, Harry R. *Noah Webster: Schoolmaster to America.* New York: Macmillan, 1936.

Warner, Michael. *The Letters of the Republic: Publication and the Public Sphere in Eighteenth-Century America.* Cambridge, Mass.: Harvard University Press, 1990.

Warren, Mark. "Deliberative Democracy and Authority." *American Political Science Review* 90, 1 (1996): 46–60.

Washington, George. *The Writings of George Washington from the Original Manuscript Sources,* ed. John C. Fitzpatrick. 39 vols. Washington, D.C.: Government Printing Office, 1939.

Washington Post/Kaiser Family Foundation/Harvard University Survey Project. "Why Don't Americans Trust the Government?" Washington, D.C.: Author, 1996.

Weber, Max. *The Protestant Ethic and the Spirit of Capitalism.* Trans. Talcott Parsons. New York: Charles Scribner's Sons, 1958.

Webster, Noah. *An American Selection of Lessons in Reading and Speaking.* Philadelphia: Young and M'Culloch, 1787.

———. *A Collection of Essays and Fugitiv Writings.* Boston: Thomas Andrews, 1790.

———. "An Examination into the Leading Principles of the Federal Constitution Proposed by the Late Convention Held at Philadelphia. With Answers to the Principal Objections That Have Been Raised Against the System." In *Pamphlets on the Constitution of the United States Published During Its Discussion By the People, 1787–88,* ed. Paul L. Ford. Brooklyn, N.Y.: n. p., 1888.

———. "On the Education of Youth in America." In *Essays on Education in the Early Republic,* ed. Frederick Rudolph. Cambridge, Mass.: Harvard University Press, 1965.

———. *A Grammatical Institute, of the English Language, Comprising, an Easy, Concise, and Systematic Method of Education, Designed for the Use of English Schools in America.* 1783. Reprint. Menston, England: Scolar Press, 1968.

Weiher, Gregory, Kent Tedin, and Richard Matland. "Age and Support for School Bonds: A Test of Voting Theories." Paper presented at the annual meeting of the Midwest Political Science Association, Chicago, 1998.

Weingast, Barry R., "The Economic Role of Political Institutions: Market-Preserving Federalism and Economic Development." *Journal of Law, Economics, and Organization* 11 (1995): 1–31.

Weingast, Barry R., and William Marshall. "The Industrial Organization of Congress." *Journal of Political Economy* 96 (1988): 132–63.

Weingast, Barry R. and Mark Moran. "Bureaucratic Discretion or Congressional Control: Regulatory Policymaking by the Federal Trade Commission." *Journal of Political Economy* 91 (1983): 765–800.

Weiss, Carol H. "The Four 'I's' of School Reform: How Interests, Ideology, Information, and Institution Affect Teachers and Principals." *Harvard Educational Review* 65, 4 (1995): 571–92.

Wells, Amy, and Robert Crain. "Perpetuation Theory and the Long-Term Effects of School Desegregation." *Review of Educational Research* 64, 4 (1994): 531–55.

Westbrook, Robert B. "Public Schooling and American Democracy." In *Democracy, Education, and the Schools*, ed. Roger Soder. San Francisco: Jossey-Bass, 1996.

Whitehead, Alfred North. *The Aims of Education and Other Essays*. New York: Free Press, 1967.

Whittington, Dale. "What Have 17-Year-Olds Known in the Past?" *American Educational Research Journal* 28 (1991): 759–80.

Wiebe, Robert. *The Search for Order, 1877–1920*. New York: Hill and Wang, 1967.

Wildavsky, Aaron B. "Choosing Preferences by Constructing Institutions: A Cultural Theory of Preference Formation." *American Political Science Review* 81 (1987): 3–22.

Wilentz, Sean. *Chants Democratic: New York City and the Rise of the American Working Class, 1788–1850*. New York: Oxford University Press, 1984.

Wilkinson, Doris. "Integration Dilemmas in a Racist Culture." *Society* 33, 3 (1996): 27–31.

Williamson, Oliver E. *Markets and Hierarchies*. New York: Free Press, 1975.

———. *The Economic Institutions of Capitalism*. New York: Free Press, 1985.

Wilson, James. *Selected Political Essays of James Wilson*. Ed. R. Adams. New York: Knopf, 1930.

Wirt, Frederick M., and Michael W. Kirst. *The Political Dynamics of American Education*. Berkeley, Calif.: McCutchan, 1997.

Witte, John F. *The Market Approach to Education: An Analysis of America's First Voucher Program*. Princeton, N.J.: Princeton University Press, 2000.

Wolin, Sheldon S. *Politics and Vision: Continuity and Innovation in Western Political Thought*. Boston: Little, Brown, 1960.

———. "The New Public Philosophy." *Democracy* 1, 4 (1981): 23–36.

Wong, Kenneth K. "Governance Structure, Resource Allocation, and Equity Policy." *Review of Research in Education* 20 (1994): 257–89.

Wong, Kenneth K., and Paul E. "Can Big-City School Systems be Governed?" Paper presented at the 1992 Annual Meeting of the American Political Science Association, Chicago.

Wong, Kenneth K., Robert Dreeben, Laurence Lynn, Robert Meyer, and Gail Sunderman. *System-Wide Governance in the Chicago Public Schools: Findings and Recommendations for Institutional Redesign*. Chicago: Department of Education and Irving B. Harris Graduate School of Public Policy Studies, University of Chicago, 1995.

Contributors

ROGER BENJAMIN, a senior researcher at RAND, is president of RAND's New York–based Council for Aid to Education.

PAMELA JOHNSTON CONOVER is a professor of political science at the University of North Carolina, Chapel Hill.

AMY GUTMANN is the Laurence S. Rockefeller University Professor of Politics at Princeton University.

JENNIFER L. HOCHSCHILD is a professor of politics and public affairs at Princeton University.

CARL F. KAESTLE is University professor of education, history, and public policy at Brown University.

JAMES G. MARCH is the Jack Steele Parker Professor Emeritus of International Management and professor emeritus of political science and sociology, Stanford University.

LORRAINE M. MCDONNELL is a professor of political science at the University of California, Santa Barbara.

TERRY M. MOE is a professor of political science at Stanford University and a senior fellow at the Hoover Institution.

JOHAN P. OLSEN is the research director of ARENA (Advanced Research on the Europeanization of the Nation-State) in Norway and an adjunct professor of political science at the University of Oslo.

LORRAINE SMITH PANGLE has taught history and English at the Groton School and the Community Hebrew Academy of Toronto.

THOMAS L. PANGLE is a professor of political science at the University of Toronto.

NATHAN SCOVRONICK teaches education policy at the Woodrow Wilson School for Public and International Affairs, Princeton University.

DONALD D. SEARING is a professor of political science at the University of North Carolina, Chapel Hill.

P. MICHAEL TIMPANE is a member of the senior research staff at RAND and a former president of Teachers College, Columbia University.

M. STEPHEN WEATHERFORD is a professor of political science at the University of California, Santa Barbara.

Conference Participants

The Democratic Purposes of Education
The Aspen Institute—July 10–14, 1996

Roger Benjamin
RAND

Pamela Johnston Conover
University of North Carolina, Chapel Hill

Gary Fenstermacher
University of Michigan

Patricia Albjerg Graham
The Spencer Foundation and Harvard University

Edmund Gordon
Yale University

Amy Gutmann*
Princeton University

Jennifer L. Hochschild
Princeton University

Carl F. Kaestle
Brown University

Joseph Kahne
University of Illinois, Chicago Circle

James G. March
Stanford University

Lorraine McDonnell
University of California, Santa Barbara

Terry M. Moe
Stanford University

Michael O'Keefe
The McKnight Foundation

Thomas L. Pangle*
University of Toronto

Nancy Pelz-Paget
Aspen Institute

Robert Reich
Stanford University

Sharon Robinson
U.S. Department of Education

David Steiner
Vanderbilt University

David S. Tatel
U.S. Court of Appeals for the District of Columbia Circuit

P. Michael Timpane
RAND

---

*Prepared a paper but was unable to attend the conference.

Index

history, 31–33, 34–35, 59, 60, 81, 111
mathematics, 34
multicultural, 7, 118, 213, 216, 220–21
political discussions facilitated by, 111–12
science, 33–35
secondary schools, 56
state standards, 7, 8, 185–86, 222
values taught in, 80–82
See also Civic education; Civics courses

Debates. *See* Discussions, political
Deliberation, 75–76, 78–79
benefits, 188–90
in education politics, 190–93, 198
issues appropriate for, 190–92
mutual respect in, 78, 79, 192
need for, 79
practical, 188–93
prospects for, 190–93
research on, 188, 189–90, 196–97
in school governance, 189, 193
skills needed, 76, 81, 92, 189
social relationships and, 194–95
Deliberative model
comparison to exchange model, 194–95, 196–97
research on, 188, 193–94, 196–97
Delli Carpini, Michael X., 11, 61
Democracy
accountability in, 158, 161–64, 166
advantages of, 32–33
agency problems, 136–37, 140, 143
in ancient republics, 26
citizen participation, 27–28, 38–39
current status, 149
essential principles, 148–49
failures of, 154–56
fair procedures, 74, 77–78
in individual schools, 80, 141, 142–43, 187
justification of, 73
lack of in workplaces, 54–55
problems recognized by Founders, 22
representative, 26–27, 28
resource distribution in, 154–55
short-term perspective in, 166
social choice view of, 129–30
values of, 74–76, 212
See also Deliberation; Governance of schools; Institutional theory of democracy
Democratic Party, 62, 64–65
Democratic procedures for dealing with disagreements, 73–76, 128–30
constitutionalism, 76, 78
in education policy, 231–32
proceduralism, 76, 77–78
skills needed, 76–77
See also Discussions, political

Democratic purposes of education
accountability, 162–63
barriers to, 4–9, 10
creation of political identities, 158–61
decline in attention to, 4–6
equal opportunity, 213
exchange perspective, 156–58
Founders' views of, 32–33, 38–39, 48, 210
institutional perspective, 158–66, 167–69
limits to, 166–67
need for study of, 9–12, 92–94
public support of, 3, 177, 216
relationship to economic goals, 2, 5–6, 51–52, 215–16
socialization, 1–2, 3, 4, 6, 12, 167
values, 159, 210, 212
See also Governance of schools
Demographics, future trends, 228–29
Desegregation, 217–19
busing opponents, 218
court decisions, 64, 184, 214
economic results, 226
effect on education quality, 218
effects of popular control of schools, 9
implementation of, 218–19, 225
Dewey, John, 3, 27, 35, 38–39, 47
Disabilities, children with, 221–22, 226–27, 230
Disagreements, persistence of, 128–29. *See also* Democratic procedures for dealing with disagreements
Discussions, political
in classes, 30, 110, 111–12, 115
in different settings, 111, 114, 116
difficulties, 160
importance, 118, 160, 167
in mass media, 49
relationship to citizen identities, 107–8, 109–11, 159
rules for, 160
skills needed, 105, 109, 114
student participation, 105–6, 107–8, 109–11, 113, 114–15
with teachers, 110–11
tolerance related to, 114–15, 116
training in oratory and debate, 29–30, 31
Diversity of population
challenge of, 188, 212–13
common schools as response to, 3
disagreements, 128–29
future increase in, 228
multicultural curriculum, 7, 118, 213, 216, 220–21
religious, 214
shared values, 3, 6–8
See also Groups; Immigrants; Tolerance